THE APPLICABILITY OF POLICY-MAKING THEORIES IN POST-MAO CHINA

To Xiuzhen and Jia

The Applicability of Policy-Making Theories in Post-Mao China

HUANG JIANRONG

Ashgate

Aldershot • Brookfield USA • Singapore • Sydney

Published by
Ashgate Publishing Ltd
Gower House
Croft Road
Aldershot
Hants GU11 3HR
England

Ashgate Publishing Company
Old Post Road
Brookfield
Vermont 05036
USA

British Library Cataloguing in Publication Data
Huang, Jianrong
  The applicability of policy-making theories in post-Mao China
  1. Policy sciences 2. Political science - China 3. China - Politics and government - 1976-
  I. Title
  320.6'0951

Library of Congress Catalog Card Number: 99-72327

ISBN 1 84014 883 7

Printed in Great Britain

Contents

PART III: ANALYSING THE POLICY-MAKING PROCESS

List of figures and tables

Figures

Tables

Acknowledgements

Research into policy-making analysis with multiple theories and models has really interested and challenged me. In doing so, my greatest thanks is to Professor Michael Hill, for his valuable guidance, help, encouragement, critical discussion and comments, which have benefited me a lot in furthering my study. Without these, I could not have completed my research work.

I am particularly indebted to Mr Vincent Riley, for his kindness and enthusiasm in giving me help in English by reading carefully all the manuscript of my drafts and correcting grammatical mistakes. I also highly appreciate his help in offering me chances to access some local community activities, which have not only enriched my experience in this country, but also benefited my research in bringing me fresh and impressive perceptual knowledge which has deepened my understanding of Western societies, which therefore gave me enlightenment in analysing and assessing the issues of China's policy-making to which my study concerns.

Acknowledgement is also due to Professor J H Veit-Wilson, for his guidance and help. I would also like to thank Dr Robert Hollands, for his friendship and help. He read some chapters of my drafts and offered me some helpful comments. Thanks also go to Dr Peter Selman, the head of the department, for his concern and support of my study. A debt is owed to Dorothy, Margaret and Caroline, the secretaries of the department, for their kindness in providing me with assistance for my research. I am especially grateful to Xiuzhen, my wife, for her support with all her strength in taking full responsibility for the family, which enabled me to concentrate on my work.

Finally, I would like to thank the editorial staff at Ashgate, particularly Kate Trew, Anne Keirby, Claire Annals and Amanda Richardson, for their valuable support and help in enabling this book to be published.

List of abbreviations

1. Organisations and projects

CAC	Central Advisory Commission
CCCPC	Central Committee of the Communist Party of China
CCID	Central Commission for Inspecting Discipline
CCYL	Chinese Communist Youth League
CEDS	Coastal Economic Development Strategy
CEDA	Coastal Economic Development Area
CMC	Central Military Commission
CMSN	China's Merchant Steam Navigation Co.
COC	Coastal Open City
CPC	Communist Party of China
CSC	Chinese State Council
CPPCC	Chinese People's Political Consultative Conference
ETDZ	Economic and Technological Development Zone
KGHK	Kumagaya-Gumi (Hong Kong) Co. Ltd.
PLA	People's Liberation Army
NPC	National People's Congress
RMB	China's currency
SBS	Statistical Bureau of Shenzhen
SEZ	Special Economic Zone
SOCSC	The SEZs Office of China's State Council
SPC	Supreme People's Court
SPP	Supreme People's Procuratorate

2. Publications

BR	Beijing Review
CEYB	Chinese Economic Yearbook
CFEL	China's Foreign Economic Legislation (1984, 2nd edition)
CSY	Chinese Statistical Yearbook
CYB	Chinese Yearbook
ED	Economic Daily

OCSE	Overseas Chinese Scholars, Electronic Edition
OL	Outlook
PD	People's Daily
PDO	People's Daily overseas edition
RF	Red Flag
SMT	Semi-month Talk
SZE	Special Zone Economy
WHD	Wenhui Daily
XSYEFC	Xiamen Statistical Yearbook of Economy linked with Foreign Countries
XTD	Xingtao Daily
YSSEZ	The Yearbook of Shenzhen Special Economic Zone

1 Introduction

To study the applicability of a range of policy-making theories in the practice of post-Mao China is really a challenging work, in view of what follows. (1) To systematically examine the applicability of those major policy-making theories developed from Western in China is a pioneering work; and (2) research into the field of China's policy-making is itself a particularly difficult task encountering many problems. Thus, to unfold this topic, it will be helpful to first briefly discuss the relevant issues below. Why is it essential to examine the applicability of those policy-making theories in China? Why does the policy-making practice in post-Mao China deserve a particular study? What are the conditions and difficulties of conducting this study? And finally, what method will be used to conduct this study and what are key issues will be discussed?

1.1 The significance of applying policy-making theories

The research about policy-making has developed rapidly over the past five decades, especially in America and Britain, and has become one of the main schemes of political science. The interest around policy-making study covers a wide range including policy content, policy process, policy outputs, policy evaluation, information for policy-making, process advocacy and policy advocacy (Hogwood and Guun, 1981 and 1984). What we discuss here is only the second part of this range: the policy-making process around which diversified theories have been created aiming to explore or explain this process. Besides these theories and models discussing policy-making process in principle, what we access in this research also includes those Sinologists' models about how China's policy is made, which were created during the last four decades. Thus, the theories and models that will be discussed in this book can be classified as two groups. The first group relating to how policy is made covers two aspects: the relevant state theories and the Sinologists' models about how China's policy is made. The former contains pluralism, elitism, Marxism, globalism and institutionalism, etc. The latter, which is actually the adaptation of the former to fit the Chinese case, comprises Mao (or Deng)-

1

in-command model, politicians-in-negotiation model, power-competition-oriented model, ideological-conflict-oriented model, and bureaucracy-in-domination model, etc. What the theories and models of the first group probe include who is involved in or dominates a policy-making, what is the dominant factor in making a policy, and also the reasons. The second group of the theories and models relating to how policy should be made, explores the way to improve policy-making, which comprises rationalism, incrementalism, optimal approach, mixed scanning method, contingent approach etc.

All those theories and models which study policy-making process in principle, including the relevant state theories and the theories exploring how policy should be made, are in the position of the mainstream in policy-making study, and of significance in Western literature. Hence, as considering to research into a concrete policy-making process of a country or a region, or a particular policy-making issue, it seems to be reasonable to first seek help from them. It should be expected that these theories and models can not only provide us with enlightening conceptual references, but with the ways of analysing policy process from different viewpoints. Furthermore, on the other hand, to analyse a concrete policy-making process with the help of the above theories and models means to examine to what extent they can be applied to observe and interpret practice, and why. Consequently, to use these theories and models to study a concrete policy event in a country or a region is certainly conducive to both testing the applicability of these theories and models and advancing the study of a given policy process. However, since China's political system and policy-making mechanism differ from those in Western countries in which those theories and models are created, two questions are inevitably raised as follows. They are: whether this method is applicable to study China's policy-making practice, and whether these theories and models are applicable in interpreting China's practice. These also need and deserve to be examined. Among these two questions, the second one is just the core issue the book aims to explore.

As for those selected models about how China's policy is made, they are produced by the concrete study of China's policy-making practice mainly before the reform period, with the relevant state theories as their theoretical bases. Since they are the creations of Western scholars, to review and re-value them is significant in view of the reasons below. First, onlookers are clearheaded. Being the observations of the foreign scholars, these models about China, to be sure, can offer us beneficial enlightenment. Second, due to the fact that China's politics and ideology differ from those in Western countries from which those scholars came, the extent to which these models can interpret China's practice, especially the practice in the post-Mao period, is really an issue deserving attention. Thus, discussion of them in detail is helpful in both expanding our viewpoint and deepening our understanding of the development and changes of China's policy-making process in the post-Mao period, which is essential to further our study.

1.2 China's policy-making in the last two decades is well worthy of study

Beginning at the end of the 1970s, triggered by the reform and opening-up strategy, post-Mao China has been in a transitional period for nearly two decades. This transition is of great and far-reaching significance in China's history. The essence of this transition, fundamentally speaking, is that China ended a two-centuries-long period characterised by closing and stagnancy, and started a brand new epoch of really opening-up to the outside world on an equal basis involving globalisation. China is rejuvenating and becoming prosperous and strong in this course. History will take note of China's reform and opening-up as one of the most influential events of the world in the twentieth century.

The changes that had brought about this transition influenced all realms of the society of post-Mao China, of which, unquestionably, economic growth is most remarkable. The last two decades witnessed a marvellous economic development in China. From 1979 to 1995, China's GNP has grown rapidly, with an annual average rate of 9.9 percent (PDO, 6 July 1996, p. 1). As a country with one fifth of the world's population, 'China's economic growth and the improvement of people's living standard is one of the greatest achievements of human being in the last two decades'[1] (PDO, 29, February 1997, p. 1).

As early as six years ago, the American Comprehensive long-term Tactics Committee, which has a great reputation in the United States, had predicated that 'in the year of 2010, China will be the second or third strongest economic country'. This report, named 'Recognise the Deterrent', was put forth based on the data of Landau Company, the famous American Brain Trust, and was signed by many popular authoritative sources of American diplomatic policy, including Kissinger, the former Secretary of State; Brezinski and Hunting, the former advisers on the State security (SZE, issue 4, 1992, Editorial).

Other influential comments, on China's achievements since 1980s, included: British *'Economist'* confirming that China's economic reform has achieved ten-odd years of economic prosperity; French *'Investment'* regarding China as an economic giant; the former American president Nixon saying that in the 21st century, China will be the country not only with the greatest population, but with the most prosperous economy (SMT, No. 5/1992, p. 5).

To be sure, the American authoritative report and the world-wide public opinions aforementioned indicated that: (1) the world acknowledged China's great economic achievement; (2) the world also acknowledged the great potentialities of China's further development and predicated its promising future. The rapid economic development brought about corresponding great changes in other aspects of China's society. China's current situation of economic and social prosperity had never appeared in the last two centuries of its history. Then, why could China achieve this significant development within only two decades? In short, fundamentally speaking, it resulted from the implementation of a series of new policies and strategies that were made since the end of 1978, which were characterised by reform and opening-up to the outside world. However, how could China's leadership since then determine these policies and strategies, which could not be made at any time in the first three decades of PRC? The available evidence suggests that, it came from the significant changes of China's policy-making behaviour and the policy-making environment. These changes concern five aspects:

- value — the standard of evaluating a desired policy;
- motivation — for what purpose a policy is decided;
- method — what approaches are used to determine a policy;
- the power mechanism — in what power structure and power operating mechanism a policy is made;
- environment — in what political environment a policy is made.

Then, what happened in these aspects during the last two decades? To answer to this question requires a careful and in-depth study. Only after clearly exploring these changes, can we understand why and how the improvement of China's policy-making behaviour and policy-making environment could produce those significant influences.

The book can not probe the changes of China's policy-making process in its entirety, instead, it focuses its study on the policy process of the establishment and development of China's SEZs, the Special Economic Zones. The reasons why the SEZ is suitable to be chosen for case study, are threefold. (1) SEZ is one of the most important parts of China's reform and opening-up strategy, and its policies have close relations with those in other realms of post-Mao China. Thus, analysing the policy-making process of promoting the SEZ course is a good visual angle to observe and evaluate China's policy behaviour in the post-Mao period. (2) SEZ's successful development had produced wide and far-reaching influences, and now both home and abroad acknowledged the SEZs' achievements as well as their significant roles as the 'Windows', 'Bridges' and 'Experimental fields' of China in carrying out the reform and opening-up policies. It is worthy of deep study to probe why and how the success of SEZ stemmed from those changed policy-making patterns. (3) Due to SEZ' features of concerning many sensitive and important policy issues and of being in the pioneering position of China's reform and opening-up strategy, the Policy-making processes for promoting the SEZ course were influenced by diversified elements and involving various forces. To probe these processes, we can see how and to what extent those internal and external factors had produced the dynamics to further the policy-making; how and to what extent those elites at different levels and in different realms had exerted their roles to intervene in the policy-making; how and to what extent a newly developing plural tendency had involved in and affected the policy-making; how and to what extent China's existing institutions, including the newly developed institutions, had structured and mediated the policy-making process; and how and to what extent those different methods had been applied in the policy-making. Therefore, it is conceivable that such a vital and colourful picture provides us with a good target for our examination of a range of policy-making theories and models.

In using these theories and models to study China's policy-making process, we adopt a method of probing the development, changes, and major features of China's policy-making behaviour in post-Mao period through the way of examining the applicability of a range of selected theories and models in China's practice, with the focus on the SEZ-related policy-making processes. This method is actually the one of killing two birds with one stone, which combines theoretical and practical analyses. To do so not only enables us to see the extent to which each of those selected theories can interpret China's practice and their reasons as well, but also to explore China's policy process in post-Mao period effectively.

1.3 The possible problems to conduct this study

However, although the possibility or advantages exist, there are still some inevitable uncertainties and difficulties to be faced, in really accessing the study of China's policy-making process. General speaking, research into politics is a kind of great challenge to the scholars, because 'it involves trying to understand and explain events in situations in which we never have complete information about what happened and why it happened, and our interpretation is influenced by our frames of reference and our ideologies' (Hill, M. J., 1993, p. 157). It is unlike observing an iceberg, although we can only see one part of it above water, we can calculate its total weight according to its specific gravity and the knowledge that nine tenth of the iceberg is under water. Further more, we also can define the shape of the part under water by using sounder or more advanced detectors. However, to observe and analyse political events including policy-making activities is quite different. When we can only see one or some parts, or the ostensible phenomenon of them, which is the extent to which they are usually to be seen, for politics especially the policy-making activities are usually secret, it would be very difficult for us to probe and illustrate the whole situation and explain their reasons actually. Because we do not have any formula or facility which can be used like observing and measuring an iceberg, to calculate and analyse those political events. Therefore, the limitation of study in this field is inevitable. What scholars need to and be able to do is just trying their best to understand and explain what they can see, according to their available information, with the help of their understanding about the general background.

Particularly speaking, much more difficulties should be expected in studying China's politics and policy-making process. This is mainly stemming from the features of China's less open political life, which would cause many inconveniences to researchers compared with the situation in Western countries. Due to the limitation of free access to the political realm by the media and researchers, some important information (including that inside or behind an open activity) was not allowed to be touched, explored and published either in or after the processing course of those political events. Thus those data are very difficult to be discovered and accumulated. Moreover, since politics in China is not a topic which can be discussed liberally, especially those sensitive issues, it would also be difficult for scholars to gather enough requisite information through different ways including interviews later.

Consequently, when deciding to research into the topic of the book, it was understood that it is inevitable that many difficulties would be encountered. However, it is essential to point out that to handle this difficult task, the author has his own strengths and weaknesses, and the strength seems to be advantageous to overcome these difficulties to a considerable extent. The strength includes two aspects. One is the familiarity of China's politics and institutions, which came from personal experience, the accumulation of the understanding of the topic, and the familiarity and language superiority to access the necessary data. The other one is that the author has more than ten years' historical academic background that is sure to be conducive in analysing a policy process with profound and complicated context. The weaknesses can be seen from two points. (1) It is difficult to have interviews with those policy makers in the SEZ course. (2) It is not easy to access some core data that closely relate the SEZ course because they are still secret of China's central authority.

To sum up, therefore, under this circumstance, research still can be conducted. By using those available data including government's publication, scholars' research works, newspapers and journals, both at home and abroad, we can try our best to portray and analyse a basic picture of the iceberg — the SEZ's policy process and the policy-making behaviour in post-Mao China as well. Although to do so is mainly according to the author's personal judgement, it is sure to be beneficial in furthering the study in this field from one aspect.

1.4 The key issues and study method

Based on combining a historical contextual analysis and a comprehensive theoretical analysis, what we aim to explore is twofold. (1) The applicability of those relevant theories and models to China's practice in post-Mao period, and (2) how and to what extent the changes occurred in post-Mao period influenced China's policy-making processes in all major related aspects including policy makers, motivation, policy-making methods, environment and institutions. In doing so, as mentioned above, we adopted a method of probing the major development, changes and features, of post-Mao China, through examining the applicability of a range of selected policy-making theories and models to the practice of promoting China's Special Economic Zones (SEZ) during the years 1978-1995.

Through this method the book explores a series of issues from two aspects. Theoretically, it probes to what extent and how these selected theories and models are applicable to explain China's policy-making process in the post-Mao period and their reasons as well. Practically, it analyses the relevant issues from the following two levels. Those that are at the first level, which directly concerns SEZ course, are fourfold. They include why did China need to establish SEZs, how could the SEZ-related decisions be made, what strategies and policies had been made to promote the SEZ course, and what characteristics can be drawn from the policy-making processes of establishing and developing the SEZs?

Then, those that need to be further discussed at the second level relating to China's policy-making behaviour and policy-making environment in post-Mao period, with the help of those selected theories and models, focus on following. (1) Who was involved in the process in different periods, and who were in the dominant position? (2) What were the purposes and motivations of determining the policy and strategy? (3) What were the main approaches with which the policy was made? (4) To what extent and how the changed political environments affected policy-making? (5) What were the main changes and characteristics of China's policy-making models and the reasons during this period? (6) What are the fundamental elements by which China's policy-making mode to be shaped? Of course, the practical discussion is taken in an integrated way with the examination of the applicability of those theories and models, and serves the latter which is the core task of our study. We divided them into two aspects here is for stating the research target more clearly.

Although this research will discuss a range of theories and models as mentioned above, we only select seven of them to particularly observe and interpret China's SEZ policy process, the major analytical object of our study. These embody the relevant state theories including pluralism, elitism and institutionalism, and the theories concerning how policy should be made, which cover rationalism, incrementalism, optimal approach and the contingent method. To make this selection stems from the following consideration, to which more analyses will be conducted in the relevant chapters reviewing theories and models, namely, chapter 2 to 4.

Pluralist account combining both descriptive and prescriptive factors, highlights the significance of the involvement of interests in influencing a policy-making, in which a balanced bargaining process could be seen. That to interpret the policy processes in the post-Mao period with this theory does not mean that China has been a politically pluralist society although a noticeable development of pluralist tendency has occurred and increasingly exerted its impacts on Chinas' policy-making process in the last two decades. To do so also does not mean China's authority has really encouraged the involvement of a pluralist competition in influencing the state's policy-making. The substance of this issue is that in a society it doesn't matter whether a regime would like to admit and accept pluralism or not, the existence of the plural forces, politically and economically, is an objective phenomenon. Even though in the circumstance that the multiple economic forces are difficult to develop due to the control by the state, the existence of groups with different political or ideological tendencies, or different policy preferences, are inevitable. They can act overtly or covertly, positively or passively, inside or outside the policy circle, which would never stop. To discuss the SEZ course with this perspective is attempting to probe how and to what extent the SEZ policy-making process was promoted by diversified forces both inside and outside the policy-making circles and both inside and outside the CPC and governmental organs, and also how and to what extent those overt or potential opposing forces had obstructed or delayed the policy process. In other words, to explain the SEZ course with a pluralist account is to see to what extent a pluralist involvement in China's political life had occurred, and to see to what extent and how a balanced bargaining process influenced China's SEZ policy-making.

Elitism is mainly a descriptive account, which considers that the key point of the complex pluralist involvement is actually the conflicts and interactions of those political elites. To observe China's policy process with elitist perspective is particularly significant in view of what follows. On one hand, the characteristic of China's existing political system, which emphasises centralised power mechanism and the political monism, and over-stresses the intervention role of the state to the social life, gives China's political elites very prominent status, compared with those in the Western countries. On the other hand, the tradition of China's feudalism politics which had developed for more than two-thousand years, also greatly increased the impacts of elitist politics. Those feudalism elements include the ideas that the power and will of an emperor are above all, that officials are more clever and important than ordinary people, and that those at high level status are more capable than those at lower level status, etc. The influences of these feudalism elements, which were reflected in China's reality of political life, included those what Deng Xiaoping had pointed out in 1980 that 'personality-cult, paternalism, paternalistic manner, and even include the life-long official term of the cadres' (Xiao, B. 1998, p. 37). Thus, to examine the SEZ course with the elitist viewpoint is to probe to what extent and how an elitist style policy-making pattern influenced the making of the SEZ-related policies, and also to see what changes have happened in China's elitist politics in the post-Mao period. Through these analyses, consequently, we can know to what extent the elitist viewpoint can explain China's policy process.

As a typical descriptive account, institutional perspective sees any possible action or element influencing a policy process as nothing but the product that is subjected to the institutional framework. All elements involving in a policy process, which include power, procedures, and theoretical principles, are determined or structured by institutions in force. Then, how and to what extent do China's institutions shape those major elements influencing China's policy process? This deserves careful study in view of the threefold reason below: China is the largest country upholding the socialist system, the largest developing country and one of the countries with the longest civilisation history. It is conceivable that to explore how and to what extent an institutional perspective can explain the features and changes of China's policy process, is significant in both benefiting the study of this theory and of China's practice. Hence, to discuss SEZ policy process with institutional method is seeking to explore how and to what extent China's institutions had influenced SEZ policy processes through shaping up the power distribution, interest distribution and the rules of the games, which were involved in policy-making.

Selecting those four major models concerning how policy should be made, which include rationalism, incrementalism, optimal approach and contingent method, to examine the SEZ-related policy-making processes, also stems from the consideration that their use is feasible and essential to analyse China's practice. To choose rationalism and incrementalism is not only because they are the most important models of the policy-making study and the two ends of this study in a continuum of searching the way to improve policy process, but also because it is particularly significant to use them to analyse China's reality. For a long time in the first three decades of the PRC, the empiricism, dogmatism, holism, aiming at too high, and idealism plus revolutionary fervour, had prevailed to the different extent, in policy-making and brought about many policy-produced disastrous consequences economically and politically, especially in the periods when extra-leflist ideology and political campaigns dominated China's social life. Then, what happened in the post-Mao era? To what extent had China departed from the old policy-making mode thus to achieve the remarkable development in the last two decades? Accordingly, to examine the SEZ policy-making course with these two rulers, rationalist and incrementalist approaches, aims at directly measuring and assessing the practice, by which to see what changes had been made and to what extent these changes had benefited China's policy-making. The optimal approach is one of the major models searching the middle way to combine merits of rationalism and incrementalism and avoid their defects. The contingent methods are trying to offer a comprehensive explanation, showing that the applicability of a policy-making model depends on whether it can match the reality of a given context of a policy-making issue, from different viewpoints. Consequently, to be sure, to use these two approaches to observe and measure China's SEZ course is helpful and also a good supplement to the analyses of pluralist and incrementalist models.

Furthermore, we need to point out that the three relevant state theories and the four models searching the way to improve a policy process, which will be introduced to deal with the core analytical object in our study, seem to fit together well. It has been generally considered that the theoretical basis of rationalism is elitism, the theoretical basis of incrementalism is pluralism, and the theoretical basis of optimal approach is trying to confine the elements of elitism and pluralism. The contingent method is aiming to explain that the adaptability of a model to practice depends on the extent to which it matches the reality of the given context. In conducting a systematic policy-making analysis, to use this method, which provides us with a comprehensive viewpoint, is of enlightenment. Institutional method is the way, which particularly observes and analyses the causal conditions why those elements can be involved in and influence a policy process, to give institutional explanation for the policy-making behaviour, in a fundamental sense. Therefore, it is conceivably an essential part to be fitted with other models in a policy analysing programme. Particularly speaking, as indicated above, to analyse policy process with an institutionalist method is also significant, in terms of China's context as the largest developing country upholding the socialist system in the world. Thus, it appears that the two groups of theories and models, which have been briefly introduced above, are linked closely.

When confirming the necessity and possibility of the use of those seven theories and models to examine the central analytical object of our study — the SEZ policy process, it is also essential to briefly explain why other theories and models including Marxist determinism, globalisation determinism and those Sinologists' models, are not introduced. The theories of Marxist determinism and the globalisation determinism, which will be discussed in chapter two, emphasise the influences producing from the economic relations, economic mode and economic force associated with the social economic life, on the state's policy-making. Accordingly, they are more feasible in observing and analysing the micro context of a big event or big social phenomenon in a given epoch, in which the elements mentioned above exert their influences through forming a causal dynamics for the state's policy-making. Usually, the role of these elements could be recognised from a longer period or a big historical change. Therefore, these two theories will be introduced to examine China's policy-making practice in general, but not to interpret the concrete SEZ policy-making course.

Those Sinologists' models about how China's policy is made are created by the practical study of China's policy-making behaviour. They provide us with enlightenment and references in researching into this realm with various viewpoints. However, it seems that their theoretical bases are still those relevant state theories, such as pluralism, elitism and institutionalism, etc. Hence, they will also not be used to examine the SEZ-related policy processes. To review them in detail aims at expanding our viewpoint and enriching the contextual background of the central analytical target so as to benefit our study.

To unfold our study, the book will be furthered in three steps. Part one, containing chapters from 2 to 4, reviews and summarises the main features of those major relevant policy-making theories and models, and discusses the applicability of some selected theories and models to China's practice in general.

Then, part two, from chapter 5 to 8, reviews the policy-making processes of China's SEZ course from 1979 to 1995, which was divided into three stages as below. The first stage was from 1979 to early 1980s, when the first group of SEZs, in which Shenzhen is the most typical one, was established and developed. The second stage was from the early 1980s to the end of 1980s, when the largest SEZ, Hainan, was established and developed. The third stage started from 1990, when Pudong New Zone, the most important and most special SEZ, was established and developed. Chapter 5 conducts a general review of the SEZ course including its background, main features and policies. Then, the following chapters discuss the three stages or three cases in turn.

Part three, covering chapters 9 to 11, analyses the applicability of selected theories and models to China's SEZ course. Chapter 9 discusses the applicability of selected state theories relating how policy is made. Chapter 10 examines the applicability of those models concerning how policy should be made. Finally, chapter 11 conducts a comprehensive and comparative analysis in which theories and models are applied in an integrated way. These examinations aim at enabling us to further deepen our understanding of the extent to which those selected theories and models can be applied to interpret China's policy-making process in post-Mao period, and also to see exactly to what extent China's policy-making behaviour had changed and why. In doing so, the fundamental features of China's policy-making in the post-Mao period are explored which leads to a conclusion of the main findings of our study.

The result of this research, hopefully, enables us to understand one of the key conditions of China's historical transition: that a better policy-making mode and environment had enabled China to make a series of effective strategies and policies, which brought about China's continuous development in the last two decades towards its desired target.

Note

[1]   This viewpoint was raised by Mr Newt Gingrich, the speaker of the House of the Representative of the United States, when he met China's vice Premier Zhu Rongji, during his official visit in China, in February 1997.

PART I:
FORMULATING THE
THEORETICAL FRAMEWORK

2 A survey of the state theories relating to how policy is made

2.1 Policy and policy-making

What is policy? In order to access the discussion of the policy-making theories, we should first try to gain a clear definition of policy. We can observe policy from different sides. First, a policy refers to the public affairs which concern a wider or narrower realm, such as a social organisation, a business company, a society, etc. It does not relate to the realm of pure private individual relations which are free from being monitored and restrained by any legal social organisation. Second, policy provides direction, regulation, standard or plan by selection, to guide the work or operation in the realm that is led by the policy-making organ. In this sense, a price stipulation, a tax rule, a piece of law or a planning scheme are all policies. Third, policy has its time limitation. It is only valid for a period of time, for example, one year, two years, fifty years, or more, but not forever like a scientific formulation. It only exists when it matches the objective environmental requirement, or it would be cancelled by the original or new decision-makers. Fourth, policy is a prescription or stipulation of dealing with an existing problem, so when a policy is being made it has administrative or legal efficacy, the people who belong to the organisation or society in which its core organ determines the policy, should be restrained or affected by it.

However, to clearly define the exact meaning of policy is not easy, and scholars hold their different opinions. For more than four decades, writers suggested a diversified ideas to describe it, in which some typical viewpoints could be listed below. (1) Policy is a web of decisions and actions. Easton holds that a policy 'consists of a web of decisions and actions that allocate ...values' (1953, p. 130). (2) Policy is a course of action or inaction. Heclo suggests that 'A policy may usually be considered as a course of action or inaction rather than specific decision or action' (1972, p. 85). (3) Policy is a selection of goals and means. As Jenkins says, policy is 'a set of interrelated decisions concerning the selection of goals and means of achieving them within a specified situation...'(1978).   (4) Policy is a stance. Friend, J.K. et al. Point out that 'Policy is essentially a stance which, once articulated, contributes to the context within which a succession of future decisions will be made' (1974, p. 40). (5) Policy is an expression of political rationality. Parsons holds that 'To have a policy is to have rational reasons or arguments, which contain both a claim to an understanding of a problem and a solution. It puts forward what is and what ought to be done. A policy offers a kind of theory upon which a claim for legitimacy is made' (1997, p. 15).

As for the scope of policy, there is a general idea commonly accepted in academic circles. That is, it 'is usually considered to apply to some thing "bigger" than a particular decision, but "smaller" than general social movements' (Heclo, 1972, p. 84).

From a broad view, we can portray policy as follows. Policy is a choice of suitable means or measures in order to reach a desired goal; policy is a balance of the interest conflict between different groups; policy is to distinguish different groups' interest and interest demand; policy is expected to serve the basic and long-turn interest of the decision-makers and to ultimately realise their theory, values and determination.

Since the concept of policy can be applied in all organisations of a society, it should be defined here that the discussion in this study is only related to the governmental behaviour, which means the scope of policy only concerns the affairs of a state and a society.

Then, what is policy-making? Generally speaking, it can be said that policy-making is a process of selecting an option for implementation. Within this process the policy makers — individuals, small groups or committees of organisations or government, are involved to react to an identified (or unidentified) problem or a set of problems by analysing information, determining objectives, formulating options, evaluating the options and finally choosing preferred alternatives. This is a narrow definition of policy-making. To be more exact, however, from a broad sense, policy-making can not be simply treated as a course of deciding a preferred policy for implementation, for it involves much more complex conceptual and functional theories which have necessarily been divided into two groups: how policy is made, and how policy should be made.

Regarding the first aspect, which mainly involves the descriptive studies, it includes some fundamental state-related theories: (1) who must have the right to participate in a policy-making process; (2) who can play the dominant roles in a policy-making process; (3) what are the purposes or motivations for making a policy; and (4) how and to what extent the state power structures and power operating mechanism (institutions) influence the policy-making process.

As for the second aspect, which mainly focuses on prescriptive studies, it contains the concrete exploration of the policy-making approaches and models: (1) what method should be used to make a policy; (2) how to use different policy-making approaches in the light of the different situations; and (3) how to judge the applicability of a policy-making model; etc. These contents just belong to the narrow definition of policy-making theories. Our study discusses policy-making theories from a broad view, which embodies those that are in above two groups.

Both these two groups relate to various schools of theories and models. In the first group relating to how policy is made, two sorts of theories and models are considered which cover the relevant state theories including pluralism, elitism, Marxism, globalism and institutionalism, etc, and the Sinologists' models about how China's policy is made. The second group relating to how policy should be made embodies rationalism, incrementalism, 'mixed scanning' approach, optimal method and contingent approach, etc. In order to examine the applicability of these theories and models to China's policy-making process, it is essential to first review and summarise their main features. This chapter discusses those relevant state theories concerning how policy is made, and also examines their applicability to China's practice in a general way.

2.2 The diverse state theories about how policy is made

2.2.1 Pluralism and neo-pluralism

Pluralism is the most influential political thought and theory in the twentieth century. With the focus on who has the right to participate and how they participate in the state's policy-making process, this theory stresses the importance of widespread political participation and holds that a state's power is dispersed amongst a wide variety of social groups. Hence, it ascribes far more importance to elections, party competition and interest groups than other theories. Also, it insists on the reality and importance of multiple channels whereby citizens can control their political leaders and shape the development of public policies.

Historically, the term pluralism was identified with a school of political philosophy that argued against the concept of an absolute and sovereign state. Both Locke and Montesquieu were the most distinguished representatives of this school. In his work, *The Spirit of the Law*, Montesquieu highly praises the eighteenth-century English system of government for separating political power into three branches — executive, legislative and judicial, and he especially emphasises the merits that a political system has more than one source of authority (Richter, M. 1977).

The classical pluralists attacked the legal doctrine of the sovereign state and argued that it did not fit empirical reality and that it was undesirable as a normative goal, because the reaction opposed the legalistic approach to political study that accepted constitutional nostrums at face value.

The key features of the intellectual origins of the classical pluralist political science summarise by Dunleavy and O'Leary (1987, p. 17), include five aspects. (1) It began first and foremost as an attack a state monism, whether expressed philosophically in the doctrine of sovereign or practically in centralised, absolutist states. (2) It valued group and organisational autonomy, activity and diversity. (3) It agreed that vigorous group conflicts must be expected in any complex society. (4) It debated the relative usefulness of institutional or social checks and balances as mechanisms to prevent state monism, and it also divided over whether the rationale for institutional or social pluralism is primarily protective or developmental. (5) It was aware of the dangers of a society where self-interest was the dominant motive and traditional social ties were absent, although it defended the merits of political individualism.

Contemporary pluralism developed in the 1950s and early 1960s, in which the representative works were written by Bell, D. (1960), Dahl, R. A (1956, 1961) and Lindblom, C. E. (Dahl and Lindblom, 1953). Although like the classical pluralism, the new pluralism still used the empirical/observational approach and followed the normative belief in limiting the power of the state (but with the focus on government rather than state), it developed as the reaction to the theory of elite and the classical democratic theory. As a response to the elitist theory, new pluralism holds that there is widespread distribution of political resources, and different interests prevail in different political disputes and different times. Arguing with the classical democratic version, it plays down the idea, which only emphasises the importance of voting as a standard of democratic system and its providing an intellectual legislation of pressure group activity.

Dahl gives an explicit statement for this version of new pluralism, derived from his studies of American politics. He stresses, 'few groups in the United States which are determined to influence the government — certainly few who are organised, active and persistent, — lack the capacity and opportunity to influence some officials somewhere in the political system in order to obtain at least some of their goals' (1967, p. 113). This is the most famous statement about the aforementioned version of pluralism.

Ham and Hill portray the source of power in contemporary society with the view of neo-pluralism from another angle: the sources of power — like money, information, expertise and so on — are distributed non-cumulatively and no one source is dominant. Essentially, then, in a pluralist political system power is fragmented and dispersed, and the basic picture presented by the pluralists is of a political marketplace where what a group achieves depends on its resources and its 'decibel rating' (1993, p. 29).

To summarise, neo-pluralism pays much less attention to elections, party competitions or interest group politics, and downgrades their social significance compared with the conventional pluralism. The main propositions of neo-pluralism include, 'the irreversible switch away from simple class-based political divisions; the anachronism of left-right ideological conflicts and the growth of new 'post-industrial' issues; the radically reduced role of representative institutions as controls on the operations of the extended state; and the privileged position of business in liberal democratically politics' (Dunleavy and O'Leary, ibid. p. 288).

2.2.2 Elite theory

Elite has always been a rather loose term in political science, for there is not a single accurate definition to describe its meaning and the relevant political and social phenomena. The originators of the modern elite theory are two Italian social scientists, Vilfredo Pareto and Gaetano Mosca. Both of them assert that the existence and the roles of the elites are objective laws of human society. In his book, '*The Ruling Class*', Mosca argues that in all societies 'two classes of people appear — a class that rules and a class which is ruled. The first class, always the less numerous, performs all political functions, monopolises power and enjoys the advantages that power brings' (G. Mosca, 1896, in Kahn and Livingston, 1939, p. 50).

It is Vilfredo Pareto who gives the term of elites a wide currency in social science since he most clearly attempted to examine elites and formulate a very general conception. According to Pareto, the elites are composed of all those having the highest ability in every human activity. In his research, Pareto concentrated his attentions on what he called the 'governing elites' which he contrasted with the non-elite or lower stratum. (V. Pareto, 1916, in Livingston and Bongioro, 1935).

The main issues to which those scholars who are involved in the study of elites theory pay more attentions are sixfold as below: the components of elites; the resources of elites' power; the relation between elites and social classes; the relation between elites and democracy; the relation between elites and pluralism, and the inevitability of elites.

The components of elites   The studies of elites by political scientists, sociologists and historians have multiplied since the 1950s. The elites groups which have received much attentions are those political leaders (including revolutionary elites), the heads of business enterprises, high-ranking bureaucrats, military chiefs, and intellectuals. However, then, what are the exact components of the elites, especially the political elites? There are many different answers to this question, among which Bottomore's classification is worthy of more attention. Bottomore's method is attempting to distinguish the political elites and the political class. According to Bottomore (1966, pp. 14-15), the former group includes members of the government and of the high administration, military leaders, and in some cases, politically influential families of an aristocracy or royal house and leaders of powerful economic enterprises; the latter is not only comprised of the political elites but also of the leaders of political parties in opposition, trade union leaders, businessmen and politically active intellectuals. This distinction defines the term of elites, both the internal components and the external extension, and sounds more acceptable.

The resources of the elites' power   It has been widely accepted that elites' power may come from various sources, such as occupying formal office, wealth, technological expertise, knowledge and so on. However, elites' power is not solely dependent on any one resource listed above. In contemporary elite theory, controlling the significant organisations (large company, trade union and parties, etc.) and important institutionalised positions has been considered as the key resources of the elites' power and received more attentions.

The relation between elite and democracy   The question of whether elite theory is feasible in a democratic society and elites are acceptable to such a society has been studied by many scholars. It has been suggested that the existence of elites is not incompatible with pluralist democracy because competition between elites protects democratic government (Ham & Hill, ibid. p. 33).

The relation between elitism and pluralism   Fundamentally speaking, there is some similarity between the theories of elitism and pluralism on the issue of who controls the political power or state's policy making. In elite theory, those political elites are clearly the minority in society and the ruling class; according to pluralism, then, although it emphasises that no one source or even a few groups are determined to influence the state in a pluralist system, the different political sources are still controlled by some small groups. Therefore, some scholars have attempted to reconcile the elitism and pluralist democracy, and some have tried to use the findings of elitist studies to argue that the power elite is but a ruling class by another name (see Ham and Hill, ibid.; Miliband, R. 1969).

The elites and the social classes   This concerns the theories of class stratification and the class origins of the elite members. Research has shown generally that there is a high degree of elite self-recruitment — from the upper-middle classes, with variations between countries and significant differences in socialist countries. Heath's study (1981) suggests that the degree of self-recruitment of the elite group has changed little between 1949 and 1972, but since 1972 there has been an important change in the overall composition of the elite group as a result of the extension of their members. The fact was that three quarters of the members of elite groups came from lower social origins in 1972. Therefore, it may be seen as the further extension of the democratic elites or democratisation in Britain and other industrialised countries.

However, some scholars disagree with the significance of the changes of the class composition of the elite members. They consider that the change of the recruitment of elite members makes relatively little difference to the situation of domination by a ruling group, so long as the ownership or effective possession of major economic resources is concentrated in the hands of a small minority, whether this is a capitalist class or a 'new class' of bureaucrats or intellectuals.

The inevitability of the elite   For explaining the inevitability of elite, scholars of elite theories give various reasons. Pareto has a complicated psychological theory, linked with a pessimistic view of the human capacity to exercise reason in social life; Mosca and Michels, emphasise heavily a theory about the nature of organisation and bureaucracy quite similar to Weber's; Schumpeter believes the masses were bound to suffer from the hysteria associated with crowd psychology; and so on (Robertson, 1993, p. 161). Although scholars of political science do not share a common view about the accuracy of elitist theories, there are few if none of them who would deny the inevitability of the existence of the elites.

2.2.3 Marxist theories

Marxism was created based on observing and analysing the basic regularity of the capitalist society. As a typical determinism, Marxism explores that the innate and insoluble contradiction of the productive relations in the capitalist society, namely the conflict between bourgeoisie and the proletariat, and the contradiction between the productive force and the production relations, would eventually lead to the fundamental class struggle, which indicates the impact of economic determinant. It asserts that in a capitalist society the state is nothing but the tool used by a small group of bourgeois who control the means of production, to carry out and maintain its rule upon the working class. Thus, it declares that to overthrow such a society by a proletarian revolution leading to socialism was an inevitable law of human history.

Although the development of contemporary society has not matched in all ways the prediction of Marx, it 'does not invalidate the whole of his analysis, particularly those parts relating to the significance of ownership or control of the means of production for power within the state' (Ham and Hill, 1993, p. 34). The state theory is one of the most important components of the huge theoretical system of Marxism, which initially developed as an critique of Hegel's political philosophy, and especially challenged Hegel's contention that in modern society the state appears as a force independent of the economic forces of the society.

According to the description of Marxist theories, the status and roles of the modern state include the following three views.

- The state is an instrument of the ruling class. This is the best known and most orthodox interpretation of Marxism concerning the state. In *The Communist Manifesto*, Marx propounded that, the modern state, far from representing common interests of a society, is nothing 'but a committee for managing the common affairs of the whole bourgeoisie' (McLellan, D. (ed.), 1977, p.223). This function is based on the economic structure of society, which is constructed by the relations of production which is the basis 'on which arise legal and political structures and to which correspond definite form of social consciousness' (Marx, K. 1859; 1973, p.181).

- The state is an arbiter in some special situations. When the class struggle is equally balanced, it will create a temporary history-making role for political leaders and state bureaucracies 'that the state power, as ostensible mediator, momentarily acquired a certain degree of independence of both.'(Engels, F. 1884)[1] Actually, Marx and Engels did not expect the arbiter state to be a typical regime under capitalism, but rather they expected it would be quickly replaced as the development of history produced decisive shifts of power towards the proletariat. On the other hand, the state's autonomy from capital on economic issues was still very limited owing to its dependence on capital, in this exceptional period.

- The state's autonomy in serving the long-term interests of the ruling class. Since the state is the superstructure, its functions should be operated to meet the requirement of the economic base. Therefore, as Dunleavy and O'Leary (1987, pp. 210-211) summarised, 'government and legal-administrative institutions are moulded in forms which optimally sustain capital accumulation, whether or not the state is directly controlled by capitalists and irrespective of the precise balance of class force'. It means that in order to serve the long-run interests of capital and against the current wishes of shortsighted capitalists, the state needs to and also can formulate and carry out some policies that benefit other social classes or even the whole of society.

The discussion about Marxism's state-related theory has always been an important part in the research of Marxism. Since the early 1970s, writing on the Marxist and Neo-Marxist theories of the state has flourished, and relevant authors included James R O'Connor, C. Offe, N.

Poulantzas, R. Miliband, and M. Aglietta, among many others (Gorman, 1985).

As a political economist, O'Connor focused his writings on fiscal crisis as well as on the role of the capitalist state in the latter part of the twentieth century. According to his analysis about the roles of different forms of modern state's expenses, i.e. social investment for increasing labour productivity, social consumption for lowering of the cost of reproducing labour power, and the social expenses which serves to maintain social harmony, O'Connor (1973) draws the conclusion that state expenditure serves the interest of monopoly capital, and the state is run by a class-conscious political directorate acting on behalf of monopoly capitalist class interest. It can be seen that although O'Connor stresses the state expenditure serves the interest of monopoly capitalist class, he still clearly points out that for the sake of this purpose the state needs to use social expanses to maintain the social harmony. This is actually one of the performances of the state's autonomy in serving its long-run interest.

Ralph Miliband advances an instrumentalist analysis of the capitalist state and attempts to probe the relationship between economic power and political power. He argues that the ruling class consists of those who own and control the means of material and mental production and are thereby also able to dominate state power. However, while pointing out the influence of the capitalist class on the state policies, Miliband (1977, p.74) also holds that the state does possess a high degree of autonomy in its operation, even though 'the state does act, in Marxist term, on behalf of the ruling class, it does not for the most part act at its behest'. He considers this relative autonomy of the state important to Marxist theory, for it gives the state the capacity to protect and advance capitalism's objective interests in ways that might be unpopular to capitalists. The degree of the autonomy varies in different forms of the state. Miliband (1983, p.65) goes further to search for the relationship between the ruling class and the state and he asserts that in advanced capitalist societies this relationship can best be characterised as a 'partnership between two different, separate forces, locked to each other by many threads, yet each having its own separate sphere of concerns'.

The distinctive contributions to Marxist state theory of Nicos Poulantzas were attempting to integrate Gramsci's notion of hegemony and Althusserian structuralism to analyse not only the state in capitalism but also the state in transmission to socialism (1973, 1976, 1978). His main ideas include two aspects.

- The state has its autonomy that serves both the interests of capitalist and the state. Poulantzas rejects the notion that the state was either a reflection of the relation of production or a simple instrument by which the capitalist class could achieve its goals. He argues that the state enjoyed a certain autonomy and therefore could pursue its own interests as well as the interests of capital.

- The state can serve the long term interests of the capitalist class. In examining how the state orchestrated the disparate interests of an internally competitive and highly fractionated bourgeoisie both to create cohesion and to serve the long-term interests of capital, Poulantzas (1973, p. 285) concludes that its relative autonomy enables the state to objectively judge some particular situations and search for feasible measures to deal with them. These actions include compromises or even sacrifices of 'the long term economic interests of one or other faction of the dominant class'. Because, 'such compromises and sacrifices are sometimes necessary for the realisation of their political class interests'.

To summarise, all discussion about Marxist state theories among scholars focus on the extent to which the state is an instrument of the dominant class of a society which is shaped by the existing economic foundation, and to what extent the state enjoys autonomy. Both these two aspects are based on the economic determinism. That means, it was the nature of the economic foundation that determines the form of a modern state and the allocation of the state's power. The ideas of those researchers mentioned above are basically similar, for instance, all these Marxist theory writers insist that the capitalist state is the main means the ruling class uses to maintain its dominance. As Ham and Hill point out, 'they represent a radically different approach both to the pluralists — who tend to see government as one set of pressure groups among many others, and to the elitists — who argue that the state elite is powerful but not tied to a particular class within society' (1993, p. 39).

However, to access a more concrete analysis about the aforementioned viewpoints, there are still some problems that need to be further discussed. First, to what extent the state depends on the will of the dominant class as it functions. Second, the conditions under which the state may enjoy certain autonomy. Third, whether the state possesses certain autonomy beyond the control of the ruling class is a universal objective law that exists in all other states with different social systems. Fourth, what are the differences in levels of the autonomy between countries with different social systems and values. Finally, and more importantly, since the class relations in contemporary industrial societies have become very complicated it is difficult to identify people's class status. For instance, many people are not the owners of the means of production and they do not even have a very small enterprise, but they do have some capital investment by having more or less stocks and shares, or capital savings. Are they then capitalists? These people are teachers, doctors, medium and lower public servants, and many other liberal career workers. Thus, how can a line be clearly drawn to distinguish the ruling class and the ruled class and how can one identify what interests belong to a given class instead of to others? Moreover, even those top managers of many big business companies are normally employees rather than owners. Do these people belong to the ruling class or the ruled class? It would be difficult to discuss the thesis that the state is dominated by the interest of the capitalist and serves the long-term interests of the ruling class, if the aforementioned issue could not be solved.

2.2.4 Globalisation theory

Globalisation theory was first produced from the study of the world's integrated economic development since the mid-twentieth century, and then was applied to the studies in other realms, such as politics and culture etc. The globalisation tendency in all these realms has been becoming more and more strong and profoundly and widely influences human society in all aspects, and so it has inevitably had powerful impacts on states' policy making. Thus, it is reasonable to treat it as one of the state theories concerning how policy is made.

To see globalisation with an economic view, it simply points to a tendency in which 'the national state is less able to control the agenda than it was in the past' (Parsons, W. 1997, p235). 'It means that all aspects of economy — raw materials, labour information and transportation, finance, distribution, marketing — are integrated or interdependent on a global scale (Carnoy et al. 1993). The history of past decades proved that the rapid development of the global economy has been eroding the integrity and even autonomy of national economies. That means, no country can decide its economic policies or strategies without carefully considering the relevant international factors and seeking essential international co-operation. Therefore, Castells clearly points out that, global economy, is 'an economy that works as a unit in real time on a planetary basis' (1994, p. 21).

The occurrence and strengthening of globalisation resulted from the rapid development of science and technology. The establishment of powerful worldwide information and communication system (telecommunication and computer network), and the improvement of advanced transport facilities, had made our earth much smaller. The restriction of time and space in the past is no longer the problem of connection among peoples under any circumstance. The more and more close connection and influences in economic activities between different countries and regions further strengthen their interdependence.

Due to the 'reordering of the time and distance in our life' (Giddens, A, 1989, p. 519), the tendency of globalisation rapidly and significantly influenced all important aspects of human society, or, in other worlds, all these important aspects had been deeply and directly involved in this tendency. Luard (1990) concretely analyses these manifestations on different sides. For instances, about the world's security, owing to the development of the military technology, the manufacture of weapons of vast destructive power, and the capacity to deliver them to any place of the world within a very short time, 'no country can any longer, unaided, defend itself and its population'. Other social issues, like taking actions to fight against terrorists, hijacking of aircraft, to prevent the spread of AIDS and many other diseases, definitely need international co-operation. Moreover, to safeguard the world's environment can only be effectively undertaken globally (p ix.). Based on his study, Luard eventually set forth a viewpoint that the focus of political action in the world had been changed to an international level and a global polity is required (p.191). He argues that, to create a more just international society only international action is significant, because,

> Only redistribution at the global level, through the establishment of a system of economic management comparable to that which operates within states, would be sufficient to remedy the types of inequality which are now most manifest. Only transnational political movements, bringing together those in all countries, rich or poor, concerned to bring about the type of changes required, are likely, to bring about the adjustment in political and economic relations which would be necessary for that purpose. And only new international institutions, more representative than those which exist today, reflecting the view of groups and individuals as well as of governments, are likely to prove suitable instruments for bringing about such changes (p. 190).

Although what Luard stresses and predicts may be too early, or, maybe as he says 'appear no doubt 'Utopian', unrealistic and perhaps misguided' to somebody (ibid.), it does explore the profound influence brought about by the globalisation, and remind people to attach enough attention to this issue.

Globalisation theory offers a new point of view to observe the manifestations, mechanism and impacts of the activities of human beings at an international level. It describes two basic facts to us that on one hand many issues of these activities could not be really or fundamentally solved at a national level (e.g. World's security, anti-terrorist hijacking aircraft, safeguard environment, preventing and controlling the spread of AIDS, etc.), and many issues could be conducted well only by widely involving into the communication of international information system, international exchange and competition (scientific and technologic researches, and all economic activities including production, finance and business, etc.), on the other hand. These indicate that the globalisation factors had inevitably played important roles in influencing national policy-making.

Unquestionably, policy-making in any state needs to be adapted to meet the demands of the globalisation situation. That means, those international factors must be carefully considered in all states' policy-making processes. Any tendency without attaching enough attention to these considerations, or without actively involving the international interchanges and co-operation, would be definitely disadvantageous to the interest of a country. For instance, economic isolation means self-departing from the mainstream of the world's economic development, and giving up the opportunity of learning, exchanging and competing with other countries, which would result in a country's economic stagnancy and backwardness. The collapse of Eastern Europe socialist countries just showed they were the victim of their economic isolation and backward, because of 'the inability of old-style, bureaucratic politics to cope with the requirements of new economic organisations and technologies' (Carnoy, M. et al. ibid. p. 13). Political isolation means self-close and self-departing from the world political arena, which would also cause many problems for a country. Therefore, globalisation tendency is a sort of challenge and stress, also an opportunity to any country. You can not escape from it, but must adapt policy-making to follow it. That is the only choice for any state in the contemporary world.

2.2.5 Institutionalist theory

Research into institutions has revived during the past two decades. This resurgence of interest in institutions is a cumulative consequence of the modern transformation of social institutions and persistent commentary from observers of them (March and Olsen, 1984, p. 734). Concretely speaking, the new attention on the institutional research resulted from the following respects: social, political and economic institutions are becoming larger, much more complex and resourceful, and have more importance in public life; most of the major actors in modern economic and political systems have been within formal organisations; and finally, the institutions of law and bureaucracy actually occupy a dominant role in contemporary life, to a considerable extent.

In general, broadly speaking, institutions include both formal and informal organisations, rules as well as the customs. Peter Hall's widely accepted definition asserts, institutions include 'the formal rules, compliance procedures, and standard operating practices that structure the relationship between individuals in various units of the polity and economy' (1986, p.19). Institutionalism examines how these customs, practices and instruments become 'institutionalised', how they take on normative forces, and become meaningful (Apter, 1991, p. 463). Therefore, institutionalism represents an attempt to illustrate how political struggles are mediated by the institutional settings in which they take place (Ikenberry, 1988, pp. 222-3). Furthermore, institutionalist are interested in the whole range of state and societal institutions that shape how political actors define their interests and structure their relations of power to other groups, which clearly include the rules of electoral competition, the structure of party systems, the relations among various branches of government, and the structure and organisations of economic actors like trade unions (Thelen & Steinmo, 1992, p. 2).

In sum up, institutionalists focus their studies on three main issues.

- To examine how the ideas, customs, practices and instruments come to be solidified or fixed, namely, institutionalised — to be accepted and observed by public in an organisation or a state.
- To probe the laws by which the political struggles and social conflicts are structured and mediated by the institutions.
- To discuss the basic relations and changes among different political and social forces within an institutionalised society.

Moreover, since goals change quickly, principles less so, institutionalism is in this sense an attempt to discuss the connections between principles and the practices (Apter, ibid.). The discussion below highlights the essential points scholars have made about the effects of institutions.

First of all, the political institutions can create the environment. March and Olsen hold that:

> Political institutions not only respond to their environments but create those environments at the some time. Such phenomena are not routinely accommodated by modern political theory, which makes political outcomes a function of three primary factors: the distribution of preferences (interests) among political actors, the distribution of resources (power), and the constraints imposed by the rules of the game (constitutions). Each of these is treated as exogenous to the political system. That is, preferences are developed within a society and transmitted through socialisation, resources are distributed among political actors by some broad social processes, and rules of the game are either stable or change by a revolutionary intervention exogenous to ordinary political activities (1989:162).

Second, the influence of the political institutions on policy-making. In his article, *From Keynesianism to Monetarism,* Hall (1992, p. 109) argues that, although institutions alone did not produce the changes made to the British economic policy during the 1970s, the institutional setting in which British policy was made contributed a good deal to the precise trajectory that policy was to follow. The institutionalised routines of the policy process structured the interpretation that policy-makers put upon the new economic developments. The configuration of the labour and financial markets intensified pressure for some lines of policy to occur rather than others, and the institutional character of the media and electoral arena added public and political appeal to some economic ideas more than others.

Desmond S. King (1992, p. 242) also asserts that, 'political parties and politicians link ideas, political institutions and policy. ... Institutional arrangements undoubtedly structure decision-making in the way Peter Hall's influential analysis suggests ...'

Third, there is an important relationship between the political institutions and political stability. Apter (1991) points out that political stability is easily fragmented under conditions of voluntarism, and whether that will happen is to a considerable extent a function of the way institutions work and what they represent or embody in terms of political norms.

Thelen and Steinmo identify four sources of institutional dynamism, by which they mean situations in which they can observe variability in the impact of institutions over time but within countries. These sources include:

(1) broad changes in the socioeconomic or political context can produce a situation in which previously latent institutions suddenly become salient, with implications for political outcomes.

(2) changes in the socioeconomic context or political balance of power can produce a situation in which old institutions are put in the service of different ends, as new actors come into play who pursue their(new) goals through existing institutions.

(3) exogenous changes can produce a shift in the goals or strategies being pursued within existing institutions-that is, changes in outcomes as old actors adopt new goals within the old institutions.

(4) when political actors adjust their strategies to accommodate changes in the institutions themselves, another source of dynamism can occur (Thelen and Steinmo, 1992, p. 2).

With the development of institutional research, a distinction has been made between 'new' and 'old' versions of institutionalism. Basically speaking, the old institutionalism derives from the political and moral philosophy issues and the new one from economics. According to March and Olsen, it would probably be more accurate to describe recent thinking (i.e. new one) as blending elements of an old institutionalism into the non-institutionalist style of recent theories of politics. Because, the new institutionalism 'deemphasize the dependence of the polity on society in favour of an interdependence between relatively autonomous social and political institutions; they deemphasize the simple primacy of micro process and efficient histories in favour of relatively complex process and historical inefficiency; they deemphasize metaphors of choice and allocative outcomes in favour of other logic of action and the centrality of meaning and symbolic action' (March and Olsen, 1984, p. 738).

2.3 The applicability of the above theories to China's practice

2.3.1 The fundamental structure and the principal features of the state's power in contemporary China

To examine the applicability of those theories that have been discussed above to China's practice, it is essential to first analyse the fundamental structure and functional mechanism of China's state power.

The most important feature of China's political structure or the state power is the multiple party co-operative system led by the Communist Party of China (CPC); then, the second is the system of democratic centralism — the minority should submit to the majority, the individual should submit to the organisation, the subordinate should submit to the higher authorities, and all levels of organisations and individuals of both party and the state should submit to the Party centre.

The power structure of the party system   The party power structure comprises five parts: Party Congress; The Central Committee; The Politburo; The Secretariat and three commissions — Central Commission for Inspecting Discipline (CCID), Military Affairs Commission (MAC) and Central Advisory Commission (CAC), of which the CAC has been rescinded in 1990.

The National Party Congress is the highest organ of the CPC, members of which are elected by a series of indirect delegates conferences from the bottom level up to the different rungs of the party ladder. Usually, this Congress is held every five years. According to the constitution of the party, The National Party congress is the most powerful organ which elects the party's Central Committee, examines and approves the party's policy and organisational changes and amends the party's constitution. Actually, since such a big meeting with more then two thousands members is only held for about one week when it is convened, the agendas and all of those decisions it will take will have been previously recommended and basically approved by the superior executive organs. Therefore, the finally ratification by the National Congress is only a formality to a certain extent. The substantive function of the Congress is to kindle massive party members' enthusiasm, give mobilisation for a new task and formally ratify the new policy and important personnel changes.

In the party centre, it is the three important executive bodies — the Central Committee, the Politburo and the Secretariat, which play the key roles in party and state's policy-making affairs.

The Central Committee is elected by the Party congress, which has about 200 full and 100 pending members. It meets in plenary session at least twice a year and is filled with the elite cadres of the CPC. These members consist of party and government officers in important positions, high-ranking military officers, intellectuals, trade union and youth league leaders, and a considerable number of local party secretaries and state officers in chief at provincial and municipal levels. Possessing a position of the central committee member is very important to a person's official career, for he or she has had the right to access some top policy-making processes of the state and the possibility of being promoted to a higher and more important position. Although the Central Committee's major tasks are to elect the Politburo and ratify policy decisions, it has its own functional departments which mainly comprise the Propaganda Department, the Organisational Department, the United Front Work Department and the General Office of The CPC Centre.

The Propaganda Department is in charge of work in the ideological field: to propagate Marxism, Leninism, Mao Zhedong Thought, and Deng Xiaoping Theory; to publicise the party's general and special policies; and specially to give guidance and supervise the works in both cultural and educational fields of the state. The Organisational Department is in charge of the party's organisational development and personnel work at higher level. One of its important duties is to examine and recommend party cadres to fill the high-rank positions. The United Front Work Department is an organ to maximise all forces which could be used to form a wide alliance for fighting against the main enemy or striving for reaching a major target, by mobilisation and organisational works in different periods. Conducting the united front work is one of the most important and effective approaches of the CPC and was used both before and after the founding of the People's Republic of China. The General Office of the CPC Centre deals with the routine works of the Party.

The centre of party's power is the Politburo, which has about 15-20 members. It is the top organ of the party's leadership and is actually in charge of making the most important decisions of both the party and the country. It assembles once a week. Those top party leaders, who possess enough experience and prestige, occupy key positions in the party or in the government or the military, are elected as the standing members of the

Politburo (now it has seven members). The standing members of the Politburo form the real core of the CPC centre and the apex of the China's power pyramid, which include the CPC General Secretary, the premier, the state president, the Chairpersons of the NPC and CPPCC. Below the Politburo there is a Secretariat, which comprises about 12 members, and functions as the assisting organ for providing the administrative back-up and co-ordinate support to the Politburo under its direction. Its tasks include formulating the new policies and dealing with the daily affairs of both party and the country. Being appointed by the Standing Committee of the Politburo, the members of the Secretariat are also responsible to it.

The other powerful organs of the party centre comprise the Central Commission for Inspecting Discipline (CCID), The Central Military Commission (CMC) and the Central Advisory Commission (CAC). The CCID was a new commission of CPC Centre, which was set up in the early 1980s. Its duty is to keep watching over ideology and discipline of the whole country, so as to enable the party's rules to be implemented, and it also supervises its subordinate committees at lower level. The CMC exerts the party's unified leadership over the Chinese Army (PLA). Like CCID, the CAC was also set up in the early 1980s, which was organised by the senior and retired high-ranking figures of party, government or military. CAC's main function was to give advice concerning the party and state's affairs to the central leaders as the central consultants. The CAC had been rescinded in 1990, for it had finished its task in the transitional period when the new replaced the old of China's cadres team.

The power structure of the State's system   The State's Constitution stipulates that The National People's Congress (NPC) is the highest power organ of the country. The deputies to the NPC are elected by local people's Congress. Since 1979, the election system has become more open and democratic. For instance, voting by secret ballot has been extended downwards to the local level, and the direct elections have extended upwards to the county rung. Meanwhile, some important changes of electing method have made elections more competitive. For instance, the number of candidates standing now exceeds the number of places available by 50-100 percent at the base level and by 20-50 percent at the higher level, and nominations are more open to all groups.

The deputies to the National People's Congress are elected every five years and usually there are about 3000 full membership deputies to fill the Congress. Now it regularly meets at least once a year for a period of one to two weeks, to examine and ratify economic plans and constitutional changes, examine and approve other important proposals concerning the state's fundamental policies and strategies, and also to elect the State's major leaders when the term of office of a government has expired. Although it has possessed more openness and independence since the later 1980s, however, it is still considered as 'a "rubber stamp" body which follows the wishes of the CPC executives' (Ian, 1991, p. 13). The leading body of the NPC is its standing committee, which is formed by about 140 members that are elected by the entire deputies of the NPC. The major duty of the standing committee is to organise the work of the congress and also to handle the daily administrative affairs between the sessions of the NPC. Its other duty includes supervising the election for NPC, making and interpreting the State's laws, overseeing the work of the state's Council and its six functional committees, and appointing those key judicial officials. The Chairperson heads the Standing Committee of the NPC.

The state president is elected by the NPC. The power of the president is subtle. Theoretically, the president is the head of the state, but actually is more like a symbol. The degree of holding power by the president depends on his or her real status within the CPC. In current China, the General Secretary of the CPC centre holds the presidency simultaneously. Under this situation, the presidency becomes much more important.

As an administrative cabinet, the actual status and role of the State Council seems more important than the NPC. It is now composed of twenty two departmental ministers, five heads of commissions and corporations, five State Councillors (some of them are also prominent departmental ministers), the secretary-general, the Auditor-General, the Governor of the People's Bank of China, four Vice-premiers and, at its head, the prime minister (Premier). The Prime Minister is nominated by the state president and approved by the NPC. All other high-level officers including the vice-premier and the departmental ministers are nominated by the Prime Minister and ratified by the NPC. This Council represents the leading executive body in the state government, which oversees the departmental and administrative apparatus, to be in charge of day-to-day management of the country and empowered to submit new policy proposals to the NPC's Standing Committee. The Council meets once a month. But its core, an 'inner cabinet' of about 14 members which comprises the Premier, Vice-Premier, State Councillors and Secretary-General, meets more frequently. Most of the members of this 'inner cabinet' are CPC Central Committee members.

At the levels of province, municipal and county, the local governments are formed and function in similar ways to the state's level.

Another important organ outside the formal elected or appointed state authority system is the Chinese People's Political Consultative Conference (CPPCC). It is a broad-front advisory body comprising representative figures from all social realms, especially those elites with excellent achievements or prominent contributions to the country. Amongst them, there are high-rank state officers, technocrats, intellectuals, artists and overseas Chinese. The CPPCC convenes usually simultaneously with the NPC. Its members are required to contribute their criticisms and suggestions for the state's affairs at the Conference. To perform their duty well, they need to devote close attention to issues of public concern or those national key issues in the aspects that they have ability to study, and to conduct an on-the-spot survey, so that they can map out their motions, before the convening of the Conference.

The Supreme People's Court (SPC) and the Supreme People's Procuratorate (SPP) are two top organs of the state's judiciary system. They are in charge of the nation-wide judicial works and supervise lower-level Courts of Justice and Procuratorates. The heads of these two organs are nominated by the state president and ratified by the NPC.

Several important relationships in the power structure To discuss China's political structure and the power distribution, there are some important relations to which further attention should be paid.

* The relation between the party and the state

  According to China's constitution, the Communist Party of China (CPC) is the core leadership force in furthering the cause of China's socialism. Therefore, it is indisputable that the party has a leading status in China. The CPC centre leads and supervises the central government and the local party committees lead and supervise the local governments at the same levels. CPC centre or the local party committees have the right to put forward important proposals for the state's affairs and recommend candidates to fill the important positions in government. Amongst the state's officers at all levels, those who have party membership account for the overwhelming majority.

* The relation between the centre and the local levels

  The principle of 'democratic centralism' stipulates that all levels of the local party committees and governments should submit to the centre.

- The relations between the top leaders and the central policy-making organs

Although all organs of both party and the government at different levels, including the centre, must carry out the principle of 'the minority should submit to the majority', the personal effects of the chief leaders on policy-making process are still very important. At central level, the top leaders of the party (most of them are also the state leaders) have the key influences on making policy decisions. They usually give new ideas, policy initiates or guidance to the policy-making bodies that include the politburo, the Central Committee, the Party's Secretariat, the State Council, etc. Moreover, in reality, many policy-making issues, are decided in the light of the chief leaders' opinion directly or indirectly, besides those which need to be decided by voting according to the party or state constitution. This is not because the other members of those policy-making organs do not know that they have the right to fully express their opinions or that party's principle is "minority should submit the majority", but because the chief leaders' authority is usually too powerful to be opposed. In the later Mao era, this problem became more serious. During the period when Deng acted as paramount leader, the situation appeared better than before, but there still had not been a fundamental change.

To understand why 'centralism' is in a dominant position while 'democracy' is not really practised, it is essential to have a brief analysis. Fundamentally speaking, in China, it would definitely cause problems for a person's political career if he or she would lose the favourable impression or even trust of the chief leader, caused by stating his or her opinion differing from that of the latter or criticising the latter, especially at the high level. The worry about their future official career prevents them from fully expressing their real ideas. The setbacks and dismissals of Peng Dehuan (Defence Minister), Liu Shaoqi (state president), Deng Xiaoping (general secretary), and many others at top and sub-nation levels, in the Mao era, showed that these worries are justified. What caused these was the lack of a reasonable and legalised mechanism for power distribution, balance, supervision, succession and replacement. Of which, for instance, even the long official term (and the life-long official term in the past) of the chief leaders, could prevent people from boldly expressing their different opinions. Similar problem occurred at different levels of China's power system. That personal wills played an important role to a great extent, was a paradoxical phenomenon in China's politics, it reflected the basic nature of politics that elite politics is actually a universal phenomenon in the world. The difference is that this elite politics is more prominent in China's experience. Therefore, the 'democratic centralism system' still is, to a great extent, the way that the minority dominates policy-making and it can not easily be changed. This issue will be discussed in more detail in Chapter Nine.

2.3.2 The applicability of the theories to China's practice

The survey in section 2.2 showed the contexts and the main ideas of those key state theories relating to policy-making (how policy is made). Each of them has its value theoretically and practically, and also some obvious weaknesses and shortcomings to a different extent as well. It is hard to say any one of them has provided a completely satisfactory explanation of the state theories they seek to study. As Alford (1975, p. 152) points out, each of them has a tendency to claim more explanatory power than it possesses and to extend the domain of its concepts to answer those questions it is actually unable to deal with. Therefore, to search for a single state theory is less useful than adopting a more eclectic approach that draws on the strengths of different theories (Cawson and Saunders, 1981). In this chapter, therefore, we use those theories that had been discussed to examine China's policy-making practice from different sides, and thereby to further assess their respective good points and problems. The following sections intend to first give brief comments on each of the theories, and then, discuss their applicability to China's contemporary policy-making practice in general.

The applicability of pluralism   The major strong point of Pluralism theory is noticing that there is a plurality of interests in any society, and so in any political system the diverse groups should share the state power. The diffusion or dispersion of power should be advocated, and there should be a rejection of the concentration of power in the hands of any one person or one group. These ideas are good to prevent totalitarianism and authoritarianism, and are conducive to enabling the state's policy-making to meet the demands of integrated interests of a society.

However, although the descriptive expression of pluralism matches the reality of modern society, its prescriptive idea departs from the political practice to a certain extent. It is essential to notice that in a society with a pluralist political system, on one hand, different interest groups are able to express their opinions and demands, or strive for their own interests through various ways according to the constitutional rights. But, on the other hand, actually, there are only some individuals or a few groups who can play the key role at any time. For all social groups, the extent to which the state's power can be influenced or shared depends on those important sources that each of them is able to control, which include wealth, expertise, reputation and social status and social influence as well. Needless to say, in a society with a pluralist political system, those groups occupying the higher social positions have greater impacts on the state's policy than those in lower positions. Those who have controlled over the main capital of a society have more right to speak on the state's affairs than those who in a weaker economic position.

Actually, those main proponents of neo-pluralist theory also recognised this when they re-thought in their late writings and revised their viewpoint. Lindblom argues that policy-making is influenced by the operation of capitalism to a great extent, the interests of business and the market being particularly important (1977). Dahl clearly points out that policy-making is not a neutral affair for the dominant force is the demands of business interests compared with other groups (1982). Thus, even in a society with a pluralist system, it is impossible to reach the real equality and fairness of sharing state power among different social groups with different social status and backgrounds; and the state's power is inevitably controlled by some small groups with superior status and power resources. Furthermore, the parties-competing system also needs to be observed from two sides. On one hand, it is one of the important components of a liberal democratic society, which is considered as the basic principle of plurality, and it does show a positive role to a society. However, on the other hand, the fact that after an election there is usually still one party to organise the government and the winning party definitely dominates the state's politics, indicates the limitation of this system. The roles of monitoring and criticising the policy makers by the other parties and interests groups are not always strong enough or powerful enough to have an important or decisive influence on the policy making. Moreover, either in an organisation (enterprise, company, association, trade union, institute or university, etc.) or a state (a government, a cabinet, a ministry, etc.), there is always one chief member who heads an organ, namely one general manager, one chairman or one president, one premier and one minister, instead of two. From this point of view, therefore, monism in any leadership system is essential and important in reality; the applicability of pluralism is relative, not absolute.

What is discussed above attempts to show that, the appearance of pluralist theory reflects the demand of people with different social backgrounds, which matches the development tendency of the modern state. Some pluralist ideas or means are the positive elements which are beneficial to promoting the development of human society; but its prescriptive ideas, on some aspects, depart from reality. In fact, the problem of inequality and unfairness in power distribution can not easily be solved. At any time and in any society, equality and balance are relative, and inequality and unbalance are absolute, economically, sociologically or politically.

Since the early 1980s, pluralist theory has been gradually studied and partially accepted by China's intellectuals. The great tide of economic reform is changing China's social structure in many ways and so the pluralistic values and interests in the society have become more and more clear, and have been gradually realised by the people in both political and academic circles. Under this situation, when using the ideas of pluralism to observe and analyse China's practice, we can see its applicability in different aspects to a considerable extent.

Before the reform period, the government and the official propaganda media always emphasised that all peoples' interests in the country are the same, or the fundamental interests of the whole people coincide, and paid less attention to the distinctions of the interests among different social groups. Actually, like any other modern countries, the distinction of interests exist in China among different social groups — government officials, intellectuals, workers, farmers and businessmen, and so on. They have different social status and income levels, and, in the reform period, these differences are becoming more and more prominent. The following paragraphs briefly discuss the pluralistic trends and their consequences within different realms in current China.

Firstly, in the economic realm. It is quite noticeable that the development of the economic reform has brought about a great change towards pluralistic interests. The decollectivelization in agriculture has produced the 'household responsibility system' which greatly improved farmer's motivation for production, for it clearly stipulated for the first time the relative reasonable relations of interests distribution between farmers and the state, which met farmers' basic demands. In the industrial field, there were four main steps that had been conducted. (1) To promote the decentralisation of management first by reducing the 'mandatory planning', while increasing the 'guidance planning', and then by initiating the development of market economy. (2) To separate the ownership and the managementship of the state-owned enterprises. (3) To readjust the tax policy and the interests distribution relations between centre and local government and also between government and the enterprises, and give more favour to the latter. (4) To encourage the development of multiple ownership enterprises, especially to promote foreign capital investment in China. With these measures, state-owned enterprises have acquired more autonomy and both local government and these enterprises can play a more positive role in the promotion of production. Meanwhile, the situation that the public-owned enterprises hold an absolutely overwhelming amount in the economic sectors of industry business has been broken. The emerging of the coexistence of diverse economic elements (ownership), including state-owned, collective-owned, individual-owned, private-owned, foreign-funded and joint-ventured economic sectors, has shown a clearer situation in which different interests among different economic groups co-exist in contemporary China. The state can not command the non-state owned economic sectors with the same methods used to command the state-owned enterprises, so when making the economic policies and other relevant policies, it has been unable to ignore the existence of these different groups and their respective interest demands.

The realm of political thought and ideology, has been a very sensitive field in China, since the philosophical absolutism and the exclusive ideology have been dominant. Marxism, Leninism, Maoism, and Deng Xiaoping theory are to be considered as unshakeable guiding thoughts and cardinal principles. Thus, it is fundamentally impossible to accept the pluralist theory. The 'Four Cardinal Principles', namely adhere to the leadership of the Communist Party, adhere to the Marxism, Leninism and Mao Zhedong thought, adhere to the proletariat dictatorship, and adhere to the socialism road (BR, vol. 40, No. 10/1997, p. 9), which were made by the party and affirmed by both Party and state's constitutions, should be upheld by the whole party and the whole nation. All theories and ideologies and their practice, either for the purposes of academic research, literary and artistic creation, or for promoting the massive cultural life and business activities and other propaganda, are not allowed to violate these principles.

However, although the four cardinal principles are claimed repeatedly, in practice flexibility in the ideological field has appeared. For instance, the policy of giving people the freedom of religious beliefs has been carried out. The number of people with religious beliefs, which include

Protestantism, Catholicism, Islamism, Buddhism and Taoism, is increasing nation-wide. Many new churches and temples have been founded. Authors of non-political writings (literature works, nature science works, etc.) can write whatever they want, as long as their writing does not embody contents opposed to the Communist party and the government, and the practising political system or has obscene contents.

In the realm of political institutions, although the one single party system has not changed, some prominent pluralistic trends have occurred. The significance of the multiple-party-cooperation system has been not only greatly emphasised, but more importantly, the system has been playing a practical role in the political life of the post-Mao period, especially from the late 1980s when Jiang Zemin became the General Secretary of the CPC centre. The status of those eight democratic parties[2] had been further raised and their political participation had been widely expanded, which enabled the mulitple-party-cooperation and political consultative system to enter a golden age (Li, D. at el. 1997, p. 4). In December 1989, according to the suggestion of Deng Xiaoping, CPC centre formulated and adopted an important document titled '*A proposal of CPC Centre about Adhering to and Perfecting the Multiple-Party-Cooperation and Political Consultative System under the Leadership of CPC*'. The declaring and implementing of this document signalled the beginning of a new stage that the multiple-party-co-operation and political consultative system led by CPC had been normalised and institutionalised. From then on, all important documents of the national conference of CPC and the plenums of CPC central committee, the government's working reports, all important state policies, important personnel arrangements, and the important laws and regulations, before being handed over for discussion, examination and determination, had been referred to the centres of the democratic parties and those famous non-party VIPs through different forms of meetings for their opinions. Since June 1989, these meetings had been held for one hundred times within eight years (ibid. pp. 4-5).

The direct participation of the non-CPC parties and non-party VIPs in the state's policy-making had produced effective results which were conducive to improving the policy-making quality and initiating some important new policies. For instance, to add a multiple-party-cooperation system into the constitutional amendment proposal, to conduct the parliament diplomacy, and to set up the Changjiang Delta Economic Development Zone, etc. all came from the proposals of those non-CPC parties or non-party VIPs (ibid. p. 6). On the other hand, to directly join the state's leadership group by the non-CPC people is also a phenomenon of the pluralistic participation to China's policy making. To the end of 1996, some forty three non-CPC people had been appointed as leaders at or above the vice minister/governor level, including one in the post of vice president of the state, while, a large group of non-CPC-party members and non-party members were appointed to the leading posts at local city level (ibid. p. 7). This is certainly unimaginable in the past. All these facts indicated, from one angle, that the involvement of the plural political forces in China's policy-making has begun to develop.

Moreover, the conducting of limited separation of the functions between the party and the government enabled the state's organs to play a greater role in dealing with the day-to-day works so as to heighten the government's efficiency. The gradual promoting of decentralisation enabled the provincial and local governments to acquire power they never had before. Some measures have been adopted to regularise and expand the power of the National People's Congress (NPC), which is the theoretically highest power organ in China. All these changes show that China's political institutions are undergoing changes towards plurality. Today more and more Chinese have realised that there had been too many bitter lessons in the past, especially the first three decades of PRC. Over-centralised and over-concentrated power would definitely bring about the problems of low efficiency, and wrong policy-making which often cause disastrous consequences. Conversely, if power monitoring and balancing mechanism were in force, policy-making powers were granted to those organs and sectors which should originally possess it, and policy-making resulted from a wide participation and public supervision, then better policy outputs could be expected and also a healthy society could be maintained.

When discussing the limitation of applicability of pluralist theory to China's practice, one of the big problems is, its view stressing the state as only an interest group among others (it is also a controversial point in the original theory!) is not applicable to interpret the reality of China. Actually, according to Marxist theory to which China adheres as a guiding thought, the state is considered quite important, which is in a central and leading position in a socialist country, under the leadership of the Communist party.

To sum up, pluralist theory is applicable in explaining China's practice of policy-making to a certain extent. It matches most in analysing the changes and development of economic structure and performance, matches to a medium level in analysing the change of the administrative system, and matches least in analysing the political thought (ideology). Generally speaking, the pluralist theory is helpful not only to explore the changes and development of China's political, economic and social life, but also to give some guidance in further promoting these changes and development, which have shown an inevitable trend in current China.

The applicability of elite theory   The virtue of elitism is exploring the fact that power may derive from a variety of sources — not only the economic force, but also knowledge, expertise, culture, ethnic origin, religious and so on; and the minority of population exercises power in all political systems in any era. These analyses enable us to pay more attention to an important aspect of the state theories that the state's policies are usually made by a minority, instead of the superficial phenomenon that they are subject to the wills of the majority of the population. Thus, to observe and study the state's policy-making should focus on the behaviour of those political elites.

However, the weakness of elitism is its simplicity. It only portrays a picture of the distribution of the power and the diversified sources of power, and fails to provide enough explanation of how that power has arisen.

Analysing the applicability of the elitist theory to China's practice, we see that it significantly matches the reality. First, the inevitability of the elite politics to a great extent in China at the present stage is most noticeable. Owning to the relatively low degree of economic and social development, a considerable amount of the common people either lack the ability to participate in the state's political life, or to be not clearly aware of how to use their political rights and how to participate in the state's political affairs, or lack participation consciousness and motivation to do so. Second, in practice, China's politics, to a considerable extent, is substantially the business of the minority of the population. The selection of the deputies of National People's Congress, for example, reflect the fact that the upper leaders control the real power of the state. Theoretically, the deputies to the NPC should be selected by election. In fact, however, they are decided not by election but by selection according to an official slate which is listed in advance in the light of the requirements of the upper leaders. On the other hand, the NPC's agenda and the draft proposals and resolutions, either for legislative, personnel appointment, or for other important issues, are also prepared before the convening of the NPC sessions by the executive organs of the state. Thus, the NPC does not really play a role as an independent legislative organ but functions as a 'voting machine'. It is the reason that some foreign political analysts consider China's NPC to be a 'rubber stamp' (Ian, 1991, p. 13). Simultaneously, the leaders above the city levels are essentially selected by the higher-ranking authorities.

The reasons why political elites are remarkably dominant in China's policy-making process are fourfold.

Historically, the old tradition of thought remains in the mind of the politicians or leaders that the officers are wiser than the ordinary people, the government is more brilliant than the public, and higher-ranking officers are wiser than lower ones. Accordingly, then, officers are always qualified to educate and guide the ordinary people; higher-ranking leaders are always able to decide the most important issues of the state without the participation of the public; the government should have unlimited power to give commands to the public and does not necessarily have to accept the real supervision from society.

Economically, it resulted from the special nature of the Chinese economy and the degree of China's economic development. On one hand, since the state-owed economic sectors account for the majority of the whole, and the exerting of political control depends on economic control, therefore, the state's policy-making is mainly controlled by the officers at the higher positions both in the party and in the government. On the other hand, in a society with the relatively backward economy, the people's enthusiasm to participate in the state's political life can not be as high as those in industrialised countries, for most people of the former still strongly need to concern themselves with earning their living.

Politically, for a long time, China's political monism and philosophical absolutism did not encourage people to really involve themselves in the state's political life and speak out boldly.

Institutionally, There are still no explicit and effective institution issued by the state to encourage the public to participate in the state's political activities, and also protect people from interference or restriction when they are expressing their different opinions.

The applicability of Marxism The most noticeable significance of Marxist state theory is its bringing to light the objective law that the social force dominating the economy also controls state power, or plays a key role in the state's policy-making process. In other words, that the domination of the means of production is significant for the control of state power. This shows a basic principle that the superstructure including the political system and power operating mechanism, etc. are subjected to the social economic foundation. On the other hand, superstructure can play a great retroaction to the economic foundation under certain conditions, in order to maintain the regime and its foundation.

As the most important vision of economic determinism, however, Marxist theory does not give enough analysis to the relations between economic power and political power, namely, the degree of the independence of the state to the capitalist force, and the possibility of the state serving the social public through its autonomy and independence. Moreover, it gives less attention to the fact that power can derive from other sources besides the economic force. Finally, with the development of the modern industrial society, the expanding of the participation of capital investment by common people has made it difficult to identify class status, which raised a new problem to Marxism theory namely to explain the relation between the state power and capital.

To discuss the applicability of the Marxist State theory to China's practice, it is essential to point out that the Marxist state theory was created on the base of observing and analysing the capitalist society and capitalist state. However, China is a socialist country. Then, a question is inevitably raised: is it applicable to China's practice? This is a complicated issue, which may not be simply answered yes or no. We know that Marxism is China's official ideology and the fundamental guiding thought of China's leaders, it has the orthodox status and has being propagated and imbued since the founding of the P.R. China. Nevertheless, in considering its applicability to China, some different situations need to be distinguished. First, the relevant theory of Marxism about how to set up a socialist state had been demonstrated to be useful in China. This can be seen in two aspects.

The setting up of CPC was in the light of one of Marxism's principle that the proletariat must strive for liberation by themselves under the leadership of their own party. The establishment of PRC had fundamentally changed the direction and course of modern China from the middle of the twentieth century.

The victory of 1949 was a successful case of applying the economic determinism. China's communist revolution resulted from the conclusion that the ruling of the Kuomingtang had not met the requirement of China's economic foundation, and only by overturning its domination could China achieve its real national independence and emancipate the social productive force. The founding of the People's Republic of China in 1949 demonstrated the applicability of this theory, in a country with one fourth of the world's population.

Second, we know that as the ruling machine of the human society at national level, all states share some general characters, such as seeking to maintain the normal order and stability of a society, and trying to prevent the country from being invaded by others, etc. According to this point of view, although Marxist State theory is mainly produced from observing and analysing the capitalist societies, it still has considerable applicability in interpreting China's practice. For instance, the ideas of the retroaction of superstructure to the economic foundation, the state's relative autonomy and independence in making policies, etc. In China's practice, the retroaction of the superstructure (here mainly indicates the state machine) to the economic foundation, focuses on accelerating the economic development by the government's positive intervention, in which there were two successful periods in PRC's history. One was in the early 1950s, with the government's mobilising, organising and commanding, China's economy soon obtained the achievements of recovery and primary development, and laid down a foundation for further development, after a long period of wars. Another period is from the end of the 1970s to now. Due to the government carrying out reform and opening-up policies, China had 'created a miracle of economic development of the twentieth century' (PDO. 21 Dec. 1995, p. 4)[3]. Some profound changes have also taken place in China's other aspects. These facts suggest that the making and implementing of government's decisions (strategies, programmes and policies) can powerfully affect China's economic and social development.

Third, to analyse the performance of China's decision makers in the post-Mao period, the actions they adopted to launch reform and opening-up strategy so as to promote China's modernisation, demonstrate the state's autonomy in serving its long-run interest. Since the end of World War Two the rapid development of the economic globalisation is significantly affecting the world's situation and the states' relations. In this course, the influence of the capitalist economic mode and the capitalist economic force are in dominance. China's reform and opening-up strategy is actually aimed at speeding up China's involvement and enabling China to enter or re-enter the world's economic order. Internally, the government reformed the economic development strategy and management system. It encouraged the development of multiple economic sectors including collective sector, private sector, joint-venture sector, and capitalist sector, besides those state-owned sectors, and loosened its control on the enterprises and allowed the latter to have more autonomous power. Externally, China devoted to rapidly expand its economic relations with the outside world. During the last two decades, China had absorbed a lot of resources which were lacking, including capitals, technology, managerial skills, administrative patterns and legal mode, from those developed countries. These indicate that China's leadership had no longer rejected those methods and resources coming from other countries, including those capitalist countries, based on the ideological consideration, as it did in the past. So long as they can benefit the development of China's economy, they could be adopted. How could China do so? It simply stemmed from the state's autonomy. By the end of 1970s, the existence of the serious backward situation economically and the big gap between China and those developed countries and regions was a great pressure imposed on China's leaders. If China's government could not fundamentally change this severe situation as soon as possible, it would be very difficult to maintain its legitimacy to rule the country. Hence, it was actually a problem concerning the survival of the regime. Consequently, the making and conducting of the reform and opening-up strategy was substantially the autonomous action of China's government to serve its long run and fundamental interest.

On the other hand, China's diplomatic and political policies had also adapted to meet the challenges of the new situation. These mainly include actively improving the state relations between China and those countries with different social systems and expanding possible co-operation between China and foreign countries in non-economic realms; and reducing the ideological control at home, etc. These also can be explained as the state's autonomous adaptability of China in policy-making, in dealing with the changing situation.

However, as has been mentioned in the previous paragraphs, Marxist State theory can not give enough analysis and attention to some issues relating capitalist state's autonomy and independence, nor address those issues concerning socialist state. Thus, how and to what extent a socialist state can use its power to manage the society, is an unsolved and also hard-to-be-solved problem. Consequently, in the practice of searching for the way to properly apply the state's power, China had fallen into difficulties for a long time before the reform. These are mainly shown as the misapplication of Marxist State theory in China's policy making.

The first three decades of PRC saw these major manifestations of misapplication in policy-making in two aspects: over-using the state's power, and over-using and abuse of the method of class struggle. Regarding the first issue, it mainly means that from the late 1950s, China's ruling party and government over-used the state's administrative power to intervene in society economically, culturally, ideologically and even in social life style. Although Marxism advocates that the proletariat can use its new state instrument to reform society and promote social development after its achieving power, however, in China, what had been done by the state's power in the past, especially in Mao's period, had exceeded its proper limits. In the economic realm, it was shown that within a command economic system the government intervened too much in social economic activities. In the ideological realm, it was shown as the strict restriction that those ideas, which (especially in political thought) differ from the party centre, were not allowed to be expressed. In the cultural realm, serious stipulations covered all aspects including literature, art, theatre, film, music, television, broadcasting, etc. which were all required to serve the state's target and meet the demands of party ideology. Even in the social life realm, powerful intervention was also in force, which included dress fashion, religion, traditional customs, etc. All these excessive interventions by the state's power in different realms caused a lot of trouble to China's society. In the post-Mao epoch, the situation has been changed to some extent. The degree of changes, which affected different aspects of China's society, can be listed decreasingly as below: the economic realm, the social life realm, the cultural realm and the ideological realm.

Over-using and abuse of the class struggle method, another misapplication of Marxist State theory, was also a big problem in China's policy making. Marxism declared that the class struggle is the driving force of the development of human history and the state is a tool of class struggles, to be used by the ruling class to maintain its regime. To analyse the viewpoint, first, it can be affirmed that the role of class struggle in the revolutionary period, as happened in any country and any epoch when a new ruling class, which represents the new production relation, replaced the old one, is important. Then, second, it is conceivable that it should be a mistake if a state over-emphasise the role of class struggle and even use the way of class struggle as the main means to maintain a society's existence and development, in a peaceful period when the new ruling class has set up its regime. During the first three decades prior to the reform, China's leaders repeated this mistake many times in many ways. For a long time, 'take class struggle as the key link' was the dominant principle in China's policy making. Class struggle was used as the dynamics to further all works, and all works in China were seen to be connected with class struggle. Using class struggle to consider and deal with everything caused serious consequences. For instance, the anti-rightist campaign treated the controversy between political ideas as the struggle of supporting or opposing CPC and socialism; the Cultural Revolution aimed at launching 'the continued revolution under the proletarian dictatorship' to get rid of the party's inner enemy— those 'capitalist roaders'. Thousands and thousands of people suffered disaster in these campaigns. To examine the consequences of upholding the way of 'taking class struggle as the key link' in state's policy-making in an all-round way, we at least can find two big problems. First, since the regime used its main energy to deal with the 'class struggle' which was mainly artificially made, and used the way of class struggle to command the economic construction, the state's economic development did not receive enough attention and therefore fell into lower efficiency and lower speed. Second, endless 'class struggle' resulted in more and more tense inter-person relations, increasing social conflicts, and frequent social instability.

What have been discussed concerning the misapplication of Marxist State theory in China show that these main mistakes were the consequences of adopting the wrong guiding thought as the motivation and purpose of the state's policy making. This resulted in the over using of the state power and abuse of the class struggle method For a long period in the past, it had naturally brought about false policy outputs and caused disastrous consequences in different social realms. These lessons demonstrat that misapplying even a correct theory would lead to the results of being punished by history.

To sum up, due to the existence of many common features of modern states, Marxist State theory can be used to interpret China's practice to a considerable extent, although it was created mainly on the base of observing and analysing the capitalist society and China is a socialist country. In analysing China's practice, the theory persuasively explains the causes of China's revolution which resulted in the founding of PRC, and the remarkable economic developments which mainly showed in the period of the early 1950s and the post-Mao Period, which were promoted by the government's feasible policies and dynamics. Of these two facts, the former indicates the inevitability that a revolution should happen and lead to success if the government in power can not maintain China's development and stability, through its policy-making and implementation. The latter demonstrates that China's government can powerfully promote the social economic development if it can exclude the ideological and political interventions in the state's policy-making and map out correct policies. In other words, it seems that if a state can exert its autonomy to a higher extent, it can make better policies. The discussion also explores the misuse of the theory, which caused noticeable disasters in China. According to these discussions, it is conceivable that Marxist state theory is particularly effective in explaining those great history events involving changes over economic foundation or political system, which contain macro-influence to a society. In view of this, therefore, its limitation should be unsuitable to explain the concrete policy-making process in which the elements including policy makers, and policy-making mechanism, must be explored.

The applicability of Globalism   This theory points to the influence of the tendency of globalisation upon the policy-making at the national level. Its significance is emphasising that the development of modern technology and economy had resulted in the 'reordering of the time and distance in our life' (Giddens, A. 1989, p. 519). Thus, to actively involve into the globalisation course which characterised by interdependence and co-operation in all realms, has become of crucial importance to a state's survival and development. To be sure, setting forth this idea is one of the most important achievements contributing to the state policy-making theory of this century.

The applicability of globalism to China's policy-making practice cannot be doubted. To demonstrate this conclusion, both China's positive and negative experiences, namely the achievements and developments brought about by carrying out the opening-up policies, and the disastrous consequences caused by the self-close and isolation, had provided persuasive evidences.

As will be discussed in section 5.2.2, self-closed policy is one of the main reasons causing China's economic stagnancy and backwardness in the first three decades of the PRC. In stressing this bitter lesson, Deng had clearly pointed out that the closed-door policy from the mid-Ming[4] period to the Opium War (1840) and the unfortunate period of 1958-1976 resulted in years of ignorance and backwardness (Deng, X., 1985b, p. 61).

Therefore, Deng considered promoting an outward-looking style economic development is particular important,

> We summed up the historical experiences, an important reason why China got bogged down into the situation of stagnancy and backwardness in the past is closing the country to international intercourse. Experiences had proved that to engage in economic construction while closing the country would make it impossible to achieve success (Deng, X. 1985b, pp. 67-68).

Deng later repeatedly emphasised the importance of opening-up to the outside world whenever he talked about China's reform and economic construction,

> Opening-up to the outside world is of great significance. For any country that wants development, it would be impossible if it isolates itself and close itself to international intercourse (Deng, X. 1987, p.105).

To sum up Deng's theory, which indicated the fundamental changes of the guiding thought of CPC policy makers, the core idea is:
- No economic development will result in danger to a state.
- Opening-up and entering the world economic order is absolute essential to achieve economic development.

The successful experiences can be seen from the end of 1970s when China proclaimed its launching reform and opening-up strategy, which embarked on China's course to widely opening and expanding the channels to connect with the world's mainstream of economy. Subsequently, SEZ programme was created serving as the 'experimental field', 'windows', and 'bridge' of implementing this strategy. As discussed in the preceding section, the leadership of post-Mao China believed that through adopting opening-up policy, China can absorb capital, advanced science and technology, and managerial skills from those developed countries, so as to speed up China's economic development. In doing so, the last two decades witnessed China's rapid involvement in the globalisation course. This change has not only brought about economic boom, but also enabled China to fundamentally depart from political isolation and greatly improved and strengthened its international status. All these facts suggest that globalisation theory is not only applicable, but also very important in interpreting China's policy-making practice.

For a long time, China's leadership in the Mao era worried about the capitalist revival from inside China. However, the available evidence showed that the real threat to China's regime was not from the internal aspects, but from the external aspect. That was the threat of international capitalism (If we search for the internal threat to China's regime, it is actually the power competition which was produced mainly by the unperfected power succession and replacement system). As has been mentioned that in the globalisation course, capitalist substances are in dominance. The tendency has developed to an extent that if a country, especially a developing country, can not follow and catch up this wave, it would find it hard to promote its economic development and very difficult to reduce the gap compared with those industrialised countries. The facts we analysed in the previous paragraphs suggest this possibility. China's unfortunate situation in the past was actually falling into such a danger.

Another reason also strengthens the significance of China's involvement in the globalisation. Although China tried to set up a socialist production system and socialist economic system since the founding of PRC, it has been proved that it is hard to achieve success without studying and using the experiences of the capitalist economic mode, which has developed for two centuries. Objectively speaking, the capitalist mode is relatively mature and successful even though many defeats and weakness of it exist. Consequently, if China would aim to speed up its economic development it has first to learn from capitalist mode. Fundamentally, a relative advanced and effective economic mode is not necessarily to be the enemy of those states holding different social systems; instead, those useful elements and resources can be drawn on or introduced from the former. China's post-Mao leadership realised this and resolutely adopted great flexibility in its policy-making in order to meet the challenge of globalisation. They believed that they could 'selectively absorb the good things and boycott the bad things from abroad' (Liu, P. 1985).

China's involvement in the globalisation, or China's adapting to the globalisation so as to enter or re-enter the world economic order, has its theoretical bases which are Deng's 'cat theory' and the criteria of 'three whethers' for judging the feasibility of adopting new policies or resources. Deng stresses that it does not matter whether the cat is black or white so long as it catch mice (Shambaugh, D. 1995, p. 88). Then what are the 'mice' in China's situation? According to the 'three whethers', they are, to be beneficial to promoting the development of socialist productive forces, to be beneficial to improving people's living standard, and to be beneficial to strengthening the state's comprehensive power of China (Deng, X, 1993, p. 372). Hence, all those methods and resources which could be used to catch these 'mice', are permitted and encouraged to use. China's experience in the last two decades indicates that it did make policy in the light of this principle.

To sum up, therefore, the applicability of the globalisation theory in China's policy-making does not only have practical necessity and urgency, but also has its theoretical basis which conforms with both CPC's current ideological guiding thought and the interests of the state and people. However, it must be noted that, like Marxist state theory, the globalisation determinism is the one which depicts and emphasises the overall influences produced by the development and changes of economic mode and economic relations, on the state's policy making. The difference between these two political economy accounts is that the latter observes the above issues from an international context, and the former focuses its analyses mainly on the internal aspects of a state. In contrast to its good point, it is logical that the weakness of the globalisation theory, like the Marxist state theory, is also not suitable for interpreting those concrete policy-making processes.

The applicability of Institutionalism   As has been analysed, the merits of institutionalism are threefold.

- It explores the important impacts produced by the institutionalised elements in framing the allocation of interest and power concerning the state's policy making.
- It stresses the significance of the institutionalised forces in structuring and mediating the conflicts in policy making. And
- it points out that in an institutionalised framework, the policy maker and the environment can interact with each other, namely the former can create and improve the latter and the latter can also exert great influence on the former.

However, as a descriptive theory, institutionalism fails to answer the question of how to set up suitable institutions to meet the demands of society, but only explains how institutions influence policy making. Actually, man is not the slave or instrument of institutions, and the institutions should serve human society. Therefore, what people need to do is not only to follow the latter and to be passively influenced by them, but also to keep making them better to meet the demands of modern society.

To analyse the applicability of institutionalist theory to China's practice, in this section, we attempt to discuss the influence of the existing institutions on China's policy-making process, and the reasons as well.

The main influence of China's institution on the policy-making processes can be seen from two sides. A highly centralised power system is the first feature. This includes the party being in the core position of state leadership; the party system intertwined with the state system to a great extent, and the power monolithism being strictly exercised. The impacts caused by such a highly centralised power system on the policy process are multiple. To be sure, it can ensure a high efficiency for making policy, especially in war time and a revolutionary period, and other specific periods, for it reduces the trouble from opposing groups and the time occupied by endless debating. However, generally speaking, in China's economic construction period, this pattern was not suitable to fully play the roles from all aspects and widely absorb the wisdom of the policy makers at different levels with different official status. Moreover, it was not good for the power balancing which is an important aspect for policy making. For a long time, the situation in China's policy-making that 'the party committee waves its hand, the government gets to work, the People's Congress standing committee vote, and the People's Consultative Congress claps' (Shirk, 1993, p. 57), was a problem. Because it confuses the duties between the party and government, between the legislative organ and the party, and reduces the role of the consultative organ (CPPCC). Fortunately, this situation has changed noticeably in post-Mao China.

Setting up and affirming an official and exclusive ideology is the second feature. This requires that the thinking of all people of the country, all members of the party must keep one accord with the party centre. Before the reform period, this situation was quite serious. It had been proved that the impacts of this tight control of ideology on policy-making was not suitable for the creation of a good political environment which can encourage the public to fully express their opinions, and it also failed to ensure that policy participants were free to express their opinions in the policy-making process.

A brief review of five state-related theories concerning how policy is made and an examination of their applicability to China's policy-making practice in general, has been conducted in this chapter. Then, in view of these discussions, three of which, including pluralism, elitism and institutionalism, are select to analyse the SEZ-related policy process The consideration for this choice could be explained as follows.

Although all these five state-related theories are applicable to interpret China's practice, their functions are different. As has been mentioned in the introductory chapter, the key point of the political economy approaches including Marxist determinism and the globalisation determinism, focuses on exploring the impacts that stem from the economic relations, economic mode and economic force, which associate with the economic life in a society, on the state's policy process. These elements, which come from home and abroad, exert their influences through forming a causal dynamics for the state's policy-making in a given epoch. However, it has been seen in China's practice that, usually, these elements can exert their role in a relatively long period and affect those big events. In other words, their role or impacts usually could be recognised from a longer period or a big historical change. For instance, as discussed in the preceding sections, that to probe the policy-making reasons why China launched the reform and opening-up strategy soon after the start of the post-Mao period we can discover these impacts. Consequently, these methods seem to be more applicable in examining those macro-contexts and dynamics of big policy events, but not suitable to interpret those concrete policy-making processes. Thus, these two theoretical accounts will not be used to examine the SEZ policy-making process later.

Contrastively, the models of pluralism, elitism and institutionalism, are sure to be more applicable in observing and analysing those elements which influence concrete policy processes including the policy-making mechanism and environment, and the behaviours of the policy makers. Accordingly, in dealing with the major analytical object of the book, these three models are introduced to examine the policy-making process of the three SEZ cases. In doing so, their applicability will be explored as well.

Notes

1   Engels, F., (1884) *The Origins of the Family, Private Property and the State,* Peking, Foreign Language press, 1978, p208.
2   These eight democratic parties are: The Revolutionary Committee of Kuomingtang, the China Democratic League, the China Democratic Construction Association, the China Association for Promoting Democracy, the Chinese Peasants' and Workers' Democratic Party, the China Zhi Gong Party, the Jiu San Society and the Taiwan Democratic self-government League. They took part in the Chinese People's Consultative Conference (CPPCC) since 1949 to form a part of the patriotic united front led by the Chinese Communist Party.
3   John Major (Premier of UK), A Speech with Chinese Officers, People's Daily Overseas edition, 27 Dec. 1995, p4.
4   Ming, (1368-1644), a Chinese feudal Dynasty.

3 A review of the models about how China's policy is made

The preceding chapter has reviewed those state-related theories concerning how policy is made, and examined their applicability to China's practice in general. This chapter surveys the Sinologists' models about how China's policy is made, which is the second aspect of the theoretical group relating how policy is made, considered in this thesis. The theoretical bases of these Sinologists' models, characterised by descriptive method, are the relevant state theories we have discussed. Hence, they are actually the versions of those relevant state theories, to a certain extent, which will be discussed in more detail later. The focus of these models is to examine particularly how policy is made in China's background. The main issues they examine are who or what elements are crucial in shaping China's policy; how and by what means those dominators could control the policy process, etc. To be sure, examining these models is beneficial to us in understanding China's policy process from a practical point of view.

3.1 The background and context

3.1.1 The development of diverse models

For more than four decades, studies of China's policy-making process have become of increasing interest to both the academic and applied study circles of politics, and to policy analysis and other relevant disciplines, in which many important Western scholars and experts of Chinese research are involved. From the early 1950s, some Western scholars had begun to conduct their study within a situation where the necessary data were very difficult to collect. However, the most important work started in the late 1970s, and especially in the 1980s, when China's rapid economic development was attracting more attention from scholars and the opening-up situation had made it possible for them to access the resources for their studies more conveniently. During this period, diverse models were created to describe and analyse the policy-making process in China.

With the deepening of these studies about Chinese policy process and the increasing of those relevant models, from early 1980s, some scholars tried to sort them out according to their analytical and descriptive focus and to evaluate their strengths and weakness. These works had been beneficial in promoting the further development of the study in this realm. At first, in 1981, Pye (1981, pp. 41-6) summarised five models developed by western scholars.

- The Yanan round-table model, which holds that the Chinese leadership 'was bonded together by a dedicated consensus — its values were homogeneous, its relations were stable, and it was a band of comrades free of tensions. All those surrounding Mao showed a spirit of camaraderie, and therefore responsibility was diffused and decision-making was spontaneous' (Pye, 1981, p. 42).

- The two-policy-lines struggle model, which is one of the various forms of conflicts-oriented models that depicts the Chinese leadership as divided between 'two lines' in policy process. Usually, it was Mao, as the correct one, against the others (Richard Solomon, Philip Bridgham, Edward E. Rice, etc).

- The structural functionalism model, which views Chinese political structure as a near-perfect blending of ideology and organisation. In Chinese politics, Lenin's dream that 'the unity of theory and action', by which the policy 'line' and organisation 'discipline' joined together perfectly, provided functional specific bureaucracies of astounding efficiency (Franz Schurmann).

- The Maoist-Revolutionary model, which stresses the roles of the revolutionary spirits of Maoism in China's politics (Benjamin Schwartz, Maurice Meisner).

- The generational model, which discusses who to follow after the Long March generation, how many generations there had been in CCP and how different their outlooks were. It presumes that change was likely in China and that tensions undoubtedly existed among the leaders (Walt W. Rostow, Doak Barnett).

Then, Pye (1981, ibid.) established his own model: the factional model, which portrays Chinese Communist politics as the clashes and struggles between different factions within China's leaderships.

In 1984, with the development of the studies, Harry Harding (1984, pp. 13-36) sorted out all models raised over the last fifteen years into eight types.

- Structural models: analyse the organisations and institutions in which policies are made, and state the allocation of power and authority among them (Franz Schurmann, Doak Barnett, Parris Chang, Kenneth Lieberthal, David Lampton, etc.).
- Normative models: stress the roles of the rules and norms, some of which are drawn from Chinese Communist doctrine, that govern policy-making in Communist China (John Lewis, Franz Schurmann, Harry Harding, Frederick Teiwes, etc.).
- Mao-in-command models: describe Chinese Communist politics as being decided by a changing paramount leader, Mao Zhedong (Michael Oksenberg, Frederick Teiwes etc.).
- Factional models: portray Chinese Communist politics as the clashes of patronage networks among the Chinese Communist leaderships (Andrew Nathan, Lucian Pye).
- Bureaucratic models: view Chinese Communist politics as the competition for resources and power among various agencies of party and state (William Whitson, Frederick Teiwes).
- Tendency models: consider Chinese Communist politics as a tension between enduring alternative policy preferences (Michael Oksenberg, Steven Goldsten, Parris Chang, etc.).
- Generational models: depict Chinese Communist politics as the competition among different generations of Chinese Communist leaders (William Whitson, Michael Yahuda, etc.).
- Interest group models: emphasise Chinese Communist politics as the interaction of various socio-economic interest groups in Chinese society (Michael Oksenberg, Alan Liu, Peter Moody).

Later, in 1988, Lieberthal and Oksenberg (1988) combined all models into two approaches. (1) Those that focus on reasoned debates by the Chinese leaders over substantive policy issues which stemmed from an implicit 'rationality model', and (2) those that focus on the struggle for power among contending leaders which arises from an individual or factional 'power model'.

Meanwhile, they introduced their own approach: to emphasise the important impacts of the bureaucratic structure in which the policy process is conducted (pp. 15-18).

Afterwards, in 1990, Avery Goldstein (1990) summarised the different approaches as four major groups:

- Stresses the political practices, norms, beliefs, and institutions of China as a Marxist-Leninist regime;
- Emphasises the distinctive role played by Mao Zedong;
- Portrays Chinese politics as a competition between actors defined according to bureaucratic affiliation, regional loyalties, class origin, occupational category, age cohort, ideological commitment, or combinations of such attributes;
- Put forward the 'factionalist' accounts of Chinese politics, in which the participating groups are portrayed as engaging in struggles for power.

Besides the aforementioned models, there is a newly advanced model — the Fragmented Authoritarianism model, set forth by Lieberthal, Oksenberg (1992), which holds that authority below the very peak of the Chinese political system is fragmented and disjointed. The structure that links the top and the bottom of the system requires negotiations, bargaining, exchange, and consensus building.

So far diversified models, raised by western scholars, have been listed above. It is indeed a fruitful development of the studies in this realm within such a short period. As mentioned above, all these Sinologists' models about China's policy-making have close relations with those relevant state theories, and start from or are based on the theoretical position of the latter, to which we now conduct a brief analysis.

3.1.2 The theoretical basis of the Chinese policy-making models

In considering the theoretical basis of the Sinologists' policy-making models, which include those that are mentioned above and those that were developed later comprising politician-in-negotiation model, bureaucracy-in-dominance model, ideology-conflict-oriented model, and power competition-oriented model etc, we can sort out those major models, as three groups (table 3.1).

pluralism	elitism	institutionalism
Politician-in-negotiation model Power-conflicts-oriented model Interest group model Factional model Bureaucracy-in-dominance model	Mao(or Deng)-in-command model Generational model	Ideology-conflict-oriented model Structural model Normative model Two lines struggle model Fragmented authoritarianism model

Table 3.1 The theoretical basis of the Chinese policy-making models

For further understanding these theoretical relations in the above three groups, some brief analyses are essential. The pluralism-basis-models, in the first group, share a feature, which stress that it is the competition, bargaining and balancing course among political groups or interests that determines the direction and outputs of China's policy-making. The differences between those four models are: politician-in-negotiation model, power competition-oriented model and factional model explore these conflicts and interactions mainly in the leaderships of the top level; the bureaucratic model probes these competitions between the centre and the local authorities, between various party and state agencies, and between provinces, in order to compete for resources and power; and the interest group model emphasises these interactions among various socio-economic interest groups in the society. The first four particularly indicate a political phenomenon of 'institutional pluralism', which occurred in the countries with a socialist system. Because, due to the features of the institutions, in these countries, political struggle or power competition which are substantially natural phenomenon in modern states, have to adopt potential or covert ways, namely the ways that are not encouraged or protected by institutions.

Then, we examine the second group, the elitism-basis-models, which contain Mao (or Deng)-in-command model, and generational model. Obviously, Mao (or Deng)-in-command model is a very typical elitist style model, which describes that China's politics was decided by the paramount leader Mao Zhedong or Deng Xiaoping. It is actually confirming the prominent role of only one top elite that stands above all other political elites. Observing Chinese politics from the viewpoint of ages, the generational model divides China's political elites according to their generations. The main issues which it concerns include who to follow after the Long March generation to control China's power, how many generations there had been in CCP, and how they act, which are seen directly to affect China's policy-making. These indicate that those political elites are considered most important in influencing China's policy-making and so it is also an elitist style model.

Finally, we discuss the third group, the institutionalism-basis-models, which comprises of the ideology conflicts-oriented model, the structural model, the normative model and the fragmented authoritarianism model. The ideology conflicts-oriented models explore an important issue that since China is a country in which an institutionalised principle determines that the ideological consideration governs the policy-making process to a great extent. Therefore, the ideological debates permeate into all issues of China's policy-making. These models analyse the manifestations, causes, and impacts of ideological controversies from different angles and in different periods. It seems persuasive that due to the institutional reason the ideological conflicts significantly influence China's policy-making processes. The structural model stresses the importance of the structure and operating mechanism of the state's power of China, which clearly suggests the application of an institutional approach. Comparatively, the normative model highlights the roles of the rules and norms in governing China's policy-making, which is also obviously affirming the influences of the institutionalised elements. More particularly, the fragmented authoritarianism model points out the character of China's politics that authority below the very peak of the Chinese political system is fragmented and disjointed, and the structure that links the top and the bottom of the system requires negotiations, bargaining, exchange, and consensus building. This finding, conceivably, is throwing a light on an institutional interpretation of China's policy-making process.

In further considering these models which we sorted out above, we can see that some of them cover more than two state theories. For example, bureaucratic model does not only portray the situation of pluralist politics to a certain extent, but also explores the role of high-rank bureaucrats, as political elites, in China's policy-making process. Therefore, it could be seen to have an elitist basis. The fragmented authoritarianism model stresses the structural influence of the institutions in China's power allocation of policy-making, whilst it also provides us with a way to observe an internal pluralist tendency in China's power system — a decentralised tendency and the competition among different interests.

Regarding to those three models include politician-in-negotiation model, power competition-oriented model and factional model, although they undoubtedly show a pluralist method, they also can be seen as emphasising the key role of those high level elites in power. Furthermore, it needs to be pointed out that some models created later, which describe the patterns of China's policy-making, seem not to have an direct theoretical connection with the state theories, but they still mainly probe the reasons from China's political system and other institutions. That means, they apply the method of institutional analysis or interpretation, and so they are defined in the institutionalism and institutions-related group.

After discussing the development and theoretical contexts of the Sinologists' models, which mainly involve the descriptive method, in the above two sections, we see that with respect to how China's policy is made, these models did create many beneficial ideas and methods to observe and analyse China's practice. These gave a great impetus to the development of studies in this field. However, with further considering these models carefully, it needs to be pointed out that it seems still to be problematic to say that any one of these models can either completely match or be fully suitably used to explain the reality of China's policy process. Meanwhile, some of these models overlap or are complementary to each other, rather than completely competitive or mutually exclusive, for they sometimes view the same issue from different aspects, or explain the same situation with different theories. Moreover, some of those models created earlier are somewhat over-simplified and over-naive, such as the Yanan Round-table models and the generation models, etc. Therefore, for absorbing the useful ideas of these models to help our study, we need to re-sort those major models emphasising the most influential aspects of China's policy process and having the most important academic value, in terms of their theoretical bases, and also give a re-evaluation.

3.2 Reviewing the models

The above discussion has re-sorted those most influential Sinologists' policy-making models into three types as (1) pluralism-basis models, (2) elitism-basis models, and (3) Institutionalism-basis and institutionalism-related models, in view of their theoretical relations. The following sections review and re-value the major models in these three groups in turn.

3.2.1 The pluralism-basis models

This group reviews four models: politicians-in-negotiation models, Power competition-oriented models, bureaucracy-in-dominance models and interest group model. The factional model is an organic part of the power competition-oriented models, and so it is not discussed separately here. These models portray a picture of China's policy-making in which policy outputs are produced by the balance of the competition, negotiation and bargaining among politicians, bureaucracies or other interest groups.

Politicians-in-Negotiation Model   For a long time, researchers on China's politics stressed the decisive role of the paramount leaders, Mao or Deng, in China's policy-making processes. However, this model suggests that: both Mao and Deng had limits in their control of the policy system. They could not play a leading role in the policy-making process. Adversaries within the party always tried to frustrate the policy formulation through their power, and the authority of the paramount leaders often encountered challenge from the former. Thus, China's policies actually resulted from negotiation and compromise among the political leaders. In the policy-making process, although the paramount leader's position was prominent, his primary role was to reconcile and balance differing interests. However, in many situations, the paramount leader had to give up his policy propositions and yield to the pressure from other leaders. Macfarquhar (1983) argues that, although Mao controlled distinct power, he could not totally dominate the policy-making process and decide the policy just according to his own will, especially in the 1950s. Conversely, some of his important initiatives encountered setbacks brought about by other political leaders. The following two cases are noticed by Macfarquhar (ibid. chapter 2 and 7) as the most persuasive evidences for explaining the aforementioned issues.

Mao's failure in launching the first Great Leap Forward, firstly, is an important case which Macfarquhar considers to demonstrate his argument. In January 1956, after solving the problem of socialisation and consolidation of the new regime, Mao turned his attention to China's economic construction. Mao considered that the scale and rate of China's industrialisation, the development of science, education, public health and so on, must be greatly expanded and accelerated. Hence, he launched the first Leap Forward with 'The Twenty-Years Agriculture Programme' as its guiding line and main policies. In this document, a series of ambitious targets was put forward. In the field of industry, Mao set forth a new slogan 'More, fast, better, and more economically' to spur the growth of production. Macfarquhar notes that although the policy initiatives were adopted by the high leaderships, they were actually not implemented for a long time. Some other top leaders even criticised the policy programme as 'Adventurism'. In the 1956 session of the National People's Congress, opened on 15 June, Finance Minister Li Xiannian summarised the economic problems that resulted from the ambitious programme, and raised a slogan to oppose impetuosity and adventurism. This slogan was emphasised in an important editorial in the People's Daily, which was drafted and revised by the major leaders who were in charge of the central propaganda sector of CPC, and finally vetted and passed by Liu Shaoqi. There was also evidence which indicated that Premier Zhou Enlai, and his colleagues in the State Council Chen Yun (Senior Deputy premier), Li Fuchun (Deputy Premier), and Deng Zihui (Deputy premier) etc., had themselves opposed this adventurism. Consequently, Mao's first ambitious attempt to launch the Chinese economy forward soon encountered a setback.

The dispute in the Eighth Congress of the CCP, is another case raised by Macfarquar. The Congress was held in September 1956, in which some prominent political leaders, e.g. Peng Dehuai, Liu Shaoqi, Peng Zhen, proposed that reference to Mao's thought should be dropped from the new constitution of the party. Meanwhile, some other party leaders, including Premier Zhou Enlai and his colleagues, insisted on rejecting Mao's radical economic policies (Chapter 8,10). According to Macfarquar's analysis, it seems that even in Mao's era, it is unreasonable to overestimate the role of the paramount leader in policy-making, and to underestimate the role of the other leaders. Therefore, to portray Chinese policy process as an absolute control by the paramount leader is not in accordance with the facts.

Scholars' controversy about the Deng-in-command model even further argue that there is no particular leader in Post-Mao China who has possessed the same absolute authority or power as Mao in the policy process. Teiwes argues that 'Although... Deng Xiaoping quickly emerged as the generally acknowledged leader, a genuinely more collective pattern now developed with many ramifications for elite interaction as a whole' (1984, p. 6). Actually, many of the most important policies were made through collective decision, which required a high degree of consensus. No one figure, not even Deng, was so dominant as to be able solely to control the policy process and impose his will to the others (Oksenberg, 1982).

Furthermore, scholars who studied the politics of Post-Mao China bring to light that this period also saw some important policy-making resulting from the sharp conflicts and negotiations among those top politicians. To explore this phenomenon, Imamual Hsu (1990) examines in particular the bargaining process that took place on the issues of Deng's rehabilitation. The fact was, in 1977, after the downfall of the 'gang of four', Hua Guofeng, Chairman of the party, faced a lot of knotty issues including his legitimacy as Mao's successor, the rehabilitation of Deng Xiaoping, the former general secretary of the party, and the reordering of economic priorities to promote modernisation. However, under this situation, Hua's disadvantage was that he did not have strong support within the party. Marshall Ye Jianying and other of Deng's supporters regarded Mao's dying words to Hua 'With you in charge, I am at ease' as only 'Mao's personal view rather than the will of the party'. Hua realised by implication that since his assumption of the Chairmanship of the CCP and of the Central Military Commission was seen unconstitutional, and, if he would agree to the reinstatement of Deng, this question of legitimacy about his succession 'could be negotiated or even withdrawn'. Thus, the two issues needed to be balanced. As a result of mediation by Marshall Ye and Deputy Premier Li Xiannian, Hua agreed in principle to rehabilitate Deng, and to revise the five-year economic plan to accelerate the four modernisations (pp. 30-31).

Also, Hsu notices (p. 36) another important policy bargaining event between Hua and Deng. This happened at the Fifth National People's Congress held in 1979, when Deng had re-established and strengthened his power base. At this meeting, Deng was in dispute with Hua over the issues of personnel arrangement, priority of economic development, and re-evaluating Mao's role. It seemed that Hua and Deng had reached a consensus: the former would support Deng's personnel changes and economic policies, and as return, the latter would agree to slow down moves toward a critical assessment of Mao's role in the Cultural Revolution, which would cause both embarrassment and injury to Hua (p. 37).

Moreover, Hsu points out the fact that even Hua's finally leaving his position both in the party (as Chairman) and in the government (as premier) was 'an orderly transfer of power', which created a precedent which 'might avoid the wrenching political turmoil and uncertainty of the past' (ibid. p. 44). Obviously, these peaceful changes were also conducted by negotiation among politicians.

All the above analysis suggests the basis of the politicians-in-negotiation models. These scholars try to prove that either in the Mao era or the post-Mao period, China's politicians often used the means of bargaining to pursue their desired policy targets; the paramount leader could not always control the policy-making situation through his will. Particularly, in the transition period from Mao's era to Deng's age, the negotiation became more important because Hua was in the top position but without majority supporters, while Deng controlled powerful political forces formally and potentially, although he had not yet possessed an important official status.

To sum up, according to what is reviewed above, the politician-in-negotiation model which stresses the important role of those high-rank political elites in China's policy process, seems reasonable. However, these evidences only came from some special periods when the power and influence of China's paramount leader had not been at its height, and therefore it seems not to be applicable to interpret the political phenomenon in the period when the paramount leader was powerful enough to dominate China's politics. For instance, in the period of the Cultural Revolution and the period of the last eighteen years of Deng's life, both Mao and Deng could control the policy-making power absolutely.

The Power-conflicts-oriented model   The power competition-oriented model emphasises the influence of power clashes between different political factions (political elites) in China's policy process, from which to search for the dynamics of Chinese politics and the determinants of Chinese policy-making process.

According to this model, power conflicts are the most important determinant in Chinese policy process. The various policy debates and fluent policy swings resulted from the competition of the participants which strove for maintenance of power positions. Therefore, policy-making has become the tool used by policy makers to realise their power goals.

A power model, developed by Lucian Pye (1981), asserts that the main factors in the policy-making process are power constellations of clusters of officials who for some reason or other feel comfortable with each other. These clusters are the so-called factions. The real motivation to form factions is to achieve career security and enhancement. Although certain policies may become the trademarks of particular factions, it cannot be concluded that factions are formed only on the basis of policy preference or ideological considerations. 'The prime basis for factions among cadres is the search for career security and the protection of power' (p. 7). On many occasions, policy-making serves the power purpose of a faction. The acute controversy of the policy makers over policies is not necessarily because of intellectual disagreements, but because the policy makers predict that the effects of the policy will alter their respective power position.

Drawing upon the findings of Parris H. Chang (1979) about policy process, Pye further described the relationships between policy issues and factional power considerations as follows: '(1) The ending or shelving of any authoritatively announced policy programme signals the existence of a countervailing power group. ...(2) A change in focus of a policy signals the existence of a contending power group that is not strong enough to be an effective countervailing power. ... (3) Policies that are not workable will not be criticised or altered unless there is a contending group to challenge for power. ...(4) A change in the responsibility for a programme implies a shift in factional power. ...(5) Persistence in clinging to unworkable policies is a sign of secure power, not of mere stubbornness. ...(6) Any public criticism, particularly at a party congress, must be interpreted as a challenge for power' (p. 162). These rules summarised by Pye show that to a great extent policy issues are dominated by factional power struggles.

Another scholar, Andrew J. Nathan (1973, pp. 34-66), studies the Chinese policy process with the power-conflicts-oriented model from a different angle. Nathan tries to place his analysis in a comparative framework. He does not adopt the usual approach to the study of Chinese power struggles that developed an interpretation on the basis of the information available, but uses a reversed procedure that presents a general and abstract framework at first, then shows that the available data on Chinese politics are consistent with the model. In doing so, Nathan first carefully examines the structural characteristics of factions and the characteristics of factional politics, by which he constructs his theoretical framework about political factions. According to his study, Nathan suggests that in an ideal-typical political system which was primarily organised by factions, the political process is characterised by a series of typical features which he lists for fifteen. Among which, include (ibid. pp. 46-51),

- a faction's most important concern is 'to protect its own base of power while opposing accretions of power to rival factions';

- ideological agreement 'is not a primary condition for an alliance with other factions';
- in policy-making 'a typical cycle of consensus formation and decline' exists among the factions;
- to weaken their rivals, 'factions try to discredit opposition faction members, dislodge them from their posts, and buy away their allies'; to do so, 'rumour, character assassination, bribery and deception are used'.

In examining China's reality from 1949 to the early 1970s with these views, Nathan demonstrates that his model is applicable to a considerable extent. Because, the available evidence shows that 'Chinese politics at the central government level had been structured largely by factions' (p. 52), so the central political arena displayed most of the characteristics of a factional system. Power consideration became the most important factor in political activities and policy-making within those political factions.

It has been seen that in employing the power competition-oriented model, to define the relations between power conflicts and policy disputes is an important issue. Kuo Hua-lun (1979) argues that in inter-party struggle, the latter is subordinate to the former, and the former is the real motivating of the latter.

> It appears that the contenders are struggling for the adoption of the correct line, whereas power is the instrument to carry out the line. In essence, the real goal is power while the supposed errors in a certain line are excuses to discredit opponents. Therefore, every top-level intra-party struggle is inevitably concealed under the line struggle, resulting in a shift and redistribution of power.' 'the correctness of a certain line, or policy, is judged by the power-holders — winners of the power struggle (pp. 25-6).

To assess the power competition-oriented model, it can be considered that it does reflect an objective fact and provide an effective way of examining China's policy-making behaviour. This means that, in CPC's high level group, the existence of factions and struggles in making policy are undeniable; and the impacts of the results of the power struggle on policy formulation are important; therefore, to observe China's policy-making process with this model is helpful, especially for some periods.

Actually, even Chinese leaders did not deny the phenomena of party's factions and power struggles. As in the early 1950s, Mao had pointed out that there are parties which exist outside the party (CPC), and there are also factions within the party; it would be very strange if there were no factions within the party. A practical example is that Mao launched the Cultural Revolution to carry out his power struggle that he considered as existing between two headquarters.

However, it should be noticed that the power model could not be applied well in all periods in China. As in any organisation, the existence of factions is absolute, but the extent of their struggle is changeable. Sometimes it appears acute, and sometimes it falls in a low wave, and even a relative peaceful period occurs. So, in China, when a round of competition ended, and the new struggle had not come to the surface, it was not suitable to use the power model to examine the policy activity. The early reform period from 1979 to 1984 is such a case, when Deng had successfully defeated other factions and controlled power, the situation in the high level party leadership was stable. The policy preference towards furthering reform and the opening-up cause dominated. At this period, the impacts of the power struggle on policy-making were unnoticeable. Another example is the period from 1990 to now. After the 1989's events, with the support of Deng, the new CPC leading group, headed by Jiang Zemin, soon controlled the situation in the same year. While, the other side of the group, headed by Zhao Zhiyang (former party general secretary), which supported more radical political reform than the former, was dismissed. Hence, from 1990, the policy-making process did not have to face strong arguments from a powerful opposing group. To observe China's policy-making behaviour form 1990 to now, therefore, using the power model is also not effective.

Bureaucracy in dominance models At the time when the controversy about who plays the key role in the policy process between the paramount leader and politicians was still in process, some scholars accessed another study object: the role of the bureaucracy. They considered that with the development of both China's party and the state's functional agency, the bureaucracy had grown up and became an important force in policy-making. In their views, it was similar to that in other modern countries, China's bureaucracies also possess some very important power resources. These resources cover many aspects. First, they control the information resources and they also have the professional ability to deal with this information for the aim of searching the desired results. For instance, Oksenbrg (1972) notices that although Mao dominated the policy-making process over twenty years from the middle 1950s, the role of the bureaucracies was quite important, for 'the alternatives available to him

(Mao) were shaped by his staff and bureaucratic subordinates. They provided the information that governed Mao's perceptions' (p. 86). Therefore, Mao 'had to devote considerable energy to retain control over the bureaucracy and to secure adequate flow of information' (ibid.). Second, they are very familiar with the process and regulation of policy-making and policy formulation so that they can exert an impact upon policy initiatives and policy-making agendas. Third, they have close relations with various interest groups and so they know more about the feasibility of a policy. Fourth, they are usually the permanent officials in the bureaucracy, and therefore, they have enough time and energy to pursue their desired policy target in a long-term competition. Thus, the bureaucracy possesses an increasing influence in the policy process. These scholars hold that in China's policy process the key role was not usually played by the political elites, but by the bureaucracy — the party or state's functional or regional organisations in various fields and at different levels. The process of shaping the policy is a competition in which various agencies struggle for resources and power.

Among those scholars who emphasised the role of the bureaucracy in the policy process, Whitson's view (1972) deserves discussion. Whitson quoted Allison's words to define the bureaucratic political model. According to Allison, 'The decisions and actions of governments are essentially intra-national political outcomes: 'outcomes' in the sense that what happens is not chosen as a solution to a problem but rather results from compromise, coalition, competition, and confusion among government officials who see different faces of an issue; political is the sense that activity from which the outcomes emerge is best characterised as bargaining...' (Whiltson, 1972, p. 382). Thus, in analysing the conflicts and results of the bureaucratic interests, values, attitudes and goals in China's policy process, Whitson considers that China's governmental decisions is the result of compromise, coalition, competition and confusion among governmental officials through bargaining and negotiation. A number of individuals in bureaucracies are the actors of these activities. These players constitute different agencies for particular decisions and actions, and the positions occupied by the players shape their stances on policy issues.

By applying his bureaucratic politics models to explain the high command's different perceptions on their strategic issues in the People's Liberation Army (PLA), Whitson suggested that there were at least six major career channels in PLA before the Cultural Revolution, which included Local force; Ground force; General Political Department; General Real Service Department; Navy and Air Force. The officers within these different fields had developed a distinctive set of organisational interests, values, attitudes and goals. They had been clearly aware of these different interests so that each of these organisations would tend to encourage their members to behave in such a way as to enhance their own collective interest (p. 383). Besides the linkage of these six formal career institutions, Whitson further defines five informal spheres, which developed from the interest relations in both historical and realistic context, which cut across the career lines and confuses the priority of collective interests of the career groups. These informal groups embody military generations, the original field armies, the military regions, the central elite and the personal relationships, from which individual differences in values, viewpoints and goals among about 1000 senior officials of the PLA were produced. Thus, each individual 'acts as a player in the bargaining process in which his informal and formal organisational affiliations could be expected to influence his choices of the issues on which he might bargain, his perspectives toward such issues, and his ultimate bargaining behaviour.'(p. 384). According to his study, Whitson draws the conclusion that owing to the close internal links through these formal and informal channels, with different interest groups, the bureaucracies in PLA play an important role in the policy process, which is characterised as bargaining and compromise in solving the inevitable conflicts.

Another author, Frederick C. Teiwes (1972) also used the bureaucratic politics models to describe the conflicts and the impacts of the bureaucracies in the policy process. Teiwes' study focuses on the provincial level as well as the centre-provincial tensions on dealing with the provincial interests. He holds (pp. 125-8) that the three-fold list as follows covers the key sources of tensions between the provinces and central authority.

- The contradiction between central policy-making and local policy implementation;
- the competition among provinces for centrally controlled resources; and
- the diversion to 'localism'— the provincial officials making their discrete policies for local interests regardless of fixed central policies.

Teiwes's study concerns China's politics in the 1950s. He suggests (p. 130) that in the late 1950s the provincial authorities had been an important force in major national decision-making. On one hand, the central elites needed to involve the provincial leaders to tip the balance in their policy debate; for example, Mao mobilised the support of the provincial officials to overcome the resistance to the new policy in July 1955 on the issue of the cooperationalisation movement in agriculture. However, on the other hand, the provincial leaders had possessed considerable force to influence central policy-making for their provincial interests, and the decentralisation measures which were adopted at the Central Committee Plenum in September 1957 indicated the increase in provincial control over industry, finances and planning.

Although the bureaucratic politics models were put forward in the early 1970s, they were less systematically developed before the 1980s due to some historical reasons. First, during that period the state structure was characterised by highly centralised power, the political elite could manage to control the formation and diversification of bureaucratic interests. Therefore, the bureaucracy actually played a minor role in the policy process before the reform. Second, the politicians did not give enough trust to the bureaucracy so that the latter could not be awarded the whole power they wanted. Since the politicians considered bureaucracy as ineffective and a morass so they sought to minimise the role of bureaucracy and even depend on campaigns as an alternative mechanism of policy implementation for a long time. It seemed as if the bureaucracies did not have the status as policy-making participants but acted as the tools in a policy process, and their actual role was neglected to a certain extent. Third, even the restricted role of the bureaucracy was controlled by the strong impacts of the political elites, especially the paramount leader.

This situation changed in the 1980s when the tendency of economic marketization and administrative decentralisation strongly promoted the relaxation of the concentrated power structure. With the realising of the significance of economic development by the political elites, professional participation in the policy process was considered more and more important. Thus, policies, especially those concerning economic issues, were increasingly made with the participation of experts and professional officials. All these elements resulted in the significant raising of the status of bureaucratic agencies and the strengthening of their power. In addition, China's opening-up situation also gave foreign scholars more opportunity to access research sources by accessing data or interviewing the bureaucratic officials (it is much more convenient to interview them than to interview politicians!), especially those in the fields of economics, culture and education. Under these circumstances, naturally, research into the roles and mechanism of the bureaucracies on effecting policy process was becoming more common.

In discussing the further development of the systematic study of bureaucratic politics models in post-Mao China, we first need to notice Michel Oksenberg's work that effectively explored the impact of the bureaucratic structure and interests on the policy process. With the purpose of examining the changes in the policy process of post-Mao China, he put forward some key questions. These included, what are the principal features of the Chinese policy process in the Deng's era, how much has it evolved from Maoist system, and whether the power now is lodged in situations more than in individuals. In order to answer these questions, Oksenberg (1982) conducted a series of interviews with officials in various bureaucratic agencies. During his investigations, he observed different aspects concerned with operations of the bureaucratic system, including the structure and mechanism of the bureaucracy, the ways in which they involved in economic policy-making, the functions of different agencies in agenda setting, the procedures of policy initiatives and design, the approaches of resolving interagency disputes, and also the ways of consensus building.

According to his investigation, Oksenberg drew the conclusion that some particular changes had happened in China's policy process.

- That the process seemed less vulnerable to the intervention of one man. At least in the economic realm, decisions were shared. The process was protracted, involving widespread consultation and modification in the face of opposition.
- Factions may have continued to exist in the politburo, but unlike the situation in Mao's last years, whatever strife existed was somewhat contained. The economic realm was insulated or cushioned from the other factional sectors.
- Rule through bureaucracy had returned. Professionalism was officially esteemed. Decisions were somewhat more based on empirical evaluations of alternatives (p. 192).

The reasons for the great change in China's agricultural policy since 1978 was one of Oksenberg's cases study projects. Through tracing the evolution of the formulation of this policy, he holds that Deng and his associates had succeeded in establishing a disjointed, incremental bureaucratic policy process, and they were obtaining 'both its benefits and its cost' (pp. 191-2). However, Oksenberg also notices that although the bureaucracy was relied upon by the leadership, 'to a considerable extent, power remained vested in individuals rather than institutions' (p. 192).

The advantage of the bureaucratic model is providing a new perspective from which to observe the Chinese policy process and overcome the biased view of the politicians in control model. The latter stresses that policy is shaped mainly at the top and the politicians play key roles; meanwhile, it underestimates the significance of the bureaucracies in determining policy outputs by either altering the information concerning the external environment or distorting the initiatives of politicians at implementation. However, the bureaucratic model holds that the structural function of bureaucracy is an important factor which can efficiently effect the shaping of the policy outputs by incorporating different organisational interests, missions, and their conflicts into the policy process. Obviously, the bureaucratic politics model is quite persuasive to some extent in explaining discrepancies between different policy outcomes, and the protracted, incremental nature of China's policy process. In contemporary China's politics, bureaucratic organisations have become a power resource that can not be underestimated.

Nevertheless, the bureaucratic approach also faces some problems. One of which is that the model seems deficient when applied to explain the Chinese policy process before 1979. During Mao's period, although Chinese politics were bureaucratic in nature, namely, the main participants in political life were bureaucratic officials, however, in fact, bureaucracy was neither strong enough nor powerful enough to play an important role in policy-making. Those endless campaigns launched by political leaders, including those to criticise 'bureaucratism', 'departmentalism', and 'localism', had successfully prevented the formation and development of bureaucratic interests and power. For a long time before the 1980s, China's bureaucracy did became a submissive tool of the politicians to the great extent.

In addition, it is essential to understand the relations between the 'bureaucratic approach' and 'political approach'. Although the former tries to explore China's policy-making process from a new perspective, it still stresses the role of elites. As has been discussed, according to the elitist theory, high level bureaucrats are also social elites although they are not considered as having as much power as those politicians, and are also at a lower level of the power hierarchy comparing with the latter. Objectively speaking, in any period of PRC, the role of the political elites (politicians) is of the first importance. The main change since the late 1970s, is that the role of bureaucratic organisations has become more and more noticeable, due to the increasing professional importance of the bureaucracy owing to rapid economic development, the decentralisation of the administrative power, and the reducing of the personality cult to the political leaders. There are two sides to this issue. On one hand, the reform had increased the significance of bureaucracy in policy formulation, especially in the economic realm. On the other hand, although the role of the political elites is not as absolute and unique as before it is still undoubtedly in the leading position. What is important when comparing these two models, is to distinguish the different roles of these two factors in different realms and different periods in shaping the policies.

Interest group model   To view China's politics from another angle, these models describe and emphasise the influences of the interaction of China's various socio-economic interest groups, on China's policy process. Researchers which contributed to these models include Moody, P., Liu, A. and Oksenberg, M. The studies of the last two writers focus on the conflicts and struggles of different factions and groups in the Culture Revolution (Oksenberg, 1968; Liu, 1976). Comparably, Moody's work (1977) accesses a relatively wider range of discussing the opposition and dissent in the first twenty-seven years of PRC, which seems particular noticeable. Therefore, this section intends to mainly analyse Moody's model.

For conducting his exploration, Moody first defines the meanings of opposition. He considers a four types' categorisation of opposition in communist systems, raised by Skilling, H. G (1968, pp. 295-9), is a useful general beginning framework. These four types' categorisation is:

> *Integral opposition*: opposition to the system as a whole.
> *Factional opposition*: opposition 'carried on by individuals and groups within the highest organs of he party of government, although support may be sought in broader social or political groupings'.
> *Fundamental opposition*: 'opposition to, or severe criticism of, a whole series of key policies of the regime, based upon crucial differences in standards of value, without, however, a rejection of the communist system itself'.
> *Special opposition*: opposition to 'special policies, without a rejection of the regime or its leaders, or its basic policies in general' (Moody, 1977, p. 2).

Moody points out that these categories may not be mutually exclusive, instead, each of them may change to one of the other positions. He goes further to argue that, as for the elites, opposition is a political act, designed 'to change policies or power relationships', and for those non-elites, opposition is 'resistance (active or passive) to policies accepted by the bulk of the elite' (ibid. p. 3).

Based on the above definition, Moody particularly examines China's different interests and the development of the opposition. In the first aspect, his detailed analyses include all sides of China's society at the background before the end of 1970s, which cover from the 'black elements', which include the landlords, rich ⁻ peasants, counterrevolutionaries, 'bad elements', and rightists, to common peasants; workers, educated youth, writers and intellectuals; and from local interests, bureaucratic interest to the Army. Moody noticed that the existence of these various interests were objective, regardless of whether the ruler would like to acknowledge the facts or not. These interests always tried to find chances to express their demands or to pursue their interest targets, actively or passively, regardless of whether the rulers would like to face them squarely and accept them or not. For instance, although the forces of China's bureaucracy was much weaker than its counterpart in the western countries, in 1962, Mao still felt unhappy about their increasing roles in China's politics. Mao criticised the Central Organisation Department both orally and in writing, in a serious manner, it 'has not made reports to the Centre, to the point that the comrades at the centre know nothing about the activities of the Organisation Department. It has locked itself and become an independent kingdom' (ibid. p. 129).

Another case, which is noticed by Moody, is the development of the regional militarism in the early 1970s. This rapid growth of these forces had been considered a problem in maintaining and strengthening the authority and leadership of the centre. This situation, therefore, finally resulted in a massive reshuffling of the regional military commands, at the end of 1973 (ibid. p. 153).

To analyse the second aspect, the opposition, Moody first defined the distinction compared with the first one. That is, the first one concentrates upon interests, and the second one upon ideology, or simply ideas. Moody mainly conducted his discussion in examining the development of opposition movements. His studies suggest that the opposition movements, namely to criticise China's policies which were dominant, or the mainstream of the ideology, had never stopped. These include the Hundreds Flowers Campaign in the middle 1950s, the critique of the Great

Leap Forward in the early 1960s, and Zhou Enlai's rational modernism in the middle 1970s.

Moody clearly states that his study is intended as 'a critique of totalitarianism'. Although he acknowledges that a totalitarian regime is one that 'does not consider itself to any standards external to itself', and it can use the 'physical' and 'intellectual' methods to limit the opposition (p. 238), he still argues that the existence of the opposition is required by the regime, because if the 'enemies were suddenly to disappear, the regime would have a hard time justifying dictatorship', and therefore, the opposition is required by the regime 'as an unintended consequence, keeps alive alternatives to the regime' (p. 239). Thus, Moody's study does not only demonstrate the inevitability of the different interests and opposition in China, but the objective role they play in China in maintaining its political system.

As relating to the policy-making process, according to the study of Moody, we see that both the existence of the plural interests and plural policy tendencies in China were objective, if they could be expressed properly, they may become a healthy and active force to be conducive to the state's better policy-making, otherwise, they would cause problems for the regime. Because, as Johnson says: 'a political order that proclaims discussion to be useless is one that invites treason, or, conversely, one that makes the concept of treason unintelligible' (p. 239).

To be sure, Moody's model provides us with a special viewpoint to examine China's policy process. That is, whether or not the government advocates and encourages a pluralist involvement in the state's policy-making, the plural interests and plural policy tendencies substantially exist and exert their roles actively or passively, overtly or covertly.

3.2.2 The elitism-basis models

These models stress the decisive roles of China's top political elites in the policy process. In this section we mainly discuss the Mao (or Deng)-in-command models, the most typical elitist style policy-making models.

The earliest one of these models was first developed by Michael Oksenberg, Frederick C. Teiwes, *et al.* It describes China's policy-making process in the period of 1949-1976 as that in which Mao was a paramount leader and the unchallenged core of China's elite politics. All other top leaders were dependent, to a great degree, on Mao's will to deal with policy-making issues. Mao was definitely in a dominant position of China's policy-making process.

Oksenberg (1972) holds that Mao had dominated the policy-making process over the past two decades. Mao's role was not to be involved in important daily decision-making but to have intervened in those key policies' formulation. According to Oksenberg, Mao's dual roles in policy-making involved playing a decisive impact in 'bringing initiatives, establishing priorities, and giving coherence to ongoing policies', and 'search for a synthesis of goals that seemed to be irreconcilable' (p. 91). In exploring the way Mao used to control the party policy process, which included 'bringing initiatives and to bend the course of events to accord with his vision', Oksenberg suggests that there were two major methods. One was through commenting on the reports submitted to him. In his comments, Mao criticised, or praised, or instructed the issues in the report, which immediately became the decisive intervention in the policy-making. Another method, the informal meeting, which was more important for Mao, was often applied (p. 98). The available data indicate, these informal meetings of top level officials were held over eighty times from 1953 to the late 1967 (p.91). These meetings were referred to by the names of the places in which they were held, for instance, 'the Chendu meeting', 'the first Hangzhou meeting', and 'the Second Hangzhou meeting', etc. On some occasions, such meetings had institutional labels, such as a Politburo Meeting, an Enlarged Politburo Meeting, or an Enlarged Politburo Standing Committee Meeting, and so on. The length of these meetings varied from case to case. Some lasted for more than a month, and some were only two or three days. According to Oksenberg, to convene these informal meetings to make policy was one of Mao's seven tactics to control the policy-making in the light of his wills. This method of disorganising the form of policy-making group, seemed good for him to prevent 'the formation of a cohesive, difficult-to-control small group' (p.96). Oksenberg notices that many important strategies and policies were determined in these informal meetings. For instances, in the Qingdao Conference, which was held in July 1957, Mao resurrected his shelved National Agricultural Development Programme, and thereby initiated the sequence of events leading to the Great Leap Forward. In Beidaihe Central Work Conference which was held in August 1962, Mao stressed the necessity of fighting bureaucracy and fostering class antagonism in society, which led to the launching of the Socialist Education Campaign, etc. (p. 88).

At these informal party meetings, usually, Mao set up the agenda, put forward important policy initiatives and general guidelines for the party and the government. Then, through the works of three key bodies: the Military Affairs Committee, the Standing Committee of the State Council, and Party Headquarters Secretariat, these policy frameworks and guiding thought soon acquired a more specific direction.

Analysing the role of Mao in the policy-making process from another angle, Teiwes (1984) argues that before the Cultural Revolution China's shifting policies can be explained by changeable tendencies in Mao's thought. It was the contradictions of Mao's overall intellectual framework that resulted in the instability of policy guidelines in China.

In searching for the reasons why Mao's shifting intellectual concern has had such an impact on China's policy process, Teiwes examines Mao's power and status in the top party leadership and the norms of behaviour which governed Mao's interaction with his colleagues. Teiwes points out that despite the fact that Mao's prestige had its ups and downs, the evidence is overwhelming that his colleagues consistently regarded him as the ultimate authority. The party leaders clearly viewed Mao's attitude towards them and the general perception of that attitude as crucial to their career (p. 24). To explore the resources of Mao's authority, Teiwes used Max Weber's concepts about charismatic authority, legal-rational authority and traditional authority. Teiwes suggests that Mao employed all three types of authority to sustain his power, and stresses that Mao's legitimacy mainly came from the first type of authority, namely charismatic authority. Because, in Teiwes' view, 'Charisma in its pure form only arises in a period of crisis when the unusual powers of the person in question are seen as providing the answers to the calamitous situation' (p. 46). Mao's absolute authority was established in a long term crisis period which included the War of Resistance Against Japan and the three civil wars, in which Mao fully showed his 'exceptional qualities' (ibid.).

History had demonstrated that, Mao's 'exceptional qualities' were recognised by his colleagues in the party leadership, through his success in dealing with the revolutionary crises. Particularly, from the 1930s to the 1940s, Mao consolidated his leadership by conducting his policies of guerrilla warfare and the independence within the 'United Front', which resulted in the ascendancy of the party and produced a vast growth of communist power. Thus, 'within a dozen years strategies bearing a personal stance led to an almost unimaginable victory which conferred on him a genuine revolutionary charisma' (p. 48). For these reasons, Teiwes believes,

> Mao stood above his colleagues, although he had sensibly fostered a democratic leadership style. His stature was such that as long as he lived, no matter how removed from daily operations or how ambiguous his position, Mao remained a factor to which all others had to adjust (p.42).

Similar to the Mao-in-command model, which emphasises Mao's role as being in a top position of the core power of the Party and none of his colleagues being able to challenge his authority, later, some scholars developed a Deng-in-command model to portray Post-Mao China's policy process. They demonstrated that there was then also a paramount leader who had the same authority as Mao to control China's policy-making.

One of these representative works of Deng-in-command model is *China Under Deng Xiaoping*, written by David Wen-wei Chang (1988). In his book, Chang argues that, although Deng was different from Mao in some important aspects he gained the same degree of authority of Mao. Through his victory against Hua Guofeng (Party Chairman from 1976 to 1978), Deng reached absolute control over the hierarchy of the party and state. The new political situation since then 'allowed Deng to have the first and definitely the last voice in all major policies. He is the final arbiter of all things, like Mao, but without being surrounded by a personality cult... his position is supreme and unique in the entire communist world' (pp. 24-25).

Chang holds that Deng was an initiator of important policies, a creator of ideology, and an architect of the current reform. He analyses (pp.25-26) the reasons why Deng was able to win the unique top leadership, which have six aspects.

- Deng's rich experiences and high positions before the Cultural Revolution had given him unique advantages over many other well-know politicians.
- Deng's age in the late 1970s qualified him as a younger and well-experienced statesman among the old generation that experienced the famous Long March.
- Deng's unfortunate experience in the Cultural Revolution enabled him to obtain sympathy from cadres within the party and government.
- Deng's policies of restoring those purged colleagues to their personal honour, to former or new positions in the party and the government won great support from millions of former leaders and cadres.

- His successful struggle against the leftists and their influence within the party and government won for him the gratitude of many individuals and groups.
- His setting up a series of new policies in saving the economy and benefiting the people greatly increased his popularity.

To analyse the Mao (or Deng)-in-command models, which emphasis the role of the paramount leaders as the most important factor in China's policy process, we need to point out that the occurrence of this policy-making style was the product of some special periods and special environments. That means, in a special period when serious crisis occurs and a charismatic authority with particular quality is required to save the situation, and in a special environment where a heavy influence of feudalism tradition exists, such an authority can more easily grow up, and can be accepted and promoted. Without either of these two factors, the style of paramount leader-in-command for policy-making could not occur. The merits of this model can be seen from two sides. On one hand, it is very persuasive in explaining the undulation in Chinese policy and the abrupt nature of some political events, for these features resulted in the changes of the paramount leaders' wishes, health, and other personal factors. On the other hand, more importantly, it can provide the explanation that only with unique and absolute authority, could these paramount leaders launch those huge-scale campaigns politically and economically without many difficulties, which often defeated the predictions of foreign observers of China. Examples of these are the Cultural Revolution and the Great Leap Forward of Mao, and the reform and opening-up strategy of Deng.

However, the deficiencies of the model are also obvious. It over-simplifies the complex policy process in China and only describes China's policy formulation as a process in which the will of the paramount leader is the unique factor playing the key role. Meanwhile, it also over-underestimates the role of the other political leaders in the party.

3.2.3 The institutionalism-basis and institutions-related models

This group includes the ideological-conflict-oriented models, the models stressing the effects of bureaucratic structures, and the models analysing the policy-making patterns. All these models emphasise the important impacts of the institutionalised elements on China's policy-making process.

The ideological-conflict-oriented models These models stress the decisive influences of the ideological conflicts upon China's policy process. It is determined by China's political system that a policy proposal could only be raised and adopted if it conforms to China's ideological principles. Namely, that it follows the line of Marxism and socialism. This was especially strict in the first three decades of PRC. Scholars focusing their studies on the ideology-conflicts-lead dynamics of China's policy-making, show us the significance of these impacts, through their diversified models.

According to their observation, some scholars hold that China's policies were produced through a course, in which different policy preferences coming from diversified and competing ideologies and values were put forward and debated in the leadership. This course involved sharp idea contentions, and value contradictions, which finally resulted in the policy output corresponding to the ideological tendency that occupied a dominant position. Consequently, the policy oscillations became the phenomenon that often occurred, deriving from the periodic up and down movement of the struggle between different opinion clusters. A simple form of the model is the 'two-line struggle' model, which was originally developed by Chinese top leaders themselves and then was modified by the western scholars. At the beginning of the Cultural Revolution, the Chinese leadership declared that there were two opposing political and ideological lines that existed in the CCP. They were the 'Proletarian revolutionary line', and the 'Bourgeois reactionary line', which also can be simplified as 'left' and 'right' lines which belonged to and served the proletarian and bourgeois interests respectively. These two lines struggled with each other and determined policy-making in China.

Later, some Western scholars applying a similar terminology to depict Chinese politics had basically accepted this dichotomy created by Chinese leadership. They described China's policy-making as a process with continuing conflicts between the 'left' and the 'right' groups. The analysis by Oksenberg and Goldstein (1974) is a typical example of exploring this meaning labelled by Chinese and westerners.

They point out that, to the Chinese, 'the 'left' represents the interest of the proletariat and peasants from poorer backgrounds, the 'left' is the sane, progressive side, committed to Maoist principles and to sound socialist development of China's culture and economy. The Chinese identified the 'right' as the side of conservatism, 'revisionism' or 'capitalism'— the side whose policies would erode the vitality of revolution' (pp. 1-3).

On the other hand, most westerners 'think of 'leftists' in China as the radicals, the extremists, the reds, the utopians, the campaigners or the ideologues... Opposed to them, in the western idiom, are the moderates, realists, experts, pragmatists, and bureaucrats, which are all seen as comprising the 'right'. In this language, these are the sane people, committed to the rational, flexible development of the economy and of the political institutions' (ibid.).

Based on the identification of 'left' and 'right' lines, western scholars employed the dichotomous labels widely on China's politics, for instance, 'Maoist' versus 'Liuist', 'radical' versus 'moderate', modernisation versus institutionalisation, the revolutionary modernizer versus the managerial modernizer, equity-seeking versus efficiency-seeking, transformation versus consolidation, etc.

The manifestation of the prominent conflicts and fluctuation of China's politics, was one of the important research focuses of those who devoted themselves to the study of the two lines struggles models. Among this literature, Nathan (1976) offered a typical analysis.

Nathan firstly listed a brief chronology of the Chinese policy fluctuation from 1949 to 1976. According to this chronology, during the early years after liberation, pragmatic or moderate policies (the right line) were in the ascendancy, because the regime faced the problems of take-over, which required the establishment of public order and the first step toward economic reconstruction. The year 1955 to 1956 saw the first swing to a left line. Agricultural collectivisation was pushed rapidly, whilst a mass mobilisation campaign brought socialist transformation to commerce and industry. A rightist interlude followed in 1956-1957, when agricultural collectives and socialised industrial and commercial enterprises were consolidated. With the launching of the Great Leap Forward of 1958-1960, mobilisation returned as the theme in all sectors of Chinese policy. The excesses of the 'Great Leap Forward' led to a period of retrenchment from late 1960 to 1965, which was characterised by a rightist line. However, since 1962, Mao had been dissatisfied with the rightist policies of the retrenchment, and so in 1966 he launched the radical counter offensive which became the Cultural Revolution. The period from 1969 to 1975 was characterised by a return to moderation and pragmatism (pp. 721-2). Then, Nathan analyses different manifestations of the 'two lines' in eight policy areas, which interlink with each other. These policy realms cover agriculture, industry, education, cadres and party life, military organisation and strategy, foreign policies towards the Soviet Union, foreign policy towards the United States, and foreign policy towards other countries. In illustrating the phenomena in the agricultural dimension, Nathan notes that (pp. 722-3) a rightist line involves a greater appeal to selfish, materialistic motives on the part of the peasants. These are shown in the form of the free markets, private plots, piecework rates, a great flow of consumer goods to the countryside, and decentralisation of management to team level. While a leftist line involves appeal to self-sacrifice, mobilizational or ideological motives, and hence a reduction in the role of the free markets and private plots, and the politicisation of remuneration systems. In accessing the industrial realm, Nathan points out that, correspondingly, a right line in industry involves balanced, planned investment and centralised management, greater technical sophistication, slower, more stable growth, and reliance on material incentives to both workers and managers. While, a leftist line involves a more rapid but inefficient, decentralised growth of a less sophisticated sector with greater worker participation in management and reliance on ideological incentives is strongly advocated.

In building the two line struggle models, some researchers did not merely describe the fluctuation phenomena and pattern of China's policy, but tried to explore the reasons. Parris H Chang (1982) argues that the policy oscillation between right and left reflected the conflicts between groups with a conservative view and groups with a radical view. 'When the radical view prevailed in the party, the political pendulum would swing to the left, policies to effect radical revolutionary changes would be pushed, and the leadership would stress mobilisation of the masses and the ability of the human will to over-come objective limitations. When the conservative view gained an upper hand, however, the political pendulum would swing to the right, the rightist policies would be moderated and 'consolidation' (retreat) would become the order of the day, and material incentives for the people as well as objective conditions would receive attention' (pp. 722-3).

The two line struggle models prevailed mainly in the early 1970s, with which scholars aimed to depict the policy-making process in the first two decades since the foundation of the PRC, particularly in the period of the Cultural Revolution. Then, it went into decline gradually from the mid-1970s, because more and more evidences had been explored that Chinese policy-making was a complex processes including many elements to which increasing attention had been attached. However, it is noticeable that some new forms of this kind of model still occurred in the post-Mao era. Those scholars who re-emphasise this model argue that the model remains an applicable way to probe Chinese policy-making process. Peter Moody (1984), for example, tries to apply the approach to analyse the policy conflicts within the Chinese leadership on the issues of political control and political liberalisation in the post-Mao China. Moody adopts an approach to divide models of political thinking and attitudes into two lines — the right and the left, or the moderate and the radical, or 'expertise' and the 'red' (means professionalism versus politics in China's background). He described the differences between these two lines as follows. The former stressed the importance of restricting the leaderships' power, asserted conducting political control over society by routine and predictability, and proposed to loosen control over people's lives. The latter affirmed the necessity of political control over all people's lives and bureaucratic agencies as well, either by the dictatorship or the 'masses'. These two tendencies had been attacking each other during the first three decades of PRC and were also continually existing in the post-Mao period. The results of the struggles shaped China's policy-making behaviour and its policy outputs.

Nevertheless, the two-line struggle model encountered criticisms from different angles. Harding (1984, pp. 20-21) points out that the model was derived from the explanation developed by Chinese Communists themselves as a tool with which to mobilise mass support in order to wage political struggles, and was then translated and edited by western scholars during the late 1960s. It 'took on a highly moralistic tone'. Thus, it depicts Chinese politics as 'Manichaen conflicts between right and wrong'. Albeit Western scholars tend to translate its labels into more respectable social scientific terminology, the basic characteristics of the models remained the same. Consequently, more recent analyses of Chinese politics have attempted to produce 'more rigorous, more objective, and more valuable tendency by rejecting each of the defining characteristics of two-line struggle (ibid. p. 21). Oksenberg and Goldstein (1974) criticise the model for oversimplifying the complex mechanism of the Chinese policy process. They hold that, Chinese politics are more complicated than the 'two line struggle models'. Therefore, to describe them only in the simplistic terms of 'left' vs. 'right' or 'radical' vs. 'moderate', 'not only precludes analysis of the process whereby coalitions are pieced together over a number of issues, but also obscures the shadings of opinion involved'. Teiwes (1984) argues that the political thinking and attitudes of Chinese leaders were not fixed but fluctuated from time to time, even 'Mao himself frequently changed his position both in terms of specific policies and by emphasising different aspects of his intellectual outlook' (p. 11). It is unconvincing to say that there were really two mutually exclusive and relatively fixed lines which exist in Chinese Communist history. Hence, the feasibility of this model is suspect.

Since the defects of the two-line struggle model had been recognised more clearly, researchers developed a similar, but more refined model to describe the ideas-oriented contention. This is the multiple-tendency clash model. The classical definition of the tendencies, made by Franklyn Griffiths (1971), referred to 'alternate possible directions of value allocation for society' or 'pattern(s) of articulation associated with a loose coalition of actors operating at different levels of the political structure, whose articulations tend in the same direction but who are unlikely to be fully aware of the common thrust and consequences of their activity' (p. 358). According to the principal hypothesis of the tendency models, policy-making is the function of competition between different tendencies, which should be described in value-neutral terms, instead of in moralistic terms, and also need not be limited to two but may be differentiated within multiple directions. On the basis of this hypothesis, scholars developed diverse forms of model, which access different issues and cover different periods and centres.

In reviewing this model, Oksenberg and Goldstein's 'four line' framework (1974) is particularly noticeable. It holds that, with the aim of responding to the challenge from the west, the key theme in Chinese society had been a search for the proper route to modernity since the 1840s. This core concern remained at the heart of Chinese politics after 1949, although it had changed in some dimensions. For dealing with this key issue, there were four opinion clusters, which could be identified among the Chinese leadership:

- the militant fundamentalists, who stressed the force of an ideologically aroused populace, and took the stance which was anti-bureaucratic, anti-urban, and anti-foreign;
- the rational radical conservatives, who pursued to preserve the traditional essence of China, and meanwhile were able to accept a selective borrowing of Western technical knowledge;
- the eclectic modernisers, who were more tolerant of a western presence in China and were willing to accept western science and technology;
- the westernised Chinese, who advocated China's pursuit of national greatness as a westernised country.

After analysing the conflicts and outcomes of these ideas, Oksenberg and Goldstein concluded that it was the struggles, coalitions, and changing positions among these schools of ideas, which decided the tendency and shaped the outputs of the Chinese policy-making (pp. 1-14).

In adopting the tendency model to depict the Chinese policy-making process, Harding (1981) first focuses his study on analysing the organisational policies from 1949 to 1976. Harding examines the different diagnoses held by Chinese leaders to deal with organisational problems and dilemmas, and he finds that there were four major policy tendencies in this field (pp. 329-331).

- Rationalisation, which stressed the importance of promulgating rules and regulations, establishing a complete network of bureaucratic auditing and monitoring agencies, systematising career lines, and expanding the role of specialised bureaucratic agencies;
- Radicalism, which advocated the complete destruction of the old bureaucracy with its replacement by a much more participatory and less hierarchical form of political system;
- Remedialism, which asserted that an organisation's problem stemmed from the personal values and political orientations of its officials, and the way to solve them therefore depended on the thorough indoctrination of cadres throughout study, criticism, and self-criticism;
- The external remedialism, which proposed to mobilised the masses to participate in party and state affairs, to oversee, discover, criticise, and rectify organisational problems. With further probing the concrete manifestation of the four tendencies, Harding suggests that this fourfold scheme determines all Chinese organisational strategies.

Harding also uses the tendency model to portray the policy process in the economic and political realms in post-Mao China. He points out (1987) that there were three schools of thought held by different groups within the Chinese political spectrum at the time when Mao passed away in 1976.

> On the left of the spectrum was a group of revolutionary Maoist, headed by Mao's wife, Jiang Qing, who wished to preserve the values and policies of the Cultural Revolution. In the centre was a second group of leaders, symbolised by premier Hua Guofeng, who believed that the wound of Cultural Revolution could be healed by restoring, in modified form, many of the political and economic institutions that existed in the mid-1950s and early 1960s before the onset of the Cultural Revolution. At the end of the spectrum, on what the Chinese call the 'right', were leaders who sought to make significant changes in both the Maoist legacy and the Soviet model of politics and economics.

This coalition of reformers was assembled and led by Deng Xiaoping... (p.40).

However, the political situation experienced a rapid development and change after 1976, the right wing of the leadership (reformers) soon enhanced its power base within the conflicting process of the tendencies. Afterwards, the reform leadership itself was divided into two groups — one seeking radical reform and one preferring moderate reform from the end of 1970s. Concerning how fast the reform should be conducted and how far the reform will be proceeded, these two groups held different viewpoints. The moderates are characterised by being more deliberate and orthodox. According to the research on the development and evolution of different tendencies during the reform period before the end of 1980s, Harry Harding concluded that the results of the contest between the tendencies in different periods shaped the formulation of reform strategies and policies.

A similar approach is adopted by Dorothy J Solinger. In her study (1982) about China's policy-making process from 1978 through 1981, the Chinese policy-making elites were divided into three groups according to their attitudes and assertions about reform. These are, the adjusters who advocated the readjustment of sectional relationships in the economy; the reformers who favoured reform or restructuring of the economic system; and the conservatives who stood in support of various elements of *status quo* and against the third Plenum of the Eleventh Central Committee of the Party (pp. 63-106). Later, in analysing the tendency clashes and policy shifts when studying the Chinese business policies from 1949 to 1980, Solinger (1984) portrays the cyclical process in Chinese commercial policy as a 'three-line struggle' —the bureaucratic approach, the market approach and the radical approach. Thus, she points out that the circling among these three competing strategies for commercial work was more than a battle over power between contending elites, but reflected a clash between generally shared values-egalitarianism, order, and productivity (pp. 297-8).

Obviously, according to the above discussion, the model with the focus on multi-tendency conflicts is more sophisticated than the two-line struggle model. The positive aspects of the former can be seen in five ways.

- It distinguishes the subtle differences of ideas involved in the policy process, instead of only sketching two general lines.
- It does not simply divide different policy tendencies into the wrong or right camp but describes them in value-neutral terms.

- It tries to identify the tendencies in lines with different issues and different periods, instead of mixing the shadings of policies in different areas.
- It highlights the phenomena of policy differentiation and policy cycles, and demonstrates that the value conflicts and ideological struggles is an important motivating factor behind the policy movements, which provides us with a convenient way of observing the Chinese policy process.
- As it classifies the different tendencies, it also devotes to searching the causal contexts of these tendencies, thus illustrating the inevitability of their existence. This way seems more feasible. Thus, this model is considered more applicable in the advancement of understanding of the policy-making process in China.

Regarding the defects of the multi-tendency models, the main one is that it takes value differentiation as the sole reason for the policy conflicts and policy cycles within the leadership and does not consider other motivating factors. To be sure, actually, the reasons of variable determining policy conflicts and fluctuations in China are diversified. The other factors, such as power struggles, institutional arrangements, factional conflicts and other socio-economic conditions also exert significant roles in motivating policy conflicts and policy fluctuations besides ideological clashes and opinion differences.

The model stresses the effects of bureaucratic structures   This model explores the significant role of bureaucratic structure in influencing China's policy-making behaviour, for the institutionalised bureaucratic structure shapes the power allocation and power operating mechanism. The most typical example of this model is the 'fragmented authoritarianism model', which developed in the later 1980s and focused on analysing China's policy process since the reform. (Lampton, D. 1987, 1988; Lieberthal, K. & Oksenberg, M, 1988; Lieberthal, K. & Oksenberg, M, 1986, Lieberthal, K. et al, 1989; Lieberthal, K. & Prahalad, C. 1989; Lieberthal, K. 1992, etc.)

The fragmented authoritarianism model argues that authority below the very peak of the Chinese political system is fragmented and disjointed; the fragmentation is structurally based on and has been enhanced by reform policies regarding procedures; and, the fragmentation grew increasingly pronounced under the reform's beginning in the late 1970s (Lieberthal, 1992, p. 8). The fragmented bureaucratic structures or authority decided that the decision-making needed consensus building at the centre and the process is protracted, disjointed and incremental (Lieberthal and Oksenberg, 1988, p. 22). As a result, intense bargaining and negotiation characterise bureaucratic decision-making.

These authors stress the influence of bureaucratic structures upon the policy process because they consider that the bureaucratic structure is closely related to the resources and authority allocation, in which the key issue is decentralisation and centralisation. To study this issue, they consider that there are three dimensions that should be accessed: value integration; structural distribution of resources and authority; and processes of decision-making and policy implementation.

Among these dimensions, the value integration is the important base of policy-making and implementation. However, according to China's current reality, it is still difficult to enter this research field for some particular reasons. Therefore, these authors focus their study especially on the latter two dimensions.

To reveal the features of China's bureaucratic structures, Lieberthal and Oksenberg (1988) divide the authority of Beijing leadership into four tiers:

- the core group of twenty-five to thirty-five top leaders who articulate national policy;
- the layer of staff, leadership groups, research centres, and institutes which links the elite to and buffers them from the bureaucracy;
- State Council commissions and ministries that have supra-ministerial status and co-ordinate activities of line ministries and provinces;
- line ministries which implement policy.

They consider that different pressures and influences shape the behaviour of officials at each level. According to their studies, then, structurally, China's bureaucratic ranking system combines with the functional division of authority among various bureaucracies. This system produces a situation in which it is often necessary to achieve agreement among different bodies, where no single body has authority over the others. In addition, the reform's decentralisation of budgetary authority enabled many locales and bureaucratic units to acquire funds outside of those allocated through the central budget, which they could use to pursue their own policy preferences. This cushion of 'extrabudgetary' funds in turn permits many locales to become less sensitive to the policy demands from higher levels. On the other hand, procedurally, some major change since the reform contributed to the fragmentation of authority, especially economic decisions. First of all, the leaders reduced the use of coercion — purges, labelling, demotions — against those who proposed ideas that eventually were rejected, thus, emboldening participants to argue forcefully for their proposals. Secondly, the stress laid on serious feasibility studies during the 1980s also, de facto, encouraged various units to marshal information to support their own project preferences, often in competition with others. Thirdly, the general decline in the use of ideology as an instrument of control had increased the 'looseness' of the system, and decentralisation in personnel management permitted many bureaucratic units additional initiative. All of these changes thus combined to reduce the extent to which organs responded in a disciplined faction to instructions from high levels (Lieberthal and Lampton, 1992, pp. 8-9).

Owing to the fragmented authority structures, consensus building is central to the policy process, and it is a subtle and complex matter in practice. Lieberthal and Oksenberg (1988, p. 23) find that, the Chinese system does permit the top leaders to bring enormous pressure to bear to advance a project over the objections of key participants. On the other hand, the consensus building needs to be achieved from both the vertical and horizontal aspects. This is because the lower level units have important resources that they can bring to bear and wide ranging efforts are made to strike balances that permit each major actor to support an effort or project with some enthusiasm.

The other feature of China's policy-making process, according to the fragmented authority model (Lieberthal and Oksenberg, ibid. p. 24), is the diffuse policy process. It means that 'the process is protracted, with most policies shaped over a long period and acquiring a considerable history that is well known to many of the participants; it is disjointed, with key decisions made in a number of different and only loosely co-ordinated agencies and inter-agency decision bodies; and, it is incremental, with policy in reality usually changing gradually'.

In making policy, the first important thing is to push an issue onto the agenda of the top level leaders. Lieberthal and Oksenberg reveal that, within the fragmented authority bureaucratic structures, there are five factors which can propel an issue onto the agenda of the top leaders — the State Council or the top 25 to 35 leaders. These factors are:

- The particular interests of individual top leaders explain many instances of problems being brought to this high level.

- Chinese bureaucrats can try to force an issue onto the agenda of the highest leaders.
- The emergence of a critical problem may capture the attention of the top leaders and force decision to be made.
- Foreigners may force an issue onto the agenda of the highest level leaders. For example, the foreign firms may require very high level assurances that the Chinese government stands fully behind a project before they will commit themselves to the effort.
- Procedural requirements also can affect the locus of decision (pp. 30-31).

This finding further explores the important effect of the fragmented bureaucratic structures upon the policy-making process.

In the book, 'Bureaucracy, Politics, and Decision-making in Post-Mao China', edited by Lieberthal and Lampton (1992), a group of authors probe from different aspects and levels the bureaucratic structural functions of China's policy-making system. They probe systematically the conditions that structure bargaining behaviour (David Lampton), examine overall reform strategy and implementation (Susan Shirk), explore the evolution, structure, and politics of the 'leading groups' headed by the top leaders (Coral Lee Hamrin) and explicate the impact on the policy process of the development of think tanks at the centre (Ina Halpern). In accessing the discussion of various bureaucratic functional organs, they examine the military system (Jonathan Pollack), education system (Lynn Paine), personnel system (Melanie Manion) and economic system (Barry Naughton). At the subnational levels, they focus their analysis on the provincial levels (Paul Schroeder), municipal levels(Andrew Walder) and county level and levels below county (David Zweig). These articles, written by using data directly collected in China and by the excellent use of interviews, contribute a lot to the study and testing of this model.

The emerging of the fragmented authoritarianism model was a significant progress in studies of China's policy process. Owing to better research opportunities for the researchers in the new period, including better access to the real world of China's politics (which embodied the high level interviews and the collecting of many first hand or second hand data), and to their hard research work, the authors had touched and revealed some important and believable facts and created a very valuable theoretical model. Its contribution, as Lieberthal and Lampton (1992) point out that, this model

...acknowledges the great insights offered from elite-oriented rational-actor approaches and by a cellular conception of the system. However, it adds a third necessary ingredient to the equation: the structure of bureaucratic authority and the realities of bureaucratic practice that affect both the elite and the basic building blocks of the system (p.11).

The researchers of this model demonstrate that the structure that links the top and the bottom of the system 'requires negotiations, bargaining, exchange, and consensus building' in policy-making, although they find that ' the system is somewhat but not totally fragmented' (p. 12).

Although this model building is a significant study which reveal some basic features of China's policy process in the reform period, it is still criticised by some scholars. Burns (1993) argues that 'fragmented authoritarianism' is something of a misnomer. Because 'fragmented' hardly describes bureaucratic interactions in contemporary China which are characterised by dense networks of communications, shared authority and inter-dependent relations. Moreover, 'authoritarianism' is usually used to describe state-society relations, not relations among state bureaucracies. In so far as bureaucracies are arranged in hierarchies, formal inter-bureaucratic relations are by definition authoritarian (p. 573). Burns also criticises (ibid.) that negotiation and bargaining, as the focus of the model, are usually found in informal inter-bureaucratic relations, and he holds that scholarly attention should focus on comparisons of the formal and informal systems over time and across political system.

In addition, the results of those researches which explore China's policy-making process in different fields with the fragmented authoritarianism model, which have been mentioned above, suggest that there seems to be less evidence to show that the applicability of this model is satisfactory enough, with the exception of the economic cluster.

The models which stress the patterns of policy-making   Before the 1970s, some scholars had begun to study China's policy-making models with a focus on the method or behaviour of policy-making. However, these studies were actually concentrating on probing the influences of the institutions in China's policy-making pattern, therefore we discuss them here as the institutionalism-basis or institutions-related models. The most prominent studies were conducted by John Wilson Lewis, Franz Schurmann and A. Doak Barnett.[1]

In discussing the mass-line method, one of the basic principles and regulations of CPC, for instance, Lewis (1963) does not only view it as 'the basic working method' of Communist cadres but also as a policy-making procedure. From the conceptual viewpoint, he divided this method into four progressive stages: perception, summarisation, authorisation, and implementation. According to his detailed analyses of these four stages Lewis demonstrates that they are actually a process of making decisions. He portrays this process as a policy-making cycle: problem identification → investigation → preliminary decision → testing → revision → report → authoritative decision → implementation → supervision → new problem (pp. 72-3).

The works by Lewis and other scholars aforementioned which were written in the 1960s were the early works of study into China's policy-making process and so they only offer preliminary results and fall short of a full assessment of the issues. On the other hand, due to the continuing great changes in China's recent political life, their 'analyses of Chinese Communist policy-making and organisational behaviour made before the Cultural Revolution are now partially out of date' (Harding, 1971, pp. 113-14).

Later, Harding (1971) constructed a compound mass-line model which emphasised the degree of mass participation and the relative use of pragmatic and the dogmatic criteria, to describe China's policy process. According to Harding, these two dimensions combine to generate the following four possible policy-making modes (pp. 119-120) (see table 3.2).

	Pragmatic Criteria	**Dogmatic Criteria**
High mass participation	Pragmatic mass-line	Dogmatic mass-line
Low mass participation	Pragmatic elitist	Dogmatic elitist

Table 3.2 Harding's two dimensions of four policy-making models

The mass-line, Harding points out, as a model of policy-making, is actually advocated by both Mao Zhedong and Liu Shaoqi. It includes procedures for information gathering, problem selection, proposal formulation, policy selection, policy implementation, and policy appraisal. As Mao says, in his essay 'Some Questions Concerning Methods of Leadership' (1943, p. 236), 'In all the practical work of our party, all correct leadership is necessarily from the masses, to the masses. This means: take the ideas of the masses (scattered and unsystematic ideas) and concentrate them (through study to turn them into concentrated and systematic ideas), then go to the masses and propagate and explain these ideas until the masses embrace them as their own, hold fast to them and translate them into action, and test the correctness of the ideas in such action'.

Harding holds that, the basic form of the mass-line is a series of interactions between an individual cadre (the leader) and the masses (the led), therefore most policy-making is performed not by individuals but by groups. This principle is called 'collective leadership with individual responsibility' as applied to the leading group and called 'democratic centralism' as applied to an organisation (1971, p. 121).

It could be noticed by researchers that both Maoists and their party opposition (i.e. Liuists) agreed about these basic principles of mass-line for policy-making, but still differed over several aspects when applying these principles. Harding summarised (p.122) these disagreements as: the criteria to be used in making decisions and resolving disputes; the best procedures for coping with risk; the range of the applicability of the mass-line as a problem-solving strategy. After identifying manifestations of the four policy-making procedures (i.e., dogmatic mass-line, pragmatic mass-line, dogmatic elitism and pragmatic elitism) and analysing the distinctions of Maoists and Liuists around these issues, Harding concludes (pp.139-140) that, neither Maoists nor Liuists seek to apply a single set of policy-making methods to all problems, rather, their choice of a policy-making method depends on the kind of questions under consideration (see table 3.3).

Issues-Area	Maoist Position	Liuist Position
Ideological and doctrinal questions	Dogmatic mass-line	Dogmatic mass-line
Political, social, and macro-economic questions	Dogmatic mass-line	Pragmatic mass-line
Technical and managerial (micro- economic)questions	Pragmatic mass-line	Pragmatic elitist

Table 3.3   Harding's classification of policy-making methods used by Maoist and Liuist under different conditions

Harding held that the major distinctions between Maoist and Liuist on the policy-making method areas were as follows. Mao considered all policy issues to be solved are 'questions of principle', and the 'divergent policy proposals stem from different class standpoints', therefore, the policy choice is 'only between two contradictory options: the proletarian (0) and bourgeois, revisionist, feudal, or imperialist (not-0)', namely, right and wrong. In Liuist's views, conversely, besides the 'questions of principle', there are also 'practical and concrete' problems among the policy issues; the policy choice to solve these different kind of problems is not 'a simple dichotomy between right and wrong (0 and not-0), but rather 'various ways and roads' (01, 02, 03, and so on), each with a degree of merit and a degree of risk' (ibid.).

Harding's analysis of his compound mass-line models is a clear depiction of China's policy-making process in the Mao era and makes an important contribution to understanding China's policy-making models in the early 1970s.

Foreign observers noticed that from the end of the 1970s China managed to carry out economic reform without conducting a radical political reform. To explain the reasons why China succeeded at economic market reforms without changing communist rule, Susan Shirk (1993) pioneers a rational choice institutional approach to analyse China's policy-making process and offers an original theoretical framework to make sense of the courses of Chinese market reform from 1979 to the present. According to her extensive interviews with high-level Chinese officials and piecing together detailed histories of economic reform policy decisions, she found the basic authority relations between party and government in the reform period to be: 'party leaders delegated more discretion to the government in economic policy-making. Delegation was intended to improve the quality of economic decisions, to tilt the policy process to favour reform outcomes, and to devise a policy package acceptable to key groups in society. This effort to separate the work of party and government sparked substantial dissension within the party ranks and was shifted largely to the government arena. Party oversight over the government bureaucracy continued to be of the tight, centralised, policy-patrol type, and the party retained the authority to select government officials, propose policy initiatives, and veto policies that emerged from the government side' (p. 69). Then, she draws four major characteristics of the policy-making process with these authority relations.

(1) Based on the 'law of anticipated reactions', policies emerging from the government bureaucracy reflect the preferences of party leaders.
(2) If the party leadership is divided and the party's line is changeable, then government reform policies are likely to shift or be inconsistent.
(3) Whenever the composition and preferences of the party leadership change, government policies will change too.

(4) Because of the party's policy-patrol oversight from within the government bureaucracy, party vetoes of policies made in the government arena are rare. The heads of government commissions, ministries, and provinces know from their participation in high-level party meetings what party leaders will find acceptable and what they would not; because their careers depend on pleasing party leaders, they will not promulgate policies of which party leaders would disapprove (ibid.).

More importantly, based on her above finding, Shirk puts forward a model named 'Delegation by Consensus' to explain China's policy process. Shirk defines delegation by consensus as:

Party leaders delegate the authority to subordinate government agencies to work out economic policies. If everyone agrees, the leaders simply ratify the policy. If some agencies disagree, then the proposal is either sent to the higher levels for resolution or is tabled. Hierarchical control gives bureaucratic agents an incentive to compromise rather than exercise their veto if the political authorities are unified and their preferences clear (p.127).

According to Shirk, the main features of the model can be summarised in five aspects.

(1) Policy decisions are more difficult and time-consuming and require more side payments than they do under majority rule.
(2) Policies emerging from this kind of system tend to be incremental because participants will veto proposals that make them substantially worse off than they are under the status quo.
(3) Highly redistributive issues are postponed or fail to pass unless the authorities impose them on bureaucratic subordinates.
(4) The larger and less stable the set of participants, the more elusive is policy consensus.
(5) When the authorities are divided and their preferences uncertain, agents are less willing to compromise and agreement on policies is more difficult to achieve (pp.127-8).

Shirk's theoretical framework is based on the analysis of the characteristics of Chinese political institutions, such as the authority relations between the CCP and the government, the party leadership incentives, the government bargaining arena and the consensus decision-making in the arena, and so it provides us with a clear description on China's policy-making process in the reform period. It shows a new development and a major contribution in this research field.

3.3 Conclusions

We have examined three groups of Chinese policy-making models with different theoretical bases, and made some specific assessments to the strength and weakness of those major models. We see that although these models have not directly used those relevant state theories concerning how policy is made to examine China's policy-making practice, they do have close theoretical relations with the latter. This fact indicates that those relevant state theories can be introduced to observe and analyse China's practice to different extents. Among these Sinologists' models, the pluralist-basis group is the biggest one in numbers, and the institutionalism-basis and elitism-basis group follow in turn. The phenomenon that there are so many models which probe China's policy-making process from the way of analysing the influences of pluralist competition does not mean either a pluralist tendency have developed to the extent of being dominant in China's policy-making, or Chinas' government positively encouraged the pluralist involvement in political life. These can be explained as what follows. First, the existence of the situation that there are different interests with different policy preferences inside and outside the ruling group, is an objective phenomenon in any society, especially in the modern world, no matter whether the regime would be ready to admit, permit or encourage this tenancy. The differences between those societies in which pluralist involvement is a legal action and those in which this involvement is not permitted or not encouraged, are as below. In the societies of the former the involvement is mainly overt and positive, and in the societies of the latter this involvement is covert or secret. Second, in China's context, although the regime does not permit and courage this pluralist involvement, these covert and potential pluralist competitions actually appear to be more complicated and diversified. This mainly resulted from the characteristics of China's politics, which are fourfold:

- the existence of the life-long official term of leading cadres and the imperfect and inadequacy of the power replacement system, especially before the reform period;
- the influences of the feudalism politics,
- the complexity and difficulty of China's politics as being the largest developing country; and
- the complexity and difficulty of China in solving the contradictions between upholding ideological principles and promoting the economic

development which needs opening-up to the outside world and the involvement of pluralist competitions, in a country adhering to the socialist system, etc.

These can be seen from the diversified analyses of those relevant models, such as power-in-competition model, politicians-in-negotiation model and bureaucracy-in-domination model, etc. Third, the periods to which those models observe the pluralist competition in China's policy-making process, mainly focus on the first three decades of the PRC, and at that time there was not a pluralist tendency which overtly and noticeably occurred as happened in the reform period. Even in the reform period, the development of a pluralist tendency is still limit due to many reasons that will be discussed in chapter nine.

The situation which there were also many scholars who researched into China's policy-making and created many institutionalism-basis and institutionalism-related models, suggests the important influences of China's existing institutions on the major elements which were involved in policy-making process. As have been discussed, these models include ideology-conflict-oriented model, structural model normative model, and fragmented authoritarianism, etc. To understand this, we only need to point out that it was China's existing institutions that determine the significant impacts of ideological tendency, the centralised power mechanism, and the fragmented authority under a centralised political system, in China's policy process. Therefore, these models are quite helpful in improving our understanding the practice

Political elites in China possessed much prominent position compared with those in western countries, due to China's political system and the historical tradition. The important one of the elitism-basis models is the Mao (or Deng)-in command model, which shows the most influential style of China's policy-making. Actually, those models emphasising the role of pluralist competition also indicate the crucial status and impacts of political elites from another angle, because all those competitions occurred in policy-making were among those political elites.

It has been seen that, as discussed above and in the earlier sections, these Sinologists' models are actually the versions of those relevant state theories, especially the pluralism, elitism and institutionalism. With drawing ideas from the latter in various ways, these models portray and probe China's policy process covering a long period from the 1950s to the early 1990s, from different points of view, which showed us multiple explanations about China's policy-making mechanism and behaviours.

Their research results are good enlightening and provide references for furthering the study of China's policy process. However, to be exact, the ways that these models observing and analysing China's practice did not exceed the ranges set up by those relevant state theories, namely the theories of pluralism, elitism and institutionalism. The contributions of the former are particularly discussing China's practice in a concrete way and drawing concrete conclusions. In doing so, the ideas of those relevant state theories are adopted, separately or integrally. Consequently, they seem unnecessary to be used in furthering the main analytical object of this thesis, the SEZ policy process. That means, in the late data analysing part, these Sinologists' models will not be introduced to examine the practice. Discussing them in detail here is aimed at expanding our viewpoint and enriching the contextual background of the central object so as to benefit our study.

Note

[1]   John Wilson Lewis, *Leadership In Communist China*, Ithaca, New York, 1963; Franz Schurmann, *Ideology and organisation in Communist China*, Berkeley, 1966; A. Doak Barnett, *Cadres, Bureaucracy, and Political Power In Communist China*, New York, 1968.

4 The diverse theories about how policy should be made

In the previous chapters, we have examined theories and models concerning how policy is made, which include the relevant state theories and the models about how China's policy is made. Most of those relevant state theories combine both descriptive and prescriptive elements to the different extent with the stress on the former. Those Sinologists' models about China's policy-making, which have close theoretical relations with the relevant state theories, are the concrete studies of China's practice with the descriptive method. This chapter surveys the different schools of theories concerning how policy should be made. These theories which are characterised by the prescriptive method explores the ways are created to probe how to improve the policy-making process. The major theories we will examine include rationalism, incrementalism, mixed scanning approach, optimal approach, contingent method, etc. These theories have close relations with the relevant state theories. For instance, rationalism is an elitism-oriented theory, both incrementalism and mixed scanning methods have a pluralism-oriented basis, and both optimal approach and the contingent approach have mixed oriented-bases from pluralism and elitism.

4.1 Examining the theories

4.1.1 Rationalism

The rational models, put forward by Herbert Simon, including the rational-comprehensive approach and the bounded rationality model, are seen as the principal and primary methods in the policy-making literature. A number of other models of policy-making are derived from the debate about its feasibility and weakness.

The foundation of Simon's rationality is his administration theory, in which decision-making is considered as the central focus (Simon, 1947, P. 1). In his early book '*Administrative Behaviour*', Simon raised the classical statement of the ideal of rationality in public policy-making, that is, the decision-maker needs 'to select that one of the strategies which is followed by the preferred set of consequences...' To make this selection 'involves three steps: (1) the list of all the alternatives strategies; (2) the determination of all the consequences that follow upon each of the alternatives; (3) the comparative evaluation of these sets of consequences' (1975, p. 67). According to Simon, the existence of goals or objectives within an organisation is of fundamental importance in giving meaning to administrative behaviour, and vice versa, administrative behaviour is purposive only if it is guided by goals. In any organisation there might be a number of ways of reaching goals, and when faced with the need to make a choice between alternatives, the rational decision-maker should chose the alternative most likely to achieve the desired outcome.

Meyerson and Christie (1955, pp. 314-15) summed up the basic features of the rational models as: 'a. the decision-maker considers all of the alternatives open to him, i.e., he considers what courses of action are possible within the conditions of the situation and in the light of the ends which he seeks to obtain; b. he identifies and evaluates all of the consequences which would follow from the adoption of each alternative; i.e., he predicts how the total situation would be changed by the course of action he might adopt; and c. he selects the alternative, the probable consequences of which would be preferable in terms of his most valuable ends.' It is quite clear that the rational model is an idealised model for policy-making. According to Simon's theoretical framework, obviously, to carry out this model requires sufficient resources. Forester (1984, pp. 23-4) argues that these conditions should include:

- A well-defined problem;
- A full array of alternatives to consider;
- Full baseline information;
- Full information about the consequences of each alternative;
- Full information about the values and preferences of citizens; and
- Adequate time, skill, and resources.

Albeit this elaboration had pushed Simon's assumption to the extreme, it does point out the main problems of the rational model. Some other scholars went further in analysing the unfeasibility of this model in detail. For example, the eight failures in the adaptation of the rational-comprehensive model listed by Braybrooke and Lindblom (1963), are as below:

- Not adapted to man's limited problem-solving capabilities.
- Not adapted to inadequacy of information.
- Not adapted to the costliness of information.
- Not adapted to failures in constructing a satisfactory evaluative method.
- Not adapted to the closeness of observed relationships between fact and value in policy-making.
- Not adapted to the openness of the system of variables with which it contends.
- Not adapted to the analyst's need for strategic sequences of analytical moves.
- Not adapted to the diverse forms in which policy problems actually arise (pp. 48-54).

To a considerable extent, in fact, Simon himself also realised some difficulties in his approach later on. These include (1964, 1983): (a) when the values of the organisation as a whole may differ from those of individuals within the organisation, it is difficult to decide whose values and objectives are to be used in the decision-making process; (b) since individuals and groups in an organisation often have discretion in interpreting general policy statements, it may not make sense to refer to the goals of the organisation; (c) in practice, decision-making rarely proceeds in such a longitudinal, comprehensive and purposive manner; (d) it seems to be difficult to separate facts and values, and means and ends, in the policy-making process.

Based on recognising the idealised nature of the comprehensive rational model, in his later works, Simon put forward the idea of 'bounded rationality' to portray the decision-making process in reality. He considers that in actual policy-making practice, the situations that the decision-makers face are:

- ambiguous and poorly defined problems;
- incomplete information about the alternatives;
- incomplete information about the baseline, the background of 'the problem';
- incomplete information about the consequences of supposed alternatives;
- incomplete information about the range and content of values, preferences and interests, and
- limited time, limited skill and limited resources.

In practising the bounded rationality, therefore, the policy alternative seeking by the decision-makers is not to maximise their values but to reach the target that would be satisfactory or good enough. That means they just do what they can (Grandner and Simon, 1958). Obviously, the 'satisfactory' standard is more realistic than the optimising alternative Simon originally advocated. Based on these, then, the standards which are satisfactory should be: the existence of a set of criteria that describes minimally satisfactory alternatives, and the alternative in question meets or exceeds all these criteria (March and Simon, 1993, p. 161).

Although it is a significant development that Simon improves his theory framework from the rational-comprehensive model to the bounded-rationality model, the former still has considerable value. As Ham and Hill pointed out, 'the rational comprehensive model remains important because it contributes to influence attempts to improve the machinery of government in various countries', which 'suggests that the idea of rational comprehensiveness is still powerful' (1993, p. 87). As known to all, one of the most prominent examples which illustrates the successful application of the rational-comprehensive policy-making model is the conducting of the projects developed by NASA (National Aeronautics and Space Administration) in the United States, to send a person to the moon for the first time in human history. The main process of engaging this project is: President John F. Kennedy firstly announced this goal; then scientists presented plans based on scientific theory to accomplish this goal; afterwards all options for implementing the plan were reviewed and a particular means was selected; towards the goal, accordingly, resources were allocated and invested; finally, in 1962, the launch was made successfully and the theories were vindicated. Some other examples (Blackstone and Plowden, 1988), in a British context, include that used in the development of the Public Expenditure Survey Committee (PESC) system for planning public expenditure, and the subsequent introduction of programme budgeting, programme analysis and review, and the Central Policy Review Staff.

As the amendment and development to the original model, the bounded rationality model tends to involve the decision-maker in choosing an alternative intended not to maximise its value but to be satisfactory or good enough. This received widely favourable comments for its great relevance to the real world. For instance, Lindblom (1979) suggests that the limitations on rationality are such that bounded rationality is the best that can be achieved.

4.1.2 Incrementalism

In the course of discussing the feasibility and inadequacies of the rational model, some scholars also put forward their own models as amendments of rationalism. Of which, incrementalism is one of those important models. As a significant descriptive and normative strategy, the incremental model was first presented by Charles E. Lindblom. The incrementalist model, according to Lindblom, is formed by three key concepts: successive limited comparisons, disjointed incrementalism and partisan mutual adjustment. Successive limited comparisons is a method to achieve simplification through limiting the number of alternatives considered to those that differ in small degree from existing policies and ignoring consequences of possible policies, it involves simultaneous analysis of facts and values, and means and ends. Lindblom argues (1959, p. 88) that although it has some acknowledged shortcoming, it is still better than 'a futile attempt at superhuman comprehensiveness'.

Disjointed incrementalism, the second concept of the incremental model, is described in detail in the book 'A Strategy of Decision' (1963), which Lindblom co-authored with David Braybrooke. According to their studies, the disjointed incrementalism is decision-making

> through small or incremental moves on particular problems rather than through a comprehensive reform program. It is also endless; it takes the form of an indefinite sequence of policy moves. Moreover, it is exploratory in that the goals of policy-making continue to change as new experience with policy throws new light on what is possible and desirable. In this sense, it is also better described as moving away from known social problems rather than as moving toward a known and relatively stable goal. In any case, it is policy-making that involves choosing those goals that draw policies forward in the light of what recent policy steps have shown to be probably realisable. The Utopian goal, chosen for its alternatives without thought of its feasibility, is not a heavy influence on this kind of policy-making (Lindblom and Braybrooke, 1963).

Lindblom's partisan mutual adjustment method is introduced to achieve co-ordination between people in the absence of a central co-ordinator. It involves adapted adjustment, in which a decision-maker simply adapts to decisions around him and manipulated adjustment in which he seeks to enlist a response desired from the other decision-makers (Lindblom, 1965, p. 33).

Later, Hogwood and Gunn (1984) summed up the main features of the incrementalism model as:

1. Policy-makers often avoid thinking through or at least spelling out their objects. This may reflect a shrewd awareness that to do so would precipitate conflict rather than agreement. It would also provide standards by which to judge performance, and why give such hostages to future?
2. When it is clear that existing policies are failing to cope, the remedial action taken by legislators and administrators will tend to be 'incremental'. That is, they will make relatively small adjustments to policies rather than sweeping changes. In doing so, they are moving cautiously and experimentally from a basis of what is known rather than taking a giant step into an unknown future.
3. Policy-makers accept that few, if any, problems are ever solved once and for all times. Instead, policy-making is 'serial'(we keep coming back at problems as mistakes are corrected and new lines of attack developed).
4. Few policies are made by individuals or even single agencies, but are instead made by the interaction of many policy influential agents operating in a power network.
5. While these actors are self-interested, they are not blindly partisan and are capable of adjusting to one another through bargaining, negotiation and compromise.
6. A value is placed in most pluralist liberal democracies on 'consensus seeking' so that what emerges is not necessarily the one best policy but rather that compromise policy upon which most groups can agree (pp. 52-3).

In late 1970s, Lindblom went further to present his strategic analysis approach as only one form of incrementalism, and he took it as a preferable idea to synoptic analysis. According to Lindblom, there is a close relationship between simple incremental analysis, disjointed incrementalism and strategic analysis. Ham and Hill (1993) summarised it as: simple incremental analysis involves analysis limited to consideration of alternatives which are only incrementally different from the *status quo*. Disjointed incrementalism involves limiting analysis to a few familiar alternatives, an intertwining of goals and values with the empirical aspects of the problem, a greater preoccupation with the problem than the goals to be sought, a sequence of trials, errors and revised trials, analysis that explores only some consequences of an alternative and fragmentation of analytical work of many participants. Strategic analysis involves analysis limited to any calculated or thoughtfully chosen set of stratagems to simplify complex policy problems. Simply incremental analysis is one element in disjointed incrementalism, and disjointed incrementalism is one form of strategic analysis (pp. 92-3).

Lindblom's incrementalism model obtains widely favourable comments in policy theory literature. In his book, *'The Art and Craft of Policy Analysis'*, Aaron Wildavsky (1980) raises a similar assumption about policy process. He holds that policy problems are not so much solved as succeeded and replaced by other problems, so that 'it is not resolution of policies but evolution that should interest us' (p. 23). He also examines some important policy phenomena that provide positive evidences of incrementalism, such as policy retreat on objectives, policy as its own cause, and co-ordination without a co-ordinator.

In analysing the feasibility of the incremental model, Dye (1984) further discusses its necessity from four aspects. Firstly, policy makers usually do not have the time, intelligence, or money to investigate all the alternatives to existing policies. The cost of collecting all this information is too great. Policy makers do not have sufficient predictive capacities even in the age of computers, to know what all the consequences of each alternative will be. Nor are they able to calculate cost-benefit ratios for alternative policies when many diverse political, social, economic, and cultural values are at stake. Second, policy makers accept the legitimacy of previous policies because of the uncertainty about the consequences of completely new or different policies. It is safer to stick with known programmes when consequences of new programs cannot be predicted. Under conditions of uncertainty, policy makers continue past policies or programs whether or not they have proven to be effective. Third, there may be heavy investments in existing programs which preclude any radical change. These investments may be in money, buildings, or other hard items, or they may be in psychological dispositions, administrative practices, or organisational structure. It is accepted wisdom that organisations tend to persist over time regardless of their utility, that they develop routines that are difficult to alter, and that individuals develop a personal stake in the continuation of organisations and practices, which makes radical change very difficult. Hence, not all policy alternatives can be seriously considered, but only those which cause little physical, economic, organisational, and administrative dislocation. Finally, incrementalism is politically expedient. Agreement comes more easily in policy-making when the items in dispute are only increases or decreases in budgets, or modifications to an existing program. Conflict is heightened when decision-making focuses on major policy shifts involving great gains or losses. Because the political tension involved in getting new programs or policies passed every year would be very great, past policies are continued into future years unless there is a substantial political realignment. Thus, incrementalism is important in reducing conflicts, maintaining stability and preserving the political system itself (pp. 35-6).

It should be noted that incrementalism especially matches the reality of the United States. Braybrooke and Lindblom (1963, p. 73) themselves acknowledge this and explain that, in the United States, 'policy-making proceeds through a series of approximations. A policy is directed at a problem; it is tried, altered, tried in its altered form, altered again, and so forth'. Some other analysts also recognise this and give more reasons to illustrate this feature. They point out that in the United States, policy-making takes place within a highly pluralistic environment dominated by interdependent interest groups, and these interest groups operate in an open system which accepts the necessity of compromise for the production of policies. (Ham & Hill, 1984, p. 82; Hogwood & Gunn, 1984, p. 53; Berry, 1974, p. 349). These match the key features of incrementalism that making policy does not aim to maximise the decision-makers' values but secures agreement of the interests for those groups involved.

Moreover, Lindblom considers his model not only a description of how policy-making occurs but also a normative strategy — a model for how decisions should be made. He argues (1965, p. 157), 'psychologically and sociologically speaking, decision-makers can sometimes bring themselves to make changes easily and quickly only because the changes are incremental and are not fraught with a great risk of error or political conflict. In a society, for example, that is rapidly changing, one can argue that it can change as fast as it does only because it avoids big controversies over big change'.

Nevertheless, Lindblom's incrementalism model is also strongly criticised for its conservative bias. In his article, 'Muddling Through — "Science" or Inertia?' Dror (1964), whilst admitting the force of Lindblom's writings as descriptive, viewed their prescriptive element 'as an ideological reinforcement of pro-inertia and anti-innovation forces present in all human organisations, administrative and policy-making...' Dror suggested that this strategy is valid only if: (1) the results of present policies are basically satisfactory; (2) the nature of the problem is relatively stable; and (3) the means for dealing with that problem are continuously available. He sees at least three circumstances in which incrementalism would be inadequate, which include: (1) present policies may be so manifestly unsatisfactory that merely to adjust them is pointless; (2) the problem requiring a governmental response may be changing so fast or so fundamentally that policies based on past experience are inadequate as a guide to future action; (3) the means available for problem-solving may be expanding, so that major new opportunities exist but are likely to be neglected by incrementalism.

In response to Dror's criticism, Lindblom argues that both in a political democracy like the United States and in the relatively stable dictatorship countries the conditions necessary for incrementalism can be met. Meanwhile, Lindblom (1964) gave response to the criticism for the conservative bias of his muddling-through approach, and holds that a succession of small steps can reach a target with significant changes, just as taking infrequent large steps can do.

The other criticisms to incrementalism are about its unreasonable standard of assessing a decision and the defect of over-stressing present interests, which is contended by Berry (1974). Regarding the first aspect, He argues that in practice, if a 'good' decision is evaluated not by the theory with objective criteria but simply by its acceptability in a particular situation, it will tend to favour the interests of the most powerful groups. Consequently, the applicability of this model is more narrow than was claimed.

With respect to the second problem, Berry suggests (ibid. p. 350) that since the model emphasises meeting the interests demand of the present rather than the future, the impact of the 'small change' on future generations may be much greater than has been generally acknowledged. Although Lindblom suggests that it is because of the cost of comprehensive analysis that incrementalism is used, actually, it tends to ignore the possibility that in some situations the cost of analysis maybe not as great as the cost for mistakes. Thus, the cost of failing to explore radical alternatives to existing policies may be higher.

Although facing criticism from different sides, incrementalism still became one of the key models relating to how policy should be made, due to its convincing good points. As the antithesis of the rationalist model, incremental approach occupies an influential position in the theoretical field of policy-making. The relationship between these two approaches is both opposite and complementary to each other. Hence, they are the two ends of seeking the way to improve policy-making process. Other methods developed later are trying to find a mid-way between them. Those models seeking 'middle ground' include mixed scanning approach, optimal approach, and contingent approach, etc.

4.1.3 'Mixed scanning' approach

Some scholars consider the virtues are as conspicuous as their defects for both the rational model and the incremental model which are not 'either realistic or satisfactory normative accounts of decision-making.'(Parsons, W. 1995, p. 297) Therefore, efforts have been made to find new approaches to combine the desirable features of both of them and reduce their weakness. The mixed scanning model of decision-making, outlined by Etzioni, is one of these attempts to seek a middle way between rationalism and incrementalism in policy-making. Etzioni (1986, p. 8) argues that his approach, is 'less demanding than the full search of all options that rationalism requires', and 'more "strategic" and innovative than incrementalism', because of 'combining (a) high-order fundamental policy-making processes which set basic directions and (b) incremental ones which prepare for fundamental decisions and work them out after they have been reached'. (Etzioni, 1967, p. 385)

Deriving from the analogy of cameras employed in satellites for weather observation, the term 'Mixed Scanning' indicates a combined method of observing and judging a policy-making situation, which can 'scan' both a general picture and the particular areas in which main contradictions or problems are confidently located and detailed information needed. To apply this approach to the policy-making process, Etzioni (1967) depicts the different goals of using rational and incremental approaches as: the former seeks detailed and comprehensive information about the whole weather scene, and the latter focuses only on those areas in which troublesome patterns have developed in the past and on a few adjacent areas. Then, the mixed scanning strategy combines a detailed examination of some sectors with a more cursory review of the wide weather scene. Thus, this model seems to have a wide feasibility with an economical operational method, which may meet the requirement of most situations.

To apply the mixed scanning approach, the precondition is to define two different kinds of decision — fundamental decision and incremental decisions. According to Etzioni, fundamental decisions are made by exploring the main alternatives the actor sees in view of his conception of his goals, but — unlike that indicated by rationalism — details and specifications are omitted so that an overview is feasible. Incremental decisions are made but within the contexts set by fundamental decisions (and fundamental reviews) (1967, p. 390). Regarding the functions of these two kinds of elements, Etzioni argues that,

> Thus, each of the two elements in mixed scanning helps to reduce the effects of the particular shortcoming of the other; incrementalism reduces the unrealistic aspects of rationalism by limiting the details required in fundamental decisions and contextuating rationalism helps to overcome the conservative slant of incrementalism by exploring long-run alternatives (ibid.).

The introduction of the mixed scanning model soon attracted increasing attentions including a series of discussions, criticisms, and applications studies. Etzioni (1968, pp. 286-8) himself set forth a model in programmatic term that could be used for a computer program, and as a basis for research designs. More importantly, based on his examination of the social context of knowledge, the nature of testing reality, the relationships between power and knowledge, the distribution of knowledge and 'societal consciousness', he argues that the rational model and incrementalism are flawed, and cannot be the basis for promoting an 'active society', because an 'active society' is the one in which people, through social collectives, can become more knowledgeable about themselves and more able to transform society in accordance with its values. Later, Janis and Mann (1977, p. 37) put forward a major improvement to Etzioni's method. They point out that while in the initial scanning when those options that have no 'crippling objectives' are kept for closer scanning, which serves as a 'quasi-satisfying' approach, then, 'each time the surviving alternatives are re-examined, the testing rule might be changed in the optimising direction by raising the minimum standard'. David Starkie (1984, p. 75) agrees with Etzioni that since the incremental model provides no guide lines for the accumulative changes which are usually random or scattered, an accumulation of numerous incremental changes is not expected to yield the equivalent of a fundamental decision. Contrastively, in applying mixed scanning approach, the fundamental decisions provide such guidance. Starkie argues that Etzioni's suggestion that an 'incremental "creep" followed by sudden changes when existing policies are no longer sustainable by modification alone' is a possible pattern combining incremental and fundamental decisions.

The criticisms of the mixed scanning model come from different perspectives. Hogwood and Gunn (1986) criticise it for two problems in applying the model in practice. First, Hogwood and Gunn raise doubts about whether there is an analogy between weather satellites and social problems. They hold that the surface of the world is of fixed geometrical proportions which can be scanned on a simple pattern and the phenomena to which closer attention has to be paid are fairly well known. However, it is not clear what the lay-out of the social world is, or what phenomena should be focused on. Second, the 'mixed scanning' model is of particular potential relevance to decisions about how to allocate analytical resources. But, Etzioni only indicates the criteria about what kind of weather formations require detailed analysis, and does not provide the criteria for determining which policy-issues should be analysed in which way (p. 61). Smith and May consider the main difficulty with mixed scanning is about how to distinguish two different kinds of decisions. They argue (1980, p. 153) that 'without further empirical data the doubt remains that mixed scanning is just as utopian as rational planning and just as lethargic as "muddling through"', because, '...the distinction between means and ends is flexible, as we have seen, so fundamental decisions in one context are incremental in another and vice versa. It is at least possible that decision-makers would define decisions in different ways either quoting or ignoring details and either exploring or neglecting alternatives as suited their purposes in particular situations'.

Ham and Hill note the problem with Etzioni's model from another aspect. They doubt whether fundamental decisions are as significant as he suggests, because 'in some situations fundamental decisions are important in setting broad directions, in other situations decision-making proceeds in a much less structured way... When this occurs, unplanned drift rather than conscious design characterises the policy process...' (1993, p. 91)

Although analysts criticised the mixed scanning model from different angles, this mode does shed light on observing a policy-making situation, because it provides 'an appropriate method of arriving at fundamental decisions because it enables a range of alternatives to be explored' (Hill, 1997, p. 106).

4.1.4 Optimal method

Another method of trying to combine rationalism and incrementalism is suggested by Dror. Based on his criticism of rationalism and incrementalism, Dror tries to create a model to increase both the rational and extra-rational elements in decision-making. Dror (1968, pp. 130-1) considers that his optimal model can avoid both extremes, by preventing pure rationality on the one hand, and by offering an optimal goal that is more than an incrementally improved extrapolation of the present situation on the other hand. He also believes his model is good at integrating and supplementing the strength of various normative models, and avoiding their weakness.

Dror's model comprises three main features including extra-rational component, meta-policy-making, and increasing rational elements. (1) Emphasising the role of extra-rational components. Dror argues that the extra-rational process must play a significant, essential, and positive role in optimal policy-making, which come from three aspects: 'First, limited resources, uncertain conflict, and a lack of knowledge place strict limits on the degree to which policy-making can feasibly be rational, so that policy makers must necessarily rely a great deal on extra-rational processes. Second, only an extra-rational process will work in some phases of policy-making. For example, policy makers need 'creativity' to invent new alternatives; Third, and this argument is more speculative and based on intuition, extra-rational processes may solve problems in some phases better than rational processes could, even though the latter by themselves could solve problems' (ibid. 157).

Dror's extra-rational elements include the use of intuition, judgements, creative invention, brainstorming and other approaches. He argues that policy makers are usually biased more toward 'intuition' than 'information' and more toward 'guess' than 'estimate', and they must work very hard to achieve an 'informed intuition' or a 'guestimate'. Consequently, in order to improve policy-making, a major way is to encourage and strengthen its extra-rational components (ibid. p. 158).

(2) Stressing 'meta-policy-making' namely 'deciding how to decide'. Dror suggests that (ibid. p. 159), broadly speaking, policy-making consists of three main stages: '(a) meta policy-making, that is policy-making on how to make policy; (b) policy-making in its usual sense, that is, making policy on substantial issues; and (c) re-policy-making, that is, making changes in policy based on feedback from the execution of policies.'

Thus, here, the policy-making system is handled as a whole by the meta-policy-making phases, with which to identify problems, values, and resources, and to allocate them to different policy-making units; design, evaluate, and redesign the policy-making systems; and determine the main policy-making strategies (ibid. p. 160). Dror highlights the importance of these phases, for it is essential to invest resources in designing procedures for policy-making in order to achieve better policy outputs.

(3) Increasing the rational elements. Obviously, this idea has close theoretical relations with the rational comprehensive model. However, Dror makes adjustments on many sides. Dror (ibid. p. 160) breaks the whole process of policy-making into eighteen specific phases and discusses them respectively. Among these phases, some of them are special, such as the seven phases of the meta-policy-making stage. Some others share the ideas of the rational model, for example, 'Establish operational goals, with some order of priority for them'. 'Preparing a set of major alternative policies, including some "good" ones.' Therefore, some scholars (Hogwood and Gunn, 1981) believe that Dror does lean toward the Simonian end of the spectrum.

Nevertheless, 'There is no doubt that Dror offers one of the most considerable attempts to devise a prescriptive policy-making model and, ...a particular strength of Dror's work is its recognition of the extra-rational elements in the process of decision-making' (Ham and Hill, 1993, p. 90).

Although Dror argues that his model avoids the difficulties of rationalism and incrementalism, some different opinions are still taken by other writers. Lindblom criticises Dror for offering no more than a series of discrete statements that do not connect and cannot be said to constitute a 'model' for decision-making. While, Smith and May (1980, p. 154) hold that,

> The weakest feature of Dror's statement is the role assigned to "intuition and experience". There are disconcerting vague, variable and hardly more than residual categories for non-rational sources of information... Again the important point is that the central feature of the dispute between rationalist and incrementalist models of decision-making remains largely unmarred by this attempt to offer this "third alternative".

For such reasons, these scholars think it is hard to credit the optimal model as an actual correction of the weakness and a supplement of the strengths of other models.

However, other scholars hold different opinions. Hill argues that, like the mixed scanning model, the importance of Dror's optimal model 'is mainly that they are attempts to meet widely held reservations about incrementalism as a prescriptive approach' (1997, p. 106). Those three aspects it suggests, which aim at 'combining realism and idealism' (Dror, 1964, p. 157) are enlightenment to seek a middle ground between rationalism and incrementalism. For instance, the extra-rational components emphasise that under the circumstances when sources for policy-making are very limited or 'creativity' is needed to invent new alternatives, which are possibly occurred in some occasions, extra-rational thinking is necessary and effective. This idea is reasonable, realistic and applicable. What could be used in these situations are 'intuition, judgements, creative invention, and brainstorming', which all come from the accumulation of experiences and knowledge of the policy makers.

4.1.5 Contingent approach

In the course of controversy and searching for the ideal approach of policy-making, some scholars have gradually realised that there is no single model that can be applied universally in all situations; different circumstances require different decision-making approaches; therefore, the policy-making approaches are not necessarily exclusive. An appropriate model (or combination of models) that might be used in a given situation should be contingent upon the contextual circumstance. Hence, these scholars suggest that policy-making methods should be varied according to the different policy-making environments. What Hogwood and Gunn (1986) describe below is a clear explanation of this idea:

> Some issues will always require highly political pluralist, bargaining, and incrementalist approach. But other issues — probably only a small minority — will both require and lend themselves to a much more planned or analytical approach'. 'Thus we advocate a "contingency" approach. ... There is no "one best way" of making decisions, just as there is no universal prescription for "good organisation". Among the diagnostic skills required is a very high degree of political sensitivity and discrimination as well as a grasp of the technical skills of planning and analysis (p 62).

The emerging of the contingent approach is a new progress in studying the policy-making process. As scholars have become increasingly involved in probing this method, they go further to explore how to assess and define the decision-making context according to diverse situations.

Based on thoroughgoing studies of the planning process, K. S. Christensen (1985) suggests that the planning process is a typical uncertain course which is a good example to be taken as a research object for decision-making in the varied backgrounds, and then he puts forward a contingent model to deal with these complex planning situations. According to Christensen (1985), the planning conditions (i.e. decision-making situations) can be divided into four types in the light of the degrees of obtaining a clear goal (purpose, desired outcome or end) and technology (knowledge of coping with the problems or means) by the decision-makers, and therefore four relevant methods for dealing with them could be suggested.

Christensen's classification of the planning conditions and corresponding approaches is fourfold. (1) The first situation is: known technology with an agreed goal. Under this circumstance, the planner needs to match an effective technology to reach the goal according to the standard and routine procedures, and he acts as programmer, standardizer, rule-setter, regulator, scheduler, optimizer, analyst and administrator. (2) The second situation is unknown technology with an agreed goal. In this condition, however, the planning becomes a learning process through which the planner will obtain the missing knowledge; inventive and creative sensitivity are needed for the planner to search for an effective means by moving pragmatically (in an incremental way), to deal with the uncertainty. So the planner acts as advocate, participation promoter, facilitator, mediator, constitution-writer and bargainer. (3) The third situation is known technology with no agreed goal. Then, planning becomes a bargaining process; each bargain must be tailored to its particular participants; mediating and concessions are necessary in the bargaining process in order to accommodate diverse preferences and reach a consensus. The planner acts as pragmatist, adjuster, researcher, experimenter and innovator. (4) The fourth situation is unknown technology with no agreed goal. Under this condition, planning becomes the searching for order over both means and goal in a chaotic situation. The planner acts as charismatic leader and problem-finder, and goes ahead pragmatically (in an incremental way), to deal with the uncertainty. Also, he acts as advocator, participation promoter, facilitator, mediator, constitution-writer and bargainer.

Compared with Christensen, John Forester analyses the planning decision-making situation from another angle. Forester (1984) holds that planners and decision-makers could make better strategy to fit the specific situation base on assessing the degree and the characters of the complexity in a decision-making situation. Forester suggests (pp. 23-31) that for the purpose of assessing the decision-making situations, it is essential to first run through the continuum from the rationalist's idealised situation to highly politically structured decision-making situations, and then to consider this continuum by beginning with the idealised assumptions followed by a slowly relaxation of them. In each decision-making situation of this continuum, different practical strategies will seem applicable, according to the level of complexity and restriction present.

Forester's continuum consists of five sections. The first one is assuming that there is only one decision-maker to consider and that he is an economic rational actor. The setting is the decision-maker's office, with an assumption of a closed system. In this situation, the problem is well defined. What are clearly provided or available in the nearest file drawer include the scope of the issue, time range, value dimensions, and chains of consequences. Information is perfect, complete, accessible, and comprehensible. Time is infinitely available. Under these conditions, therefore, rational problem solving or optimisation through the available methods and solution techniques, is a clear, applicable strategy to adopt.

The second section of the continuum is that the situation has become restricted: the decision-maker is fallible, he permits intuitions, localities, and doubts to creep into the picture. The setting is opened to the environment. The problem is not so well defined and its scope is a bit ambiguous. Moreover, information is imperfect, time is a scarce resource. Under these conditions, a satisfactory decision will have to suffice. Investigations into the consequences and environmental changes now become bets to be hedged. In this course, shortcuts need to be taken, and estimation and approximation are essential to be made.

Then, the third section of Forester's continuum is the situation that the decision-maker faces an increased number of restrictions as below. The decision is made by a co-operative group that consists of decision-makers, staff, and clients, whose skills and insight vary from one to another. The setting is socially differentiated. Interpretations of the problem are also differentiated. Information is not only imperfect but also greatly varied. Time becomes a socially precious resource. Within this situation, satisfying alone will no longer do. It must be supplemented by strategies of search through social intelligence networks. Search depends on the ongoing cultivation, maintenance, and nurture of the networks. Here the decision-making situation is no longer simply in a cognitively bounded or limited environment; it is now socially differentiated, and decision-making strategies must take that environment into account. The decision-makers must now be able to gather information by bridging organisational boundaries, using social networks, and tapping sources of expertise, in order to achieve a desired target.

The fourth situation of the continuum is in a pluralist world in which the decision-making setting becomes more complex. It is not only social differentiation, but also competing organisations that further complicate the practical decision-making conditions. In such a pluralist environment definitions of problems are diversified. Towards the problems presented, interest groups make diverse sense and valuations. In this circumstance, information becomes a political resource. The actions of contest, rejection, manipulation, and distortion are involved. While, time becomes a scarce resource. Under these conditions, strategies of search and "networking", etc., are not enough, instead, bargaining and adjustment are essential, and short-term political compromise becomes a practical incremental approach to apply.

The fifth situation of Forester's continuum suggests that in reality, social actors in political organisational environments are not simply randomly and diversely interacting actors, clashing and competing with one another, but rather they are often positioned with and against one another in social and political-economic structures that display significantly non-random continuity. Within the decision setting which is characterised not by random plurality, but by highly structured plurality, where structure and power are rarely neatly separable, definitions of problem are reflecting their social sources. The information of the decision-maker seems to reflect the interests of the participants. Time is power, and power appears to be distributed equally. Under these conditions, incremental strategies are hardly responsive to the realities at hand. The appropriate strategies should be restructuring strategies in which strategies work toward effective equality, substantive democratic participation and voice, and strategies that work away from the perpetuation of systematic racial, sexual and economic domination, are involved.

According to his aforementioned analysis of the strategies for decision-making in a continuum, Forester concludes (1984, ibid.) that an increasingly sophisticated set of decision-making approaches is required as the contextual complexity of the decision-making situation increases.

Differing from Christensen's model which copes with four types' situation in the light of the extent of availability of goal and technology, and Forester's continuum which focuses on the varying contextual complexity by which to decide the corresponding policy-making method, Patsy Healey contributes a more subtle contingent approach which shows a particular perspective. Based on criticising the tendency which discussed policy process forms in isolation from their situations, Healey stresses the importance of considering the context within which the process forms arise or are put to use. She argues that the discussion should be related to the substance of the issues addressed in any instance, and the crux of the study lies in how the relations between context, substance and policy processes may be made. Furthermore, Healey holds that policy processes are interpenetrated by the social relations of the wider society, not independent of them or 'slotted into' them. Then, the context itself may be defined and transferred through the way policy processes operate. Hence, she points out that this conception

> firmly locates the discussion of policy process within the economic and political dynamic of social change in society. Policy process is thus inherently political (Healey, 1990, p. 92).

Consequently,

> The task for analysis then focuses on identifying the distinctive qualities of the processes by which the power relations among the interests with a state in and/ or involved in, collective or public agency operations are mediated and transformed'(ibid.).

In defining the relations between the social interactions forming policy processes and wider social relations, Healey (p. 98) raises three sets of criteria to analyse policy processes. (1) Criteria concerning who is involved which include who gets access to the process and on what terms, who controls the process and to whom must the process be legitimated. (2) Criteria concerning the relations between those involved which cover what should be the style and procedure of debate. (3) Criteria concerning the judgement of an acceptable decision, which comprise which values should govern a decision, and in what way should decisions be presented to the relevant constituency.

According to these criteria, Healey further discusses a continuum of process forms of decision-making, which flows along the line from clientelist, political-rational, pluralist politics, open democratic debate, bargaining, special committees, corporatist, bureaucratic legal, judicial/semi judicial, techno-rational, to market rational. The order of these processes, in a continuum as listed above, moves from the more directly political forms, to other forms involving a direct relation to interest groups, and then to an indirect relation with interest groups ostensibly separate from formal and informal politics.

Healey (1990, p. 100) considers this approach stressing the distributive tendencies within particular processes, irrespective of the context in which they are developed. Clientelistic processes will have great difficulty in mediating complex interest conflicts and addressing external effects. Bargaining processes will exclude those who have no power over other participants. Bureaucratic, judicial and tech-rational processes mediate interests indirectly... Therefore, she concludes that process forms are the products of interest mediation around a specific set of issues. The decision rules embodied in a process will reflect the power games of the particular mediation process, shaped but not determined by the structuring forces which both distribute power among the interests involved and set up decision rules within process forms.

In this section, so far, we have discussed three sorts of models of probing policy-making process with contingent method from different perspectives. According to this discussion, to sum up, it could be deduced that all these contingent approaches to policy-making emphasise the importance that a policy-making method is effective only if it can match the given situation under which a policy issue should be decided. In exploring the way to use the contingent approach, their works provide us with multiple viewpoints in both analysing the policy-making situation and applying corresponding policy-making methods, which seem convincing to different extents.

4.1.6 Garbage can theory

The garbage can model was first raised in early 1970s by Cohen, March and Olsen (1972). They based their description of this model heavily on the studies of the decision-making processes at universities. This model is actually a critique of those prescriptive approaches. It emphasises that policy-making situations often involve many uncertainties, which include not only goals, problems, and solutions, but also organisations and participants. Therefore, it denies any idealised decision-making process.

This idea describes the phenomenon that opportunities for choice in decision-making attract all sorts of unrelated but simultaneously available problems, solutions, goals, interests, concerns, just as garbage cans attract garbage, which was labelled the 'garbage can theory of decision-making' by its authors. Although the authors apologise for introducing this pungent phrase into social science literature, but 'the phenomenon is real enough and important (and it is too late to banish the label).'(March and Simon, 1993, pp. 26-7)

The model attempts to identify a situation of "organised anarchy" in decision-making, which is characterised by unclear or inconsistent goals, a technology which is obscure and little understood by members and a highly variable member participation.

According to this theory, organisations can be viewed as collections of these elements: (1) problems; (2) solutions; (3) participants; and (4) choice opportunities; and (5) situations in which participants are expected to link a problem to a solution, and thus make a decision. Hence, organisation 'is a collection of choices looking for problems, issues and feelings looking for decision situations in which they might be aired, solutions looking for issues to which they might be the answer, and decision-makers looking for work.' (Cohen, March and Olsen, 1972, pp. 2-3)

In such a 'garbage can', usually, these elements are more or less randomly mixed together. Combinations arise almost unpredictably and there is also no a priori chronology. Sometimes, solutions can precede problems, or sometimes problems and solutions can wait for a suitable opportunity for a decision. Thus, the traditionally assumed order: 'identification and definition of the problem,' 'generation of decision alternatives,' 'examination of their consequences,' 'evaluation of those consequences in term of objects,' and finally 'determination of the selection', is often a poor description of what actually happens. (March and Olsen, 1976)

According to March and Olsen (1976), within a garbage can process, decisions are made in three different styles:

- By *oversight*. If a choice is activated when problems are attracted to other choices and if there is energy available to make the new choice quickly, it will be made without any attention to existing problems and with minimum of time and energy.
- By *flight*. In some cases, choices are associated with problems (unsuccessfully) for some time until a choice 'more attractive' to the problems come along. The problems leave the choice, and thereby make it possible to make the decision. The decision resolves no problems (they having now attached themselves to a new choice).
- By *resolution*. Some choices resolve problems after some period of working on them. The length of time may vary greatly (depending on the number of problems). This is the familiar case that is implicit in most discussions of choice within organisations (p. 33).

The garbage can theory emphasises the important structural influences of an organisation on the outcomes of the garbage can process. The structural elements can impact upon these outcomes through: (1) affecting the time pattern of the arrival of problems, choices, solutions, or decision-makers; (2) determining the allocation of energy by potential participants in the decision; and (3) establishing linkages among the various streams.

Although the authors of the garbage can model deny an idealised decision-making process, they do not assert that no systematic decision-making can be discovered in organisations. Instead, they emphasise that the seeming anarchy has a structure and an organisation, which form a reasonable, although not optimal, answer to the great environmental uncertainty in which the participants find themselves. For the purpose of decision-making, it is essential that the organisation manages to attract sufficient attention from the participants to solve the problems in question. However, participants generally have more on their minds. Thus, it is not unusual for decision-making to take place without explicit attention to the problem, or by simply postponing the problem. The authors, however, see it as the task of management to co-ordinate and steer the required attention in a desired direction by the organisation.

March and Olsen (1976, pp. 34-5) identify eight major properties of the garbage can decision process. First, resolution of problems is not the most common style for making decisions except under conditions where flight is severely restricted or under a few conditions of flight load. Second, the process is thoroughly and generally sensitive to variations in load. An increase in the net energy load on the system generally increases problem activity, decision-maker activity, decision difficulty, and the uses of flight and oversight. Third, decision-makers and problems tend to track each other through choices. Both decision-makers and problems tend to move together from choice to choice. Fourth, there are some important interconnections among three key aspects of the 'efficiency' of the decision process. These three aspects are problem activity, problem latency and the decision time. Fifth, the decision-making process is frequently sharply interactive. Sixth, important problems are more likely to be solved than unimportant ones and early-arriving problems are more likely to be solved than later ones. Seventh, important choices are much less likely to resolve problems than are unimportant choices. Eighth, although a large proportion of choices is made, the choice failures that do occur are concentrated among the most important and least important choices.

A major feature of the garbage can process is the partial separating of problems and choice. Although decision-making is thought of as a process for solving problems, which is often not what happens. Cohen and Olsen (1972, p. 16) hold that problems are worked upon in the context of some choice, but choices are made only when the shifting combinations of problems, solutions, and decision-makers happen to make action possible. Quite commonly, this is after problems have left a given choice arena or before they have discovered it.

The garbage can model provides an attempt to deal with the decision-making issue in a sceptic situation of 'organised anarchy', the idea that goals are discovered by acting, action precedes intent, and solutions search for problems seemed to match some characteristics in decision-making practices in some circumstances. As Cohen and Olsen point out (ibid.) that, 'it does enable choices to be made and problems resolved, even when the organisation is plagued with goal ambiguity and conflict, with poorly understood problems that wander in and out of the system, with a variable environment, and with decision-makers who may have other things on their minds', although it 'does not resolve problems well.'

Thus far, in section 4.1, we have examined various policy-making theories and approaches relating to how policy should be made. Although they view policy processes from different angles with different methods, and draw diversified conclusions respectively, there are some relations that exist among them. Incrementalism is produced as a critique to rationalism, other policy approaches are trying to find the middle ground. These relationships can be seen in figure 4.1.

Rationalism	Optimalism	Other methods	Contingent method	Incrementalism

Figure 4.1 The relations of different policy-making approaches

As have been pointed out, these theories and models are mainly characterised by the prescriptive factor seeking approaches to improve the policy-making process. Based on understanding their main features including the merits and weaknesses, we now need to go a step further to examine the applicability of some selected theories and models to China's policy-making practice in general.

4.2 The applicability of the selected theories to China's practice

Before examining the applicability of some selected theories and models to the practice of China's policy-making in general, it is helpful to first briefly discuss the necessity of studying these theories and models in current China. The modern policy-making theories were produced and developed in Western countries. In China, there was hardly anyone systematically undertaking research into policy-making theories until the early 1980s. This situation can be explained from various aspects historically, politically and theoretically. First of all, it had been a forbidden academic discipline before the end of 1970s. For research into policy-making would definitely touch upon and discuss the political affairs concerning the party and the state from the top to the local levels, which is not allowed to be accessed by ordinary scholars. Secondly, the classical Marxist works were seen as the encyclopaedic works of social science, and were considered to embody all social and political theories. They were considered correct and sufficient enough to deal with any political and theoretical problems, therefore, it was not necessary to search for other theories to cope with policy-making issues.

Thirdly, there was a lack of the research drive. The emerging of the policy-making theories resulted from the demands of the rapid development of the modern economy and the modern governmental administration, because both the greatly increasing complexity and the speedy operation of the modern economy and the society, demand highly efficient and scientific policymaking. For a long time before reform, politics and class struggle, instead of the economy and social development, were the focuses to which China's leaders attached their attention. Therefore, the need of this research is not as urgent as in the developed countries. For making policy to deal with the political and class struggle issues, Chinese leaders always had enough self-confidence. However, it was in this period that many big policymaking mistakes occurred, economically and politically. These facts show that, it does need a scientific and systematic theory to guide policy-making actions in China so as to reduce or avoid the possibility of falling into error. Fourthly, the new situation which appeared since the beginning of the reform brought about rapid economic development and corresponding political relaxation which had never occurred before, and provided the practical possibility and demand for undertaking research of policy-making theories.

Since it is only at the initial stage of studying policy-making theory in China, it should be beneficial to first employ those ready-made theories to analyse China's practice, then to find what we can absorb from them and what we can further develop. This section examines the applicability of some selected theories including rationalism, incrementalism, mixed scanning approach and optimal method, in China's practice in general. In this examination, the following crucial issues will be discussed: whether they are applicable to China; and if applicable, then, to what extent and in what way can they interpret and improve China's policy-making process.

4.2.1 About rationality theory

To use rational approaches to examine China's practice, we see that as an idealised and elitist style model of policy-making, it is to a considerable extent in accordance with the basic policy-making method in China. To speak more clearly, theoretically speaking, China's policy makers usually preferred to use this method (comprehensive rationality). The method of trying every possibility to find the best measures (policies) only within some small groups in the core of the policy-making circle to solve the problems was quite popular before the reform period. For a long period before the reform, the top Chinese leaders as well as most of the leading cadres at different levels, were always exceedingly confidential about the force of the human being and the force of the newly established regime, and neglected the limitations of these two aspects. They simply would like to have believed that which was one of the major theoretical bases, as Mao said, under the lead of the communist party, any miracle of human society could be created as long as the human resources are available. Therefore, they always thought that they could find the best policy alternative from those, which could be chosen in any situation, to solve the problems they, faced, even in a very short time.

However, unfortunately, there was a contradiction here, namely that China's leaders theoretically tended to utilise the rational policy-making approach and believed it could reach perfection, but actually China's policy-making behaviour often departed from the way the rational model pursues. This meant that they often failed to really conduct a comprehensive analysis by examining all possible alternatives and their consequences, including those which either would be favourable or offensive to the chief leaders, before making a policy. What caused this phenomenon included some political and social reasons. For example, because the power for policy-making is too concentrated, the number of the people that can directly participate in the policy process is quite limited. On the other hand, both the possibility and conditions of public involvement in the state policy-making are also limited. Thus, the channels to widely absorb necessary information and ideas from all sides and throughout the whole state for making policy were restricted considerably. Moreover, on account to the impacts of political monism and the officialdom-will, the opposition opinions could not easily to be expressed, and even if they would have been expressed they would not easily have been considered and accepted by the chief leaders. This situation was particularly serious before the reform period and a lot of big mistakes were made due to the irrational policy-making approaches which dominated in many policy-making occasions.

As known to many people, the typical cases of these mistakes in the economic realm were the failure of the setting up of the People's Commune and the launching of the so called Great Leap Forward. These two programmes aimed at rapidly promoting the development of China's agricultural and industrial economy, increasing the national strength and improving people's living standards as well over a short period. However, when making these key strategies China's leaders had not considered all the realistic conditions which existed at that time. These conditions should include: China's very weak economic foundation, the backward technological level, the insufficiency of the wanted funds, and the limitation of people's ability. They also neglected the important distinction of the basic laws between launching and commanding the war, and organising and managing the economic construction. In addition, they had not clearly considered all the possible consequences, which would be caused by conducting these programmes. Hence, they raised the very unrealistic slogan 'to exceed Britain and catch up America within fifteen years', and launched massive campaigns to realise these giant but dreamlike economic goals at that time. The actual consequences are known to all, not only the total failure of these campaigns, but also the great disasters caused by these campaigns in both the national economy and society.

By tracing the history of the Communist Party with the focus on policy-making issues, one can further find that the extents to which the rational approach could be applied by the leaders varied in different periods and on different issues. In the war period, they could better use the rational method to deal with warfare issues, and they were also relatively successful in handling the political situations with a rational approach. Then, in the peace period since 1949, the situation varied in different fields. As the victors of the civil war, although they still tried to cope rationally with various problems they met, it was not easy to do so in practice, especially before the reform period. Due to the increasing arrogant feeling of the leaders, particularly some top leaders, they became too self-confident and eventually often used intense revolutionary emotion to replace profound intelligent thinking. Hence, it was quite easy to fall into mistakes in political issues. Meanwhile, for making economic policies, owing to the lack of the necessary knowledge and experiences, as well as always intertwining economic matters with the political issues, they also often made mistakes. The determination of other policies were similar with these. As some exceptions, the relatively better realms of policy-making were the state's diplomatic affairs and the national defence affairs. These two aspects could be dealt with more practical rational ways and avoid making big mistakes can be explained as what follows. On the one hand, China's leaders possessed successful political and warfare experiences accumulated in the very long period; on the other hand, the crucial significance of the diplomatic and defence affairs which directly related to the survival and development of the state, forced them to be very prudent in making decisions for these issues.

Moreover, when the non-political issues were intertwined or involved in the ideological or political arguments, which were mainly artificially imposed, the decision-making would receive less overall rational consideration. Since the beginning of the reform, the situation has been improving greatly, although some mistakes were still made especially on the political aspect. However, generally speaking, the situation became much better. To observe the policy-making processes of formulating the reform and opening-up strategies including the SEZ programme, solving the resuming of the sovereignty of Hong Kong and dealing with the Sino-America relation, etc. it is believable that they were the successful issues in finding solutions to deal with problems, in which more rational elements were involved.

To summarise, according to China's experiences in the past and *status quo*, the rational method was often advocated to be employed in policy-making process, but in many occasions it was not easy to apply, especially in the period before the reform, due to the reasons which have been analysed above. However, conceivably, in a specific state like China in which the philosophical monism and absolutism are still dominant in political and ideological circles to a considerable extent, and the individualistic arbitrary and the personality cult still exist to some extent and have an impact on social life, to emphasise the use of the rational model for policy-making is beneficial in reducing the impacts of those negative elements aforementioned and improving China's policy-making process. Of course, in the process of using this model it is necessary to eliminate its demerits by combining other feasible approaches. Furthermore, for promoting the feasibility study of policy-making, some major elements of the bounded rational model could be or should be applied in China's practice in the current situation where policy-making power has been expanded to a relatively wider range although centralism still exists.

4.2.2 About incrementalist model

It is unquestionable that this model is applicable and helpful in China's practice. To a considerable extent, the theory or thinking pattern which is now dominant in China as the basic guiding principle for promoting the reform and opening-up course, is an incrementalism model. This principle is well expressed in Deng Xiaoping's well-known saying: 'Groping pebbles to cross stream.' Since both reform and opening-up strategies are extremely new attempts of China to speed up the economic growth and promote social development, China's leadership of party and government does not have any such experiences, and there are also no ready-made methods which have been tried in other developing countries that can be used as references. Thus, generally speaking, the feasible way in this situation for China to carry out these two tasks is to try those new programmes step by step toward their final goals. That is, for the purpose of achieving the desired goals without making big mistakes and getting lost, to try a series of small steps incrementally, while adjusting the policies continuously as feedback is obtained from their application, instead of taking the big risk to take a large step toward the pursuing target.

Furthermore, one of the key features of the incrementalism model is to reach agreement by mutual-adapting of the ideas among the participants involved in the policy process, which is an important pursuing target of policy-making; meanwhile, Lindblom stressed that in order to seek faster change it is essential to avoid big controversies over big changes. These ideas are particularly applicable in China's contemporary practice. As known to many scholars, for nearly three decades before the reform, there were so many fundamental policy-making issues relating to China's development, which had to first be involved in time-consuming arguments. Because at that time these were usually closely connected with some sensitive political principles or ideological issues, hence, it often became difficult to reach agreements owing to the existence of the leftist thinking. On the other hand, some people considered that to show their leftist stance was more politically safe than expressing a viewpoint or stating something objectively. Thus, many policy issues were not easy to decide by mutual-adapting of the opinions among the policy-making participants but failed in endless debates which finally often led to the ends that leftist opinion were in domination, which had resulted in the great loss that many programmes for economic development failed to be passed in these debates. Deng Xiaoping had summed up this lesson and strongly argued that: 'It is an invention of mine not to carry out controversy. The purpose of doing so is to save time to do more work. The situation will become complex when we engage in controversy, and then time will be lost and nothing can be done' (1993, p. 374). Deng's idea clearly suggests that, first do something that is considered necessary and then check whether it is really good according to fact. This political pragmatism was expressed clearly in his well-known 'Cat theory' that 'It does not matter if it is a black or white cat, it is good cat as long as it catch mice.'

It is a coincidence that Deng's above ideas are somewhat similar to those that Lindblom stressed. However, there is some difference, in the method to avoid controversy for making practical progress on a policy-making issue between Lindblom and Deng. That is, Lindblom advocated reaching this goal by securing an agreement of the participants' interest through mutual adapting, and Deng, mainly depended on the authority of the central leadership, especially the authority of himself. Nevertheless, we might be sure that this idea of avoiding those useless and unnecessary arguments while doing what should be done for seeking the desired concrete goals reflects a political wisdom of human beings in modern society. Only those politicians or thinkers who possess rich experience or have studied the issue in depth can discover and apply this key important idea.

In examining China's practice, we see that some principles of the incrementalism model, such as to reach the target with a great change only through a series of small steps, are applicable in many but not all situations. Fundamentally speaking, some great changes can be achieved by conducting a sequence of small steps, but some can not. For instance, one of China's biggest programmes now in process for social development, is to build up the social welfare system. It is definitely a giant and comprehensive project that needs the investment of huge funds and takes a long time, but it can be implemented step by step and reach the target gradually no matter how long it will take. It is very clear that due to China's relatively lower economic level, the lack of financial sources and also experience, this programme can not be realised completely at once or even in a short period. Instead, this big project should be divided into many small branch systems and small targets according to the possibilities of available resources, which could be realised one by one with many relatively small decisions. In the future when the programme has been finished completely it will be a vast project indeed. But in the initial stage it is neither necessary nor possible to declare that a comprehensive welfare system commences implementation in an all-round way.

Another case, however, to make the decision whether to build the Three Gorges Dam in Changjiang River, can not use the incrementalism model basically. Of course, in the preparation period when the data of geology, hydrology, meteorology and other relevant sources is being collected, the decisions can be made incrementally as it is an accumulative process. These works had been carried out for nearly forty years from the mid-1950s to the early 1990s. But to decide whether to approve this construction scheme of the great dam it was impossible to adopt the incremental method. In order to answer 'yes' or 'no' to this issue, the rationality model should be used, for it concerns a huge investment and important safety issues. Both that withdrawal in the course of conducting the project and that failure after its completion would be definitely unforgivable (This giant project was started in 1994).

For further analysing the importance of incrementalism to China's practice, it is necessary to briefly examine the related situation before the reform. During the first thirty years of PRC, one of the main problems of policy-making was to be eager for quick and big success without carefully considering the realistic conditions. For instance, launching the 'Great Leap Forward', was aimed to speedily and fundamentally change China's very backward economic situation and catch up with America and Britain within twenty or fifteen years. But it naturally resulted in failure. Another typical case is the collectivisation in the early 1950s and the following Communes campaign started from 1958 in the countryside, which tried to reform the organisational structure of farming production thoroughly within a short time so as to enable a speedy development of agriculture. However, the two decades after 1958 saw the bitter consequences caused by these adventure efforts, which had brought about a more and more low efficiency in farming production. As known to many people, this system had been thoroughly replaced by the 'household responsibility system' from the end of 1970s. When re-thinking these events, we can know that if the incrementalism method could be introduced for making policy for those issues, many fewer mistakes which resulted from holism, aiming at too high, and idealism plus revolutionary fervour, and less loss would have occurred.

What we discussed above is actually a kind of manifestation of radicalism, or a simplistic approach in policy-making. For further exploring the roles of the incremental approaches, we need to add some more discussion about the relations between incrementalism and the radical action in China's practice. It has been noticed by many scholars that China is a country in which it is easier to produce the radical thinking and actions politically and economically, particularly in the modern age. As Sheng Hua and his co-authors pointed out, no matter how ridiculous ultra-left radicalism was in the Cultural Revolution, it was by no means a fantasy of one person or even one generation. Because, 'modern Chinese radicalism is far more deep-rooted than most people realise or are willing to acknowledge'. Therefore, 'It can only be understood against the background of China's specific history of transformation under the great external pressure, which engendered impetuous action and anger stemming from both the glory and greatness of the past and the repeated defeats and humiliation of the modern era' (Hua, S. at el. 1993, pp. 22-4). Hua listed many facts to prove the phenomenon of radicalism in modern China from the last century to the period before the 1980s, which include the prevailing slogans that 'Catching up Britain in seven years and surpassing the United States in fifteen years' and 'Running into communism', appeared in the Great leap Forward, and the situation of 'doubted everything and condemned everything' during the Cultural Revolution. (Hua, S. at el. ibid. pp. 15, 23)

Why was China's policy-making behaviour so easily linked with the radicalism? Briefly speaking, we can analyse the reasons economically and historically. First, current China is still a developing country with a very great number of small-scale farmers which account for about three quarters of China's population; and many cadres, especially those at mid-and-low levels have the background of being closely linked with this small-scale rural economy, to different extents. The background in which these small-scale peasant economy existed, before the founding of the PRC, was a society that was far behind the full development of a capitalist economy and so was lacking great-scale social industrial production; thus the soil of the society with small-scale peasant economy in dominance is the one in which petty bourgeoisie fanaticism is more easily produced. In the first two decades of the PRC prior to the reform period, although some great economic development had been achieved, the social economic base had not changed fundamentally. Second, historically speaking, before 1949, during a period of more than a century since the Opium War, China fell into backwardness, poverty, and repeated defeats and humiliation, owing to the corruption and incompetence of the regimes and the continuous invasions by Western imperialism countries. Under these circumstance, both the leading intellectuals and the common people eagerly wanted to change the *status quo* as soon as possible so as to strengthen the national power and improve people's life. China's great and glorious history provided people the confidence and encouragement to fight for the state's destiny, while the extreme poverty and backwardness in reality forced them to act radically and often want to solve the problems at one go. Thus, radicalism kept increasing for a long period. Examining the manifestations of radicalism in contemporary China, what we need to see are not only the launching of the Great Leap Forward and the Great Cultural Revolution, etc. but more importantly, why these radical campaigns were accepted, carried out and supported by China's masses from many (not all of them) high-rank officials to the common people, especially the former campaign. The possibilities and conditions of doing so were just the broad and profound social foundation of the radicalism. Considering this context, unquestionably, therefore, to emphasise the practise of incremental approaches is particularly significant in China.

To sum up, incrementalism, which is an important and effective approach of policy-making, is particularly applicable in China's practice, especially in the new situation since the start of the reform at the end of 1970s. Facing so many uncertainties in promoting the modernisation course in such a big country, to employ the incremental approach as the main guiding principle of making policy is reasonable indeed, for it can be beneficial to overcome the radical tendency in China's policy-making and to enable more reliable policy to be made.

4.2.3 About mixed scanning model

The basic features of the mixed scanning approach are threefold: (1) To observe and analyse both the general situation and the particular situation of a crucial part within a whole policy issue when accessing a policy-making process. (2) To distinguish fundamental decisions and incremental decisions. (3) Stressing that fundamental decisions set the basic direction and provide the contextual conditions for making incremental decisions. Thus, it helps decision-makers to undertake a broad review of the situation as a whole, and the broad review enables longer-run alternatives to be examined and leads to fundamental decisions. Then, incremental decision can be made on those necessary aspects, under the guidance of the fundamental decision.

Generally speaking, this model is acceptable to China's practice. China was a country carrying out a planned economy mode before 1980s. Since the conducting of the reform from the end of 1970s it has been transformed gradually towards a market economy system. But, the central government still plays a considerable important role in China's economic and social development, through formulating guiding plans instead of the instructive plan as in the past to give the general direction. For instance, China's government now continues to make five-year plans and some even longer-run plans as in the past. These plans, formatted on the base of considering both the national and provinces' situations, conditions and possibilities, are the fundamental decisions for the country. In the light of these plans the ministries of the government and provinces can make their concrete developing schemes.

A current important case of setting the long-run development plan as the fundamental policy-making is the enacting of 'The Proposal of CPC Central Committee for Formulating the Ninth Five-Years Plan for the National economic and Social Development and the long-term Target for the Year 2010', which was adopted at the Fifth Plenum of 14th Central Committee of CPC.

Only by glancing at some major contents of this proposal, can we find some features that are similar to the elements of mixed scanning methods. This proposal (*BR*, vol. 38, No.46, 1995, pp. 12-6) consists of six parts:

- Important Period for China's National Economic and Social Development
- Major Targets and Guideline
- Economic Tasks and Strategic Distribution
- Reform and Opening Plans
- Major Tasks and Basic Policies for Social Development
- Unite to Accomplish Established Goals

From all these titles, we can deduce that this proposal was formulated on the basis of an overall view and the consideration of the whole country's situation for the present and the near future. It is just a scanning for a long-term strategic target of China's economic and social development.

The major targets fixed by the proposal are required to reach by two separate times:

> By the year of 2000, ...the GNP will quadruple the figures of 1980; poverty will basically be eliminated; the people will have relatively comfortable living standards; the establishment of a modern enterprise system will be accelerated; and the socialist market economic structure will be basically in place (ibid. p. 12).

Then, by the year of 2010, the main target set in the proposal

> is to double the 2000 GNP, thereby enable people to live an more comfortable life, and ensuring that a relatively complete socialist market economy will have been established (ibid. p. 13).

Needless to say, to map out these targets based on a detailed scanning in both different economic and social fields and different regions with focus on those most important aspects. That means, they came from the concrete examination and study. Thus, the process to formulate this proposal was the one involving the mixed scanning approach. In other words, to apply the mixed scanning approach is conducive to this kind of policy-making.

The document also stipulates nine major principles for social and economic development, which must be implemented over the next 15 years. These principles include maintaining the sustained, rapid and healthy development of the national economy; actively promoting a shift in the mode of economic growth, and regarding increased economic returns as the central task of economic activities; using science and education to revitalise China, while at the same time integrating the economy with science, technology and education; adopting agricultural development as the primary task for promoting the national economy; and so on (ibid.). These principles provide basic methods and directions to realise the main targets.

To sum up, these main targets and measures are the state's fundamental decisions of China, which resulted from a mixed scanning of the general examination and assessing of China's *status quo* and the objective conditions. They set up the basic direction and provide the contextual conditions for incremental decisions, namely, provide the base (put forward the key important targets in various fields and formulate the basic policies), for the concrete policy-making for the reform and opening-up course in the coming years. This process is seen as the mixed scanning which first enables decision-makers to undertake a broad review of the situation as a whole; and then the broad review enables longer-run alternatives to be examined and leads to fundamental decisions; and finally, these fundamental decisions will guide the concrete incremental policy-making at different levels of the state, to be conducted without missing the defined direction and general policies in future development.

From what have been discussed above, we see that the mixed scanning model is quite applicable and effective to China's macro-policy-making practice in economic realm, for its central leadership still keeps an important position in guiding the state's economic development, and each province and even the lower level authorities also play similar roles.

4.2.4 About optimal approach

It has been known that the main part and a particular strength of Dror's optimal method is the extra-rational elements, which comprise the use of judgement, creative invention, brainstorming, etc.

Examining China's practice with these ideas, we can see its applicability in many occasions. Three years ago, the Beijing — Jiulong (an area of Hong Kong) railway, one of the most important main lines links north and south of China, had been completed. This railway is 2536 km long and connects 9 provinces and municipalities. The accomplishment of the main project of this railway was a great achievement of China's modernisation construction. To analyse how the decision to conduct this giant programme was made will enable us to discover the extent to which the optimal approach is applicable.

To build the Beijing—Jiulong railway was a century long dream of the Chinese nation. In his book 'The General Plan of Founding a State', Mr Sun Yat-sen, the chief leader of the 1911 revolution, had thought to build a bridge in Jiujiang (a city of Jiangxi province), 'to enable it to become one of the centres of the railways connecting the north and south'. In 1958, a plan of 'small Jing-Jiu' (Beijing to Jiujiang) railway had been put forward. Then, in the April of 1991, the plan to build the 'Big Jing-Jiu' (Beijing to Jiulong) railway was finally listed in the Eighth five-year Plan. It has been 32 years then since 1958! Why did China's leaders urgently need to make the final decision to build this railway after a long period's procrastination? It needs to be examined in some detail. In the reform period, the railway transport has become one of the key measures for securing the sustained, rapid and healthy development of the national economy. In the main stations of both the Beijing — Guangzhou railway and the Beijing — Shanghai railway, only 40 percent of the freight transport plan can be met, and the situation for passenger transport is also seriously overloaded (Yan Bing, 1995, p. 1). Then, if the Beijing—Jiulong railway is built, 'It will not only greatly improve China's railway distribution, and greatly relieve the tense situation of the railway transport connecting the north and south, but also help some poor areas in central Henan province, Anhui and Jiangxi Province, to eliminate poverty and gradually become rich; moreover, it will be of benefit for keeping the stability and prosperity of Hong Kong and of promoting the unification of the country' (PDO, 17th Nov. 1995. P. 1).

According to the arrangement of 1991, the project was planned to finish in 1997 when China would resume its sovereign rights in Hong Kong. However, in the autumn of 1992, in accordance with the situation, the CPC Centre and the State Council resolutely made a decision to concentrate efforts to complete the railway project in three years (in 1995). From then on, two hundred thousand builders participated in this great programme and finally finished it ahead of time.

This case shows that the final determination of building the Beijing—Jiulong Railway ('Big Jing-Jiu') and the deadline to complete the project were based on some urgent reasons as below. (1) To solve the serious problem that the railway transport linking north and south could not meet the demands of the state's economic development. (2) To strengthen the connection between inland and Hong Kong, and between Beijing and Hong Kong, so as to keep Hong Kong's stability and promote the unification. (3) To help some poor areas in the middle parts of China to eliminate poverty. Among these reasons, obviously, the second one is particular urgent and significant. These considerations and the way to determine the 'Big Jing-jiu' project and its progress according to the considerations, showed a pattern of optimal thinking, or extra-rational thinking. It indicates that in those policy-making processes concerning some key issues, while resources (time, data, or knowledge, etc.) are limited, the extra-rational model can be introduced and then usually better policy outputs can be expected.

The meta-policy-making, another feature of the optimal model — to decide how to make decision — is also an issue that both politicians and scholars are interested in discussing. To employ this method should be beneficial to improving China's policy process, for China needs to overcome the drawbacks which developed from the past in which non-scientific and non-democratic factors were involved, so as to adopt better policy-making approaches.

4.3 Conclusions

This chapter, has surveyed a variety of policy-making models, which were created to improve the policy process, and also discussed the applicability of some selected models to China's practice in general. Then, four of these models, which include rationalist approach, incrementalist model, contingent approach and optimal method, as mentioned in the introductory chapter, are selected to conduct the major analytical task of my research — to examine the policy-making process of China's SEZ course, in view of what follows. It seems to be conceivable that, according to the discussion in this chapter, to select rationalism and incrementalism is of significance theoretically and practically. On the one hand, these two are the most important models of the policy-making study and also the two ends of this study in a continuum of searching the way to improve policy process. Therefore, to introduce them in analysis can observe the practice from a contrastive way in which two models are completed each other to a considerable extent. On the other hand, it is particular important to examine China's practice with these two models. As what has been analysed, the main defects of China's old policymaking pattern, which were characterised by dogmatism, holism, and radicalism, etc, indicate the necessity of greatly increase the involvement of rationalism and incrementalism. Therefore, it is essential to see how and to what extent the influence of these two elements had increased in China's policy-making practice in the post-Mao period, as we know that significant changes had occurred from the end of 1970s. Moreover, it needs to be pointed out that although these two models seem to be theoretically contradicted, they are actually not absolutely exclusive with each other but emphasising the thinking mode from two ends of a continuum in selecting the policy-making approaches. Accordingly, to stress the importance of applying both of them in China's practice should not be a contradiction. The optimal method is one of the attempts, which aim at searching a middle way between rationalism and incrementalism so as to combine their merits and avoid their weaknesses. Compared with the mixed scanning method, the optimal approach appears the one with more dynamic force in interpreting or being applied in the practice of the post-Mao China in which the great and rapid development occurred and the policy-making needed to handle many urgent and crucial issues. Hence, optimal method is also selected to examine the SEZ course. The contingent approaches illustrate diversified ways to observe and analyse the applicability of policy-making methods, and emphasise that the applicability of a policy-making method depends on to what extent it can match the given contextual situation, in which the elements of either substance, or complexity, or the relations of interest mediation is considered. Hence, they can be helpful in examining the SEZ course in which a variety of policy-making methods were involved, and so it is introduced to conducting the analysing task. The garbage can model is an attempt to deal with the decision-making issue in a sceptic situation of 'organised anarchy'. Thus, it is obviously not suitable in interpreting China's policy-making practice in the post-Mao period. To be sure, analysing the SEZ cases with those four selected models can serve two purposes: further examining the applicability of these models and deeply probing the changes and characteristics of China's policy-making behaviour in post-Mao period.

PART II:
THE POLICY-MAKING
PROCESS OF THE SEZ
COURSE

PART II

THE POLICY-MAKING
PROCESS OF THE SEZ
COURSE

5 A general review of China's SEZ course

Before discussing the concrete policy-making processes of establishing and developing Special Economic Zones (referred to as SEZs hereafter), it is essential to first understand the issues concerning why China needed SEZ, the main characteristics and policies of China's SEZs and their major development course and achievements. To access this contextual analysis will benefit us to further unfold our study.

To set up SEZ in a country is not a pioneering work contributing by China, and even to set up SEZ in a socialist country is not the creation of China. Why did China need to set up SEZ? It resulted from an understanding of its significance. That is, SEZs can play an important role in accelerating a state's economic development, and to set up SEZs had been an essential and universal measure adopted by most countries in the world. China drew a great deal of enlightenment from the successful experience of the world's SEZs which has existed for a long time.

When discussing China's SEZs, it is necessary to firstly identify the meaning of SEZ. The term of 'SEZ', i.e. the Special Economic Zone, can be explained from two aspects. In a broad sense, it refers to all those zones which being particularly marked off in a country or a region, to engage in economic activities with special policies granted by the government. These embrace Free Port, Free Trade Zone, Export-Originated Processing Zone, Traffic Free Zone and Scientific Industrial Park, etc. In a narrow sense, it only refers to those comprehensive economic zones with special policies, like current China's SEZs. We use the broad sense when mentioning the world's SEZs, and use the narrow sense when discussing China's SEZs.

5.1 The main characteristics and policies of China's SEZs

5.1.1 The main features and policies

The whole name of China's SEZ is 'Special Economic Zone', in which the key word is 'economic'. It means that China's SEZs are neither special

145

political zones, nor special administrative regions like Hong Kong and future Macao when its sovereignty returns to China, and Taiwan when the reunification can be realised. They are still directly under the leadership of the local municipality governments (such as Pudong), provinces (such as Shenzhen, Santou, and Xiamen) or central government (such as Hainan). On the other hand, they are also not like export processing zones in other countries, for they are the comprehensive special economic zones giving the first place to industries, combining industries and commerce, and also promoting the development of other trades. Furthermore, it should be noticed that, China's SEZs are also not zones with special social and economic systems, but with some special economic policies and special economic management systems.

As in other countries, foreign businessmen who invest in SEZs must observe China's constitution and laws; and, their investment direction, size and the location of the enterprises must obtain the approval of the relevant departments of China's government. According to the SEZ Office of China's State Council (SOCSC, 1988, p. 730), the main policies implemented in the SEZs can be summarised as six aspects.

Firstly, the SEZs' economic development mainly depends on foreign capital. The principal of SEZs' economic structure is the coexistence of different economic sectors predominantly joint ventures, co-operative and sole foreign invested enterprises, under the general condition of upholding the socialist direction.

Second, the SEZs' economic activities are principally regulated by the market demands under the macro-guidance of the state's planning economy.[1]

Third, to promote efforts to develop the outward-oriented economy; the selling of the SEZs' products must be mainly in the international market.

Fourth, according to the direction of the central government, the SEZs governments provide special policies, preferential treatments and convenience to the foreign investors. For instance, the joint ventures, co-operative and solely foreign invested enterprises only have to pay 15 percent business income tax. The additional local income tax may be deducted or exempted by the SEZs' governments. Concretely speaking, those foreign invested enterprises that engage in productive trades, such as industry, agriculture, communication and transportation, even enjoy more special preferential treatments of 'two years' exemption' and 'three years' deduction'. That means, the income tax of these enterprises of productive trades can be exempted in the first two years, and only levy half of the 15 percent from the third year to the fifth year. After these five years, so long as the value of the export products accounts for more than 70 percent of the total value of the enterprises' products in the same year, this enterprise is only levied by 10 percent business income tax (Zhao, G. 1992, p. 21). The tax on the income from the exports produced by SEZ enterprises or of hi-tech and knowledge-intensive advanced enterprises may be cut down to 10 percent. Moreover, the profits earned by the foreign investors are exempted from the remittance tax when remitted to foreign countries. Usually the exports are exempt from the industrial and commercial tax.

The degree of this preferential tax treatment could be seen more evidently when compared with those in non-SEZ areas. According to the Article 3 of 'The Income Tax Law of the People's Republic of China Concerning Chinese-Foreign Joint Ventures', the income tax rate on joint ventures shall be 30 percent. In addition, a local income tax of 10 percent of the assessed income tax shall be levied (*CFEL*, 1984, p. 36). As for the exclusive foreign invested enterprises, in accordance with the Article 3 of 'The Income tax Law of the People's Republic of China Concerning Foreign Enterprises', they shall be levied income tax at progressive rates on accounts in excess of specified amounts of taxable income, which vary from 20 percent to 40 percent. Meanwhile, a local tax of 10 percent of the taxable income shall be levied, under Article 4 of the same law (ibid. pp. 64-5).

Fifth, for the convenience of engaging business activities, the procedures for the foreign investors' entrance into and exit out of China have been simplified. In Hainan SEZ, the system that foreigners' visa for entrance can be obtained as they arrive is practised.

Sixth, the SEZs are granted some considerable autonomy by the state to make economic decisions. For example, the SEZs possess a greater authority in approving construction projects than the common provinces and autonomous regions; the quotas of capital construction can be made outside the gross fixed investment controlled by the central government (SOCSC, 1988, p. 730).

The preferential treatments also include those related to the policies of utilising and developing lands, financial policy, import and export policy etc. All these preferential policies and other conveniences offered by the SEZs are aimed at creating a better environment for foreign investors.

5.1.2 The relations between the SEZs and the reform and opening-up strategy

Defining this relation may enable us to understand the significance of SEZs in China's modernisation course. Reform and opening-up to the outside world are two wheels of China's development locomotive towards the modernisation since the end of 1970s. To set up and develop SEZs is one of the important parts of China's reform and opening-up strategy. To carry our reform means to change those productive relations and superstructures that do not correspond with the development of the productive force, to change all those managerial patterns, thinking patterns and behaviour patterns, that do not accord with the reality, which is a wide and profound revolution. To conduct opening-up policy indicated that China had changed some dogmatism ideas and no longer only divided the world into two camps of socialists and the capitalists, or exploiters and exploited, but also considered the world as two parts — developed and developing countries, with the economic view, by which to formulate political and economic strategy and policies. China now holds that peace and development are the two key subjects of today's world. The developing countries, such as China, should be able to utilise the advanced technology and capital of those developed countries to speed up the economic development. As Deng points out that 'if socialism would aim to win a superior position over capitalism, it must boldly learn from and absorb all civilisation achievements created by human society, learn from and absorb all advanced management model and managerial skills, which reflect the modern socialised production laws, from the foreign counties of current world including those capitalist developed countries' (Deng, X. 1993, p. 373).

Since one of the main targets of SEZ is serving as the 'experimental field', 'window' and 'bridge' of promoting the opening-up strategy, this paragraph discusses opening-up policy in more detail. With carrying out the opening-up policy, from the end of the 1970s, China has been encouraging and attracting the participation from developed countries to China's economic construction with great efforts. In doing so, China would like to show that 'they can, far from being exploited, manage foreign capitalism for national profit within their socialist borders' (Kleinberg, 1990, p. 2). The contents of conducting the opening strategy covered many aspects. Of which, the major parts included expanding and increasing foreign trade, absorbing investment of foreign capital, sending young scholars and professionals to study abroad, expending and increasing the exchanges between China and other countries in terms of culture, science and education, etc., letting foreigners travel considerably more freely in China and also allowing Chinese people to get to know more about the external world through the state controlled mass media, setting up special economic zones, and economic and technological development zones to increase the involvement of external participation in China's modernisation construction.

To sum up, carrying out the opening-up policy is to open all possible channels to link China and the outside world, to obtain information, technology and capital, and to join the international competition, so as to accelerate China's development.

Then, what is the relation between SEZ and the opening-up strategy? First, SEZ is one of the most important parts of the reform and opening-up strategy for it involved several key aspects of aforementioned contents, such as absorbing foreign capital and technology, expanding foreign trade and expanding the exchanges and co-operation with foreign countries, etc. Second, SEZs are at the forward position in carrying out the reform and opening-up strategy, and operating as their experimental bases, for many of China's important reforms and opening-up schemes. Policies were firstly implemented there and then expanded and spread to other parts of the country after some experiences were accumulated.

5.1.3 The relations between the SEZs and the CEDS programme

That to define the relations between the SEZs and the CEDS is essential to further clarity the value and significance of the SEZs, and also the significance of our study to select SEZs as the main cases of probing China's policy-making models in the reform period.

The CEDS (Coastal Economic Development Strategy), was formally put forward in 1986 after the Thirteenth National Congress of CPC, and was affirmed by the Fourth Plenary Session of the CPC Politburo in 6th February 1988. The core idea of the CEDS is to develop the outward-oriented economy. It stressed that: China must seize the opportunity of present readjustment of the international economic structures, actively participate in international economic competition; it is of key importance to push the coastal regions to the international market, and it must give full use of the advantages of the coastal regions in technology, trained personnel and economic foundation, to develop the outward economy; with the development of the coastal economy, to accumulate funds and technology so as to give impetus to the economic development of China's central and west parts and finally accelerate the rapid development of the entire national economy of China (Quan, Q. 1992, pp. 1-2).

The structure of CEDS consists of four levels:

- Special Economic Zones (SEZs);
- Economic and Technological Development Zones (ETDZs);
- Coastal Open Cities (COCs);
- Coastal Economic Development Areas (CEDAs).

SEZs was the starting point, path-explorer and experimental ground of the CEDS, which was initiated in 1979 and has kept growing in both the sizes and strength since then on.

ETDZs were setting up in COCs. From 1984 to March 1992, 16 EDTZs were established in Dalian, Qinghuangdao, Tianjin, Yantai, Qingdao, Lianyungang, Nantong, Ningbo, Fuzhou, Wenzhou, Guangzhou, Zhanjiang, Hainan and Shanghai. There are three in Shanghai.

There are some obvious differences between ETDZs and the SEZs. First, SEZs are the comparatively independent administrative areas while ETDZs are the areas implementing some preferential policies, under the leadership of the respective municipal government. Second, all the SEZs are now the comprehensive special Zones while ETDZs lay their stress on the development of new technology and industrial production. Third, SEZs impose an enterprises' income tax of 15 percent on the enterprises that utilise foreign investment which include both the productive and non-productive enterprises; whereas, ETDZs offer the preferential treatment only to those productive enterprises. Fourth, upon the completion and operation of the extent of control in SEZs, most consumer goods enjoy tax deductions or exemptions; while, imported consumer goods and materials on market are all taxed as regulated in ETDZs (Xie, B. 1991, pp. 537-8).

The decision to open 14 coastal port cities (i.e. coastal open city COC) was made by the meeting jointly convened by the Secretariat of CPC and the State Council in Beijing in April 1984. The putting forward of this scheme resulted from the summary of the practice of China's opening policies, especially the development of SEZs, which aimed at further accelerating the progress of China's reform and economic development.

These 14 coastal open cities embody all the important port cities along China's coastal line from north to south. They are: Dalian, Qinghuangdao, Tianjin, Yantai, Qingdao, Lianyungang, Nantong, Shanghai, Ningbo, Wenzhou, Fuzhou, Guangzhou, Zhaijiang and Beihai. Although the population of these 14 coastal cities only account for less than 8 percent of the total of China, they occupy an important place in the national economy: their industrial output value record 23 percent of the total, the export value account for 40 percent of the total, and the productive efficiency is 60 percent higher than the average level of the country (Chang, H. 1992, p. 17).

The purpose of defining the COCs is to give full play to the roles of the coastal cities which possess relatively developed economies, rich professional sources, better industrial foundation and transportation conditions, by which to further actively absorb and utilise the foreign funds and advanced technology in order to speed up the scientific and technological progress and economic development; to further expand the international market in a much wider background while changing the inward economy into a combination of inward and outward economies; to carry on the economic co-operation with interior regions in terms of the transfer of technology, skilled personnel, funds, materials, commodities, etc., so as to push the economy forward.

The CEDAs — the Coastal Economic Development Areas were set up in February 1985 by the approval of CPC centre and the State Council, according to the suggestion of Premier Zhao Zhiyang (SOCSC, 1988, p731). This important innovation was made upon the experiences of the SEZs and COCS which had greatly shown the significant roles on accelerating the economic and technological development.

Compared with SEZ and COC, a CEDA usually covers a large area instead of one city or a small region. The first three CEDAs are: Changjiang (Yangtze River) Delta, Zhujiang (Pearl River) Delta and the triangle area that covers Xiamen, Zhangzhou and Quanzhou in southern Fujian province. In March 1988, another two CEDAs were added: Liaoning Peninsula and Shangdong Peninsula. The total CEDAs include 288 cities and counties, covering total area of 320,000 square kilometres, and the population of 1.6 billion. CEDAs share some similar purposes and policies with the COCs, but since they possess much more wide hinterland which are the bases of their development, so they can do more in terms of adjusting the agricultural structure, building up the health interchange with both the domestic and abroad markets, and building up a rich and developed rural and urban area with highly modern civilisation.

So far, the CEDS, consisting of SEZs, ETDZs, COCs and CEDAs four levels, has been basically shaped up. With practising this ambitious strategy a considerable wide coastal opening belt has been formed which starting from the most northern coast of Yellow Sea to the most western coast of the South Sea, covers all coastal provinces and coastal port cities. This wide belt of CEDAs, which contains all SEZs, ETDZs and COCs, attracts innumerable investors from both home and abroad, and has been called 'the Golden Coast'.

Among the structure of the CEDS programme, according to the previous analysis, SEZs are the highest level outward economy, ETDZs are the second level outward economy, COCs are the third level outward economy, and the CEDAs are the fourth level outward economy. Obviously, one conclusion could be drawn from the course of shaping up the CEDS: SEZs are the trigger, pioneer and motive force of the CEDS. It was the development and success of SEZs which enlightened and accelerated the formulation of the CEDS.

That is just one of the important reasons why this book selected the SEZs among many other aspects related to the opening-up and reform programmes as the cases to make a thorough study.

Then, how could China realise this situation and determine to establish SEZs? In a fundamental sense, it was promoted by carrying out the reform policy. China's SEZ was one of the direct and important products of the reform. Here, it is necessary to point out that although reform and opening-up are usually to be stressed at the same time, actually, they are not entirely parallel concepts, for the opening-up policy is one of the major contents of reform. Therefore, we need to clearly define that the producing of China's SEZs resulted from launching the reform which was the policy-making background and dynamics of the former.

5.2 Policy-making background: China urgently needed and had launched the reform and opening-up

As known to all, by the end of the Cultural Revolution, China's national economy had been driven to the brink of bankruptcy, and the entire country had fallen into the grim economic and social crises, which seriously threatened China's regime. This unfortunate situation, undoubtedly, was directly caused by the evil consequence of the ten years' upheaval. Fundamentally speaking, it resulted from more profound reasons. At the end of the 1970s, when was the eve of the producing of the SEZs, China urgently needed to launch a reform which had become an inevitable tendency. To understand this background, namely the inevitability of launching the reform or the reasons why China fell into crises, an analysis can be conducted from three aspects: the old economic management system strongly impeded China's economic development; the self-closed state seriously prevented China from sharing the interests of the economic globalization; and the policy-making pattern which was characterised by over-centralised and even personal caprice to a certain extent, did not conform with the demands of a modern society.

5.2.1 *The old economic management system strongly impeded China's economic development*

China's old economic management system was mainly copied from the Soviet Union and began to practise in the first Five-Year Plan period. It was a highly centralised plan system, which was also called the 'command economy system'. It was in dominance in China for nearly thirty years. Some analysts, like Brown, Neuberger, Ward and Shirk revealed some key features of this planning system as:

(1) State ownership of industrial enterprises; organisation of agriculture into large-scale collective and state farms. (2) Centralised bureaucratic management of the economy with government planners setting output and supply quotas, prices, and wages. (3) Capital investment provided as free government grants; no land rents or land-use fees. (4) An extensive growth strategy designed to achieve high rates of growth and establish a heavy industrial base. (5) State revenues based almost entirely on industrial profits. To increase the profitability of industrial production, planners set the prices of agricultural commodities and raw materials low, and manufactured goods high. The result was a system of rich industry and poor agriculture. (6) Disparagement of the service sector and prohibitions on private business. (7) A closed economy with foreign trade plans treated as addenda to domestic plans; foreign trade held to low levels and aimed at the goal of import substitution; no foreign investment; a central foreign trade monopoly; nonconvertible currency; and the prevalence of barter trade (Shirk, 1993, pp. 24-5).

This command economic system contained many fatal weaknesses. Gao Shangquan,[2] a well-known economist of China, the vice minister of China's State Commission for Restructuring the Economic System, argued (1996, p. 1) that these defects at least had four aspects: (1) state's excessive control deprived enterprises of autonomy; (2) denying the laws of value, market, and commodity production; (3) the egalitarianism of distribution; and (4) no competition environment for the enterprises owing to the unique ownership and economic structure. 'Together these systemic defects severely dampened the creativity, initiative and enthusiasm of enterprises and their workers' (ibid.).

The serious consequences caused by these defects had many aspects. First, it resulted in the gravely irrational and uneven development of the national economic sectors. From 1949 to 1978, the value of heavy industrial output increased 90.6 times, but agriculture only increased 2.4 times, and the light industries 19.8 times (Dong, 1982, pp. 5-7).

Second, the price to achieve a high rate growth of industry was too steep. During the period of 1951 to 1980, the average annual increase of the total investment in industrial fixed assets (11.7 percent) exceeded the average annual growth of industrial output value (8.6 percent) (Liu, R. 1987, p. 5). Hirszowicz (1980) considered this industrial growth to be a 'self-consuming growth', with the growth eating up an ever larger share of industrial output.

Third, the inefficiency in most sectors of the national economy especially the industries and agriculture. Due to the tight control from different levels and the prevalence of egalitarianism, the local governments were short of motivation to develop their local economy, the enterprises had poor incentive to develop their production, the individual workers, farmers, and other employees in different sectors as well, lacked incentive and enthusiasm to create efficient and high quality products. Hence, the entire economic activities of the society got stuck in an operation with very low efficiency.

Fourth, as the investment in industry and other economic sectors increased, the people's living standard stagnated and even declined. From 1952 to 1980, the gross output value of industry and agriculture increased by 810 percent and national income grew by 420 percent, while the average individual income only increased by 100 percent (Ma Hong, 1982, pp. 6-12). Taking the factor of inflation in this long period into account, the individual income actually declined. Moreover, even the grain available to each person was not enough, because from 1953 to 1978 the grain output only grew by 55 percent while the population increased by 64 percent (CSY, 1989,1990). Before the reform, three-fourths of China's population lived in the countryside and about 25 percent of them were in poverty.

5.2.2 The self-closed state prevents China from sharing the advantages of the economic globalization

Since the end of the World War II, economic globalisation developed more and more rapidly, which has been an unchangeable tendency. Involving into this wave means participating in a wide international exchange and co-operation in terms of information, science and technology, commodity, labour force and capital, and sharing the advantages of this course. Conversely, to separate from this system means to be isolated form the world and would result in falling behind the world's development wave. Unfortunately, from the late 1950s, especially after the Sino-Soviet split in the early 1960s, China was actually closed off from the mainstream international society. The main reasons causing this self-closed state were fourfold.

- The restriction of the doctrinairism ideology that worried about the impacts from capitalist countries.
- The effects of the ultra-leftist ideas in the leadership that over-stressed the importance of economic independence and the method of self-supported economic construction.
- Due to the hostility of some western countries which headed by the United States, during the cold word period. They imposed an economic blockade and embargo on China for a long time for their purpose of curbing communism.
- Some other traditional reasons, in which one was the natural economic tradition, and another was a lack of a realistic attitude to face the rapidly developing and changing world squarely, also strengthened the self-closed tendency.

The closed state produced a lot of troubles to China. For nearly two decades before the reform, China's foreign relations, especially foreign trades and international exchange of the science and technology, were quite restricted. The emphasis of China's foreign relation then was with the developing countries to which China provided a lot of aid although China itself was still in a difficult situation, due to the ideological consideration. This meant that China was basically apart from the mainstream and the leading part of the world's economic, scientific and technological development. The consequence was disastrous: China was excluded from international competition environment which was one of the most important conditions for promoting modern economic development; the channels to absorb the advanced science and technology, advanced managerial skills, and foreign funds to help China's economic construction, were greatly restricted or even closed to a great extent; and even to obtain the latest information became difficult, which was rather unfortunate in an information age. As a developing country, China suffered a great deal from all these difficulties during the long period prior to the reform.

5.2.3 The old policy-making pattern failed to meet the demands of a modern society's development

China's old policy-making pattern, prevailing in the Mao era, was characterised by over-centralisation and even personal arbitrary to a certain extent. The practice had proved that this mode was not suitable for a modern society. The failure and the disastrous consequences of the Great Leap Forward and the Proletarian Cultural Revolution were the typical cases which indicated that this pattern was so prone to cause the mistakes of radical, ultra-leftist and blind-commanding. Because it could not make policies depend on gathering enough data for all possible channels and listening to all opinions including supporting and opposing ones. Thus, under this condition, the resources for the policy-making were usually not fully reliable. To make policy with this mode was unreasonable either for political issue, economic issue or other issues.

Through profoundly examining China's historical lesson and the status quo of the world, China's leader realised the necessity and urgency of conducting a large-scale reform in the late 1970s after the ending of the Cultural Revolution. The launching of the reform was at the Third Plenary Session of the Eleventh Central Committee of CPC, which 'signalled the rise of Teng Hsiao-p'ing (Deng Xiaoping) as the paramount leader and adopted the key decisions of accelerating economic development and opening the door to the outside world' (Hsu, I. C. 1995, p. 841), which was convened in December 1978. It has been fashionable to regard this conference as the third turning point in China's twentieth-century history, after the revolution of 1911 and 1949 (Goodman, 1994, p. 90).

The Third Plenum ended the situation that China was going forward at a walking to and *fro pace* since the October 1976, began to correct the 'leftist' mistakes in and before the Cultural Revolution in an all-round way, and determined a series of fundamental policies and strategies. These significant resolutions, which were all reform measures in the fundamental sense, included, setting up China's new guiding thought for socialist construction, by overthrowing the 'two whatevers'[3] and re-established the correct principle of 'seeking truth from facts and the practice is the sole criterion of testing truth'; realising the shift of the state's work to the economic construction; setting up the fundamental strategies and formulating general policies for China's economic development; setting up the strategy and policies of reform and opening-up to the outside world.

The launching of reform and opening-up was a strong force to promote China's modernisation cause, which soon brought about a series of great changes and development. The rise of SEZs was one of these important achievements.

5.3 A basic development course and main achievements of China's SEZs

The years from 1979 to 1995 saw the experiences of three stages in setting up and developing the SEZs in China. In the first stage, which started in 1979, the first group of the SEZs came to being. This group of SEZs includes Shenzhen, Zhuhai, Santou and Xiamen. Among these four, the first three are in Guangdong province and the last one, Xiamen, is in Fujian province. What was accomplished during this period was initiating the theories and general policies of setting up China's SEZs, and gradually accumulating experience. The time from 1979 to 1985 was an experimental and probing period, and from 1985 onward some successful methods and policies were accumulated. With the success of building up the first group of SEZs, China's opening-up strategy was further pushed forward. Some policies applied in the SEZs had been expanded to other coastal cities and regions.

The second stage began from 1988 when China's largest SEZ — Hainan island, with the territory of 33,920 square kilometres and 6 millions population, was set up. Hainan Island had been an administrative region of Guangdong province. In April 1988, the First session of The Seventh NPC approved the State Council's proposal to establish Hainan province and build it as a new SEZ of China. From then onward, the development of China's SEZs entered a new period, for this new SEZ is not only the largest one, which is nearly 36 times as large as the total territory of the first group of SEZs, but it was granted some more particular policies compared with the first group of SEZs.

The third stage started from the early 1990s. On 2nd July 1990, the Centre of CPC and the State Council formally approved the establishment of the Pudong New Zone — the most special SEZ in China. The speciality of Pudong New SEZ includes two aspects: (1) it was granted some most special policies; (2) backed by Shanghai, China's most important and advanced industrial base and economic centre, Pudong New Zone developed very fast and achieved success within only a few years, which gave a significant impact on China's reform and opening-up situation.

The main achievements of the SEZs have been shown on two respects: one was the rapid development of their own economy, the other was their role to promote progress of the reform and economic development of the whole country.

First of all, to set up SEZs had enabled these cities and regions to achieve extraordinary economic development. Among China's SEZs, except that Pudong is a new area with a certain industrial foundation, and Xiamen had a relatively developed economy, the rest were in an absolute poverty before setting up the SEZs. For instance, Shenzhen, a region under the administration of Bao-an County before establishing the SEZ, was a seriously poverty-stricken place. According to an internal report wrote by a Xinhua News Agency correspondent, in Shenzhen then, walls were falling down, houses had collapsed, farmlands ran wild and people had moved away, as if Japanese invaders had plundered this area. Before 1979, many people had stowed away to Hong Kong and Macao which are adjacent to this area. Even in 1979, 84,600 people were recorded as having tried to move to Hong Kong. Of which, 32,900 succeeded, and 85 percent of them were young people. Shenzhen's total CCYL (Chinese Communist Youth League) members were 8406 at that time and more than 5000 (60 percent of the total) stowed away to Hong Kong (Xie, B., 1991, p. 528).

Another case is Hainan, the largest island of China, although rich in natural resources, there were at least one million people (about one sixth of the total population) who were in absolute poverty, with an average annual income of only RMB 200 yuans[4] before the setting up of the SEZ. The financial revenue of the island in 1988 totalled not more than 400 millions yuans while its expenditure was 900 million yuans. The central government had to cover the difference (ibid. p. 529).

Since setting up the SEZs, these cities and region's economy developed rapidly and brought about an earth shaking change within a short period. Shenzhen, Zhuhai and Santou had become the flourishing cities brimming with vigour, occupying an important position in the state's economy;

Xiamen gained greater development; Hainan become one of the China's most important focuses that fix the eyes of both home and abroad investors in 1990s; Pudong, the new zone of Shanghai, is developing with exceptional speed, like a bright pearl rising from Shanghai. Some major statistical figures listed below portray a fundamental picture about these historical changes. Shenzhen, for instance, even compared with the 'four small dragons' of Asia, its economic Goth rate was still much faster in 1980s. (see table 5.1)

	Korea	Taiwan	Hong Kong	Singapore	Shenzhen
1970-1985	7.6	6.5	5.7	6.1	51 (data of 1983-86)
1985-1987	11.4	11.3	12.7	5.3	20 (data of 1985-89)

Table 5.1 The economic growth rate of Shenzhen comparing with some countries and regions of Asia (%)

(Source: Guangjun Shui, 'SEZs' role in the sino-foreign countries economic co-operation', *Jinan Journal*, 4, 1990, p8)

Comparing Shenzhen's economy of 1991 with that in 1979 (CYB, 1992:560; TES, 1992, **3**, p. 56), we can understand why the term of 'Shenzhen Speed' is popular in China (see table 5.2).

	total value of domestic production	national income	total industrial value	total value of export
1979	1.928	1.60	0.599	0.094
1991	174.46	127.57	271.97	34.46
increase	8950 %	7870 %	45300 %	36400 %

Table 5.2 Shenzhen's economic development from 1979 to 1991
(unit: billion yuan RMB.)

From 1979 to 1993, Shenzhen imported foreign investment for 13489 projects from more than 40 countries and regions. The imported capital that was agreed by contract was 148.3 billion US $, of which 59.8 billion US$ had been actually used. The enterprises that foreign businessmen directly invested in made up to 10326 (Ni Tu, 1994a, p. 5). For a dozen years, Shenzhen has been keeping a high rate of increase in its economic development, even as early as eleven years ago when the SEZ had been set up for just five years it was called an 'One-Night-Built-City', for it seemed as if the building of a flourishing city from a poverty-stricken small town only took one night.

The preferential policies and other conveniences attracted rapidly increasing foreign investors to develop their businesses in SEZs. From 1980 to 1990, the direct investment from foreign countries imported by the first group of SEZs accounted for one fourth of the total amount of the foreign investment in China during this period. The total value of the industrial production of these four SEZs reached 283 billion yuans, an increase of 22 times over the figure prior to setting up the SEZs. The export of the foreign trade accounted for one-tenth of the total for the entire nation (Liu, L. 1995, p. 17).

Hainan's development also received world attention. In 1991, only four years after setting up the SEZ in the whole province, Hainan's total value of national production was 109 billion yuans, which made up 146.7 percent of the figure for 1987; the provincial revenue obtained 88.6 billion yuans, which accounted for 143.2 percent of the 1987 total. By the end of 1991, there had been 1874 enterprises which involved foreign capital (including joint-venture, co-operative and sole foreign capital enterprises) in this province. The total value of the foreign investment was 6.74 billion US $. Meanwhile, the investment environment has been improved greatly. A network of modern transportation and communications has been built up (CYB, 1992, p. 500; Zhao, G. et al. P. 17).

The economic development in Pudong new area is particularly outstanding, due to its location within Shanghai — the most important industrial centre of China with an ideal geographical position. Nowadays, there is a common view shared by the World Bank's statistical data and the international authoritative persons in economic circles, that since the beginning of 1990s, the globe's investment focus is in China, the key point of investment in China is in Shanghai, and, the central area of investment in Shanghai is Pudong New Zone (PDO, 8 May 1996, p. 2).

From April 1990 when Pudong was declared as a new zone for opening-up and development, there have been companies from 55 countries or regions which came to invest in this zone with 3748 projects. The foreign capital imported into this area by agreement made up US $ 9,850 million. Of which 274 were the big projects that each invested more than 10 US $ million. The total imported foreign capital of these big projects by agreement was US $ 6,800 million (69.04 percent of New Zone's total).

Among 500 of the world's most famous transnational corporations, there have been 55 which had investment in Pudong for more than 80 projects (ibid.).

The enterprises built up by monopoly capital in Pudong have increased fast. In 1992, these enterprises were only 52; however, by the end of 1995, this figure had increased to 1218, accounted for one third of the total enterprises that involved foreign capital (ibid.). Besides these 3748 foreign investment projects, there are more than 4000 enterprises absorbing home capital invested by state's ministries, committees and other provinces and cities. In 1995, Pudong's total value of the domestic production recorded 410 billion yuans, which was 12,000 million more than that for 1994 and was 6.83 times as much as the figure of 1990 when this area was just starting to development (OL, No. 17 1996, p. 8).

The raising and successful development of China's SEZs' gave great impetus to China's course of reform and opening to the outside world, in the following ways.

First, they opened a window to the world and created an objective environment to let foreigners get to know more about China whilst allowing the Chinese people to get to know more about the world. For reasons which had been briefly discussed in a previous part, after its founding the People's Republic of China, experienced nearly thirty years of isolation. By the end of the Cultural Revolution, both the world and China were unfamiliar with each other. The people of Hong Kong, Macao and Taiwan even had some fear of China in their minds to different extents. In 1980, the tourists of foreigners, overseas Chinese, the fellow Countryman of Hong Kong, Macao and Taiwan, visiting Shenzhen via Luohu, were less than 1500 (YSSEZ, 1985, p. 605); Xiamen, one of the most beautiful coastal cities of China, only received 1600 tourists (XSYEFC, 1989, p. 100). With the setting up and fast development of the SEZs, the conditions to meet this urgent need of increasing the understanding between China and the world were provided. From 1985 to 1988, the tourists from foreign countries and regions who visited the first group of SEZs (4 cities) accounted to 6.64 million (SBS, 1987:151-3; 1988, p. 100). The foreigners' visiting, observing, examining and comparing in the SEZs greatly expanded their understanding about China's reality and China's reform and opening policies. Also, the foreign businessmen investing in SEZs and building up more and more enterprises of different types provided the Chinese people with the opportunity to learn more about the world economic situation. This included the advanced management methods to run modern enterprises, advanced technologies, and the laws of international trade. All these accelerated the opening of China, rapidly increasing the participation of foreign investments in China's economic construction. This is the role SEZs served as the 'window' of China's opening strategy.

Second, SEZs' highly effective efforts in terms of absorbing foreign capital, importing advanced technology and scientific management experiences, expanding export, developing international economic co-operation and exchanges and gradually building up the economic operation mechanism that meet the demands of an outward economy, were a successful exploration and contributed a lot to promoting China's reform, setting up and perfecting China's opening mode, and formulating the Coastal Economic Development Strategy. This is the role SEZs served as the 'experimental ground' of China reform and opening strategy.

Third, SEZs' pattern that through both importing from abroad and joining with resource from inland, and expanding the horizontal economic coalition to develop the economy, gave great enlightenment and impetus to many inland cities and regions to enter the international market. This is the role SEZs served as the 'bridge' linking inland of China and abroad.

Fourth, SEZs always went one step ahead of the other cities and regions on many aspects of conducting economic management system reform, so they provided many important experiences for promoting the development of the economic management system reform of the whole country. This is the role SEZs served as the 'path-explorer' of China's reform.

Fifth and finally, SEZs' rise contributed to promoting the course of China's reunification. The setting up and development of the SEZs had produced strong repercussions in Hong Kong, Macao and Taiwan. From the fact that China allowed the existence of the capitalism in SEZs, the people of these regions further understood China's political and economic policies. At present there is a saying common outside the mainland of China: 'Taiwan is watching Hong Kong, and Hong Kong is watching Shenzhen'. Those external people considered Shenzhen as the barometer of China's policies (Liang Xiang, 1985, p. 54). Ten-odd years before, some comments from Hong Kong newspapers said, Shenzhen's image had become the latest sign of confidence to China in the minds of Hong Kong capitalists since the capitalist enterprises are allowed to be developed in Shenzhen, so Hong Kong has nothing to be worried about its future (ibid. pp. 54-5). Now as Hong Kong's sovereignty had been smoothly returned to

China, the significance of SEZs' role can clearly be understood as an example of China's policy when tracing back the history of 1980s.

All these available evidences show that to build up a series of SEZs along China's coastal areas as the forward position of economic reform and opening-up strategy has achieved noticeable success. This fact indicated that the policy-making actions around mapping out and carrying out this strategy were correct and effective. Therefore, it deserves further study to access the concrete processes, by which to probe China's policy-making behaviour in the Post-Mao period.

Notes

[1] This principal was formulated in 1980s when China still stressed the importance of upholding the planning economy. However, in early 1990s, the situation changed and the top leaders of China started to call for developing the market economy in the whole country, which affirms that the market demands' regulating should play a principle role, and the state's planning regulating is second. This new idea for economic reform had been confirmed by the formal documents of the CPC centre and State Council.

[2] Gao is an authoritative person in both the research and promoting the practice of China's economic reform, for he is now the vice minister of the State Commission for Restructuring the Economic System, the president of China Reform and Development Institute, the vice president of the Chinese Society of Industry, and the vice president of Chinese Society of Urban Economy. He is also the professor Doctorate Supervisor at Beijing University.

[3] The idea of 'two whatevers', which was supported and affirmed by Hua Guofeng, the then Chairman of the Centre Committee of CCP, insisted on that 'we will resolutely uphold whatever policies decisions Chairman Mao made, and unswervingly follow whatever instructions Chairman Mao gave'. The two whatevers was first contained in a joint editorial by *People's Daily*, the Journal of *Red Flag* and *Liberation Army Daily*, entitled 'Study the Documents Well and Grasp the Key Link', in 7 Feb. 1977. Hua Guofeng supported and stuck to this principle, he reaffirmed this stand in his speech at the Central Working Conference of March 1977. It would be absolutely impossible to launch China's reform without overthrowing this 'two whatevers'.

[4] RMB yuan, the unit of China's currency, 100 yuans equals about $11.4 at present.

6 Policy-making for setting up the first group of SEZs

From what was discussed in chapter five, we know that to set up SEZs in the territory of China was only possible after launching the reform. As a socialist country, that China boldly used SEZs as 'window' and 'bridge' to widely absorb technology and capital from capitalist countries was absolutely unimaginable in the past. To do so was thought to be a serious political mistake, which many people considered would not be good for the state's economic development. Around this issue, there were many bitter lessons.

Due to the special geographical position, Guangdong became the main base of China's SEZs, in which four of the total six SEZs (before Hainan Island being granted the status of a Province and established SEZ, it was one region of Guangdong) have been set up. Of which, three are in the first group, which are the cities of Shenzhen, Zhuhai and Santou. Why could Guangdong become a breakthrough opening for setting up China's SEZs? Besides the geographical reason, some historical elements were involved which mainly concerned the lesson Guangdong had experienced. To briefly review this lesson could be conducive to deepen the understanding of the policy-making context of setting up the first group of China's SEZs.

6.1 Refusing a golden chance: the big lesson in the 1950s

One of those bitter lessons happened in the 1950s. As for looking back in that period, many senior officials in charge of the economic and foreign trade sector, or heading the local government of Guangdong province were very aware that they were loosing a valuable chance to use foreign funds to help China's economic development (Ni Tu, 1994b, pp.8-9). In the middle 1950s, owing to the sharp political change in many Asia and Africa countries a number of capitalists including a lot of overseas Chinese, were in a hurry to transfer their capital from the countries they lived in to Hong Kong which was viewed as a safety harbour, within a short time. Hence, huge idle funds of hundreds of billion US dollars came from Indonesia,

Thailand, Malaysia and other countries and regions, poured into Hong Kong's banks. All these idle funds were urgently needed to find the out ways of investment or loaning. However, it was not easy to do so in a short period, as Hong Kong is a very small place and the financial market was very limited at that time. Consequently, the banks in Hong Kong had to reduce the interest rate of saving one after another, and finally the depositors even needed to pay interest to the banks in reverse. Under this situation, Hong Kong's bankers offered loans with very low interest rate, so as to solve this problem. At this moment, Hong Kong's entrepreneurs, both great and small, opened their pockets as wide as possible to take loans with a very low interest rate, with which to set up new factories, open new shops, and develop the real estate. As a result, afterwards, huge profits came into their pockets continuously.

Just at that moment, in the summer of 1956, Mao Zhedong, the Chairperson of the CPC Centre, came to Guangzhou, the capital of Guangdong province, to have an inspection. As one of the contents of his inspection, one day, Mao invited some local leaders to report the works about Hong Kong and Macao both which were closely adjacent to Guangzhou. These leaders came from the Middle Southern China Bureau of CPC and Guangdong province and included Tao Zhu, Lin Liming, Yao Zhangfeng and Huang Shiming. When Huang Shiming reported on Hong Kong's economic situation that huge idle funds were floating into Hong Kong and Hong Kong's entrepreneurs were taking full use of them to develop their business, and suggested that those fourteen Chinese banks in Hong Kong should also take advantage of this opportunity to greatly absorb this international capital by which to expand their business on one hand, and more importantly, to use these funds to support the inland construction with forms of investment or deposits, on the other hand. Mao nodded again and again. Mao said, 'that sounds quite good. We can make use of those idle funds. There were so much of them. The fund to set up a light industrial enterprise, either from loans or from investment, can be earned back after two or three years, and then returned to them.' Then, Mao emphasised that, it is really not easy to find such an opportunity! Your thinking is very good and I will bring it back to Beijing for further discussion (ibid. p. 8).

Unfortunately, as the time passed, month after month, there was no any answer from Beijing. In March 1957, when Huang Shiming went to Beijing to report work to the CPC Central Office, he asked for the result of this event. To his surprise, the reply was a total rejection. The answer was, the request had been studied, some leaders considered that to accept loan from foreign countries is just to borrow money from them, and this will result in a bad reputation for our country, and also will be harmful to the state's system. As a consequence, when Hong Kong's entrepreneurs fully utilised the golden opportunity to develop their business and create a marvellous economic achievement, and also many small banks in Hong Kong, took full use of this chance and went all out to run their businesses so they developed rapidly. Some financial groups with British capital or overseas Chinese capital also had similar stories. Meanwhile, however, those fourteen banks of China in Hong Kong were just eagerly watching those funds floating through their front gates (ibid.).

Looking back at the setback in the past, enabled those in the leading positions of Guangdong province and Hong Kong's Chinese enterprise, and of other relevant aspects, to see more clearly how China should develop its economy in the contemporary world. As soon as the reform started and the opening-up policy began, they raised their brave ideas to open the door from Guangdong to the outside world.

6.2 The policy-making process of setting up the first group of SEZs

This policy-making process could be divided into three stages: the initiating of the suggestion, the deepening and finalising of the scheme, and the determination, legitimisation and implementation of the decision.

6.2.1 The first stage: the initiative of the suggestion

The initiative of the idea to set up SEZs was an incremental process, which was produced against a background that China's recently started economic reform. It was the result of join forces from different respects.

Before the third Plenum of the Eleventh Central Committee of CPC, the Party committee of Guangdong province had got some new ideas about how to promote the economic development in Guangdong. These ideas came from three aspects. (1) Careful studies of the successful experiences of the economic take-off of the four small dragons in Asia (i.e. Singapore, South Korea, Hong Kong and Taiwan) and other countries' experiences. (2) Understanding the special superiority of Guangdong compared with other provinces. Guangdong is adjacent to Hong Kong and Macao, and a huge amount of its residents and family members or relatives, are living overseas. The amount of overseas Chinese that come from Guangdong province are 8.2 million. This is much greater than any other province. Furthermore, most of the residents of Hong Kong and Macao are also Guangdongese. In short, Guangdong has the closest, widest and most convenient connections with the outside world. (3) Summarising the historical lessons. One of their new ideas was that by taking advantage of Guangdong's better condition, and using the experiences of the outside world as reference, to set up some large-scale export-orientated bases in Guangdong province. Then, being encouraged by the third Plenum's strategy which focuses on reform and accelerating the economic construction, in order to set up the export bases in Bao-An and Zhuhai counties, Guangdong provincial Party Committee made a decision to raise the administrative status of Bao-an and Zhuhai from county to municipality, on 23 Jan. 1979. Only one month late, The State Council approved its request (Wang, Z. 1995, p. 7).

At the same time when Guangdong's leaders were thinking about how to develop an outward-oriented economy, there were also some other people who were considering the similar issue. Yuan Geng, the standing vice chairperson of the board of China's Merchant Steam Navigation Co. (CMSN) in Hong Kong, which is a direct subsidiary of the China's Transport Ministry, had just got a new idea. CMSN was then the only enterprise of China's capital with considerable economic force in Hong Kong. Yuan Geng was thinking to build up an industrial zone in Shenzhen, the county town of Bao-an. At the very beginning, the advantages of doing this he thought embraced three aspects. First, it was suitable to build up docks in Shekou, a peninsula of the south end of Shenzhen. Second, Shekou was the nearest place to Hong Kong by sea, so Hong Kong's electric power could be used in this area. Third, to build up a group of enterprises at the nearby of Shenzhen's Xili lake could use the water source conveniently and recruit the labour force from inland. Bao-an, is the hometown of Yuan Geng, he left there to join revolution in the 1930s. By the end of 1970s, he was very shocked at the sight of the poverty of his hometown when he came back to have an inspection. As Yuan Geng returned to Hong Kong he happened to meet Ye Fei, the deputy minister of Transportation, who had just finished his investigation trip in West Germany. Yuan Geng talked over his idea with Ye Fei and obtained full support from the latter (Jiang, W. 1981, p. 4; Chan, T. *et al.* 1986, pp. 88-

91). Thus, Ye Fei immediately left for Guangzhou from Hong Kong, to meet Guangdong's major leaders to specially discuss the issue that CMSN in Hong Kong should set up an industrial zone in Shekou of Shenzhen.

The ideas of the Transport Ministry and Guangdong province fitted together easily. In promoting this programme, Xi Zhongxun and Yang Shangkun, then the provincial first and second party secretaries respectively, were the firm advocators. So later they were identified as early supporters of SEZs (Chan, T. *et al.* 1986, p. 88), and Xi was referred to as 'one of the founders of China's SEZs' (CEYB, 1986, p. 18). Both of Transport Ministry and Guangdong province considered that in the situation in which China had embarked on the reform and opening-up, Guangdong, being in a good location and possessing some better conditions, should be able to open as soon as possible by using these advantages. Hence, on 6 Jan 1979, these two sides jointly submitted a report to the State Council, which formally put forward a request to build up an industrial zone in Shekou. In this report, they stated the advantages as, 'it can not only utilise the land and labour force in home which are relatively cheaper, but will be also convenient to absorb the foreign capital, advanced technology, and raw materials. To combine these advantages of two sides will give great impetus on the accomplishment of the modernisation of China's transportation and navigation and the promoting of the industrial construction of Bao-an county and Guangdong province as well' (Ni Tu, 1994c, p. 10).

The idea of setting up a production zone in Bao-an and Zhuhai of Guangdong province aimed at increasing exports, also came from an economic investigation group visiting to Hong Kong and Macao dispatched by the State Council. In this group's investigation report, submitted at the end of June, 1979, one of the main suggestions was to mark off Bao-an and Zhuhai which are adjacent to Hong Kong and Macao, as export-orientated bases. The target of setting up these zones is to build up the outside-toward production bases to a considerable high level, and provide attractive sight-seeing zones for the tourists from Hong Kong and Macao, after three or five years' hard efforts (ibid. 1994b, p. 9).

The facts mentioned above indicated that within the first half of 1979, there had been three groups of China's higher level officials considering the idea of setting up the export-oriented or industrial zone in Guangdong province. They were: the economic investigation group to Hong Kong and Macao sent by the State Council, the Ministry of Transport and its direct subsidiary CMSN in Hong Kong, and the Party Committee of Guangdong province. This background showed that the idea of opening the door of the country as soon as possible and developing close economic relations with the outside world had been not only the determination of the Central leaders, but had also become the common view and concrete action of those senior officials and local leaders.

6.2.2 The second stage: deepening and finalising of the scheme

The joint report submitted by Guangdong authority and the Transport Ministry aroused great attention from the central leaders. Li Xiannian, the vice Chairman of CPC Central Committee and the deputy premier, then in charge of the day-to-day work of the CPC Centre, carefully studied the report with Gu Mu, the then deputy premier in charge of economy and foreign trade, and immediately decided to invite Peng Deqing, the Minister of Transport and Yuan Geng, the deputy Chairperson of the board of CMSN in Hong Kong, to discuss the issue face to face.

Just before this meeting, also in Jan. 1979, when Xi Zhongxun, the first secretary of the Party Committee and governor of Guangdong province, arrived at Beijing to report Guangdong's work to the Centre, he had clearly asked Centre to give Guangdong more autonomy and allow Guangdong to refer to the successful experience of the 'Four Small Dragons' of Asia, to try an experiment of setting up export zones in Guangdong. Guangdong's bold idea obtained support from many central leaders.

An important meeting to discuss the joint report, presided over by the vice Chairman Li Xiannian, joined by Gu Mu, Peng Deqing and Yuan Geng, was held on 31 Jan. 1979, in Zhong Nanhai (the place of the CPC Centre and the State Council) (Ni Tu, 1994c). At that moment, as the chief leader in charge of the state's economy, Li Xiannian thought not only to mark off a small area to set up an industrial zone or export zone, but to find a way and a place to make a breakthrough so as to promote the reform and opening-up of the entire coastal areas. Therefore, when Yuan Geng finished his introduction about their plan and asked Li to give a small piece of land for their construction, Li definitely confirmed the necessity of setting up this zone, and further emphasised the significance of this direction. He pointed out that there was a need to combine the superiority of Hong Kong and inland and make a full use of foreign capital. It was not only Guangdong that must do this. Fujian province, Shanghai and other places should also consider it. Thus he agreed to give the whole peninsula of Shekou in Bao-an county to CMSN for its industrial zone construction. Yuan Geng was surprised to hear Li's offer, for he originally was only going to ask for a small piece of land of about two square kilometres. Then, Li said, for formulating some special policies for this zone, it was essential to have discussions with all those related organs, i.e., the State Custom, Financial Ministry and the State Bank, etc. Finally, Li Xiannian wrote down his opinion on the joint report. It said, 'Approved in principle. Would comrade Gu Mu hold another meeting with those related comrades for further discussion, and then implement according to this resolution' (ibid. p. 11).

Only one day later, on the 2nd Feb., according to Li Xiannian's instructions, Gu Mu presided over a special meeting to work out the essential policies for the industrial zone which would be set up. The participants in this meeting, included Yuan Geng and all those senior officials in chief from the State Planning Commission, the State Construction Commission, Foreign Trade Ministry, Financial Ministry, Transport Ministry and the People's Bank. Gu Mu firstly stated the purpose of this meeting and the relevant instructions of the central leaders. He stressed that in the light of Deng Xiaoping's opinion, Guangdong and Fujian provinces should enjoy more opening policies. Gu Mu pointed out that in order to develop the industrial zone in Shekou, there was a need to grant some special policies, namely to give it a special status like Hong Kong, such as the freedom of import and export.

Then, Yuan Geng presented the main issues of his idea that including the context, conditions and possibilities. He first summarised the 107 years' history of CMSN and analysed its experiences and lessons, and also the feasibility of its further development in the near future. He talked especially about the grave lessons that China had learned after missing a golden opportunity to use the international idle funds for China's economic construction in the mid-1950s, which has been discussed above.

As for explaining why CMSN did not attempt to build up the export base in Hong Kong, Yuan Geng listed three main reasons (ibid. p. 12) (1) The land price was too expensive. In central Hong Kong, one square foot cost HK $ 15,000, which was only second to the Silver Place area of Tokyo. Even the land for industrial use in the suburbs cost at least HK $ 500 for one square foot. (2) The banks' interest rates of loan were too high. (3) Labour costs were too high. Therefore, it was quite difficult for CMSN to accomplish the financial target of expanding foreign trade and increasing foreign exchanges which were determined by the central government. Yuan Geng said, that after carefully studying Hong Kong's economic situation CMSN reported to its higher authority and also discussed with Guangdong Party Committee, and finally reached a common viewpoint. That is, to make full use of the land and the labour in Guangdong's territory adjacent to Hong Kong, and use Hong Kong and foreign countries' capital, technology, blueprints, data, patents, and the complete set of equipment, by combining which it will posses the advantages of both Hong Kong and inland while avoiding the disadvantages of building up enterprises in Hong Kong. Yuan Geng stressed that these are the advantages that no Hong Kong financial group can obtain.[1]

Finally, Yuan Geng concretely introduced the idea about the export base which are fivefold. (1) The ownership of the land and enterprises, and also the power of the administration should belong to the state. (2) Guangdong province should appoint administrative personnel which would be in charge of the running of the zone. (3) Hong Kong's managerial mode would be used to run the enterprises by CMSN. (4) They should export the products of this zone's enterprises through Hong Kong, in order to repay the foreign debt and the foreign investment. (5) To build up this industrial zone would not use even one yuan (the unit of China's currency) of the State's Financial Ministry and the State Bank, but only ask for remission of tax for 10-15 years, and after that all profits obtained from this zone would be completely turned over to the State. Regarding to the types of enterprises which will be build up in the first stage, Yuan Geng listed about six which all related to the navigation.

After Yuan Geng's introduction, the other participants of the meeting gave their opinions according to their respective working field. They basically agreed with Yuan's suggestion and plan, and further studied the concrete policies which should be formulated for this new zone. The main ideas of this discussion focused on the following aspects (ibid.).

- Reference would be made to Hong Kong's method of levying income tax.
- Most of the products of this zone should be exported, so as to repay the debt which came from foreign capital; the state would not give any funds.
- If the products of this zone were sold inland, they would be treated as imports and import tax must be levied.

- To consult some foreign free trade zone, by which to map out a law to be used in this zone.
- The administration of this zone must follow economic law, with reducing the state's intervention in economic activities.

To summarise, the basic principle had been decided in this meeting. Gu Mu finally emphasised that Deng Xiaoping thought not only Bao-an and Zhuhai could do this, but other counties of Guangdong and Fujian provinces could also do the same. This obviously indicated that the central government would allow the CMSN in Hong Kong to build up an industrial zone in Shekou not only to solve the problem of CMSN, but also to let CMSN go ahead first, thus achieving some experience for the large-scale action launched later. During the course of this meeting, Gu Mu referred three times to Deng Xiaoping's opinion which showed that Deng had given much attention to this issue.

6.2.3 The third stage: the determination, legitimisation and implementation of the SEZ strategy

In April, 1979, when Xi Zhongxun and Yang Shangkun, the first and second secretaries respectively of Guangdong provincial Party Committee, attended the Central Work Conference in Beijing, Xi was asked to directly report on their plan to Deng Xiaoping and other central leaders. Xi's report again focused on requesting the centre to give permission to Guangdong to mark off certain areas in Shenzhen, Zhuhai and Santou, as 'co-operative trade zones' in which to develop their outward-oriented economy, mainly depending on absorbing the investment from Hong Kong, Macao and foreign countries. Xi stressed that the production of these zones would be operated in the light of the demands of the international market, and these areas would be administrated separately.

Deng Xiaoping supported Xi's ideas. When discussing an exact name for these zones, Deng suggested the name of 'Special Zones'. Deng said, 'We can mark off some pieces of zones, call them special zones. In the past, the Shan-Gan-Ning Border Region was just the Special Zone.[2] The central government has no money, so your people need to look after themselves. It must to fight a bloody way as breakthrough!' (Ni Tu, 1994c, p. 14). Deng's last word fully highlighted the centre's determination and the significance of doing this.

Soon after the central work conference, in the middle of May, Gu Mu was dispatched with a working group, to engage in an investigation of the feasibility of setting up SEZs in Guangdong and Fujian provinces, and to help these two provinces to map out the request reports for implementing special policies and adopting flexible measures. Then, on 15 July of the same year, CPC Centre and the State Council formally ratified the two reports from Guangdong and Fujian and circulated them to all ministries and provinces. This was the well-known Centre's No. 50 document, which signalled the rising of China's SEZs. In this important document the Centre had clearly announced that some special policies and flexible measures were to be implemented for the outside-toward economic activities in Guangdong and Fujian provinces, and granted the local authorities more autonomy so as to enable them to give full play to their superiority by which to grasp the advantaged international situation; then to go one step ahead to strive for a remarkable economic development. As for setting up industrial zones, the document approved that, 'to firstly try experiment in Shenzhen and Zhuhai, and then after obtaining experiences to consider expansion into Santou and Xiamen' (Wang, Z. 1995, p. 8).

Hence, the Shekou (in Shenzhen) industrial zone formally started construction in July 1979. To sum up, the period from mid-1978 to mid-1979 witnessed a series of development of the idea of setting up SEZs. This idea came from different aspects and experienced an important deepening course. In March 1980, nine months after embarking on the Shekou zone, Gu Mu was dispatched again to Guangzhou to preside over a conference for discussing the issues of initiating the SEZs. The participants to this conference included the leaders and scholars from Guangdong and Fujian provinces. In May, the summary of this conference was ratified by the CPC Centre and the State Council. One important issue in this document was that the name of the new industrial zone was formally confirmed as 'Special Economic Zone', instead of 'export special zone' as original decided.

Five months later, in 26 August 1980, the fifteenth session of the Fifth Standing Committee of the National People's Congress formally approved 'The Regulation of the Guangdong Special economic Zones' set forth by the State Council, and publicly announced that China set up the SEZs in Shenzhen, Zhuhai, Santou and Xiamen (SOCSC, 1988, p. 730). From then onward, the setting up of SEZs in China possessed a legitimacy granted by the State's law.

Since the general direction and policies had been determined, the construction of China's SEZs therefore went faster. In October 1980,

Zhuhai SEZ began to be set up. From May to June of 1981, the State Council convened a Working Conference on SEZs in Guangdong and Fujian provinces, which inspected and summarised the works of initiating the SEZs and studied the measures for further implementing the Centre's instruction. In July, CPC Centre and the State Council approved the summary of this conference, and stated that to attempt the experiment of setting up SEZs must further emancipate the mind and lead to the adoption of special policies and flexible measures. In addition, this document concretely stipulated the developing directions of the four SEZs (including Xiamen and Santou, which were set up soon) (Wang, R. 1995, p. 944). This document laid a foundation for a complete set of the Special policies and measures for the SEZs. In October 1981, Xiamen SEZ started building. In November, Santou SEZ began construction, which signalled the start of the overall construction of the first group of SEZs.

The size of the SEZs increased several times after they were initiated. The area of Shenzhen SEZ is 327.5 square kilometres, which accounts for 16.21 percent of the total area of Shenzhen. There is an administrative line which lies 84.6 kilometres long between the SEZ and non-SEZ region. Originally, the area of Zhuhai SEZ was only 6.81 square kilometres; in June 1983, the SEZ's area was expanded to 15.56 square kilometres; finally, in April 1988, the State Council approved the expansion of this SEZ area to 121 square kilometres, which embraces all the town area of the city. At the very beginning, only 2.5 square kilometres was marked off as Xiamen SEZ; in 1984, a decision was made to expand the SEZ to the whole Xiamen island (including Gulang islet), which covers 131 square kilometres. In May 1989, a special investment zone was marked off for the Taiwan businessmen, which contains the whole Xiamen SEZ and two other regions (Xinglin and Haichang). The area of Xinglin and Haichang is 126.64 square kilometres (CYB, 1992, pp. 560-4).

Notes

[1]   With the development of the opening-up course, later, Hong Kong's local businessmen began to invest in inland of China and they then got same advantages of land and labour with lower prices.

[2]   This Border Region was set up by the CPC during the anti-Japan War, in the Northwest China.

7 Policy-making for establishing the largest SEZ — Hainan

Hainan SEZ, compared with other China's SEZs, has five major characteristics: it is the largest SEZ of China, which is 65 times as great as the total areas of the first group of SEZs; it was set up as a SEZ at the same time as it was defined as a new separate province from an Administrative Region; its entire province is a SEZ, unlike other SEZs which are only a city or a part of a city; it is a huge island; and, it possesses very rich natural sources but was in a very backward situation economically and culturally before it started to be opened to the outside world in the early 1980s. The establishment and development of the SEZ in Hainan experienced a long period with many twists and turns, and even some great setbacks, which had shocked people at home and abroad.

7.1 A brief introduction of setting up SEZ in Hainan

The fact that the entire Hainan province — the whole island was defined as a SEZ, indicated the special significance of this unusual strategy for China to accelerate its opening course and its economic development. For understanding this it is essential to firstly see the basic conditions of this island, its location, natural resources and environment, as well as other relevant information.

7.1.1 Some features of Hainan Island

Hainan is a beautiful island, which is like a bright pearl inlaid in the South China Sea. Its features can be summarised as four aspects.

An ideal location and a wide territory Situated between the South China Sea and the Baibu Gulf, Hainan Island faces Leizhou Peninsula across the Qiongzhou Strait. Hainan is a tropical and subtropical area. Its average annual temperature is between 22°c and 26°c, and its rainfall is about 2000 mm a year. These conditions are very good for agriculture. As China's second largest island, Hainan's area is 34,000 square km, only a little smaller than Taiwan which covers an area of 36,000 square km. The sea area of Hainan is over 2 million square km. Hainan is good for international transportation by sea, for its 1500 km coastline is dotted with over 60 well equipped harbours, and it is convenient to Hong Kong, Taiwan, Japan and other Southeast Asia countries and regions, so it could very well become an important shipping centre for the Asia-Pacific region (Yang, X. 1988, p. 14).

A treasure island with rich resources   Hainan's rich resources include minerals, tropical plants and marine products. Its mineral resources are more than fifty sorts. The reserves of these minerals are very rich, such as, iron reserves of 316 million tons; and those of titanium of 18.6 million tons; bauxite 22.28 million tons; lime 2500 millions; quartzite 50 million tons; brown coal 170 million tons; oil shale 2800 million tons; etc. Its energy resources also attracted people's great attention: the reserve of petroleum is estimated at one billion tons while the natural gas is over 200 billion cubic metres; the potential of hydroelectric resources is put at 650,000 kilowatt, as compared with the current 128,000 kilowatt (Chao, Y. 1987, pp. 7-8).

The resources of Hainan's tropical plants are above all rubbers; it produces upwards 130,000 tons a year, about half China's total output. Pepper and coffee are also important products of Hainan's farming. Other economic crops, including sugar-cane, tea, oil cashews, sisal hemp, pineapple, lychees, mangoes, bananas, lemons, and oranges are all produced on a considerable scale.

Hainan's major marine products include groupers, Spanish mackerel, silver pomfrey, hairtails, ink fish, abalone, tuna, lobsters, green turtles, sea cucumber, sea horses and agaragar. Annual catches amount to about 100,000 tons. Specialists estimate that the water around Hainan Island is 100-200 metres deep, with potential annual catches of over 200,000 tons (CYB, 1992, p. 499;Yang, X. 1988, p. 15).

A wonderful tourist area   Hainan's tourism potential is one of its most important resources. The beaches are superb, particularly at Sawan. The Dadong Offshore Bathing Grounds are well-known, and the Yalongwan's seven kilometres magnificent coastline scattered with white sand beaches is very attractive, the annual average temperature of the surrounding water is 20 °c. These conditions indicate that they are among the best beaches in the world. In 1986, Zhao Zhiyang, then premier, suggested making tourism one of the main industries and the main force in the island's economy (CYB, 1992, p. 499; Yang, X. ibid. p. 16).

A poor development island Although possessing a very nice natural environment and rich resources, Hainan had been in a poverty-stricken situation for most of its history. As it is far from China's hinterland, it was called 'the end of the earth' since ancient times, and was once a place for exiled prisoners for a long period. Even after the founding of PRC, it was only an outpost for national defence, and was not considered as an economic development base. Before 1980s, in this island, the rural populace accounted for 80 percent of the total population. In 1978, the annual per capita income of rural populace was only 56 yuans RMB, which is equivalent to US $ 33.30 at that time (Chao, Y. 1987, p. 8). Since 1960s, the economy of those countries and regions surrounding the Hainan Island, such as Singapore, Japan, Hong Kong, Taiwan, developed very fast, making Hainan become the most backward and undeveloped area of the Asia-Pacific region. This unfortunate situation of Hainan was indeed in sharp contrast to its excellent natural environment and rich nature resources.

7.1.2 The relations between turning Hainan into a separate province and establishing a SEZ

Hainan's poverty is indeed not worthy of its name of the Treasure Island. One of the major reasons causing this unfortunate situation is that, its development and construction had never been given enough importance owing to its status in the old administrative system and structure. As a huge island, Hainan is a relatively independent geographic unit and economic region, but its status was only an administrative region belonging to Guangdong province. According to Hainan's features, it should have had certain autonomy to deal with its own affairs in the light of its concrete situation, but it had never obtained this power. On the other hand, however, due to its lower administrative status, the remote position, and the existence of a huge farming and mineral industry systems directly controlled by the central ministries, it had also not got enough guidance and support from the province. In other words, Hainan was neither being led directly by the Centre, nor obtaining full consideration and help from Guangdong province. Guangdong province, actually, did not have the full power and ability to tackle Hainan's problems fundamentally. In short, Hainan's administrative status had not been suitable for the demands of its development for a long time. Therefore, to grant Hainan a separate provincial status had become a prerequisite to promote Hainan's economic development, and also a prerequisite of setting up SEZ in Hainan. This issue is rather complex, hence further discussion will be given later.

7.1.3 A tortuous road towards setting up the SEZ

Due to the very special conditions and background, the establishment of SEZ in Hainan experienced a very tortuous process, in which three tides appeared:

- the first tide, from 1980 to 1983, when Hainan was a quasi SEZ;
- the second tide, from 1983 to 1987, when Hainan was a SEZ without' an official SEZ status;
- the third tide, from 1988 onward, when Hainan became a new province and a real SEZ.

By tracing this course we can see how complex and prolonged the decision-making was towards the final target of setting up the SEZ, in which various factors were effective.

7.2 The first opening wave — Hainan as a quasi SEZ

The idea to defining Hainan as a SEZ and a separate province did not appear suddenly, instead, it was produced in an incremental way. At the very beginning, the general policy for Hainan's development was just to open to the outside world, which was raised in 1980 when China's economic reform had been launched and the construction of the first group of SEZs was in its process.

According to the instruction of the State Council's leaders, a forum about the development of Hainan Island was convened from 30 June to 11 July in 1980, in Beijing. This forum further affirmed the significance of Hainan's economic development, and explored ways and policies to develop Hainan (Zhong, Y. 1989, pp. 150-1). The participants fully discussed the *status quo* of Hainan and their reasons, and finally reached an assessment. It was pointed out that during the first three decades of the PRC, although some certain economic achievements in Hainan had been obtained, its development was actually too slow, the whole economic conditions were too poor, the people's living standard was in a very low level, the local government had very little reserve financial force, and its ability to develop social production was very limited. This situation arose mainly because good strategies and policies for Hainan's development had never been formulated. However, Hainan has a great potential for its development, as long as it were able to draw on lessens from the historical experiences conscientiously and well adjust the developing direction and strategy, a faster development in Hainan's construction could be expected.

Zhao Zhiyang, then premier, in the reporting meeting of the forum on 8 July, clearly stated that some special policies had been defined for implementation in Guangdong, and wanted the provincial leaders to consider giving Hainan a certain autonomy for its foreign trade, to allow Hainan directly to export the products of its tropical crops and distribute a part of its foreign exchange income to it. Zhao's instruction actually pointed out the direction of making policies for Hainan, namely, to grant it more autonomy, give it more relaxed policies, so as to enable Hainan itself to play a full part in developing its economy rapidly. Two weeks after this forum, the State Council ratified and circulated 'The Summary of the Forum about Hainan Issues' in 24 July, which is the first important document — State Council [1980] No.202 document. This document stressed that, at present 'Hainan's task which is to stimulate the economic development mainly depends on both enforcing and relaxing the policies.' Of these policies, the first one is, 'for the import and export trade, its main target is exporting to Hong Kong; to grant Hainan some greater autonomy; the method of Hainan's foreign economic activities could be referred to those of Shenzhen and Zhuhai, giving them greater power; the increasing part of its foreign exchanges income from foreign trade and others, could be kept more by Hainan so as to benefit its further development' (Zhong, Y. 1989, p. 151).

This No.202 document is the first one to set forth the issue of opening Hainan to the outside world and developing its outward-oriented economy, which formally pulled off the prologue of Hainan's opening. Since the special policy had been confirmed that the principles of Hainan foreign economic activity could be referred to the first group of SEZs, Hainan had actually got a 'Quasi SEZ' status from then on.

Unfortunately, this first opening wave in Hainan, pushed by the No. 202 document, did not produce the expected fruit. Hainan's opening situation had not really occurred. During the three years from 1980 to 1982, only some 23 agreements of direct investment by the foreign businessmen were signed, which introduced US $55.02 million by agreement, in which only US $1.95 million were actually used. The total value of Hainan's exports in 1980 was US $ 18.29 million, and recorded US $ 20.27 million in 1982. The annual average rate of increase was only 5.3 percent. It received 21.8 thousand tourists from 1980 to 1982, and created tourism foreign exchanges of only US $ 0.82 million (ibid. pp.151-2). These facts showed that during the first stage of Hainan's opening, the size of the foreign economic activities was very small, the development speed was very slow, and therefore the entire achievement was far from satisfactory.

Actually, this first tide of opening was a defeat. Then, what caused this setback? Gu Mu, then deputy premier, in his letter to Premier Zhao Zhiyang in 13 December 1982, argued that The State Council's No. 202 document was correct. But due to the existence of different views about this document from those relevant aspects, some important stipulations in this document (mainly related to the foreign economic activity) had actually not been implemented (Zhong, Y. ibid. P. 164).

Further analysing the setback of this stage, more reasons could be found. Firstly, the urgency of developing Hainan had not been fully realised by the central leaders, therefore, the issue of developing and opening Hainan had not been put on the most important agenda of the Party Centre. Secondly, due to the background of a special period when China's national economy was in the course of adjustment, the state could not invest enough funds to support Hainan. Thirdly, since the national opening situation was just coming to being, the first group of SEZs was in the initial stage, many relevant ways to develop an opening economy were in the course of probing and adjusting, so there were no mature experiences which could be drawn on to guide Hainan's development. To launch a large-scale construction with an opening strategy in such a wide region like Hainan was indeed not an easy thing. Fourthly, since Hainan had been in a closed state for a very long time, when the opening prologue was pulled off, Hainan's own preparation was far from being ready. This point embodies three aspects. (1) The thinking for engaging in the opening economy was not ready among the leaders and cadres, so that they lacked of initiative and creativity to conduct the new works. (2) The personnel preparation was not ready. The issue of the quality of cadres, especially the selection of the leading group had not been really solved. Thus it was impossible for Hainan to make the first good step without a good leading group and a lot of qualified cadres. (3) Hainan's infrastructure was too poor to absorb the foreign investment. For a long period, the construction of the infrastructure in Hainan was ignored, which therefore resulted in a very bad investment environment. From 1952 to 1980, the investment from the state to Hainan was only RMB 43.38 billion yuans, of which the amount used in improving transportation conditions was only 2.5 billion yuans (5.8 percent of the total investment). As the deputy premier Gu Mu said, in December 1982, Hainan's infrastructure is too poor; ports, roads tele-communication conditions were all very backward, most of those overseas Chinese businessmen and foreign businessmen who considered investing in Hainan were deterred by what they found there (ibid. p. 152).

Albeit the first step of Hainan towards the opening was a defeat, its significance is still important, for it definitely was a great historical turning point in Hainan's development. It was the first time Hainan was open to the outside world after thousands years of isolation. Thus, this setback also recorded an important beginning of a new era.

7.3 The second opening wave — a SEZ without the SEZ's status

In late 1982, when Hainan's first opening tide suffered setback, the general situation of China's opening-up was going well, the first group of SEZs had been successfully launched. At this moment, China's top leaders began to devote more attention to Hainan's development.

In October 1982, premier Zhao Zhiyang, in his written instruction on a report, clearly confirmed that, 'Hainan is not to be set up as a SEZ, but it can be granted more autonomy in its foreign economic cooperation. ... Hainan is isolated in the sea, the policies therefore to be implemented there can be more relaxed'. Following his instruction, a series of investigations and studies were conducted (ibid. pp. 153-4). In November, vice premier Wang Zheng presided over a forum in Guangzhou, to discuss the Hainan issue. Then, vice premier Gu Mu, together with Wang Zheng, invited Guangdong's leaders and the relevant officials in chief of the Ministry of Agriculture and Forestry, to further discuss the issue of Hainan's development, in Beijing. In January 1983, Premier Zhao Zhiyang arrived at Hainan to specially convene a forum about Hainan's development. In February, Hu Yaobang, the then General Secretary of the CPC Centre, made an inspection tour during the period of the Spring Festival, Chinese New Year, in Hainan. All these activities showed that the urgency of developing Hainan had commanded China's Central leaders' attention, and they were striving for new ways to promote its development. Under this situation, from late February to early March, 1983, Vice premier Gu Mu called together the officials in chief from the relevant sectors and departments of the State Council, to further study this issue systematically. Then, on 18 March, a meeting of the Standing Committee of the State Council was convened, which formulated a document titled 'A Discussing Summary about Accelerating Hainan's Development and Construction'. Two weeks late, the CPC Centre and the State Council jointly ratified and circulated this 'Summary', which is the CPC Centre [1983] No.11 document, the second milestone of Hainan's opening course. In this document, the issue of Hainan's development and construction had been considered as having a high level of importance among the state's political and economic strategies. It had been considered that to speed up Hainan's development and construction would be not only conducive to supporting the country's modernisation construction and strengthening the nationality unity, but would contribute to strengthening China's state's defence in the South Sea, and promote Taiwan's return to the motherland and complete the course of China's reunification.

This document clearly defined Hainan's development strategy as 'to promote the internal development by opening to the outside world.' It gave Hainan more autonomy in its foreign economic co-operation with more relaxed policies from eight aspects, by which to enable it to be 'a SEZ without a SEZ status'. These special policies included an agreement that Hainan could retain considerable foreign exchanges and use them to import scarce consumer goods including the seventeen categories the import controlled by the state.

As for the fundamental requirements to Hainan, the document stipulated some clear rules. (1) Hainan's development and construction must be based on the resource superiority of the island, with full tapping of the internal potentialities and seeking a better economic structure. (2) To positively and safely utilise the foreign funds, introduce advanced technology, develop import and export trade as well as tourism, so as to promote the internal development by opening to the outside world. (3) That a policy to import those goods which were usually controlled by the state, must be examined and approved strictly; and those import goods could only be used and sold in Hainan Administrative Region; to sell them to outside the Region is not permitted.

In order to be better in implementing the No. 11 document, the Centre asked Hainan to make a general programme for its development. Hence,

Hainan invited over sixty experts from more than thirty different units all over the country, to study and map out Hainan's development scheme with scientific methods. In early September 1984, their research result titled 'A Programme for Hainan's Social and Economic Development (1986-2000)', was formulated. The programme put forth that by the end of 1985 the total industrial productive value should be double its present level; in 1990, a target to double the figure of 1980's total value of industry and agriculture, should be realised; in the year of 2000, Hainan's total GNP should reach US $187.5 billion, so as to enable Hainan to catch up the 1980's level of Taiwan in the three aspects of production development, science and technological advance and people's living standard.

With the guidance of the No.11 document and the Development Programme, Hainan's steps towards a new opening target were accelerated and some distinct achievements were soon obtained. In the four years from 1983 to 1986, some 265 programmes of foreign direct investments were signed, which introduced US $ 1.99 billion by agreement, which was four times as much as the total figure from 1980 to 1982. The total export value in 1983 was US $ 15.77 million, and that of 1986 was US $38.40 million; the annual average increasing rate reached 34.5 percent. From 1983 to 1986, the annual average rate of increase of the total value of the industry and agriculture reached 13.6 percent (CYB, 1988). These fruitful developments showed that during this period both the size and speed of Hainan's opening course and economic construction were considerable.

To be sure, the general situation of Hainan's opening was quite good at that time, a very promising target was to be approached step by step. However, it was just at this very moment, that the 'motorcar incident' which involved some of Hainan's leading cadres, including Lei Yu, the deputy Secretary of CPC Hainan Regional Committee and concurrently a member of CPC Guangdong provincial Committee, was exposed in July 1985. These leaders and officials purchased US $ 570 million worth of foreign exchanges at high rates on the black market outside the island for the import of a huge amount of motor vehicles and other electronic consumer goods from 1 January 1984 to 5 March 1985. These embraced, motorcars 89,000 (over 90 percent of them are cars and mini buses), of which 79,000 had arrived; TVs 2.8 million sets, of which 0.347 million had arrived; Video players 0.252 million sets, of which 0.134 million had arrived; motorcycles 122,000, of which 45,000 arrived. Of all these imported goods, more than 10,000 motorcars and most of others had been resold to the 27 provinces in the mainland at high prices. At the same time, other cadres and departments at Hainan's different levels were also actively involved into this kind of dealing.

The exposure of this illegal trafficking scandal which was the most serious one since the beginning of China's reform programme, shocked those at home and abroad. This 'motorcar incident' seriously violated the stipulation of the No.11 document and the State's relevant administrative rules about foreign exchange, collided with the State's plan and home market, destroyed the State's credit, and also corrupted social values. Moreover, the gravity of this event provided the conservatives with an opportunity to criticise the reform and opening policy. They had opposed such reforms as bringing in capitalist ideology and culture, and causing the increasing of corruption and economic Chaos. This event was seen as a good example for them to prove the correctness of their ideas. After the exposure of this scandal, the leaders who had responsibility for this event were dismissed, some special policies which had been granted to Hainan were taken back, and Hainan became heavily in debt to in excess of RMB 1 billion yuans. More specially, this grave incident caused ideological confusion among Hainan's people. Hence, Hainan's economic development was bogged down in a stagnant state again, and a heavy depression appeared. The enthusiasm of foreign businessmen to engage investment in Hainan reduced greatly. In 1986, only 24 programmes of foreign investment were introduced, with the total value of foreign funds only recorded at US $ 7.77 million by agreement, which made up 6.48 percent of the 1984's figure and 13.5 percent of 1985's figure. In 1986, the total value of Hainan's industry and agriculture only increased 8.9 percent, compared with the figure of 13.6 percent percent as the annual average rate of increase from 1983 to 1986.

These serious consequences indicated that the second opening wave of Hainan had fallen into a low tide. Hainan's road toward opening and development was covered with a heavy shadow again.

7.4 The third opening wave — Hainan became a new province and the largest SEZ

As Hainan sank into the second low tide, the leaders of CPC Centre and the State Council still kept giving it help and support. From 30th October to 6th November 1985, only three months after the exposure of the motorcar incident, vice premier Gu Mu had an inspection trip in Hainan. He reaffirmed that the principles of CPC Centre's No.11 document and the State Council's No.202 document had not changed; the general direction and policy for Hainan that to promote development by opening to the outside world had not been changed. He stressed that Hainan should sum up the experiences and lessons, understand the situation clearly, so as to go ahead with new steps. In the New Year of 1986, Hu Yaobang, the General Secretary of CPC Centre, gave important instructions in Hainan for its development. Later, Premier Zhao Zhiyang and other central leaders also had inspection trips in Hainan, to concretely study the problem Hainan encountered. They held a series of forums to discuss how Hainan should carry out its long-term development strategy which had been formulated, and encouraged Hainan's cadres and masses to re-new their efforts toward further opening and economic development of Hainan, by which to strive for a bright future of Hainan.

Simultaneously, all aspects including the central and local authorities, and experts, scholars in the academic, economic and political circles, were thinking about Hainan's way-out. The lessons of the two setbacks in Hainan had attracted people's attention. Why was it not easy to promote Hainan's opening-up course? Why was it so easy to slip on a wrong way when more relaxed policies and autonomy were being granted to Hainan? With these serious re-thinking, a new idea was being brought to light gradually and shared by more and more people. That is, first, the direction of Hainan's development must be clear, and a corresponding status must be affirmed to develop Hainan's economy with the special policies. Second, according to Hainan's *status quo* and history, the original administrative status had been unsuited to its administration and economic development. Hence, the conclusion should be: to turn Hainan into a new separate province and formally define Hainan as a SEZ as well.

7.4.1 A new strategic step — the whole Hainan Island became a province and a SEZ

Actually, to change Hainan's administrative status to a separate province was not a newly produced idea. This idea had been first set forth in 1887. Some thirty five years later, in 1912, Dr Sun Yixian, the chief leader of China's 1911 Revolution, raised this proposal again. Dr Sun stated five reasons for the necessity of his proposal. (1) It is important for strengthening the state's defence. (2) It will be conducive to developing the rich natural sources. (3) It can promote the cultural development of the island from its very backward base. (4) It is good for home immigration. (5) It is convenient for the administration, for Hainan is quite different compared with Guangdong in respect to custom, tradition and even languages. These reasons appeared correct not only at that time but also at present. Dr Sun therefore thought it would be good for both Hainan and the State if Hainan could be granted provincial status (Zhong, Y. 1989, p. 170). Unfortunately, Dr Sun's proposal was never put on the State's agenda.

During the first three decades of PRC, this issue was never put forward again. In the early 1980s, with the development of Hainan's opening-up, the inadaptability of Hainan's administrative status became more and more prominent and came to the attention of the authority. On 31 May 1984, the Second Session of the Sixth National People Conference discussed and adopted the State Council's motion of establishing the People's Government of Hainan Administrative Region, and determined to set up the People's Conference and the People's government in Hainan Administrative Region, which are the first level local regime authorities of the state. After the motorcar incident, according to the State Council's instruction, the State Planning Commission agreed to give Hainan a separate planning account within the state's planning system, to allow it to have the same status as the provinces, autonomous regions and municipalities which directly leaded by Centre,[1] and granted Hainan the same power as a province for its economic administration.

Finally, with great efforts which came from many aspects, the State Council formally put forward the proposal to annul the Hainan Administrative Region and establish Hainan province, in August 1987. This proposal suggested that to turn Hainan into a province could benefit by simplifying the administration and improving work efficiency, by reducing middle links and giving the more local power, and could be conducive to implementing more relaxation and more flexible policies in Hainan, and also benefit to the whole country to support Hainan. In short, it will enable Hainan to develop faster by making full play of its own superiority.

On 13 April 1988, the First Session of the seventh NPC adopted the State Council's proposal and formally decided to annul the Hainan Administrative region and establish Hainan province, and to set up SEZ in the whole Hainan province (ED, 14 April 1988, p. 1).

Some 8 years had passed since Hainan started its opening course which experienced many setbacks, in which changes occurred in determining its direction, and now Hainan at last was given its SEZ and Provincial status.

The Central authority finally realised the significance and urgency of clearly defining Hainan's suitable position for its economic development and the improvement of its administration.

With the defining of the status of both province and SEZ, Hainan was granted some more special policies. The major principles of these policies included: Hainan being allowed to conduct the political system reform of trying to set up the system of 'small government and big society', and conduct the economic system reform which did not rely mainly on the development of the public-ownership economic sectors (Qu Zhang, 1989, p.4). In addition, to the basic policy to develop Hainan namely 'to promote development by opening to the outside world', which was put forward at early 1983, was added 'to promote opening by reform' (Zhong, Y. 1989, p.158). This meant that in order to meet the demands of the new situation of the third turn of Hainan's opening tide, the central authority had formally raised its target to thoroughly reform those relations and superstructures which did not adapt to the development of social production, and thus build Hainan into the SEZ and province with new features.

In mapping out the new scheme of Hainan's economic development, Hainan's leaders put forward a key project — the Yangpu programme, for which the policy-making process had been considerably delayed because of controversy.

7.4.2 Yangpu programme — a key project of Hainan SEZ course

Since the general direction and policies had been determined, it was now necessary to consider what Hainan should do to create the appropriate conditions for its economic development as a new SEZ. At the very beginning, Hainan province proposed three alternatives. The first was that a zone should be set up to push the province into the world market and make it a special bond district. The second one was that a few places should be chosen for development, breaking through restrictive policies which were still in existence in the province. These places, as the 'head of the Dragon', would push forward the province's economy. The third alternative was that the province remain unchanged, with the economy neither stagnating nor flourishing. Hainan policy makers finally opted for the second proposal, and chose Yangpu as their experimental target (BR, No. 41/1992, p. 29).

The raising of the scheme for developing Yangpu in September 1988, was an important event in Hainan's opening course. However, it was not foreseen that the programme would suffer a serious set back and that the resulting issues would be hotly debated making Hainan the focus of attention both at home and abroad again.

Located in Danxian County which in the north-western part of Hainan province, Yangpu is a peninsula covering 150 square km, which possesses superior conditions for the construction of an economic development zone. Surrounding by the sea on three sides, Yangpu is a natural harbour with a coastline of 110 km. Its harbours are deep, wide and silt-free. According to the surveys, some 26 berths for vessels of at least 10,000 tons can be built in the area. The largest dock capacity would be some 100,000 tons. Experts pointed out that this area, located in the Asia-Pacific economic and the international shipping lane centre, could be developed into a major distribution centre for international goods (PD, 14, March 1992, p. 1).

Additionally, there are rich resources at the nearby area of Yangpu. The reserves of natural gas and petroleum are plentiful. There are also other important mineral resources which could provide energy and making building materials. Moreover, Yangpu's flat terrain, a reasonable amount of earth and thick bedrock layer, are ideal conditions for building a city and factories (BR, No. 41/1992, p. 29.).

All those people with foresight include the major new leaders of Hainan province and the foreign businessmen had envisioned the great development future of Yangpu. However, to embark on the construction of Yangpu firstly needed heavy capital investment which was surely the main problem of the new province and the new SEZ.

Nevertheless, Hainan's leaders were no longer willing to wait, headed by Xu Shijie, the provincial party secretary, they defined a principle to lease the land of Yangpu — a whole stretch of land to the foreign investors, and then allow them to undertake Yangpu's development. They attempted to try this experiment of allowing foreign businessmen to contract for entire development of the land, by which to promote the development of the entire Hainan. After conducting many negotiations the province signed a contract with Kumagaya-Gumi (Hong Kong) Co. Ltd. (referred to as KGHK Ltd hereafter) for developing and using of 30 square km of Yangpu's land by the latter. The Chinese side would lease the land and be responsible for administration and law enforcement, and the other side would have the full management rights for development and enjoy 'free harbour' policies like those in force in some countries. At the beginning, the investor was exclusively the KGHK Ltd. which had full rights to develop Yangpu, but later, Yangpu's development was jointly participated in by some seven companies, headed by KGHK Ltd. and others came from Hong Kong, Taiwan and mainland of China (BR, No. 42/1991, p. 29; No. 41/1992, p. 29; Jiang, S. 1996, p. 2). It was believed that the successful development of Yangpu would be a locomotive of growth for the largely agricultural-based and sparsely populated island of 6.6 million (Cheng, E. 1992, p. 65).

The Yangpu programme immediately attracted much attentions both from the media and from society in general. Some people who had conservative ideas toward the reform and opening-up cause viewed this programme with sceptical attitudes from the very beginning. The emergence of those strong criticisms soon caused many disturbances.

7.4.3 The breaking out of the 'Yangpu Incident'

Only a few months after the raising of the programme for developing Yangpu, which was later called 'Yangpu Mode', much contention followed its publication in early 1989.

On 18 January 1989, a small group of the committee members of the Chinese People's Political Consultative Conference (CPPCC), headed by Zhang Wei, the former president of Shenzhen University, went straightway to Yangpu to conduct an on-the-spot investigation. Knowing this news, Xu Shijie, the provincial Party Secretary, immediately detached Li Huandu, director of the Planning Office of Yangpu Development Zone, to urgently push on with his journey to Yangpu by a specially-sent car, to report the Yangpu development programme to the CPPCC group. Li was asked to try every possible method to catch up with the group to explain the programme in detail. Why was Xu so eager to do this? When this small investigating group, sent by the Committee of Science, Education, Culture and Public Health of CPPCC, arrived in Haikou, the capital of Hainan, it was received directly by its subordinate organ of Hainan. By chance, the main leaders of Hainan province were not then at Haikou, so both Xu Shijie and the governor Liang Xiang, the former mayor of Shenzhen, had no chance to meet this group. Hence, the former lost an opportunity of directly introducing their Yangpu plan to the group, which would have allowed them to thoroughly understand the issue from the angle of the decision makers. Xu worried that if the group could not clearly get to know the essential points and the context of the programme, it would definitely cause misunderstanding and blame, for the programme being new to China was very controversial.

As Director Li hurriedly got to Yangpu at the dawn of 19 January, the small group of CPPCC had finished its inspection and heard the relevant report from other people. Li stated that he was sent by the Party Secretary Xu to report their work to the group when he met Mr Zhang, but Zhang said that the report had already been heard. However, Li did not insist on giving the report again, nor did Mr Zhang ask any more questions. At this moment, the time was just 7:30 am. Then this group left Yangpu in a hurry.

Also on the same day, 19 January 1989, there was an other event that was considered much more important by Hainan's leaders. Only one and a half hours after Zhang Wei's group left Yangpu, Tian Jiyun, the vice premier, came to Yangpu for an inspection, accompanied by Hainan's main leaders including Xu Shijie, and Yu Yuanping, the General Manager of the KGHK Ltd. Vice premier Tian defined the name of this development zone as 'Yangpu Economic Development Zone' when he finished his inspection, Xu Shijie smiled knowing that he had got support from the State Council. He had forgotten the matter of committee member Zhang's inspection, and he did not foresee that Zhang's inspection would cause a 'Yangpu Incident'. On that day, an agreement between Hainan and the KGHK Ltd., for developing Yangpu, was signed (Zhang, J. 1996, pp. 36-7).

Two months later, the 'Yangpu Incident' broke out. On March 25, the Fourth Plenary Session of the Seventh CPPCC had the last meeting for making speeches. Committee member Zhang Wei, the head of the inspection group to Yangpu, was the last speaker. After reporting his investigation at Yangpu, Zhang then strongly criticised Hainan's programme for Yangpu's development. He started his talk from the cession of Hong Kong by Qing Dynasty, and then he pointed out that even this national humiliation has not been avenged, Hainan again is to lease Yangpu, which covers the land of 32 square km, equal to a half of Hong Kong, to foreigners with the very low price of RMB 90 million yuans, which could not be lower. More specially, Zhang emphasised, this foreign business company was from Japan — the same country which invaded China 44 years ago. Zhang censured indignantly that 'Hainan's action was like inviting a wolf into the house and opening the door to robbers!' (Zhang, J. ibid. p. 37).

Zhang's speech, only a few thousand words, was repeatedly punctuated with warm applause. According to the report of a newspaper, this speech was the one with the highest record of receiving applause, in the Fourth Meeting of the Seventh CPPCC (ibid.).

Unquestionably, Zhang's speech and its repercussion aroused great grief and indignation among Hainan's leaders. When Yao Wenxu, the deputy Party Secretary of Hainan, who then was attending the CPPCC meeting, phoned Xu Shijie immediately to tell him the news, Xu was greatly surprised. He had expected that the Yangpu programme would cause contention but he had not foreseen that it would be accused of 'betraying sovereignty' and 'humiliating the State'.

Before Xu Shijie could get time to meet the challenge which was definitely a heavy attack to him, the 'Yangpu Incident' had become an earthquake of magnitude 7, and rapidly spread to the world. Firstly, on March 26, the second day of Zhang's speech, Shanghai's 'Jiefang Daily' (Liberation Daily) published a 'Special News From Beijing', titled 'Five committee members, headed by Zhang Wei, delivered a joint speech to criticise Hainan's leasing a large stretch of territory for a long term at a very low price.' Immediately, the whole country was shocked by this report which was like the explosion of a giant bomb. Over one hundred committee members of CPPCC jointly signed a letter to the State Council urging that the approval of Hainan's report for developing Yangpu must be stopped.

Some newspapers outside China also made a stormy sea stormier over 'Yangpu Incident' issue by prominently reporting this news. On the 'Dagong Daily' (Hong Kong), the report title was: 'Zhang Wei opposed the proposal of allowing Japanese businessmen to contract the development of Yangpu, for it concerned the sovereignty of China'.

Also Hong Kong's 'Ming Daily' reported: 'Yangpu is to be leased to Japan, five committee members strongly opposed, for it will result in the reappearance of the concession which will become a new national humiliation'. The Los Angeles' 'International Daily' reported 'The defence of national honour should not be forgotten when carrying out economic reform. Hainan's action in surrendering sovereignty for monetary gain is an act of betrayal'. On April 22, Shanghai's University students staged a demonstration march. The slogans 'Return our Hainan!' 'Down with the traitor!' were on their placards they held. They shouted loudly their protest as they passed the streets. On May 22, in Xi an, the capital of Shanxi province, the students also held a demonstration march. Their slogan even included 'Indignantly denounce the betraying action of Hainan!' (Zhang, J. ibid. p. 37-8).

All these mentioned above were just like fuel added to a flame, which made the event even more complicated and confused, and cast a shadow on the reform and opening situation of both Hainan and China. The possible failure of the lease of Yangpu made Hainan people feel very uneasy. Many of those people including technicians, researchers, and university graduates, etc. who came from the mainland to work in Hainan were prepared to leave the island (Xie, B. 1991, p. 552). For seeking the solution of this contention about 'Yangpu Model', which constituted one of the main reasons for delaying decision-making, some great efforts were contributed from different aspects.

7.4.4 The efforts toward saving the Yangpu programme

When Xu Shijie got to read the reports in the newspapers, he smote the table and rose to his feet immediately, and stated that he must strike back to this attack. Needless to say, Xu could not endure this censure. He had left school and joined the revolution when he was eighteen; he participated in the War of Resistance against Japan and the Liberation War; and he had been a political commissar of a guerrilla force. He did all these, even risking his life, just to defend China's sovereignty and integrity and to set up new China by driving out the invaders and throwing down the reactionaries. But now he was censured for betraying China's sovereignty when he was doing his best to accelerate Hainan's economic development. No words could describe how complex and confused of his frame of mind was at that moment.

On the evening of 26 March, Xu decided to see Wang Zheng, the vice president of the State. He asked his secretary to print the report about the context and reasons for Hainan's development with giant characters. Only a few days before the breaking out of the 'Yangpu Incident', Wang Zheng, accompanied by Xu Shijie, met Yu Yuanping, the general manager of the KGHK Ltd., for the matter of Yangpu development. Xu remembered how Wang gave full support to the Yangpu project. When Yu Yuanping said that 'President Wang, I have been all ready for the work. I will start the construction as soon as Beijing grants approval.' Wang answered, 'That's all right! I guarantee that...' Therefore, in this emergent moment, Xu was keen to see Wang to seek his support, and he also wanted to inform Yang Shangkun, the president of the State, and Deng Xiaoping, through Wang.

Since Wang was out when they went to his home at about 10:00 p.m. at night, Xu left the report. Very soon, Xu got Wang's written instruction on his report. It said, 'The development of Yangpu which covers 30 square km, to be contracted by KGHK Ltd is entirely feasible. So I suggest that the Party Centre and the State Council give ratification' (Zhang, J. 1996, p. 39). Meanwhile, Xu's other copy of the report had been submitted to Yang Shangkun, the State President, who promised to pass it to Deng Xiaoping.

On April 6, ten days after the happening of the 'Yangpu Incident', the CPC Centre held a special work conference, to solve the Yangpu issue. At this meeting, Xu Shijie got an opportunity, in the presence of those central and provincial leaders, to state his viewpoints in an all-round way. He explained the detail of the ideas and reasons of the Hainan provincial party committee to lease Yangpu to the foreign company, and criticised the media for incorrectly reporting on the true position and disregarding the consequences; meanwhile, he listed many cases in the world about the land's dealing that not to be linked with the state's sovereignty.

Xu's speech lasted for about half an hour. Then, vice premier Tian Jiyun delivered a speech. Tian argued that the pattern of the Yangpu programme is accordance with the revised constitution and the policy that the State Council granted to Hainan, namely that to sell land and to develop a tract of land for 70 years are in compliance with the law. Hainan should not be given the cap of 'betraying the country' (ibid. p. 40).

Shanghai's leader of the Party committee (possibly Jiang Zemin, then the Party Secretary of Shanghai) held that nothing was wrong with Hainan's programme, Shanghai would do likewise to develop Pudong. Li Ruihuan, then Party Secretary of Tianjing, now the president of CPPCC, stated that Hainan's model is of benefit, Tianjing also wanted to lease the land by payment to allow foreigners to develop the tract of land; since we have no money ourselves to conduct the development; it would be good if our country could allocated the funds to us (ibid.).

Hearing this supporting opinion, Xu and his colleagues felt some relief. After this conference, Xu and Yao (Hainan's deputy party secretary) did not return to Hainan straightway, instead, they went to Shenzhen to meet Mr Yu Yuanping, the general manager of KGHK Ltd, who was invited to Shenzhen from Hong Kong by the former. Since the breaking out of 'Yangpu Incident', Mr Yu had become unsure whether to forge ahead against a swift current or just withdraw from the whirlpool which was linking so many matters that concerned right and wrong, and he found it very difficult to make up his mind. At this moment, Xu told him about the attitudes of several central leaders towards the Yangpu issue, and specially suggested Yu 'never waver in this situation'. Xu's words set Yu's mind at rest (ibid. p. 40).

Mr Yu, sixty-nine at that time, was also a committee member of CPPCC. Although his general company is Japanese, his KGHK Ltd is a Hong Kong-based branch company. During the past twenty years and more, the KGHK Ltd has completed many excellent projects in Hong Kong under his leadership. The fact that Mr Yu was very enthusiastic about developing a tract of land in Yangpu, resulted from his full confidence in China's reform and opening policies, and the full confidence to China's government. Therefore, he was very pleased to be able to complete an important beneficial project for China in the remaining time of his life (Jiang, S. 1996).

More importantly, another item of news made Xu and Hainanese much excited. On April 28 1989, twenty-two days after the central work conference, the hot line phone from Zhongnanhai (the place of CPC Centre) transmitted Deng's written instruction about Yangpu development issue to Hainan, it said,

> After making some investigations, I think the Hainan provincial Party committee's policy-decision is correct. The current opportunities are rare, and the plan should not be postponed. But, explanations should be made to people holding different views both inside and outside the party. The formalities should be completed quickly (Lin, L. 1997, p. 9; Zhang, J. 1996, p. 40).

This written instruction showed Deng's very clear-cut stance in backing up Hainan, as its leaders suffered the censure of 'betraying sovereignty' and 'humiliating the state', and had fallen into trouble. Deng's opinion, with taking a broad and long-term view, was a great support in the crucial moment to Hainan's opening development.

As Yu Yuanping, who was then in Hong Kong, got to know Deng's view, he clearly stated that Deng's words 'It is not good to delay' matches his thinking. He hoped the State Council would ratify Hainan's report as soon as possible, and he stressed that as long as the State Council's 'Red title document'[2] is available, the starting project of Yangpu development will begin at once with firing a gun salute. He guaranteed the project could be in operation in that year, and start production in three years.

Since the latter half of 1989, groups from NPC and CPPCC had inspected Hainan many times. After examining Yangpu's situation concretely, they voiced their support of Hainan's plan to introduce foreign funds to develop a large stretch of land in Yangpu (BR, No. 41/1992, p. 29).

Unfortunately, Deng's instruction and the favourable opinions did not lead to quick ratification of the Yangpu project, to which a long protracted course followed. It was pointed out by a Chinese scholar (Xie, B. 1991, pp. 554-5) that in July 1989, Chinese State Council had approved the lease of Yangpu to the KGHK, but due to other reasons the lease was in suspension. However, this news has not appeared in any official media and publications then and after. In all these relevant official sources it was stated that Yangpu project was approved in March 1992 or the Letter of Intent about the Programme of KGHK LTD's Investing in the Development of YEDZ was signed in September 1991 (see PD, 19, May 1990, p. 1; BR, No. 41/1992; Zhang, J. 1996; Lin, L. 1997, p. 9, etc.). In considering this issue, some questions, which inevitably to be raised, are, if it had been approved in July 1989, why this news could not be released? If it were not convenient to declare at that time due to the political climate, why it still could not mention the fact long time after this event in any official publications and still emphasised that the formal approval was in the early 1992? It seems that even we can not clarify this issue now, the facts have shown us that this policy event did involve sharp contradictions and conflicts, which occurred at high-level policy makers. Actually, even though Yangpu programme did have been ratified by the State council in July 1989, the fact that it could not be publicly confirmed until 1992, and also this approval could not be mentioned then or later indicate the existence of the problem in solving this issue.

During the course of tackling the Yangpu contention, in late 1989, another event occurred. On September 14, Liang Xiang, Hainan's first governor, who had been in his official position for only one year, was announced being dismissed for his corruption, and replaced by Liu Jianfeng, Hainan's former deputy Party Secretary and the former vice-minister in the Ministry of Electronics. Liang, aged seventy, was accused of abusing his power for personal gain: allowing his wife and sons to speculate in property and to import motor vehicles, and arranging for his son to reside in Hong Kong and use public funds to pay for private banquets and even for personal clothing. However, some analysts believed that Liang's removal was mainly because he promoted radical reform and was too close to Zhao Zhiyang, the newly dismissed General Secretary of CPC Centre after the Tiananmen event (Rosario, 1989, p.10). The occurrence of the Liang Xiang incident increased the complexity of the policy-making about Yangpu programme and relevant issues of Hainan.

In this period, some major leaders at the top level still showed their support to Yangpu programme in different occasions. For instance, Jiang Zemin, the General Secretary of the CPC Centre, stated his clear-cut stance in Hainan. From May 12 to 17, 1990, Jiang, accompanied by Xu Shijie, went to Hainan for an inspection. When talking about the construction of Yangpu Economic Development Zone (YEDZ). Jiang clearly confirmed that the Party Centre and the State council supported the whole-stretch-of-land development of Yangpu; introducing foreign funds to develop a tract of land was to be purely commercial, and this could not be linked with harming the sovereignty of China (PD, 19, May 1990, p. 1).

What Jiang stated about the Yangpu issue was the same standpoint of Deng who gave his supporting instruction one year ago. However, after the passing of another year and four months, as 'the Letter of Intent about the Programme of KGHK LTD's Investing in the Development of YEDZ which Covers 30 Square km' was being signed by the representatives of Hainan and KGHK Ltd., on September 16 1991, Xu Shijie, a brave solider in promoting the Yangpu project, the provincial Party Secretary, had passed away a few months before, due to the stomach cancer. Afterwards, the State Council's formal approval for YEDZ's programme was delayed again for another year, until March 9 1992, which indicated a particular conspicuous prolonging decision-making process in China's SEZ course.

As the People's Daily (overseas edition) reported in August 1992: 'Deng Xiaoping's remarks during his tour through South China early this year (1992) have finally put the development of Yangpu on the State agenda. On March 9 1992, a meeting convened by premier Li Peng approved the establishment of the Yangpu economic Development Zone and the use of foreign capital to develop and manage the area' (BR, No. 41/1992, p.29).

This report indicated that Deng, although he had retired, still played a key role in those most important policy-making issues and had the power of final say. On the other hand, however, it could also be found that somehow Deng's opinion could occasionally not be carried out right away by the party Centre and become policy. The fact was that albeit Deng expressed his full support for the Yangpu project in April 1989 on his written instruction, it still took three years for Hainan to finally obtain the formal ratification from the State for its request of Yangpu programme.

Although the Yangpu programme, the key project of Hainan's opening course in its third opening wave, had experienced a lot of troubles, it had eventually been put into operation. According to the State Council plan, YEDZ, the largest programme of introducing foreign capital to Hainan since it was set up as a SEZ, will be built into an export-oriented industrial district based on advanced technology and appropriate development of tertiary industry. It will introduce a tight management system and implement appropriate bonded zone policies in order to provide a good environment for foreign investment and facilitate exports and imports. The General Administration of Customs, the provincial government and other administrative organs will establish offices in the area and exercise unified and effective administrative management and supervision (BR, No.13/1992, p. 30).

After the formal approval of the State Council, the construction of the YEDZ was conducted in an all-round way. By the end of 1995, some RMB 42 billion funds had been invested in this zone's development. The closing of the Yangpu Custom had been ready for a long time. YEDZ was enclosed by a segregated line of colour wire netting which extending 11.4 km (since this zone is surrounded by sea on three sides). The construction of the power station, communication facilities, and the high-grade motor way had been completed. A lot of huge buildings for commercial or residential use were being constructed. Some of them had been finished, such as the thirty-eight-storey, 138m high Yangpu Commercial Building, and a twenty-eight-storey apartment house.

The State and Hainan province also carried out some great and concrete measures to support YEDZ's construction. For instance, the State invested RMB 7.8 billion to build the second term project of the Yangpu port which includes three 10,000 tons deep water berths; Hainan province, with the permit of the State Planing Commission, had started to build the high way from Haikou, the capital of Hainan, to Yangpu, which will cost RMB 22 billion.

The preferential policies, granted by the State Council when YEDZ was set up had been fundamentally in force. So that YEDZ had become a very special zone with the features of both SEZ and the free tariff zone.

Now the situation concerning YEDZ is that, everyone from the leaders at the centre to those at local level now attaches great importance to the programme. Because, 'to develop Yangpu, has been a matter not only related to the business of profit or loss of the contractor, but a concrete symbol of China's opening policy; the promise to Yangpu has been not only the promise of Hainan or some top central leaders, but also the solemn promise of 12 billion Chinese people and the People's Republic of China' (Jiang, S. ibid.).

Notes

1   According to China's economic administrative system which is currently still in force, all those central commissions and ministries only formulate the state plan for allocating resources and setting up budgets at and above the provincial level, each of these provinces, autonomous regions and municipalities directly leaded by centre, and also some particular important cities, therefore has a separate account in central government.

2   Since all the titles of China's print central documents are red, including those of both CPC Centre and the State Council, which are very important in guiding China's political and economic life, so people are accustom to call them as 'red title document'.

8 Policy-making for establishing the Pudong New Zone

The project of developing Pudong area, the east bank of Shanghai's Huangpu River, was formally declared by China's premier Li Peng, in April 18 1990. Then, two years later, in the governmental work report, Li further proclaimed that the Pudong project has been determined as the key point of China's development and opening up strategy in the following ten years, at the Fifth Session of the Seventh NPC, in April 1992.

Concerning the issue of Pudong development, Deng Xiaoping had voiced a self-criticism, also in early 1992. He said, 'Now we look back on the last decade, a big mistake of mine was not choosing Shanghai when establishing the first group of four Special Economic Zones. Otherwise, the Changjiang River Delta area, the whole Changjiang River valley, and even the whole reform situation of the country would have been totally different now' (Deng, 1993, p. 376). Why did China's leaders attach such importance to Pudong's development and opening up to the outside world? It is due to Pudong and Shanghai's particular conditions and status in many ways.

8.1 The advantages of Pudong

The ambitious project of Pudong New Development Zone, is to develop a triangular area adjoining the present city proper, which stretches along the east of Huangpu River, the Southwest of Changjiang (Yangtze) estuary and the north of the Chuanyang River (see figure 8.1). This area is like an isosceles triangle: the top angle is the confluence of Huangpu and Changjiang Rivers; the left base angle is the confluence of the Huangpu and Chuanyang Rivers; and the right base angle is the confluence of the Chuanyang River and the Changjiang estuary. Most of the area is within a radius of 15 km from the heart of Shanghai City. With a population of 1.1 million (1989), Pudong New Zone primarily covers 350 sq. km (Ni Tianzhen, 1992, p.137) which is as big as the present Shanghai downtown

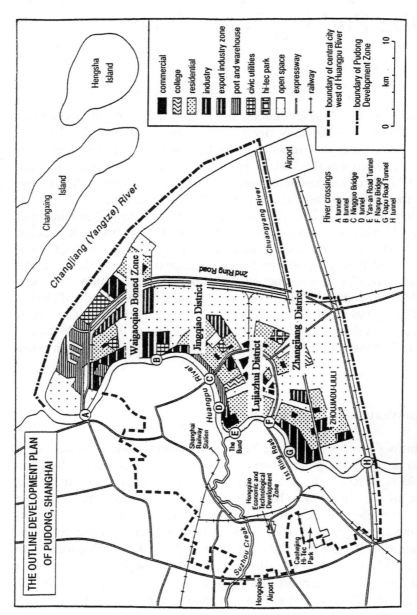

Figure 8.1 The Pudong project: The outline development plan

Source: Tony Binns, 'Shanghai's Pudong Development Project', *Geography*, vol. 76, 1991, October, p. 364

area. Later, the New Zone was enlarged to 522 sq. km. (You Yuwen, 1995, p11).

Skirted by Huangpu River and Changjiang estuary, Pudong can easily develop river and sea transportation because the navigation route surrounding it is more than a dozen metres deep. Meanwhile, the entire area covering several hundreds sq. km has great potential for the development of manufacturing industries and tertiary industries as well.

Besides the good geographic condition, more importantly, Pudong's superiority is being one part of Shanghai municipality. What Shanghai can directly offer, to support Pudong's development from divers aspects, is unmatched by China's other provinces and municipalities. The name of 'Pudong', in Chinese, means the east of the Huangpu River, for 'Pu' indicates Huangpu River, and 'dong' is the east. Puxi, the centre of Shanghai, indicates the west of Huangpu River, for 'xi' is the west in Chinese. Therefore, Pudong is an important part of Shanghai and is closely linked with the present Shanghai proper. For two reasons, this zone is called 'Pudong New Development Zone', or 'Pudong New Zone', instead of SEZ or ETDZ. First, since Puxi is the old part of Shanghai's proper, the Pudong should be called the new zone. Second, and more importantly, as discussed later, Pudong is said to be the most special one with the substantial status of SEZ or ETDE, compared with others in China, for the policy privilege granted to Pudong is most powerful in intensity. Consequently, to only name it SEZ has been not fully appropriate to indicate its feature. Comparatively, using the name of 'New Zone' is more acceptable.

As known to all, Shanghai is one of the world's largest metropolises. Its rapid growth occurred in the late nineteenth and early twentieth centuries, and owed much to the involvement of Europeans. The western bank of Huangpu River was the central development area, which is known as The Bund and has been called an 'architectural museum of all countries', with many magnificent buildings of different styles. Most of these buildings constructed in the 1920s and 1930s were the branch offices of the major international banks (You, Y. 1995, p. 10). In the early 1930s, Shanghai had become the world-known metropolis and the biggest financial and trade centre of Asia. Owing to Shanghai's rapidly development and prosperity, it was regarded as 'the Paris of Orient' and 'Paradise of the Adventurers' (Binns, T. 1991, p. 362).

Being the largest city of China, after the founding of PRC, Shanghai continued to play its part as the economic heart of China, and has led the country in the decades before reform in industry, science, technology and commerce. With just one percent of the country's population and 0.1 percent of Chinese territory, Shanghai turned out one-tenth of the country's revenue and hence became the backbone of the country's central finance system (You, Y. ibid.). Moreover, Shanghai is one of the world's ten major ports, which can handle 147 million tons of cargo a year, accounting for more than one third of the total of the country. It's industrial production accounts for 15 percent by value of the whole of the country. The total value of its exports accounts for more than one seventh of the total of the country. Shanghai is also one of the most important bases of China's science, technology, culture and education, with 50 universities, more than 1600 research institutes, and over one eighth of the academians of the Chinese Academia Sinica (CYB, 1992, p. 477).

Compared with Hong Kong, now known as a 'Pearl of Orient', Shanghai was in the lead for more than half century. In the 1930s, Hong Kong lagged far behind Shanghai, few people wanted to go there. Even in the early 1960s, Hong Kong was still inferior to Shanghai, and it was only in the following ten to fifteen years that Hong Kong began its great development leap, mainly based on its success with entrepot trade, monetary circulation and variety of real estate business. Nevertheless, Shanghai's superiority over Hong Kong in terms of industries, technology, science, culture and education has never been lost.

Due to Shanghai's decisive role in China's development, some people with breadth of vision saw the strategy to develop Pudong as adopting a 'Bow and Arrow Model'. They compared China's coastline to a bow, the Changjiang (Yangtze) River an arrow, and Shanghai, situated at the centre of the coastline and the estuary of Changjiang River, to the head of the arrow, with the end of the arrow: Chongqing, the largest city of Southwest China. Once Shanghai takes off, it will carry with it the development of China's coastal areas and the Changjiang River Valley and exert an incalculable impact on China's overall economic growth (Jing Bian, 1990, p. 24).

Actually, to conduct the project of developing Pudong has been the hope of Shanghai and Chinese people for generations. In his well known work 'The Programmes of National Construction', Dr. Sun Yat-sen included a tentative idea of developing Pudong and building a large harbour there. Likewise, the Kuomingtang authorities, in the 1940s, also drafted a plan to build a greater Shanghai that also included Pudong (Dai,

G. 1990, p. 16). Unfortunately, all of these efforts finally resulted in nothing more than plans on paper, due to the various reasons.

After 1949, Pudong had gradually constructed a sizeable industrial and agricultural foundation. Before 1990, some 1930 industrial enterprises, with 0.38 million employees, had set up in this area, and its annual industrial output value had roughly accounted for 10 percent of Shanghai's total (ibid.). However, its development is still far from what it should be, considering its advantages compared with Puxi, the central Shanghai.

With the deepening of China's reform and opening-up course and China's overall rapid economic development, the importance and urgency of developing Pudong which is being considered as 'the last treasure land of the world's metropolises in the 20th century' by the most famous city planners and architects of the world (Ni Tianzheng, 1992, p. 140), were gradually recognised by the leaders of both Shanghai municipality and China's government. Therefore, the development of Pudong was finally decided as a key strategy of China's reform and opening-up course.

8.2 The policy-making process for establishing Pudong New Zone

8.2.1 Pudong project: the origin and development

The scheme to develop and open Pudong has been brewing for a long time, in fact, since the early 1980s. As discussed in the chapter five, the strategy of China's opening course was arranged to be conducted and promoted step by step, from South to North, and from East to West. In doing so, SEZs were first set up in Guangdong and Fujian provinces, and then the fourteen coastal cities which including many Economic and Technologic Development Zones, were opened, followed by the five Coastal Economic Development Areas (CEAD) and finally the Coastline Economic Development Strategy was established. In the middle 1980s, when the reform and opening-up course had yielded prominent achievements in the Pearl River Delta, the Southern part of Fujian and the Southeast coastline regions, Shanghai was just beginning its development as one of the 14 coastal opening cities. At that time, Shanghai had not only lagged behind the 'Four Small Dragons' — Hong Kong, Singapore, South Korea, and Taiwan, but also behind many of China's Southeast coastal cities and areas both on economic development speed and economic vigour. Having been the largest central city of economy, finance and trade of the Far East in the 1930s, Shanghai had become somewhat overshadowed. From 1986, in Shanghai Puxi area, three Economic and Technologic Development Zones (ETDZ), Minhang, Hongqiao and Caohejing, were set up successively. Due to Shanghai's superiority in the aspects of geography, economic foundation, technology and science, these three zones aroused great interest to both foreign and home investors. Within a very short period, they successfully attracted many investment programmes with a huge capital, which brought about the boom of these ETDZs.

In Minheng ETDZ, for instance, before September 1990, some ·11 countries and regions, including the United States, Japan, Germany, Australia, Canada, Singapore, Thailand, Switzerland, Italy, Hong Kong and Taiwan province, had signed contracts for the establishment of 61 foreign-funded enterprises in the zone; 41 of which had begun operation. By the end of March 1990, a total US $ 221 millions foreign capital had been · invested in the zone which only covers 2.13 sq. km. More than 84 percent of these foreign-funded enterprises are export-oriented or equipped with advanced technology. In 1989, the foreign exchange earnings of productive business hit US $ 49.08 millions. For years, the zone's net foreign exchange earning had ranked the first among the 14 coastal economic development zones (BR, No. 36/1990, p. 29).

Hongqiao, the smallest one of China's ETDZs, with only 65.2 hectares area, created the best achievement for absorbing foreign capital (US $ 620 millions) in the late 1980s (WHD, 3 May 1990, p. 1).

Caohejing ETDZ's development also attracted people's attention, for gathering a group of enterprises in high-tech fields, such as microelectronics, aeronautics and astronauts, optical fibre communications, biology engineering, computer and new materials. More than 60 foreign and home enterprises were constructed in the zone. In 1989, the total industrial output value of the zone accounted to RMB 1.84 billion yuans, and the foreign exchange earnings from exports reached US $ 43.933 million. A booming high-tech industrial group was taking shape there (ibid.).

As introduced above, these three ETDZs' development was rather fruitful, which shows the great potentials of Shanghai to create a rapid economic growth in the new period. However, these ETDZs are too small in size, as they only cover in total 8 sq. km, to launch a greater economic development strategy for such a metropolis, China's biggest industrial centre. To promote the further development of Shanghai's opening situation, and to find a way to restore Shanghai's prestige as soon as possible, a much larger development zone needed to be inaugurated. Where was a suitable place? Shanghai's high density of population is known to all: some thirteen million residents crowed the Shanghai's 6340 sq. km area; and on average, only 48 sq. metres land for one person, which only made up one third of the national average level. Moreover, the 141 sq. km city centre was densely crowded with more than 20,000 industrial productive sites of over 4,500 enterprises (Cheng Y. 1996, p. 13). Under this situation Shanghai's authority further intensified its idea to develop Pudong area, the West Bank of the Huangpu River.

At the very beginning, when was the early 1980s, various schemes were put forward: some suggested to develop Shanghai toward the Baosan (a county of Shanghai municipality) direction, some considered to extend the industrial area into Jingshan county, and some thought developing Pudong the ideal scheme, etc. After comparing these diverse schemes again and again, Shanghai's leaders finally reached the same opinion that to go ahead toward the east and across the Huangpu River, and to develop the Pudong area in an all-round way. Pudong then was decided upon as the new economic growth point from which to promote the rejuvenation of Shanghai.

Then, in 1984, Shanghai's government put forward a suggestion to develop Pudong as a new zone through creating the necessary conditions, in a proposal titled 'The Synopsis of the Report about the Economic Development strategy of Shanghai', which was submitted to the State Council. When the State council gave written reply to this report, the suggestion was affirmed (Xie Jinghu, et al. 1996, p. 6). However, at this stage, this initial scheme to develop Pudong was only a local level's economic strategy for Shanghai. In other words, it was only a local government's plan and had not been considered as a national economic development strategy, as Deng pointed out in early 1990.

From 1986, the idea of developing Pudong was gradually deepened. The State Council stressed, in its written reply to Shanghai's report 'The Overall Planning Scheme of Shanghai Municipality': 'At present, it is necessary to pay specific attention to constructing and reforming the Pudong area... to develop business of finance, trade, technology, higher education and commercial service facilities in the Pudong area, and also build up the new residential zone, so as to enable the Pudong new zone to become a modernised new zone' (ibid.). Although this instruction confirmed again the necessity of Pudong development, it was still not seen as a state project.

In order to carry out the above two instructions of the State Council, the Shanghai government formally set up a joint consultative group which included experts from both home and abroad, to study Pudong new zone's development, in June 1987. This group undertook one year's feasibility study and formulated a general schematic idea for Pudong's construction. Many experts positively put forward their good opinions and suggestions. Professor Lin Tongyan, for instance, a very famous bridge expert with an international reputation, an American Chinese, was the earliest and the most enthusiastic exponent of the Pudong project from abroad. He went to Pudong many times to engage in inspections and investigations. He asserted that nowadays many metropolises were developed across the two banks of a river, such as London on the Times River and Paris on the Seine River. Pudong is just like Manhattan which is on the bank of New York River. He said with certainty that among all those famous metropolises in current world, Pudong is a sole treasure land which could be developed. Therefore, he set forth seven times successively the suggestion of 'Developing Pudong and constructing a modernised great Shanghai'. His important ideas including those that to raise funds by leasing land to the investors, to conduct infrastructure construction must formulate a general plan, etc., were valuable for the Pudong's development (Ni Tianzheng, ibid. p. 140).

In May 1988, the Shanghai government held a large-scale international conference to discuss how Pudong new zone should be developed, and more than one hundred scholars and specialists were invited to participate in this conference. Jiang Zemin, the then Secretary of Shanghai Party Committee, and Zhu Rongji, the then mayor of Shanghai, attended this meeting and delivered important speeches. Jiang Zemin pointed out that 'Shanghai is a world-known big city and it had become the largest centre of international finance and trade of Asia as early as the 1930s. Since 1949, the government has paid attention to its economic development, especially its industrial development, however, it has not had enough time to conduct the city reform and construction effectively, due to various reasons known to all. Therefore, Shanghai's function as the economic centre and its pivotal position at home and abroad have been reduced. From now on, this situation should not be allowed to continue'. (Xie Jinghu, et al. ibid.)

After this international conference, the early stage's studies for Pudong's development proceeded rapidly. Then, in early 1990, with Deng Xiaoping's direct involvement in promoting this project, Pudong development finally became a state's economic development strategy.

8.2.2 From local development scheme to a national key development strategy

In early 1990, Deng Xiaoping spent the Spring Festival, the Chinese New Year, in Shanghai. While staying at the largest economic centre of China, he thought more about how to accelerate China's reform and opening-up course, although he had retired. Seeing the great changes and marvellous achievements of the original five SEZs and the rapid development of the Southeast coastal areas promoted by SEZs, Deng had one regret that he had not included Shanghai in his short-list for the first group of SEZs a decade ago. He thought that too much time had been lost in speeding up Shanghai's and the whole country's economic development. Speaking to the leadership of Shanghai, at the top rotary hall of the New Jingjiang Hotel, on 18 February, Deng explained the reasons for not selecting Shanghai into first group of SEZs ten years before. He said, 'Why we defined those four SEZs in that year, was mainly because we considered geographic conditions. Shenzhen is adjacent to Hong Kong, Zhuhai is near Macao, Santou has many people from Chaozhou (one part of Santou) doing business in the Southeast countries as overseas Chinese, and Xiamen also has many people undertaking business around the world. However, we didn't recognised Shanghai's superiority of talented people. Shanghai's people are wise and have good quality.' He said with certainty that ' If Shanghai were defined as a SEZ at that time, the situation would be totally different now. Although Shanghai was listed as one of the 14 coastal open cities, that was only a general treatment. It would have been very good if Pudong had been developed, like Shenzhen, a few years ago...'(Xie Jinghu, *et al.* ibid.).

Actually, that Shanghai was not designed as a trial SEZ and put to the forefront of China's opening experiment in early 1980s, might be a result of another important and sensitive factor. That is, due to Shanghai's significant status as China's industrial centre and the State's revenue backbone, to chose Shanghai as a SEZ experiment would mean taking a great risk. If this trial SEZ went wrong, China's economy would be influenced to a great extent.

Nevertheless, it had been proved that China's SEZ programme had not led to disappointing results. Therefore, Deng thought it was the time to apply those successful experiences to Shanghai. He believed that, backed by the superiority of talent, technology and management of Puxi, Shanghai's existing industrial area, the development of Pudong would be a key step with great profound significance for promoting the restoration of Shanghai and also the economic development of the Changjiang River Valley as well as that of the whole country. Hence, Deng entrusted Zhu Rongji, then mayor and Party Secretary of Shanghai to do his best to promote its progress (ibid. p. 5). With Deng's close attention and support, then, the Pudong project as a state's economic development strategy soon came into existence, through a series of high efficient works conducting by relevant aspects from the centre to the local governments.

As Deng returned to Beijing from Shanghai, he talked about his idea to some chief leaders of the Party centre. He said that although he had retired from the first front of the Central leadership, there were some things he still wanted to mention, and one of these issues was the development of Shanghai's Pudong. He specially stressed that 'Shanghai is a trump card of ours. To keep on grasping Shanghai's development is definitely a key measure, which is a shortcut to promote the economic development of the whole country' (ibid. p. 4).

Due to both the significance of Deng's idea and the authority of Deng's words, Deng's suggestion immediately aroused the attention of the Party centre and the State Council. Zhou Jiahua, the State Councillor and the director of the State's Planning Commission, who had newly taken up his official post, delegated by the Centre, went to Shanghai at once, to make an on-the-spot investigation in Pudong area, and soon reported to the Centre.

A few days later, with the guidance and support of the Centre, Shanghai's Party committee and the government put forward a formal report, which was titled 'A Request about Developing and Opening Pudong Area', to the Centre. Then soon followed the submission of Shanghai's report, from 28 March to 8 April, Yao Yilin, the vice premier, delegated by the Party Centre and the State's Council, who headed a group of the leaders of the relevant Commissions and Ministries of the central government, went to Shanghai again to have a ten days' study about the feasibility of Pudong's development. And then, as the result of this study, an important document of 'An Outline of the Report on Several Issues about Developing Shanghai's Pudong Area' was formulated.

Two days later, in April 10th, Premier Li Peng presided over a State Council's meeting to listen to the report from vice premier Yao Yilin. Then, after another two days, Jiang Zemin, the Party General Secretary, chaired a meeting of the Political Bureau, which studied and adopted in principle the scheme for developing Pudong area put forward by the State Council.

After another two days, on April 14th, Premier Li Peng started a working inspection in Shanghai. Then, on April 18th, in delivering a speech at the Celebration Conference for the Fifth Year Anniversary of the Founding of the Shanghai's Dazhong Motorcar Company, he declared that the Centre of CPC and the State Council had formally approved Shanghai's proposal to speed up the development of Pudong area, and agreed to give Pudong the same policies of the Economic and Technological Development Zone and some policies of the Special Economic Zone. He particularly emphasised that 'This is an another great strategic arrangement for deepening the reform and expanding the opening-up of China, which is a matter with important strategic significance both to Shanghai and to the whole country' (PD, 19, April 1990, p. 1; Xie, J. et al. ibid. p. 5). He stated that the centre would give necessarily support for Pudong's development, and he also asked all other regions of the country to give their positive support.

Li expressed the view that China welcomes the entrepreneurs of the foreign countries and the fellow-countrymen from Hong Kong, Macao and Taiwan, as well as the overseas Chinese to invest in the development of Pudong, and he promised that China would provide them with preferential conditions for co-operation and an improving investment environment. Li's declaration soon spread all over the world through the media.

Two years later, in 'The Work Report of the Government' which was delivered by premier Li Peng at the Fifth Session of the Seventh NPC in April 1992, the importance of the Pudong project was further emphasised. This report confirmed that 'Shanghai's Pudong New Zone is the focal point of China's development and opening-up in the following ten years... Through developing and opening Shanghai's Pudong, to promote the economic development of the Changjiang Delta region, and also the whole Changjian valley, and so gradually enable Shanghai to become one of the centres of international economy, finance and trade of the Far East'.

Also, in 'The Political Report', delivered at the Fourth National Conference of CPC in October, 1992, the General Secretary Jiang Zemin declared that 'China will take the development of Shanghai's Pudong as the driving force, to further open the cities along the banks of the Changjiang river, and thus make Shanghai one of the centres of international economy, finance and trade, by which to give an impetus to the new leaps of the whole Changjiang Delta region' (Xie, J. et al, 1996, p.6).

It can be seen that Jiang and Li's above-mentioned announcements marked a new important turning point for the Pudong project. That is, two years after starting Pudong's development, the Pudong project has been finally determined as China's key economic development strategy of the 1990s.

8.2.3 To keep giving guidance and impetus in the course of implementing the project

Since the declaration on Pudong's development, China's top leaders, including Deng Xiaoping, and all the standing members of the Party Political Bureau, the heads of the NPC and CPPCC, and the premier and vice premiers, all attached great importance to it. They grasped it tightly and kept offering guidance and supervision on its implementation. They went to Pudong to make inspections and investigations every year, and worked together with Shanghai's leaders to analyse and solve the problems emerging in the process of conducting the project.

In early 1991, only one year after the start of the Pudong project, Premier Li Peng, headed a group of the chief leaders of the relevant commissions and ministries, which went to Pudong to conduct an on-the-spot investigation. After listening to the report and engaging study, Li Peng gave four opinions. First, to develop and open Pudong is a long-term project, which should be conducted step by step according to the general scheme. During the period of the Eighth Five-Year Plan, the main task is to complete the infrastructures construction by which to create a good investment environment, and to lay down a firm foundation for the Ninth Five-Year Plan and the 21st century's development. Second, to develop Pudong full use must be made of Shanghai's existing advantages, which included its economic and technological conditions, and the superiority of a developed market system. Third, it is necessary to well handle the relations between the tertiary industries and the second industries from the very beginning of the Pudong development. Forth, to use the method of inviting bids to make Pudong planning, by inviting the top master designers from both home and abroad.

Then, later in October 1991, Li Ruihuan, the standing member of the Party Political Bureau, had an inspection in Pudong. He encouraged Shanghai's cadres and masses to speed up the development of reform and opening course, to do their best for the big project of developing Pudong and restoring Shanghai, which had the great strategic significance.

More importantly, from mid-January to late-February of 1992, as known to the world, Deng Xiaoping had an inspection tour in South China, which included Wuchang, Shenzhen, Zhuhai and Shanghai. While staying in Shanghai, Deng told Wu Bangguo, Shanghai's new Party Secretary, and Huang Ju, the new mayor, '1990s is the last chance for your Shanghai, you can not miss this chance'.

Then, within only three years from early 1992 to early 1995, Deng, Jiang, Li, and Zhu inspected Pudong and Shanghai separately for totally ten times to urge and help the works of development.[1] Among these inspections, four were particular important. One was Jiang's inspection in early May of 1993. At that time, since China was carrying out some macro-adjustment policies in the economic field, some people both at home and broad, worried about whether the policies of developing and opening Pudong would be changed. There were also many conjectures in the media outside the mainland of China. To counter this situation, Jiang Zemin solemnly declared that, the Centre's policies concerning developing and opening Pudong were firm and unshakeable, and would not be changed. 'The Centre has great hopes for Shanghai's future development.' Another three were the inspections which conducted respectively by Jiang, Li and Zhu in early 1995. After these inspections which involved many careful studies according to Pudong's new situation, China's central government agreed that in the period of the Ninth Five-years Plan, Pudong would implement the strategy of developing infrastructures construction and functional development simultaneously, and offer Pudong a series of new policies to accelerate its functional development. These new policies caused repercussions at home and abroad.

As listed above, since the beginning of the Pudong project, many centre leaders frequently went to Pudong and Shanghai to conduct inspections and give work guidance. This had never happened since the founding of PRC. It could be thought that these frequent inspections served some special aims: (1) to keep informing the world that China's determination to develop Pudong was firm and unshakeable, so as to increase the confidence of those investors, especially those foreign investors, who had been engaged in programmes, and attract more new investors; (2) to show local authorities the importance the centre attached on this project, and encourage them to do their utmost; (3) to keep offering solutions to problems arising during the implementation of the project, and thus to ensure Pudong's smoothly and rapidly development.

8.2.4 New Zone's planning: a key point of Pudong's policy-making

Planning is a special type of policy-making. Ever since its very beginning of Pudong's development great importance has been attached to construction planning. Deng Xiaoping, the 'general architect' of China's reform, had given an instruction for Pudong's planning, which emphasised that Pudong's development must be conducted from a high starting point, and in the light of the direction of opening to the outside world; its general functions should be able to meet the demand of being one of the international centre of economy, finance, trade and high-tech industries; its city construction should reach the target as an ideal new zone ranking with the world's best, with multiple-functions and modernised facilities. (Xie Jinghu, 1995, p. 4) Deng believed that with a higher starting point Pudong could surpass other SEZs which developed earlier (Xie, J. 1996, p. 4). Obviously, the core of Deng's opinions is to hold up a high starting point and a high standard in Pudong's development and is based on the following factors: (1) Shanghai's special advantages; (2) Shanghai's important status and influence both in China and in the world; (3) the enlightenment from the ten-odd years' experiences of planning in other SEZs.

Unquestionably, to reach the above target of both a high starting point and a high standard requires a high level planning work. To be sure, what Pudong's planning has shown and is continuing to show the world is an excellent example in doing so, which includes some main features as below.

Compared with the development courses of other metropolises of the world, the most obvious advantage of Pudong in planning is that the Pudong area can be projected in its entirety at one time from the very beginning, therefore its construction can be planned systematically and scientifically to the highest standards in a comprehensive manner. Awakening to that, Pudong's planners treasured the conditions Pudong owns and held up a target that Pudong's planning should reach a leading position in the world. This target was implemented concretely in heir works. Firstly, they clearly defined a long-term plan of Pudong New Zone for the period from 1990 to 2010 which fixed the general targets for three stages as follows. In the first stage (1990-1995), the task is to accelerate the infrastructures construction and the development of those key districts. In the second stage (1996-2000), the first rank civic infrastructures of China should be completed so as to enable Pudong to become China's largest centre for commercial activities and to develop a group of highly opening up financial and trade zones, comprehensive bonded zone, export-oriented processing zone, and the modernised agriculture of outskirts style; meanwhile, that the high quality residential districts with full sets of living services conditions can fully meet the demands. In the third stage (2001-2010), a modernised new zone, with world's top level, outward-oriented style and multiple-functions, should have been taken shape basically.

In order to obtain the best design to ensure that Pudong's construction held a leading position in world's metropolises, Pudong's authority invited the best designers of the world to join in the planning work. The design of the core zone of Lujiazhui district which is in the heart of Pudong, the would-be financial and trade centre, provided a typical case of Pudong's planning which gathered the best wisdom of those leading experts. This central district which is situated at the opposite bank of Puxi's Bund, covers only 1.7 sq. km. To develop it experts from the United States, France, Britain, Italy and Japan were invited to join in the work. Like Pudong's decision-makers, those designers were also highly aware of the advantages of the Lujiazhui central zone. As a foreign designer said, 'it is a sole treasure land among the large-scale city construction in the world's metropolises, in progress in this century. Therefore, it needs the most brilliant design. Its significance and influence will far exceed Pudong, Shanghai and China' (Zhang, S. 1996, p. 2). In making their designs, all these experts were very confident of their own outstanding talent. As they finished the presentation of their respective plans, they left without caring what comments the others would give. Nevertheless, when the final perfected scheme, which emerged after conducting three rounds and seventeen stages of studying, comparing, revising and selecting by both Chinese and foreign experts, was produced, they were all attracted and convinced. This scheme reflected the merits of each designer, and also had strong Chinese characteristics. According to this scheme, some 88 huge buildings, with different functions and styles, would appear in this district, forming a special feature combining the best strong points of home and abroad, China and Western, and also integrate the historical tradition with and future tendency. The overall arrangement of this scheme sought the integration of functions for economic development and social life, with the full consideration of the ecology environment, while providing plenty room for their further development.

One of the world-known masters designer from Britain, Rogers G. Richard, stood at the exquisitely made planning sand table for a long time, and sighed, 'A brand new conception of China will appear at the first time

214 The applicability of policy-making theories in post-Mao China

in the 21st century's textbook of the architectural design' (Zhang, S. 1996, p. 2).

It could be said that, in planning this tiny area to the highest standard, Pudong authority had spared no expense, and some FF. (French Franc) 400 millions had been spent.

Upholding 'rational and orderly development' is an important principle of Pudong's planning. Great attention has been paid to the integration of the second industries and the tertiary industries during the planing process. The degree of the tertiary industries' development is one of the important measures of the development of either a city or a state. Compared with those developed countries, Shanghai's situation can not be optimistic. In 1985, tertiary industries in Japan and the United States made up 49 percent and 51 percent of their respective GNP. In Shanghai, the most developed area of China, the figure was only 29 percent. This was very low when compared with that of Tokyo and New York, which was as high as 70 percent (Dai, G. 1990, p. 19). Awakening to this reality of lag, therefore, Pudong's planers attached great importance to the design of the functional structures for different districts, so as to ensure an ideal structure and good overall arrangements for Pudong's economic distribution.

To date, as the first stage programme, four districts have been parcelled out and are already in construction. These four districts have their respective special function and main development target, and each of them is a essential part of Pudong as an integral whole which serves the defined general target.

Lujiazhui, the heart area of Pudong, which covers 16 sq. km, was designed to concentrate most of the tertiary industries, which include finance, trade, information, service, science, technology, education and culture course. Its stress laid on establishing a financial and trade centre, by which to great change Shanghai's economic structure and thus help it regain its unique status as the largest financial centre of Orient.

Jinqiao district, with an area of 19 sq. km, was designed as an export-oriented processing zone. Besides accommodating hundreds of factories, some 3.1 sq. km of land will be devoted to luxury houses, apartments, office buildings, hotels, markets and recreational centre. Moreover, in this district, bonded storehouses will also be set up to guarantee its open trade capacity and attract more foreign investment.

The third key functional area is Waigaoqiao Free Trade District, which is also called a bonded zone and covers 10 sq. Km. This Free Trade District will be a comprehensive development zone which allows for both free trade and export-oriented processing. The ultimate goal is to build a completely free port. The district will be isolated from the neighbouring territory by a separation belt.

The fourth key district, Zhangjiang high-tech zone, with an area of 3.5 sq. Km is designed to concentrate on the promotion of high-tech industries. It is planned to create China's largest high-tech development zone through merging education, scientific research, development, production and sales.

As listed above, different functions had been determined for the districts when mapping out Pudong's planning. Thus, it can be ensured that the ambitious development project will be conducted as perfectly as possible from its commencement.

In planning Pudong's construction, the planners did not only consider the demands of economic development, but considered thoroughly the overall development of the society so as to provide each resident with the best culture and life environment. With this target, to protect the ecological environment is considered to be very important. Needless to say, the land in Pudong is very valuable, however, the proportion of land reserved as open space must be a target which aims at an average of 20 sq. metres for each person, and the total area covered by trees, flowers and grass-plot should hit 35 percent of the whole Pudong New Zone. In addition, a forest wall covering 38 sq. km along the coastline has been planned. Moreover, in the heart of Pudong, a central park covering 160 hectares, will be constructed.

Facilities for culture, education, health and physical culture have been considered in Pudong's planning. A group of buildings forming the important symbols of Pudong, including an Oriental Concert Hall, a large-scale Stadium, Astronomical Observatory, Nature Museum, etc., will set up there. Meanwhile, universities, colleges, schools of the first rank level and top science and technology parks will also to be built.

Since the starting of Pudong project from April 1990, foreign investment flowed into Pudong continuously with an average speed of 1.5 projects and US $ 5.6 millions per day, and this speed has been kept up for more than 5 years. For selecting the best projects which can meet the demands of the New Zone's development, Pudong's decision makers insisted on high standard examining rules. This resulted from their 'treasure land consciousness', for they are clearly aware of the great value of Pudong's land. Based on this recognition, they uphold an unshakeable standard of examining every investment programme seriously and never accepting 'sunset industries' or pollution-making industries, regardless of who introduces the programme, or how great the investment. For instance, a traditional textile programme set forth by a Taiwan businessman, although the capital he was preparing to invest hit US $ 35 millions, was politely refused.

Due to keeping high standards for the selection of investment programmes, the quality of Pudong's foreign investment is very good and embodies three features as follows (Xie J. et al. 1995, p. 5). First, the size of these investment items is large. An average item involves the capital of nearly US $ 4 millions, which ranks as the top of China's ETDZs. Of all foreign-invested projects, more than 202 programmes are over US $ 10 millions, making up seven tenths of the total foreign investment capital, 60 of which were invested by 44 of the world's most famous transnational companies. Second, the industrial structure of the investment programmes is excellent. Up to the middle of 1995, there were 1370 programmes invested in the tertiary industries, such as finance, commerce and trade, forming the key point of Pudong's development. The total investment in the tertiary industries accounted for 2.22 times as much as that for the secondary industries. Third, the technological content of the programmes is high. Among those 11 high-and-new-tech fields encouraged for development by the state, nine of them have settled down in Pudong and basically formed a group of industries, thus giving a great impetus to the adjustment and reconstruction of Shanghai's industrial structure.

Carrying out the principle of integrating city with countryside is an important creation in the course of setting up China's SEZs and the ETDZs. Within Pudong New Zone's 520 sq. km area, there are 33 countries (with bureaucratic rank between county and the village) and towns. For matching Pudong's general development planning and the concrete schemes of different districts, these countries and towns have been correspondingly planned for their development according to the principle of integrating city with countryside. In doing so three methods were adopted (Xie, J. et al. 1995, p. 6).

- To adjust the structures of township enterprises to link or match the New Zone's construction, which could ensure that the New Zone's defined general plan could be implemented, and also those township enterprises development can be advanced.
- To reform the existing agriculture by shifting the extensive cultivation into the intensive cultivation, to meet Pudong's new farming demand. For instance, in Yanqiao country, a vegetables-producing base, even though its vegetable land had been reduced by 83.3 percent from

1990's 800 hectares to only 133 hectares in 1995, improvements in planting methods resulted in its total farming income increasing from 1990's RMB 7.2 billion yuans to RMB 22 billion yuanss (ibid.).

Meanwhile, through the thorough feasibility studies, a plan has been formulated that Pudong's agricultural development will break away from the traditional old pattern of planting farming, and shift to a much wider development direction which includes sightseeing, tourism, green ecology, foreign-exchange-earning farming, etc. With these measures, the farmers will be able to get rich more rapidly and the countryside of Pudong will naturally become an organic part of a great international metropolis.

- To strengthen the education on farmers and enhance farmers' quality. In 1995, some one fifth of Pudong's farmers, nearly 260,000 people, were in adult education courses including 120,000 who were urgently needed to complete the transition from farmer to city residents, for their land had been taken over for the use of the New Zone's development. In 1994, 14,000 people took part in the Shanghai's computer user skill examination, and seven tenths of them were awarded certificates. By the end of this century, about 0.2 million of Pudong's farmers will have finished their adult education with qualified certificates (ibid.).

In Pudong, as soon as the planning is determined, it is given the force of law. The planning of the overall arrangement of Pudong's development was examined and adopted by the Standing Committee of Shanghai People's Congress, and all those districts' plans which derived from Pudong's overall planning, needed approval of the respective government at different levels. For carrying out the agreed planning, Pudong authorities adopted three measures: to set up a planning exhibition hall to enable all Shanghai's residents to study the plans and enhance their planning consciousness; to set up an accusatory system to encourage people to report those contravening the plans to the relevant authorities; and to set up a special team to check and deal with those offenders against the defined planning. By implementing these serious measures, Pudong's development construction has being rapid and orderly.

Being a new zone of the State's key programme in 1990s, Pudong has been granted a series of new and powerful policies by central government, so as to guarantee its successful speedy development. Simultaneously, Shanghai and Pudong authorities also made many corresponding policies to ensure those state's policies could be carried out effectively.

8.3 New policies for the New Zone

A defined policy is the first and immediate result of a policy-making process. The formulation of correct policies is essential for success of a leadership. Since the Pudong project was launched on the base of ten-odd years' development of China's SEZs and ETDZs, it could be based on successful experience accumulated elsewhere, and so the policies which mapped out for the New Zone could be more systematic and comprehensive. As a result, policy guidance in Pudong was more concrete, powerful, and successful.

8.3.1 The sources and types of the Pudong policies

All those policies carried out in Pudong were from three aspects: (1) granted by CPC Centre and the State Council; (2) made by the relevant Commissions and Ministries of the state; (3) set forth by Shanghai and Pudong authorities.

To analyse these policies, their three major functions can be identified.

- To give Shanghai authority more power, which focuses on two aspects: one to grant local authority more autonomy to examine and approve investment projects in a considerable wide range, and the other to allow the local authority to keep a favourable rate of financial income earned in the New Zone and give it special financial support.

- To provide investors with three preferential conditions: tax reduction or remission; more convenience in going through the formalities for their investment; creation and improvement of the infrastructure with the aim of providing a better investment environment.

- To stipulate the administrative work methods and work procedures of local authority, with which to enhance the work efficiency and improve the work quality in the New Zone.

8.3.2 The main policies and their features

What the following paragraphs attempt is to concretely analyse Pudong's main policies and discover their features. Up to the end of 1995, the most important policies in force in Pudong made by the central and local authorities included: the ten preferential policies on Pudong which were announced on April 30 1990; the nine laws and regulations released on

September 10 1990; ten more preferential policies granted on March 10 1992; and some other regulations about work methods and procedures.

On April 30 1990, Shanghai municipal government held a press conference at which, Zhu Rongji, the mayor of Shanghai announced ten preferential policies and measures, approved by the CPC Centre and the State Council, for the Pudong New Development Zone (PD, 2, May 1990, p.1). The content of these policies included some new provisions, besides those general items which had been implemented in other SEZs and ETDZs, such as the methods and conditions of tax reductions and exemptions, and the exemption from the industrial and commercial consolidated tax, encouragement to invest in the infrastructure construction, etc. Those new provisions are fivefold.

- Foreign business people are allowed to build tertiary industries in the zone. Financial, retail sales and other trades, for which foreign businessmen are banned or restricted from operating in other places according to the current stipulations, may be run on a trial base in the New Zone with official approval.
- Foreign business people are allowed to set up foreign-funded banks in Shanghai and the zone.
- Within the bonded area of Pudong, foreign trade agencies are allowed to engage in entrepot trade.
- Clearly confirming the policies of transferring land-use rights with remuneration, and encouraging foreign businessmen to contract for developing large tracts of adjoining land.
- The New Zone's newly generated financial income may be retained by the New Zone for its further development (ibid.).

Only a few months later, the nine regulations on opening and developing Pudong New Zone, were published, on September 10 1990, at a press conference held by Shanghai's government (BR, No.39/1990, September, p. 19).

These nine regulations were the concrete implementation of the ten preferential policies and measures declared on April. Of which, three were approved by the State Council and promulgated by the departments concerned under it. They were:

- The Measures for Administration of Foreign-Funded Financial Institutions and Financial Institutions with Chinese and Foreign Capital in Shanghai (published by the People's Bank of China);
- The Regulations on Reduction and Exemption of Enterprises Income Tax and Industrial and Commercial Consolidated Tax to Encourage

Foreign Investment in Shanghai Pudong New Development Zone (published by the Ministry of Finance);

- The Customs Measures of the People's Republic of China for Control over Goods, Means of Transport and Personal Articles Entering or Leaving the Waigaoqiao Bonded District of Shanghai (published by the General Administration of Customs) (Ge Wu, 1990, pp.12-5).

The six other regulations were published by the Shanghai's government, they were decided after consultation with various State Council departments. While those relevant leading bodies gave firm guidance and approval. These six regulations included:

- The Regulations of Shanghai Municipality for the Encouragement of Foreign Investment in the Pudong New Development Zone;
- The Measures for Administration of the Waigaoqiao Bonded District of Shanghai;
- The Provisions on Land Administration In Shanghai Pudong New Development Zone;
- The Provisional Measures on the Programme for the Construction and Administration of Shanghai Pudong New Development Zone;
- The Measures for the Examination and Approval of Foreign-Funded Enterprises in Shanghai Pudong New Development Zone; and
- The Guide to Industries and Investment in Shanghai Pudong New Development Zone (ibid.).

In making these documents, both CPC centre and the State Council had attached great importance. Even General Secretary Jiang Zemin and Premier Li Peng had personally involved themselves in the legislative work (BR, No.39/1990, p. 19). Since the work was considered significant and urgent, it was conducted with high efficiency. The drafting of these documents was finished in August after only four months efforts following the announcement of the Pudong project and then they were translated into English and Japanese within another one month, so they could be presented to a press conference held on September 10 1990.

After two years, on March 10 1992, Huang Ju, the mayor of Shanghai, released the important news to the domestic and foreign correspondents that, in order to further support Pudong New Zone's opening up and development, the central government had agreed to grant Shanghai ten new policies, which are said to be more preferential than those given to Shenzhen (BR, No.12/1992, pp. 6-7). These ten policies consist of five for expanding Shanghai's power to examine and approve the investment programme, and the other five for increasing Shanghai's power of raising funds to support Pudong's development.

The first five policies are:

- empower Shanghai to examine and approve those entrepot trade industries with foreign or domestic funds in Waigaoqiao Bonded Zone;
- authorise Shanghai to examine and approve the import and export right of those State-run large and medium scale enterprises in Pudong New Zone;
- expand Shanghai's power of examination and approval for establishing those non-industrial projects in the New Zone;
- grant Shanghai the power to examine and approve those industrial projects with investment of less than RMB 200 million yuans in the New Zone;
- allow Shanghai to issue its own stocks and bonds to be used for Pudong development, and allow the stocks in other parts of the country to be traded in Shanghai.

The key points of the other five policies for raising funds, for forming a complete set for the first five, are as below:

- permit Shanghai to issue RMB 500 million yuans worth of industrial bonds annually;
- apart from the annual loan of US $100 million that has already been secured for Shanghai, the central government would give the city another US $ 200 million in low interest loans every year;
- allow Shanghai to float an additional RMB 100 million yuans worth of shares, apart from the ordinal quota;
- Shanghai can float US $ 100 million worth of B-shares for foreign investors every year;
- give Shanghai RMB 100 million worth of additional allocation funds in 1992, on the base of those funds of 200 million yuans already allocated (PD, 11 Mar. 1992, p. 1).

Some considerable space has been used above to introduce the main points of those important policies relating to Pudong New Zone. This was necessary for understanding the policies in a comprehensive way. These facts clearly demonstrate the following: (a) China's central authorities treated Pudong New Zone as very special; (b) all policies carried out in Pudong were made in a very short period; (c) these policies included many which were new and had not been implemented in other SEZs and ETDZs, and also policies that were similar with those in other SEZs and ETDZs but much more powerful; (d) both central and local governments showed a strong sense of urgency in executing these measures.

It is essential to emphasise that those new policies specially granted to Pudong are very significant. For instance, the central government granted financial allocation and bank loan quotas for Pudong's infrastructure construction. This is a departure from the approach for existing SEZ policies. Without exception, all other China's SEZs and opening zones were only given policy privilege to facilitate local capital accumulation, but no direct grant from the central government. It is just as Deng said to the Guangdong province's leader in April 1979, 'The central government has no money, so your people need to rely on their own efforts.' Thus, the special treatment to Pudong showed the determination of the central government to guarantee Pudong's successful development, for it was not going to leave Pudong's infrastructure construction to the uncertainty of foreign investment or the ability of local government to solicit domestic funding from newly found sources (Chan, T. M. H. 1991, pp. 11-3).

Besides making those policies directly related to economic activities, some policies about work methods and work quality were also made, the most special being the regulation stipulating a time limit for examining and approving investment projects by the foreign businessmen. It stipulates that, from receiving the relevant documents, the work must be finished within: 20 days for a project proposal, 30 days for the feasibility study report, contract and articles of association, 7 days for issuance of an approval certificate and 15 days or checking and granting a business licence. (Ge Wu, ibid. p. 15) With these regulations Shanghai and Pudong New Zone's authorities have greatly enhanced their work efficiency and improved their work quality, enabling an ideal investment environment to take shape in Pudong and Shanghai, which brought about the booming of the New Zone.

8.4 Pudong's booming

From what was discussed in the previous paragraphs, one conclusion might be drawn: that compared with other SEZs and ETDZs of China, Pudong New Zone possesses a leading position in three aspects. These are: its comprehensive conditions for development and opening up are the best; the intensity of the preferential policies granted to it are the greatest; and the starting point of its development is the highest. Naturally, therefore, these also produce its fourth 'the most'— its development speed is the fastest.

Pudong's booming is a marvel which has focused the world's attentions. First, the great achievement of its infrastructures construction has brought about a thorough change in the investment environment. Up to April 1995, just at Pudong New Zone's five years anniversary, more than RMB 2500 million yuanss had been invested to Pudong's infrastructure construction, which enabled a brand new Pudong to take shape, which included roads, bridges, docks airport, communication facilities, water, electricity and gas supply, and various huge buildings with different functions, as well as the residential area with its necessary supporting services. As recently as 1990, Pudong was still seen as a countryside by the Shanghai's residents, and it is now becoming a modern metropolitan district. A famous phrase in Shanghai for a long time was 'I would rather own a bed on the Western bank (Puxi) than an apartment on the Eastern bank (Pudong)'. Now this phrase had become history forever (You, Y. ibid. p. 12).

Due to the good conditions in many ways, Pudong offered a great attraction to both foreign and domestic investors. Even at the very beginning of the Pudong project, a lot of foreign businessmen with foresight poured into the zone to find investigate the possibilities for their development. Within only five months from when the Pudong project was announced in April 1990, some 1500 groups of foreign businessmen with investment interests had gone to Pudong, which made up for 4000 people, and more than one hundred programmes of the secondary and the tertiary industries were under consideration (Huang, J. 1990, p. 10).

From 1990 to 1995, the amount of the foreign investment pouring into Pudong increased rapidly (see table 8.1). The total funds of foreign investment by contract had reached US $ 9094 million (Xie, J. & Zhang, C. 1996, p. 2).

Table 8.1 The rapid increase of foreign investment in Pudong New Zone (1990-1995)

year	1990	1991	1992	1993	1994	1995
investment	34	101	1353	1757	2593	3265

* unit: US $ million.

The total projects invested by foreign businessmen totalled 3748, which included 33 bank branches and 87 financial companies' agencies (XTD, 4 May 1995, p. 8). Of these foreign investment projects, the sole foreign-funded projects are 1218, which accounted for one third of the total. More specially, Pudong's introduction of foreign capital has been in a leading position in the country in the respects of the total amount of projects, the level of the investment items, and the total funds of the investment. For instance, in the Jingqiao Export Processing Zone of Pudong, which had involved 200-odd foreign-funded projects, the average investment funds is US $ 13 million, which made up ten times as much as those of the country's average figure (Xie, J. & Zhang, C. 1996a, pp. 7-8). Within the period of Pudong's first five years, foreign investment poured into Pudong at an average speed of US $ 5.6 million on 1.5 projects every day (You, Y. ibid. pp. 10-11).

Besides, a huge domestic capital was also absorbed in Pudong New Zone. By the end of 1995, some 4000 enterprises invested by the state commissions, ministries and other provinces or cities, had been set up in the zone (Xie & Zhang, 1996a, p. 8).

Because the infrastructure construction is proceeding with high speed, and the huge amount of investment projects from home and abroad has become established in Pudong, production output value has increased rapidly. It is known to all that investors are well rewarded with a rapid increase in their capital when their enterprises start to operate. Pudong's facts indicated that it is the ideal place to get good returns. Among those 3700-odd enterprises with foreign capital, in 1995, 2320 had started operation. Of which, more than 90 percent would earn profits after one year's production; in 1995, these enterprises had a sales income of RMB 56400 million yuans, and created 410 million yuans worth of interest (Xie & Zhang, ibid.). The Shanghai Hitachi Electrical Company Ltd, set up in Jingqiao Export Processing Zone, with an investment of US $ 55 million, was built and went into operation in one year and earned 300 million yuans in less than one year of production. This Japanese investor said, 'Hitachi has never had such efficiency with an overseas branch before'(You, Y. ibid. p. 12). In 1990, the total value of Pudong's domestic production was only 6000 million yuans, and this figure had increased to 41 billion yuans in 1995, which is 5.83 times that of 1990.

Five years are only a twinkling of an eye in history, however, an earth-shaking changes had occurred in Pudong New Zone within this period, which is as brilliant as an epic. Pudong's development attracted great attention from the outside world. Some 4000-odd groups of foreign guests, which included more than 200 international political VIPs and the magnates of the economic circle, specially went to inspect Pudong. Pudong's achievement persuaded them that it is the place which possesses the greatest potential for investment in the current world.

Note

[1] During this period, Deng Xiaoping inspected for one time, Jiang Zemin for four times, Li Peng for three times and Zhu Rongji for two times. See Xie Jinghu, et al. 1996.

PART III:
ANALYSING THE POLICY-MAKING PROCESS

9 The applicability of the selected theories about how policy is made

In the preceding four chapters, the second part of the book, the main policy-making process and the outcomes of the establishment and development of China's SEZs, including its background and *status quo*, have been reviewed. This last part of the book, which covers three chapters, is to examine, analyse and interpret these empirical data in detail from different angles with selected theories and models which have been discussed in the first part. In doing so, the applicability of these selected theories and models to China's practice, and the major changes and features of China's policy-making process in the post-Mao period, are explored.

9.1 Methodologies

As has been defined, the theoretical framework discussed in the first part of the book comprises theories and models of three aspects in two groups. Those that are in the first group, concerning how policy is made, include the relevant state theories, and the models about how China's policy is made. Those that are in the second group, concerning how policy should be made, cover the theories and models seeking the way to improve the policy process. The following theoretical analyses consist of three steps. This chapter interprets the SEZs' policy-making process with three selected theories about how policy is made, which embody pluralist perspective, elitist theory, and the institutional approach. Chapter Ten, then, analyses the SEZs' policy process with four selected theories and models about how to improve policy-making, which comprise rationalism, incrementalism, the optimal approach and contingent method. Chapter Eleven, a conclusion part, first accesses a comprehensive analysis with the basic ideas of different theories and models, in an integrated way, and then discusses the differences in the policy-making behaviour for the three cases of the SEZ course. Finally, the main findings of my research are summarised.

Whilst in discussing the applicability of those selected theories and models to China's policy-making practice and their reasons as well, this last part of the book, the major analytic part, examines in depth some important issues as following from different viewpoints. (1) What were the motivations of China's authority in making the SEZ strategies and the relevant opening-up policies? (2) How and to what extent those different elements, both internal and external, became pressures which affected the policy-making process? (3) Who was involved in the policy-making and who played the key role in which and why? And (4) what are the main methods of China's policy-making and why were they applicable?

Among those diversified theories and models that were discussed in Chapter 2 and 3, concerning how policy is made, we will use three of them, as mentioned above, to analyse the SEZ practice here. It has been pointed out that in the earlier parts, Marxist determinism and globalisation determinism are mainly suitable to be used in observing and analysing the general situation and condition of the macro policy-making events; those Sinologists' models are actually the versions of the relevant state theories in conducting the practical studies of China's policy-making behaviour, so they are not used to examine the SEZ-related policy process here.

To discuss the SEZ practice with pluralism, elitism and institutionalism in this chapter is unfolded through examining the three SEZ cases separately in turn. In discussing each case, these three theories are introduced one by one. In this course, the extent to which these theories are applicable in interpreting the SEZ policy process and why, are discussed in detail from different angles.

9.2 Examining the establishment of the first group of SEZs

This is the first stage of the development of China's SEZs, when China just started its reform and opening-up strategy, for which many issues concerning the direction, methods, and policies needed to be probed. As a pioneering programme of implementing this strategy, inevitably, the SEZ-related policy-making faced considerable uncertainties, to handle which was actually a process of paving the road for the development of both China's SEZs and the reform and opening-up course. Therefore, to examine policy process at this turning period with different theories has a particular significance.

9.2.1 Pluralist view

We had known that with the development of the reform and opening-up course in post-Mao China, an economic plural tendency had occurred noticeably, then, was there a plural involvement that appeared in the policy-making realm? And to what extent did this involvement influence SEZ policy process? To answer these questions, leads us into an analysis with pluralist account.

Pluralist perspective considers that power is diverse and fragmented among interests in a society. Power is accessible to all, theoretically; but inequality is unavoidable practically. Those who control most important economic power usually play the key role in influencing a policy process. However, the policy outcome is uncertain, since it depends on the changes of a concrete circumstance, which favours certain interests against others (Hill, M. 1993, pp. 32, 42. Blowers, 1984, p. 214). To examine the initiating course of SEZs with pluralist view, the discussion below will be conducted from three aspects, by which to see how and to what extent a plural involvement had affected the policy process, and also to what extent a pluralist view is applicable to interpret this course.

Interests involved and a bottom up pattern in making SEZ programme   The original idea of setting China's SEZs did not come from the creation of the brain tank or a few leaders at the central level, but was the product of multiple interests working through a typical bottom up pattern. Those interests involved in this course behaved actively with each several motivation and different ways, and eventually became a strong joint impulse to the central decision-makers, thus powerfully promoted the making of SEZ programme.

The interests involved in the course include CMSN (China's Merchant Steam Navigation Co.), Guangdong provincial authority, Transport Ministry, Central government, Party's top leaders, etc. (section 6.2). CMSN is a state-owed enterprise which is located in Hong Kong. In order to complete the financial target of creating foreign exchanges set up by the state, it wished to enlarge its business by establishing an industrial zone in Shekou of Shenzhen that is the nearest place to Hong Kong. CMSN considered that by making use of both the advantages of Hong Kong (electric power, etc.) and Guangdong (cheaper labour force and land, etc.), the products of the industrial zone would have much stronger competitive ability in the international market. CMSN put forward its suggestion at the earliest time among all the advocators.

As the direct high authority of CMSN, the Ministry of Transportation, a functional sector of central government, firmly gave CMSN full support, for whether CMSN could fulfil the financial target directly concerned its responsibility. The involvement and support of the latter strengthened the impact of the CMSN's initiative.

Guangdong province was a special interest in this event. Owing to its nearness to Hong Kong and the closest connection with overseas Chinese, it was deeply affected by the external pressures caused by the rapid economic development of the outside world, directly and heavily. For changing the backward economic situation and solving the problems of maintaining social stability, Guangdong adopted many measures focusing on setting up an outward-looking economy and speeding up its economic development (section 6.2.1). Their efforts also represented the wishes of Guangdong's common people to improve their living standard and to get rich. These were the reasons why the Guangdong authority kept requesting the Centre to let it go one step ahead and go faster than other provinces to develop its economy. In the early January of 1979, Guangdong had put forward its idea to set up the export bases in Bao-An and Zhuhai counties. Later, that three of the first group of SEZs were determined to set up in Guangdong's territory, further increased the interest concern of Guangdong.

Those officials in Central government, of course, were concerned with state interest and had their direct responsibility to the state. In the course of initiating SEZ programme, those centre-dispatched inspection and investigation groups to abroad, strongly suggested the setting up of an outward-looking economy as soon as possible, and also gave a very persuasive theoretical base, which provided the necessary condition for producing the SEZ programme later. One of these groups, which went to Hong Kong and Macao for its survey, also clearly raised a suggestion of setting up of an export-oriented zone in Guangdong (section 6.2). Then, in bringing the SEZ plan into conductible policies, those functional sectors of central government, were positively involved with accomplishing a series of down-to-earth works.

A pluralist view would also consider those top leaders of the centre, like Deng Xiaoping, Li Xiannian (then the vice Chairman of CPC Central

Committee and the deputy premier), Yao Yilin (then vice premier), as a special interest. Since they fortunately survived the Cultural Revolution, and re-controlled China's power in the post-Mao epoch, they knew particularly clearly about China's situation and had a strong sense of responsibility for CPC's revolutionary cause, and of extricating China from a very difficult position. Considering the importance of developing an outward-looking economy to the state, they did not only give full support to the SEZ programme immediately as they got to know the original ideas, but concretely gave guidance and assistance to solve the problems which were produced in the policy process. When Deng expressed his support and raised the name 'Special Zone', he asked Guangdong's leaders 'to fight a bloody road'. This word seemed to be very strange as pointing to an economic event. However, substantially, it did reflect the real thinking of those top leaders at that moment. It indicated that they did not only clearly realise the heavy pressures which came from both external and internal sides, which were caused by the backward situation then and the enlargement of the gap between China and those developed countries and regions economically, and the difficulty of China in making a breakthrough for its economic development, but also had strong determination to accomplish their desired goal.

Pluralists would highlight the involvement of interests from different sides. Under the situation that all those accessing this issue, in which the local authority and enterprise had more direct interest, had intense motivation to promote China's outward-looking economy, the initiation of the SEZ programme could be promoted efficiently through a bottom-up pattern. The CMSN set forth its suggestion and obtained support right away from the Ministry of Transportation; Guangdong made its own plan and meanwhile was willing to co-operate with the Transport Ministry. In the meantime, those investigation groups to abroad dispatched by central government also raised their proposal to set up exported-oriented zones in Guangdong a few months later. That these three sides put forward their similar suggestions separately within a short period can be explained as the recognition of a common request of conducting such a programme at that time. These demands, then formed a joint force to advance the centre's policy process. To pluralists such a wide involvement in promoting a policy-making issue is significant in increasing the extent to which the would-be-made policy represents the wishes of the society and the feasibility of implementation.

The interaction of interests in promoting the policy process   The pluralist view would confirm the significance of the interaction between interests in the course of initiating, deepening, crystallising, and finalising the SEZ programme. To set up SEZ in China's territory was considered an important issue relating to a series of key state policies about importing foreign capital and technology, expanding foreign trade, and leasing land to foreign businessmen, etc. Therefore, decision-making power was retained at central level. In the policy-making process, those interests at different levels interacted with each other through their own channels and tactics, and finally influenced the policy outputs produced by the central authority.

As a direct subordinate enterprise of the Transport Ministry, CMSN has a convenient channel to express its suggestion to the centre and to ask for support directly or through the Ministry (sections 6.2.1-6.2.3). Although the original idea which CMSN raised was mainly for its own business target, later, it was the head of Transport Ministry who represented CMSN to negotiate with Guangdong for searching the possibility of setting up export-oriented zone in Guangdong. In the first meeting of studying the feasibility of those proposals, held by Li Xiannian (then vice CPC central Committee and standing vice premier) and Gu Mu (vice premier), on 31 Jan. 1979, Yuan Geng, the head of CMSN, and Peng Deqing, the head of Transport Ministry got the chance to report their idea, with which to directly influence the central decision makers, and obtained full support from the latter. It was in this meeting that Li promised to give CMSN the whole peninsula of Shekou in Bao-an County to CMSN for its export-oriented zone. Later, in another meeting which was held by Gu Mu, for all those senior officials in charge from relevant commissions and ministries including finance, banks, foreign trade, etc., Yuan Geng further won concrete support for policies in which the basic principles for setting-up the zone were confirmed. According to these facts, we see that at the early stage, CMSN and the Transport Ministry had more direct chances to access the policy process and influence the central decision makers effectively.

Being the first level sub-nation authority of China and the host of the original place of China's SEZs, Guangdong provincial leaders could access and influence the policy process in different ways. Pluralists would point out the importance that Guangdong could have more say since it possesses the major resources for establishing the zones, which include land, funds and labours. For setting up an industrial zone in Shekou, CMSN and the

Transport Ministry, its higher authority needed to ask for support and permission from Guangdong. The central government, when considering the feasibility of these suggestions, also needed to discuss with Guangdong. Therefore, the Guangdong authority was in an initiative position in this policy-making process. Of course, Guangdong itself also had the wish to build up exported-oriented bases. It could take advantage of these favourable conditions to meet its target. Owing to the inner-relations of China's leadership system, the heads of Guangdong's party and government had several opportunities to talk directly with the central leaders including Deng and Li, to explain their requests and suggestions in detail. Also, they conducted the formal official procedures to state their demands through submitting reports separately by themselves and jointly with the Transport Ministry. Moreover, due to another important reason, the opinions of Guangdong's leadership were particularly influential in impressing the Centre. At that moment, Xi Zhongxun was both the first secretary of the provincial party committee and the governor of the province. Xi was also a survivor of Cultural Revolution and he had been a vice-premier before the Cultural Revolution. Hence, it could be sure, he had close relations with profound influences in high level officialdom. To pluralists this was also an important political resource that could be used for pursuing Guangdong's desired target. Deng's astonishing words 'to fight a bloody road' and suggesting the name of 'Special Zone' were just spoken to Xi and Yang Shangkun, then the second secretary of the provincial party committee, when discussing Guangdong's scheme with the latter.

Those functional sectors of central government and the investigation groups had their direct responsibility to central government. They were active in raising suggestions, engaging theoretical research, carrying out on-the-spot surveys, conducting feasibility studies, and drafting concrete policies, under the command of the state's senior leaders at and above vice premier level. Obviously, they represented the state's interest and based on which they supported and promoted the SEZ programme. The most important role they exercised in influencing the SEZ programme was formulating those concrete SEZ policies covering tax, finance, import and export, and the land administration, etc. In doing so, they had practical and decisive power (section 6.2.2). This was actually controlling the resource of legislative power to a great extent for the zones. To make these policies, which would determine a basic framework of the mode and direction of the would-be-SEZs, was the action of those functional organs representing the state, to balance the interest relations between different sides.

Those who stood at the top of SEZs' decision-making circle were the central leaders above vice premier level. They were not only concerned with the state's economic demands but also the state's political goals that included consolidating the regime. Therefore, as soon as they found those ideas relating to establishing an export-oriented zone or industrial zone, they identified and affirmed their value at once with a broad and long-term view, based on the consideration of the overall situation of China. Furthermore, in making the SEZ decision, what they did was not simply to accept the original suggestions from subordinates, but to deepen, develop and perfect them. What Deng and Li had done in the policy process showed this significant role, which indicates a powerful influence produced by a special interest.

Then, what were the relations of different interests in this policy process? The pluralist approach suggests that interests involved in a policy process are not in an equal position. Even though there was basically no direct conflict that occurred in determining the would-be-SEZ programme, the extent to which interests could affect the policy-making varied from one to another according to the political and economic resources which could be controlled by each of them. Since Guangdong province controlled the most important resources (capital, land and labour) for setting up the zones, it occupied a significant position in influencing the policy process. At the very beginning the central government studied this issue with CMSN and its higher authority, the Transport Ministry, on many occasions. However, with the development of the event, gradually, the object to which the central government negotiated was turning to the Guangdong authority. That meant, the negotiation relation gradually changed from Centre vs. CMSN to Centre vs. Guangdong. In handling this issue, Guangdong authority was of key importance. Since the Centre would not provide money for the zones' development, it actually meant that Guangdong needed to raise funds itself besides arranging land and labour. Therefore, Guangdong had much more right to influence the decision-making issues. We saw that those policy outputs (Central instructive documents) concerning setting up SEZs and the relevant policies were finally all issued to Guangdong province, instead of to CMSN or the Transport Ministry.

CMSN had played an important role especially at the early stage in promoting the SEZ course. But, later, with the development of the policy process and more and more clarity about the interest relation, Guangdong authority had replaced its role. As controlling the power of formulating the relevant economic policies for the SEZ, the impacts of those functional sectors of the central government was considerable in shaping the framework of China's SEZ.

Finally, it is essential to point out the influences of top leaders. As mentioned above, pluralists would see them as a special interest, compared with others. Since the state-owed enterprises were in a dominant position in China's economy, those top leaders actually acted as the general managers of the state's economy (if the state were seen as a super-company). If we neglect this fact and only admit their importance because of their political positions, reputations and authorities, we would find it difficult to fully understand their influence. As we know that the classical pluralist considers those central leaders as passive elements, like a football in a match, in the policy process. However, they can play a positive role and are not an entirely passive force. In pursuing their desired target, whilst being influenced by others, they need to and also can influence others. They need to convince others, both inside and outside the policy-making circle, to accept their ideas, and to guide the public sentiment and also the trend of policy-making. Hence, as we have examined, the central decision-makers exerted a crucial role in determining the direction and policies of SEZ. Without their direct interventions with a far-reaching and broad view as standing at the highest position of a state, the original ideas of setting up an industrial zone or exported-oriented zone could not have been developed into a scheme of building-up the comprehensive economic zones, the SEZs. This issue also concerns an elitist explanation, which is the topic of next section.

The interaction relations and interest overlap relations, which existed among different sides in promoting SEZ policy-making, formed a joint force in promoting the SEZ course. These relations can be seen from the figure 9.1.

To pluralists, the interactions of those interests and their different impacts upon the policy process in initiating, deepening, crystallising and finalising the SEZ programme, show that the extent to which the participants can exercise their influence varied according to their power and status economically and politically.

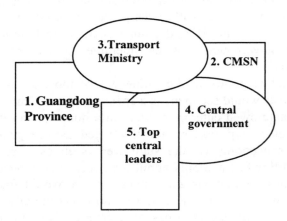

Figure 9.1 Interaction and interest overlap relations in policy process of initiating SEZ programme

Legend:
1   Guangdong province. Aimed to set up an export-oriented zone in order to develop an outward-looking economy.
2   CMSN. Hoped to establish an industrial zone in Guangdong's Shekou so as to increase its ability to fulfil its financial target of creating foreign exchanges.
3   Transport Ministry. Supported its subordinate, CMSN's plan to develop an industrial zone in Guangdong.
4   Central government. Tried to find a way as breakthrough to set up an outward-looking economy.
5   Top central leaders. Firmly promoted opening-up strategy and speeding-up China's economic development, which served the purpose of consolidating the stability of the regime.

Interest integration and policy evolution A policy process usually, but not necessarily always, involves conflicts in which different groups compete for their goals. A pluralist approach would suggest that the initiating of China's SEZ was an interests integrating course, in which different interests were involved and each of them showed its demand and tendency in the light of its own interest through different ways, and tried its best to pursue its desired target. The joint efforts of interests finally led to the producing of SEZ programme.

Although there were not direct interest crashes that occurred during this course, those interests did contend, negotiate, bargain and search for balance as well, in pursuing their desired targets. In this course, different interests were integrated, the goal was adjusted, and the direction was becoming more and more clear, and then a ultimate target was reached, which not only could be accepted by all sides, but seemed to be better than that expected (figure 9.2).

To pluralists this policy output proves the positive role of a wide involvement in advancing a policy process. CMSN originally only wanted to have a small area of land of two square km to build its industrial zone, and finally it got the whole Shekou peninsula to do so. The Transport Ministry did a good job in promoting its subordinate to enlarge business. The central government sectors enjoyed their success of realising a breakthrough in promoting the development of setting up an outward-looking economy. Guangdong was going to set up one or two export-oriented bases, then it was permitted to establish a group of SEZs which enjoyed much more favourable policies than could be predict. As for those top central leaders, their efforts in carrying out an opening-up and reform strategy achieved a good start, which greatly increased their reputation and consolidated their political status.

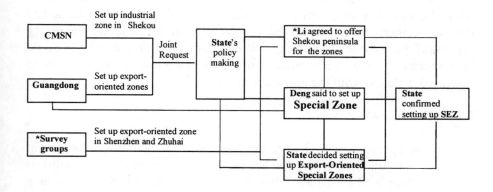

Figure 9.2 Interests integrating and policy adjusting process in making SEZ decision

Legend:
1   Li is Li Xiannian, the then vice Chairman of CPC central Committee and standing vice premier.
2   Survey group means the investigation groups sent abroad by Centre.

In examining the policy process of initiating SEZ programme, the pluralist approach would contend that in China's early reform period a tendency of wider involvement in policy-making had occurred, which was conducive to making better policies. This course illustrates that an effective plural involvement in a policy process in the post-Mao period requires three conditions as below. (1) A dynamics motivated by direct interest of pursuing a policy target. (2) An unobstructed channel for accessing policy process. And (3) an environment within which it is possible to accept those constructive opinions by the policy-making authority. Furthermore, the course also indicates that the extent to which the participants could influence the policy process depends on their resources they possess, and the degree of interaction and integration among interests.

However, we can not credit a pluralist explanatory mode too much in analysing the policy process of initiating SEZ programme. Pluralism has difficulty in exploring the issue of who dominates a policy process, and in handling the idea that those key decision-makers have an autonomous capacity to take decisions. If we deeply examine this course, it could be conceived that the substance of the competitions and interactions among interests, was the performance of those political elites, especially those key decision-makers, who played the crucial role in influencing the policy process. To a considerable extent, this defect of the pluralist account could be corrected by the elitist model. Hence, it is necessary to go ahead to discuss this course with the elitist approach.

9.2.2 Elitist view

The elitist approach would consider that both the works of theoretical guidance and practical promotion are the important roles of those political elites in China's SEZ-related policy process. Actually, the former appears to be more crucial in many occasions. Hence, it would not be reasonable if we did not point out this significance, but only attached attention to the concrete policy-making works that those elites did in furthering the SEZ course. The available evidences suggest that it was the renewing of the thinking mode, and the making of the new theoretical principles and guiding thoughts that provided the bases and essential conditions for the creation of the SEZ programme.

Political elites, in the research, mainly refer to those leaders or senior officials at and above provincial/ministerial level. Besides, those who are members of CPC central committee, members of CPPCC, high-rank bureaucratic officials and leading official theorists, are also included. To discuss the elites' role in initiating China's SEZ programme, first of all, we need to notice what they did in building up the basic theoretical framework and the general strategy, which is the foundation of creating China's SEZ. Being a turning point of PRC history, the Third Plenum of the 11th Central Committee of CPC set up new theoretical principles, new guiding thought of developing China's socialist economy with Chinese characteristics, and decided to shift the work focus to economic construction. These important strategic decisions had been recorded as paving the road and laying down the foundations of China's opening-up and reform course. For making these strategic decisions, those key political elites, with Deng Xiaoping as its core, played a decisive part. What they contributed included that Deng and his flowers firmly advocating and supporting the discussion on the criteria of judging truth, advocating the principle of 'seeking truth from fact', opposing and throwing down the erroneous idea of 'two whatevers', setting forth the principle that to develop the economy is the first important task, and raising the assertion that the science and technology is the first productive force, etc.

All these viewpoints, principles and theories provided the possibility for making China's SEZ-related programmes and policies, both then and afterwards. Unquestionably, setting up these theoretical frameworks in the early post-Mao period was an important milestone in CPC and PRC's history. Without this break-through, it would be absolutely impossible for China to make reform and opening-up strategy with SEZs as its experimental fields and windows. History had credited those elites a lot for these theoretical and directional making works.

The course of initiating the SEZ programme also saw a series of concrete parts played by those elites. The SEZ-related policy-making emerged in a period — the early stage of post-Mao China, when China was just ending an old era which was characterised by a highly centralised political system and a closed economic system, and trying to pave a path for reform and opening-up. Therefore, in this period, the old tradition still affected the operation of society to a considerable extent. Accordingly, a plural involvement in the policy-making process was still quite limited. Comparing with the second and the third stages of the SEZ course, we can see very clearly that in the first stage there were not public forces from different levels and different sides of the society including media, nor those from abroad, involved in the policy process. Under this circumstance, consequently, the role of those political elites appeared to be much more prominent than that which occurred later.

First, elitists would point to the crucial part played by those politicians and high level administrators. We saw that the original ideas of either setting up an exported-oriented zone or an industrial zone did not come from common people, but from the leaders of CMSN, Guangdong authority, and the officials of bureaucratic organs. It is not surprising that their official positions determined that they had the responsibility and the corresponding status in the bureaucratic system to view and consider this issue. In fact, to set forth such a constructive plan, which concerned many general policies and the overall situation of the state, is really not the affair of the ordinary people or even those bureaucratic officials who are at middle and lower levels. This could be seen basically as a universal phenomenon in all countries. Usually, except at those crisis moments when a state is facing a danger to its survival or is facing a very important issue, those ordinary people do not have the energy and enthusiasm to directly involve themselves in the state's affairs.

The process of deepening and crystallising the SEZ-related ideas also witnessed the active role of those elites. Both the leaders of CMSN and Guangdong tried every possibility to report their ideas to the top leaders and state the importance of their schemes, through different channels including formal report, individual meetings, and also informal channels. As soon as the central decision-makers recognised the significance of these suggestions, a 'bottom-up' pattern soon became a 'top-down' method in promoting the course. The central leaders immediately adopted a series of measures to further the feasibility study. According to the instructions of Li Xiannian, the vice chairperson of CPC centre and the standing deputy premier, within only three days from 31 January to 2 February 1979, two meetings for hearing the report and discussing how the related policies should be made for setting the zones, were held separately. Then, a working group, headed by Gu Mu, the deputy premier, was dispatched to Guangdong and Fujian provinces to conduct an on-the-spot investigation. With these powerful and prompt promotions, the decision-making for the would-be-SEZ developed fast and efficiently. It only took six months from when Guangdong and the Ministry of Transportation jointly submitted their request for setting up an industrial zone in Shekou, to when the CPC centre and the State Council formally approved the report coming from Guangdong and Fujian provinces asking for setting up SEZs. We notice that, more particularly, during this course, Deng Xiaoping had personally invited Xi Zhongxun, the first secretary of the CPC Guangdong Committee and the governor of Guangdong, to directly discuss the relevant issues of the zones. It was in this meeting that Deng formally set forth his opinion to set up the 'Special Zone'. All these facts indicate that it was the elites in the leading positions who played key roles in promoting the determination of the SEZ programme. Without their works of sparing no efforts with a long-term view it would have been impossible to make those decisions.

To evaluate the elitist style policy-making mode that occurred in the course of initiating the SEZ programme, it might be reasonable to say that the relative concentration of the decision-making power in the central authority, and the direct involvement of those key top leaders, had made the policy process including implementation quite efficient indeed, which is worthy of notice in the context of post-Mao period.

Examining the course of producing the SEZ programme with the elitist approach, to sum up, it could be conceived that political elites were in the dominant position of the policy-making process. There was little doubt that they had ample ability and power both to build up a new theoretical framework with which to launch a series of noticeable strategies, which are the theoretical strategic making from which SEZ programme could be produced, and to govern the concrete policy process efficiently. It was their powerful involvement that made it possible to determine the SEZ programme. However, on the other hand, we can also say that it is quite natural for those elites to do so because their responsibility and status require and enable them to perform in such a way. This is concerned with the issue of the resources and mechanism of their power and motivation, to explain which an institutional viewpoint could be helpful.

9.2.3 Institutional view

The institutionalist approach confirms the significant influence of institutions on policy-making through shaping the distribution of interests, the distribution of power and the rules of the game (March and Olsen, 1989, p.162). As have been analysed in section 2.2.6, institutions, in its theoretical account, cover a wide range of political and social issues. In the discussion of the SEZ-related policy process, therefore, we can not access them in a comprehensive way, which is too wide to be dealt with in the research. Instead, we focus our analysis only on those most important influences produced by the political system and power mechanism, upon the policy-making processes of the SEZ course.

In doing so, as observing the course of initiating the SEZ programme and developing the first group of SEZs, an institutional view would indicate that it was China's institutions which ensured to those political elites and high level officials very prominent status and power in dealing with policy issues, provided a centralised power mechanism, and shaped the importance of ideological controversy, which significantly influenced the policy processes.

When Yuan Geng, the head of CMSN got the idea of setting an industrial zone in Shekou, he immediately reported to and discussed with his direct leader, Ye Fei, the deputy minister of Transportation, in Hong Kong, without holding any relevant meetings as routing work. Ye supported Yuan and went to Guangzhou right away to meet Guangdong's leader for pursuing the co-operation. Then, after a special discussion on this issue, a joint report for the request to build up an industrial zone in Shekou was submitted to the centre within a very short time. In this course, the major leaders of CMSN, the Transport Ministry and Guangdong handled the decision-making issue directly and efficiently.

A few weeks later, this proposal was identified and put on the central agenda. The following works, the interactions between central leaders to the CMSN, and to the Guangdong authority, between the individual top leaders and the leaders of the relevant local authorities and central functional organs, with central leadership having the final say, were also conducted rapidly. These leaders and senior officials, including those at central and local levels, were in key positions of the party and the state's leading organs they belonged to. Owing to the features of China's party-led instead of state-led, administrative-led instead of legislative-led power system, it was not easy for other forces to challenge and obstruct these methods and actions taken by the SEZ advocators in advancing the policy process. Then, in pushing along the implementation of the agreed programmes and policies for the establishment and development of SEZs, a 'top-down' method was quite noticeable. In this course those chief leaders at and above vice-premier level played a dominant role, which enabled these works to be grasped directly and firmly from end to end, by which to secure a very high efficiency.

Obviously, this centralised power mechanism is beneficial in dealing with those policy-making issues that the state and CPC centre considers urgent and crucial, with particular efficiency. This is because that the decision makers 'don't have to go through a lot of repetitive discussion and consultation, with one branch of government holding up another' (Deng,

X. 1983, p.75) and can avoid the situation that 'decisions being made but not carried out' (ibid.).

In analysing the course of making the SEZ programme, furthermore, institutionalists would agree that as one of the major organic parts of China's institutions the ideology was of key importance in shaping the direction of policy-making. This feature indicates a decisive influence of ideology in a socialist country such as China so that whether a policy can be raised and adopted depends on whether it can meet the requirement of China's guiding theories and principles. Therefore, it seems not surprising that it was the noticeable changes of China's guiding theories that made it possible to determine a range of new policies and new programmes giving the first priority to the economic construction over others and conducting reform and opening-up strategy as its core. These changes that occurred in and after the Third Plenary of the Eleventh conference of the CPC, included advocating 'the practice is the sole criterion of test truth', and opposing 'two whatevers', etc. Unquestionably, it would have been absolutely impossible for China to make the reform and opening-up strategy and the SEZ-related policies, if it had not renewed its ideological thinking and still 'resolutely upheld whatever policy decisions Chairman Mao made, and unswervingly followed the instructions Chairman Mao gave', like Hua (Chairman of CPC centre, 1976-78) advocated, in the post-Mao period. It is simply because those new policies, which embodied shifting the focus of work of the party and the state to the economic construction, reforming the economic system, widely importing capital, technology and managerial skill, and all other useful resources from industrialised countries, and setting up SEZs etc., would be definitely considered ideological wrong in the Mao era.

Furthermore, in the development course of promoting the first group of SEZs, ideological conflicts also often occurred, which focused on following major aspects. Whether a socialist country can learn from capitalist countries, whether it was acceptable to allow foreign businessmen to invest in China for setting up joint adventure or sole foreign capital enterprises, and, whether a SEZ might become a foreign concession like those which existed in Shanghai and Tianjing before 1949, since it involved so many capitalist enterprises and capitalist factors, etc. All these conflicts inevitably brought about influences on SEZs' policy-making to a varied extent. For instance, it was defeating the 'whatevers group' that created the precondition for setting up SEZs, which served as the pioneering programme of implementing the reform and opening-up strategy.

To sum up, the above analysis suggests that the institutional approach is applicable to a great extent in interpreting the practice of the first stage's SEZ-related policy process. Conceivably, those three features including the prominent role of those political elites, the centralised power mechanism and the important impact of ideology, which stemmed from China's existing institutions, exercised a significant role in shaping the policy-making mode and direction.

9.2.4 Conclusions

The initiating of the SEZ programme occurred in a phase when it was just two years after China ended a decade's upheaval period and those key politicians who were purged in the Cultural Revolution were just controlling the central power again. At this stage, to determine a new strategy and new policies for the state's economic development became a very important and urgent central task. Therefore, the brewing and formulating of the SEZ programme benefited greatly from this powerful impetus. In examining this policy process, three approaches have been introduced. The pluralist view illustrates that the positive involvement of different interests formed joint dynamics to promote this course, in which the original idea of SEZ was produced through a 'bottom up' pattern. However, a plural participation in the policy process of this stage was still limited, being restricted only to the policy-making circle and only among those political elites at higher levels and different aspects, including those bureaucrats in higher status. In observing this situation, the elitist approach provides a more reasonable explanation. It was the elitist style policy-making mode with the centralised power mechanism as its main feature that gave a high efficiency to promote the policy process. However, the special status and power of elites came from China's existing institutions. It was the institution that provided those elites prominent status, shaped the centralised power mechanism and ideology-dominated principle, which framed the behaviour of those elites in making SEZ programme and SEZ-related policies. From this viewpoint, the institutional approach is applicable to a considerable extent in interpreting China's practice.

9.3. Examining the Hainan case

The setting up of SEZ in Hainan is a very particular case. Before setting up a separate province, as a remote island at the southern end of China, Hainan was in a rather marginal position in China geographically and politically. It possessed a large territory but only had a very low administrative status. Due to this reason, it appeared that it was easier to develop the local force and reduce the influence of the control from the centre on one hand, but not easy to successfully pursue its own interest on the other hand. Consequently, the policy-making course of promoting its development involved a lot of uncertainties. The potential conflicts of three interests between the Central government, Guangdong province and the Hainan region, and the conflicts of two crucial issues concerning the direction of Hainan's development and Hainan's administrative status, had got tangled up. During the SEZ-related policy process, a plural participation came to a considerable degree, and serious conflicts, arose, both overtly and covertly among the political elites and social forces, while the direct intervention from economic interests became relatively less significance.

9.3.1 Pluralist view

To observe the SEZ-related policy process for Hainan in an overall way, it can be seen that the interaction of three interests including the centre, the province and Hainan, governed the development of Hianan. Since this interaction has a closer relation with the influence of the institutions because the latter directly structured the relations of interest and power among these three sides, therefore, in this case, to examine this course with the institutional perspective should be much more appropriate.

In this account we mainly discuss the 'Yangpu Incident', which is a typical case of plural involvement in influencing the policy process about Hainan. The breaking out of the 'Yangpu Incident' pushed Hainan onto a national-wide background in which diversified interests were involved in the process of the debate about the feasibility of the Yangpu project (referred as YP hereafter). In this sharp controversy, a more particular plural participation was evident. By tracing this course we can see how complex and prolonged the decision-making was towards solving this incident, in which various factors were effective.

The 'Yangpu Incident' erupted in early 1989. Under the condition that China's reform had been further advanced when the political environment had been noticeably loosened, a plural involvement with much wider range and deeper extent in influencing this policy process, became possible.

Yangpu, an area in Northeast Hainan with good conditions for development, was planned for the setting up of an Economic Development Zone by Hainan province, soon after the Central government determined to set up SEZ in the whole Hainan Island. The focus of the debating on YP was whether it was legal and reasonable to lease a big tract of land covering 31-sq. km., to a foreign business company for development for a long period.

Compared with the policy process of initiating SEZ programme, in which fundamental conflict did not occur, the making of YP involved acute and strong opposition. The contradiction was comprised of many aspects (section 7.4.3). Diversified forces accessed the process and tried every possibility to show their opinions overtly or covertly, in order to influence the decision-making. Crisis broke out continuously. Four years had passed when the problem was solved and YP was eventually approved.

Interests involved in the YP conflict   Interests involved directly or indirectly in the protracted policy-making process of YP included: (1) KGHK (Kumagaya-Gumi (Hong Kong) Co. Ltd.); (2) Hainan province; (3) CPPCC; (4) media; (5) public; (6) central government; (7) politicians; and (8) hidden opposition in central level. Pluralists would emphasise the significance of the interest relations in shaping the motivation of people to access and influence a policy process. Among these interests, as discussed in section 7.4, Hainan province and KGHK were the most positive promoters. Due to lacking funds to develop Yangpu Economic Development Zone, Hainan province decided to lease a whole stretch of land which covered 31 square km. to the KGHK, a foreign company, and allow the latter to undertake Yangpu's development. The contract stipulated the rights and obligations of both sides under the condition that the power of administration and law enforcement in the zone belonged to Hainan. Obviously, this was a mutually beneficial co-operation. With this program Hainan would solve its big problem of urgently wanting huge funds without which it would be impossible for Hainan to start its ambitious construction scheme in Yangpu. As for KGHK, it could get a good opportunity to develop a large tract of land in such a promising area, and the repayment for its investment would be very attractive. For these reasons, both sides were eager to realise this plan, and hoped it could be approved by the central government as soon as possible.

However, in pursuing the desired goal, the role of these two sides was quite different. A pluralist view indicates that Hainan could play a much more important part than KGHK, for Hainan possesses the most fundamental resources for Yangpu's development. These include cheaper land and labour, and rich natural resources as well, which were the cards with which it could negotiate. But, its weaknesses were also prominent: it lacked capital on the one hand, and its political and economic foundation was relatively weaker, as a newly setting up province, on the other hand. Concerning the political foundation, Hainan's inadequacy in personnel relations in the power system seems a special weak point in seeking supporters in handling YP incident. This relation is an important political resource in China's reality, which could be used in influencing a policy process. As a foreign business company, the superiority of KGHK (the owner of its parent company is Japanese) was its possessing capital, with which it could either go ahead to develop YP, or withdraw if permission for YP was not available. The problem for it was that the state leaders did not consider YP as a very important programme of China at the early stage, so it had not been attached high attention. Under this condition, then, KGHK could not do more to influence the central decision-makers. Furthermore, the Japanese background of its parent company greatly increased its trouble when people discovered that a large tract of land would be leased to it. What KGHK could do in promoting YP, was to urge Hainan or express its demand to China's government if a suitable opportunity were available. In doing so, its role appeared quite limited.

CPPCC, as a national political consultative commission, is one of China's four most influential power organs at top level which include CPC centre, the State Council and NPC (Parliament). Among these four, CPPCC is listed as the last one and seems not to exercise any real power. However, its role lies on its important influence on China's politics, for it is composed of those representative figures from all social realms of the country (section 2.3.1). Pluralists would see it as an active and representative force in China's state's political life. Those CPPCC members involving in YP incident, which was headed by Zhang Wei, the formal president of Shenzhen University, viewed Hainan's YP style to develop an economic zone as 'selling state sovereignty' and 'betraying the country', so they thought that what they did to oppose YP was defending

China's national interest. Due to CPPCC's political status, this group's actions produced a great and profound impact on YP policy process.

It is conceivable that the media is the most powerful force in a society in influencing public sentiment, especially in a society which advocates a pluralist involvement in the state's political life. The media referred to here includes those at home and abroad. Usually, in reporting news, there are four attitudes in the media's performance: providing true fact with objective comment; providing true fact without comment; providing fact with unreasonable comment; providing wrong fact with wrong comment. Pluralist perspective emphasises the importance of the media in accessing and influencing the political life, in which it can play the role of communicating, advising, criticising and monitoring. It could be said that, among these four attitude, the first one represents the interest of the public, the second one seems to stand at neutrality, the third one confuses readers and then leads to a wrong direction, which appears maybe serving a given interest, and the last one absolutely safeguards an interest it supports. What attitude the media adopted towards the YP incident and what interest they represented, we will discuss later.

Public assessment in the YP Incident also included the student movement, which seemed like one kind of interest. The problem is that the nature of the student movement usually involves uncertainty to a considerable extent. Therefore, that whether they can represent the interest of the majority of the population or the fundamental interest of the state, needs to be analysed according to the concrete situation.

Politicians involved in YP policy-making process comprised those at provincial and central levels. At top level, they included Deng Xiaoping, Yang Shangkun (then state president), Wang Zheng (then state's vice president), and Tian Jiyun (then vice premier), etc. At provincial level, Xu Shijie, the Party secretary of Hainan, was a main figure. Besides, some chief leaders of other provinces also had accessed to the policy action. Xu, of course, represented Hainan's interest and performed as a firm defender of YP. He considered that YP project was completely in accordance with the state's interest. Other politicians mentioned above seeing that their actions were safeguarding the state's interest, were also supporters of YP.

Pluralists attach particular attention to the existence of those opponents of the YP at central level, which also can be called conservative force. Although the relevant reports or materials are still not available to list their names with certainty, the existence and positive actions of them in opposing YP were undeniable. The fact that the YP policy-making at central level was seriously obstructed indicated their force. They must have included politicians and senior officials in bureaucracies.

We saw the backgrounds and status of interests in the YP incident which show us how the conditions of each of them could influence the policy process. However, in this static observing, pluralism can not offer an explicit explanation. Therefore, a further analysis of the course in the situation when conflict happened and developed must be conducted, by which the pluralist approach might probe the essence of the issue. In this course, we can see how Hainan and KGHK, fighting in a pluralist condition, sought possible supporters to resist heavy stress from other interests, in order to pursue their desired goal.

Interests in conflict For Hainan and KGHK, they had expected some different opinions which would be raised after they declared their plan to develop Yangpu, but they never foresaw that the force opposing their plan would be so strong, the criticism to them would be so acute, and the range of the impact of the YP decision-making would be so broad. However, if they had enough preparation in their mind for this situation, were they able to manage the challenge? Was their force strong enough to solve this problem and lead the policy-making to the way they preferred? The answers to these are definitely negative. This is simply because the power to approve YP was not in Hainan but in the central authority, and even one or several chief leaders at the top could not decide it. A pluralist explanation for this might be that although different interests could access or influence the YP issue, the crucial impact on it mainly depends on those who control the most important resource (politically or economically), and so the changing circumstance favours some interests and ignore others in different period. We know that in some policy issues, it is even difficult to assess the policy output with a simple standard of right or wrong in a given phase, for the policy only reflects a consequence of the actions performed by some joint forces in searching for a desired target. What is important and needs to be examined, is whether decisions are made by a lawful majority through a lawful procedure. But, if the policy-making were conducted with a 'black box' style, it would be even difficult to assess from this aspect.

It was a dramatic consequence that when two inspections, the CPPCC survey group headed by Zhang Wei, and the State Council group headed by vice premier Tian Jiyun, went to inspect Yangpu, on the same day but only at different times, in January 1989, for they arrived at entirely opposite conclusions. CPPCC's group collected powerful evidences which it considered could be effectively used to deny the feasibility of YP fundamentally; while vice premier Tian Jiyun praised the YP programme and expressed his full support on the spot, and he even immediately defined the name of this zone as 'Yangpu Economic Development Zone'. An agreement between Hainan and the KGHK, for developing Yangpu, was signed, on the same day.

Pluralists highlight the significance that different opinions can be heard in a policy process. When Zhang challenged the Yangpu project overtly two months latter, by delivering a provocative speech to severely condemn YP, at the Fourth Meeting of the Seventh CPPCC, over one hundred committee members of CPPCC supported Zhang and strongly asked the State Council not to approve Hainan's scheme. Media, from home and abroad, also immediately became involved. These led to a national debate in which Hainan's YP became a target of public attacks, within a very short time. These evidences indicate that in this stage, nearly ten years after China launched its reform and opening-up strategy, the public outside the policy-making circle had been able to influence the state's policy process through different ways to a certain extent.

In order to change the disadvantaged situation, Hainan's authority had tried every possibility to seek support, which included directly submitting a report to the major central leaders and explaining their stance in the central meeting (section 7.4.3). Pluralists would see Hainan's efforts as defensive reaction for its interest that was challenged by so many others. A Pluralist view would also admit the uncertainty to determine a solution when a policy process encounters pressures from various sides. Although some major leaders including Deng and Wang Zheng (then vice president of state) expressed their clear-cut support to YP, and so did some provincial leaders, in and after the Special Work Meeting of CPC Centre, which was convened to deal with the YP issue, the tide of criticising YP was still very difficult to turn round. It seemed that the opponent was a strong force that could obstruct YP powerfully at that moment.

To further consider the YP policy course, pluralists would not be surprised about why Zhang Wei could still deliver his speech at CPPCC meeting to challenge YP even though he knew that the vice premier was stating support for YP which seemed to represent the opinion of the State Council, why a Special Work Meeting of CPC Centre could not solve this issue, and why Deng's instruction was not powerful enough to lead to a determination of YP.

Actually, in YP Incident, Zhang Wei was only a common committee member of CPPCC. That he dared to challenge YP to which he had known the opinion of the State Council, was not because his own status was powerful enough to enable him to fight against the latter, but because he stood on the position of CPPCC. As a national consultative organ, CPPCC possesses a high status which is not only at least at the same level as the State Council, but has the right to access and examine any policy relating to state affairs. Therefore, when more than one hundred members of CPPCC jointly asked the State Council not to approve the YP, which was the first time CPPCC publicly opposed the stance of the State Council, it gave the latter great pressure. This action, which enabled people to hear different sounds directly from China's top political arena, could be seen as an important symbol of the rise of a pluralist tendency in China's politics in the post-Mao period.

The special work meeting of CPC centre on YP, gave Xu Shijie an important opportunity to explain and defend his stance. However, also some leaders of the State Council and provinces warmly gave support to Xu, it seemed that the result of this meeting did not favour Hainan. More particularly, the fact that Deng's writing instruction of supporting YP also could not lead to a favourable result, indicated that some obstructions existed at central level, which provided us with evidence that Deng's words were not always the final say, and could still be challenged by others.

Furthermore, pluralists would like to analyse the role of the media in YP Incident particularly. The performance of the media in YP incident was noticeable. They had rapidly reported the situation that YP was seriously accused in CPPCC meeting and the reverberation in the country including the students' demonstration, which caused great influence both at home and abroad. However, they did not offer comments about whether YP was 'betraying sovereignty' and 'humiliating the State', like the cession of Hong Kong one and a half century ago, as it was accused. Actually, it seems not difficult to understand that they were completely different. YP only leased land to foreign businessmen for their development, and the power on the land of carrying out administration and law still belonged to Hainan, while the latter lost sovereignty. What the media did in their reports actually had made a stormy sea stormier over the YP incident, which produced much more pressure on the policy makers.

The students' actions including those large-scale demonstration marches, like the media, had a great instigating role. Their slogans, such as

'Return our Hainan!' and 'Down with the traitor!' etc., were easily able to trigger a patriotic feeling in Chinese people, for China had suffered invasion and insult from foreign countries for more than one century before 1949. Although the students' performance seemed radical, a pluralist view would emphasise this role as representing one kind of public opinion to access and influence the YP policy process, which had greatly increased the pressure on both Hainan and the Central policy makers.

Who dominated From the breaking out of YP Incident, the debating lasted for more than three years. In the postponed policy process, various interests had been involved. Contradiction and conflicts were interlaced at different levels. All relevant interests, including those inside and outside government, at higher or lower status, acted with their possible efforts. Pluralists would find it hard to explicitly point out which force was in a dominant position. Hainan's strengths lie in two aspects: it controls the local assets which include rich natural resources, land and labour; and being a newly set up province and SEZ, it had the right to ask the centre to give more favourable policies as support. However, its political foundation was not strong for it lacked essential power relations. More importantly, Hainan did not have the decision-making power on YP issue, although it could defend itself through all possible ways. Those top leaders, like Deng, Li, Wang and Tian, who were in the powerful positions, seemed unable to control the changeable situation for a quite long period. Their opinion, which favoured YP, failed to reach their goal by determining an acceptable solution. The pressures that came from different sides including opponents inside party and government made it difficult to make a final decision.

Those other oppositions including some CPPCC members which triggered the YP Incident, media and students which actively accessed the course, played great parts in obstructing the approval of YP. Before Deng's South China inspection, which aimed at striking back conservative force and launching a new round of opening-up and reform, the pressure of opposing YP eventually could not be excluded. To summarise, a pluralist view would point out that the YP policy process was complex and difficult due to the influences which came from different sides and also due to the significance of a plural involvement in a policy process in post-Mao China. In this postponed course, for the central decision-makers, the situation had been out of control. Different forces had shown their impacts, in which the opposing force seemed to be in domination and obstructed the issue for a long time with the result that both Yangpu and Hainan lost the best opportunity for their development in that period. However, the YP Incident showed us typical evidence of the rise of a plural involvement that occurred to influence China's policy processes in the post-Mao period. Although it had caused many troubles to YP, it did indicate a noticeable progress in China's political life.

A pluralist interpretation provides us with a picture that various interests can influence the policy process concerning Hainan's SEZ course, in the light of the extent to which each of them possesses the resources that could be used to do so. But, it can be argued that this explanation fails to explicitly point out who is really dominant in the policy process and why the YP was secured eventually. To seek an answer for this, applying an elitist view is essential.

9.3.2 Elitist view

Elitist approach would confirm the dominant role of those politicians at and above the provincial level, in influencing Hainan's SEZ policy process. Although a plural involvement significantly influenced the YP course, policy-making power was eventually still in the hands of the political elites, especially those at central level. The issue of setting up SEZ in Hainan got tangled closely with Hainan's administrative status. Due to Hainan's marginal position politically and geographically, for a long period, the direction of Hainan's development was quite ambiguous. This fact can be explained as below. Since the decision-making power over this issue, which concerned a remote island with large territory and important military significance, was highly concentrated, neither the region itself nor Guangdong province had much say on it. However, it would be impossible to determine an explicit and satisfactory solution unless the central authority could really discover Hainan's potential value and fully understand the necessity and urgency of its development. During the course towards setting up SEZ and a separate province there, both Hainan's administrative power and preferential policies that the central authority granted to it increased bit by bit, and they were also changeable. Owing to the existence of many uncertainties and a relatively limited involvement in this crucial issue by those inside or outside the policy-making circles, it had not been easy for those central decision-makers to deeply study this issue and to get enough information for making up their minds. Therefore, they needed to adopt an incremental method to promote this policy process, to which more detailed discussion will be conducted in chapter 10. This postponed course may also show the limitation or weakness of the elitist policy-making pattern in which the lack of both enough strong motivation and enough essential information in some occasions appears to be an unavoidable problem.

This conclusion seems to be in contradiction with that stressed in section 9.2.2 that an elitist style policy-making mode with centralised power showed high efficiency in the course of initiating the SEZ programme. Actually, they are not contrary to each other. The efficiency of the latter can be shown only when a powerful motivation was set up and the essential information was available for those elites. For instance, in the case of initiating the SEZ programme, a bottom-up pattern of involvement in advancing the policy process contributed greatly in helping and promoting the determination of the central leaders. And then, a series of actions of top-down policy-making and implementation with high efficiency could be conducted. However, in the process of making decisions for Hainan's development, these two sides mentioned above were not enough.

Although the policy process for determining Hainan as a SEZ, which was closely linked with setting up a new province in Hainan, lasted for a long period, a solution was eventually made by the central decision-makers. In this course, local authorities, experts and scholars in the academic, economic, and political circles, participated. But, as shown in reality, unquestionably, in determining such an important issue, which related to the state's affair politically, administratively, economically and militarily, the role of those central elites was decisive.

The elitist view would not only confirm the decisive role of those elites in making the final solution in the policy process towards setting up Hainan SEZ, but also point out their diversified influences, promoting or obstructing, in all those events which occurred in the course. In the 'Motorcar Incident', some people abused the favourable policies obtained from the centre to engage illegal traffic, in order to obtain Hainan's financial incomes. The fact was, Hainan's high level leaders manipulated this economic scandal, which shocked home and abroad. Stressing the fact aims to illustrate that only those people who controlled key power in Hainan could use the financial and power resources to purchase US $ 570 million worth of foreign exchanges on the black market for their illegal traffic. It indicated that it was this force formed by those key elites, instead of the people at lower status, which could fundamentally affect the policy process for Hainan's SEZ course. This action increased the conflict between central and the local governments, for it challenged the policy and authority of the former. Then it eventually made the central government re-consider the policies granted to Hainan, because this incident inevitably caused the centre's suspicion over the feasibility of granting so mach power to Hainan, a remote and large island. In this course, we see that those elites, representing central and local governments respectively, adopted actions they considered necessary to pursue and safeguard their interests. However, the weakness of Hainan in controlling resources politically and legally, contributed to its defeat. The action of those key elites in Hainan actually pushed them to a disadvantageous position, for some of those important favourable policies were taken back by the centre soon after this incident. Consequently, it further postponed the policy process of making the strategy for Hainan's development including the setting up of SEZ.

To further examine the course of YP Incident, the available evidences also suggest the crucial significance of those elites in the policy process. Although a plural involvement had been noticeably affecting the situation, the decisive role was exerted by those elites at high levels. It was the CPPCC group, headed by Zhang Wei, who first challenged the YP in the CPPCC Conference, and triggered the YP Incident. Without the important status and impact of CPPCC in China's political life, Zhang Wei's opposite opinion would certainly fail to attract attention both at home and abroad and produce a great pressure immediately.

However, could this challenge and the following pressures produced from various sides of the country change the minds of those politicians supporting YP programme? The fact was: from the early phase of this event to the final stage of the policy process, neither the challenge from CPPCC, nor the broad attack from the media and student movements, could enable those politicians persisting on supporting YP to concede. Xu Shijie, the party secretary of Hainan, still spared no pains to defend YP, until he deied of stomach cancer, half a year before the YP was approved. Tian Jiyun, the vice primer, inspecting Yangpu at the same day with Zhang, the leader of opposition in CPPCC, still held up his stance and firmly confirmed the lawfulness and necessity of YP project in the Special Work Meeting of CPC. Those major central leaders, including Deng Xiaoping, Wang Zhen, and some provincial leaders, also showed their clear-up support from end to end. No matter what happened inside and outside the policy-making circle, they had not made any concession and did not yield to pressure. These facts fully prove that either the external or the internal pressures had not changed, and also had been unable to change the thinking and wills of these mature politicians. Similarly, on the other hand, the opinions of this group favouring opening-up and the YP project, also could not change the minds of the hard opposition within the top policy-making circle. Although the names of this opposition cannot be identified from the available data, it was definitely the fact that they had been strongly opposed the YP project all along and successfully obstructed its adoption for more than three years. The situation could not be turned round until Deng struck back in the early 1992 by launching a new wave of reform which defeated the conservative force and enabled the YP programme to be approved eventually. Fundamentally speaking, it seems beyond controversy that those political elites dominated the policy process about YP, either making the event, or increasing the obstruction, or bringing it to the end by determining a solution.

When pointing out the significance of the competition among those elites in shaping Hainan's SEZ policy process, we can not neglect the influences of China's existing institutions. It was these institutions that framed the behaviour pattern and the mode of the policy process, to which we now turn.

9.3.3 Institutional view

In examining the policy process for setting up SEZ in Hainan with the institutional approach, what most attract our attention are the influences from three aspects: the fragmented centralism, the 'democratic centralism system', and the controversy of ideology. As has been identified in the earlier section, one of the main features of China's existing political institution is the centralised power mechanism. However, we know that when one side of an issue is particularly emphasised, it usually indicates that the converse side had become a problem or had been a tendency needed to be controlled. Since the founding of the PRC, or even the most periods of China's history, to advocate and consolidate a highly centralised power system was always an important task of the ruling group. This fact suggests, from the opposite side, that China is a country in which localism and power fragmentation are quite easy to develop. These are the two sides of one issue. In PRC's history, particularly speaking, either in the Mao era or post-Mao period, this contradiction often occurred and affected the policy-making processes. To observe the Hainan case, this phenomenon is also noticeable.

The fragmented authoritarianism model (section 3.2.3) argues that authority below the very peak of the Chinese political system is fragmented and disjointed. That for a long period the issue about Hainan's economic construction failed to be put on China's central agenda before the reform, and the development direction of Hainan could not be decided even after Hainan embarked on its opening-up course. These can be explained as resulting from the influence of this feature. Because it was China's existing institutions that determined the interest and power allocations and the rule of the game.

We know that since 1949, Hainan had never been considered as an economic development base, but only an outpost for national defence, especially in the cold war period. Due to Hainan's lower administrative status before the middle 1980s, the central government did not directly guide its development or include it in the state's development scheme by offering an overall consideration and arrangement in terms of the state's plan. However, the central government controlled many productions by use of those key resources in Hainan including important mines, farms (tropical plant farms, e.g. rubber farms), and also controlled the military bases there. This means that the central government had many interest relations in Hainan, but it did not have the direct responsibility to consider Hainan's comprehensive development, nor did it wish Hainan to be controlled too much by the Guangdong province. Thus, there was a subtle relationship between province and the centre. The attitude of the latter towards Hainan was quite confused. It seems that if a higher administrative status were granted to Hainan it would not be convenient to deal with the economic interests there which were directly controlled by central government. Politically speaking, if Hainan, a remote island with a quite wide territory, were granted a higher status, for instance, as a province, it would be easy to develop a local force. Therefore, the centre hesitated to change its stance towards Hainan for a long time, although the former understood that without a corresponding higher administrative status it would be difficult to manage Hainan's development in such a large island. Although as early as 1887 the idea of setting up Hainan province had been raised and Dr Sun Yat-Sen put forward this proposal again in 1912, it did not come true until 1988. From the early 1980s to 1988, the central government raised Hainan's status and increased its power gradually: from giving a status of administrative region, to granting a status with separate planning account like a province, and finally setting up a new province. Needless to say that if a suitable administrative status of Hainan could not be determined, it would be very difficult to make the decision for Hainan's development. Hence the central government's attitude towards Hainan, which involved some key interest considerations economically and politically, inevitably affected the policy course for Hainan's development.

As for Guangdong province, Hainan's poverty was a financial burden to it, and to improve the condition was not easy. On the other hand, Guangdong also could not challenge the situation that central government directly dominated some important economic activities in Hainan, and so for a long time Guangdong was inactive over this issue.

During this period, Hainan was neither led directly by the Centre, nor obtaining full consideration and help from the province, for the latter actually did not have the full power (politically) and ability (economically) to tackle Hainan's problems fundamentally. Hainan was in a very weak position until the middle 1980s. Hainan's involvement in the policy process varied in different stages according to the changes of its status and powers. When it was in a weaker status as being only a common region of Guangdong province, taking actions to influence the policy-making for its general development was basically impossible and also useless. Therefore, there was not any active part performed by Hainan on this aspect in the early 1980s when Hainan had been granted some special policies by which it actually got a 'Quasi SEZ' status to promote its economic development. Later, in the middle 1983, the No.11 document, issued by the CPC centre, offered Hainan more favourable policies enabling it to be 'a SEZ without a SEZ status'. A noticeable change of Hainan's Status and the corresponding power happened in 1984 when the State Council's motion of establishing the People's government of Hainan Administrative Region was adopted by the NPC. Under this circumstance, Hainan's leaders began to use their power resources to realise its interest pursuing, which appeared to be too hurried to consider the relevant stipulations of the state. Their action aiming at rapidly increasing Hainan's financial revenue, focused on the illegal trafficking in motorcar and electric goods, which eventually became an economic scandal known as the 'Motorcar Incident'. This action actually challenged the authority of the centre and undermined the state's interest. As a balance of this conflict which showed a competition between the centre and the local authorities, some of the most important preferential policies granted to Hainan were taken back. This was the first time Hainan clearly pursued its local interest. Unfortunately, it used an inappropriate and even illegal method and was defeated by the central authority. After that Hainan was defined as a separate province and was granted a SEZ status in the whole province, in 1988, and so it had much more power resource to seek and defend its own interest.

From what was discussed above, we see that the central government actually could not offer careful consideration for Hainan since it did not govern the latter administratively. In the meantime, neither Guangdong nor Hainan could decide this issue themselves. Consequently, this very important issue with great multiple-significances relating to the state, province and the island, failed to be considered for more than three decades. It seems undeniable that a fragmented centralised power mechanism did reduce the efficiency in policy-making when this contradiction become serious. After Hainan commenced its opening and economic construction course from the early 1980s, the issues about its administrative status and the corresponding development strategy still could not be decided for eight years until 1988. In this course, policies granted to Hainan increased by bits and appeared changeable. Institutionalists would see this phenomenon as the continuous influence of an established power operating system in which the defects were not easy to eliminate even if they had been recognised. However, it is now still not clear whether these defects had been realised by those key decision-makers at that time.

Furthermore, it is noticeable that the fragmented authoritarianism model considered the development of reform beginning in the late 1970s to enhance the fragmented and disjointed feature of the Chinese power system, because of the three reasons below. (1) The new situation that China's leaders reduced the use of coercion — purges, labelling and demotions for those who proposed ideas that eventually were rejected had emboldened policy participants to argue forcefully for their proposals. (2) The stress laid on serious feasibility studies during the 1980s actually encouraged various units to marshal information to support their own project preferences, which were often in competition with others. (3) The general decline in the use of ideology as an instrument of control had increased the 'looseness' of the system, and decentralisation in personnel management, permitted many bureaucratic units additional initiative (Lieberthal and Lampton, 1992, pp. 8-9). These changes combined to reduce the extent to which organs and authorities at different levels responded in a fixed fashion to instructions from high levels, and to increase fragmentation of authority to a considerable extent.

The policy process for determining YP project did reflect these changes resulting from a new political environment in post-Mao China. This new environment was the creature of nearly ten years' reform in China. That Zhang Wei, the head of a CPPCC investigation group to Yangpu, dared to voice a strong opposing opinion on YP programme, even after he knew the preference of some major top leaders, was just encouraged by a changed and loosening political environment. Under this circumstance Zhang and some other CPPCC members supporting him had no longer worried about the consequence that would follow their action. It was absolutely impossible to do so in the first three decades of the PRC. In that period, if someone expressed ideas that differed from the official standard, he or she would probably be treated as a rightist or anti-party person and then endless disasters would follow. Later, the occurrence of a serious divergence at the Central level about YP also indicated that the new situation had emboldened participants of policy-making to argue forcefully for their proposals even though they faced the disagreement of the top leaders, due to the noticeable reduction of the political and ideological stresses. Up to now, there is no evidence to show that anyone who insisted on his or her different opinions over this issue had been punished.

The changing political environment in post-Mao China also encouraged officials to publicly and directly compete for the interests they represented. For saving YP scheme, Xu Shijie, the party secretary of Hainan province, had tried every possibility including formal and informal political measures, to strive for support from the policy makers at central level. Xu did not know whether YP would be approved when he died in the middle September 1991, due to his stomach cancer resulting from too much hard work and anxiety. Institutionalists would consider that although the changing environment had been beneficial in emboldening people to pursue their desired interests and preferred policy targets, it greatly increased the complexity and difficulty of policy-making on some issues, compared with the past when the centralised authority was very powerful.

The fragmented authoritarianism model holds that under the structure and procedure with fragmented authority, the policy process is 'protracted', 'disjointed' and 'incremental' (Lieberthal and Oksenberg, 1988, p. 24). This conclusion seems to catch the main features of the policy process for Hainan's SEZ course, which lasted from the middle 1980 to early 1988 when Hainan was finally decided to set up SEZ in the whole island and to establish a new province. This is a typical protracted, disjointed and incremental policy-making process. This incremental feature will be discussed in more detail in the incremental interpretation account in the next chapter.

The reinforcement of the fragmented centralism in post-Mao China was actually a tendency of decentralising the power system. It might reduce the efficiency of the policy-making to a certain extent, however, it greatly increased the involvement of a plural participation. From this point of view, therefore, it can be also considered as a progress of China's political life in the post-Mao period.

The ideas and wills of the paramount leaders were usually decisive in influencing a policy process either in the Mao or Deng era. However, this was not absolute. Sometimes, they also encountered challenge from oppositions and even failed to turn round the latter. In Hainan's case, that Deng's instruction favouring YP project was obstructed in the policy process for a long time showed this situation. As China's paramount leader in the post-Mao period, Deng enjoyed a very strong authority and power in governing both the state and the party's affairs. But, why couldn't his clear-cut instruction of supporting YP change the tendency of the event after the eruption of 'YP Incident'? Institutionalists would illustrate this phenomenon from the following two aspects. The loosening political environment had emboldened people inside and outside the policy circle to express and persist in their opinions, and the principle of 'democratic centralism system' which emphasises that the minority should be subject to the majority in making decision, was still effective in post-Mao China. Deng was unable to change the situation until he struck back the conservative force through his South China inspection in the early 1992. Nevertheless, the role of paramount leader in the policy-making process in post-Mao China is well worthy of study, to which further discussion will be conducted in the next section.

Although a general decline in the use of ideology as an instrument of control has occurred, especially in the non-political realms, ideological considerations still often influence some people's thinking to a great extent. In Hainan's case, the controversy about the feasibility and lawfulness of YP project was closely linked with ideological issues. The debate focused on whether a big tract of land of a socialist country could be leased to KGHK, a foreign company from the capitalist world, for a long time, particularly since the parent company of KGHK is a Japanese enterprise. Forty-three years ago, Japan was the fierce enemy of China. The opponents of YP strongly condemned the YP project as 'humiliating the state' and 'betraying the sovereignty of China', which produced great pressure on those supporting the YP. This sharp debate involved people from different sides and different levels of the society. Those conservative forces also took advantage of this event to criticise reform and opening-up programme. All these made it very difficult to decide the YP for a long time. Examining this fact, it seems that ideological controversy can still influence China's policy-making process to a considerable extent.

9.3.4 Conclusions

Hainan's SEZ policy process involved many uncertainties. At the beginning of its opening-up course a clear development target could not be decided, which had been searching in the practice step by step. Although setbacks and incidents occurred during this course, a series of feasible SEZ-related policies was eventually determined for Hainan's development. To pluralists the uncertainties in the policy process came from the difficulty in dealing with the indefinite *de facto* interest and power relations between the centre, province and the region, relating to Hainan's status and development. A variety of forces had influenced the policy process, and the extent of their impacts varied in different periods in terms of the resources they could control. Elitist perspective emphasises that although those social forces had played a great part in influencing Hainan's events they could not be the decisive element; instead, those politicians at and above the provincial level actually governed the decision-making to the last analysis. Elites' prominent roles embody those positive and passive aspects. The institutional approach would see the protracted, disjointed and incremental policy process for Hainan's SEZ course as the result of the fragmented-centralised power operating mechanism. The new environment in post-Mao China characterised by less political coercion and less ideological control emboldened people to voice their opinions and pursue their interests. These changes noticeably increased the plural involvement in the state's affairs although they might reduce the efficiency in policy-making to a certain extent. Moreover, it needs to be pointed out that although ideological control had been reduced in China's social life generally, in some important occasions the influence of ideological debates on policy processes still can not be neglected.

9.4 Examining the Pudong case

Pudong's development occurred in a stage when many experiences about SEZ had been accumulated and many SEZ policies had been tested and approached maturity. Moreover, the advantage for Pudong's development also came from Shanghai's special status in China and the relatively high quality of Shanghai's leadership and cadres. Under these conditions, the policy process for developing Pudong New Zone should have been promoted with high efficiency from end to end. However, the reality seemed not to follow this way completely. In the period from 1984 to 1995, the first five years were a protracted process and then the last five years showed a rapid development. Besides, some other features are also noticeable. How could these situations occur? Explanations are varied in different theoretical approaches.

9.4.1 Pluralist view

Pluralists would see the producing of the Pudong project as the result of the contribution of various forces through a bottom-up pattern in the new condition. Those who were involved in this course included Shanghai's local authority, experts from home and abroad, and the central decision-makers. The enthusiasm of each of them to access and to promote this course varied in different stages. These changes affected the evolution of the policy process to a considerable extent. With the wish to restore Shanghai's prestige as a world-known metropolis and the biggest financial and trade centre of Asia in the 1930s and 1940s, Shanghai's authority was very keen to speed up its construction. As early as 1984, Shanghai government had set forth the idea to develop Pudong. At that time, three ETDZs had been set up in Shanghai and achieved fruitful development, but their sizes were too small to realise Shanghai's ambitious scheme. Consequently, Shanghai decided to develop Pudong and two reports about Shanghai's development strategy were submitted to the State Council (CSC) in 1984 and 1986. In these reports Shanghai repeatedly put forward the suggestion of developing Pudong as a new zone. But, the target for Pudong's development, which means following what mode and using what way to undertake the Pudong project, was still not very clear by Shanghai itself then. However, a pluralist view would highly value this initiative that represented a request of local interest and sought support from the centre. Whether or not this proposal could be put on the centre's agenda and adopted as a State's programme, it had been a beneficial action in promoting the State's policy-making for Shanghai's development.

As for the State Council, its responses to Shanghai's reports were also the general treatments, which considered the Pudong programme as a local scheme. Although the written instructions from CSC confirmed the necessity of developing Pudong again and again, it was neither seen as a state's project with offering special policies nor considered as being urgent. This attitude was not changed until the early 1990 when Deng became involved in this issue. This fact indicates that although the CSC has the right to decide whether Pudong should be treated as a special zone, and although it had the time for six years to consider this issue, it failed to realise the particular significance of Pudong and grant the latter with special policies. It seems to be conceivable that with the applicable resources the inaction of the CSC towards Pudong was actually missing a good opportunity, which was a disadvantage to both Shanghai and the State. Since the CSC had the decisive power in dealing with this issue, it should take the major responsibility for the stagnancy of studying the proposal about Pudong for six years.

It needs to be noticed that whether Pudong is defined as a SEZ or SEZ-like zone is very important. If it is, some favourable policies are available to Pudong, which would be conducive to its development; if it is not, then, Pudong would be only treated as a common development area without special policy offer, as in the period from 1984 to the early 1990. Since the imparlance between The State Council and the Shanghai government had failed to produce an initiative result towards a SEZ direction, what could be expected to break this balance was the involvement of another powerful force with foresight.

This force did eventually come. To pluralists, Deng's intervention in the Pudong issue from 1990 indicated the active involvement of China's most positive reform group at high-level policy-making circle. This group represented the core interest of CPC and the State. Deng's involvement signalled the turning point of the Pudong policy process. Since then, the policy-making for the Pudong project was speeded up remarkably. Only two months later after a series of highly efficient works from the centre to the local authorities, the project of developing the Pudong New Zone was confirmed by the State. Making this decision finally ended a six years' protracted and hesitant process. These fast responding actions could be adopted was not only because the decision-makers had realised the significance of the Pudong issue, but more importantly, because the interest controlling the most important power resources could have the decisive say. Furthermore, the prominent increasing of the attention on the Pudong project and the remarkable improving of the working efficiency for Pudong policy-making may be linked with a major change in China's top leadership. That means, Jiang Zemin, the original Party Secretary of Shanghai, became the General Secretary of CPC centre in the middle 1989, replacing Zhao Zhiyang after the Tiananmen event. It is not clear whether Jiang was directly involved in promoting the Pudong project. But even if he did so it seems not to be irrational, for Shanghai is his political base. The fact that two years after Jiang became the General Secretary the importance of Pudong New Zone was further emphasised and determined as China's key project in the 1990s suggests that it is unnecessary to exclude the influence of Jiang on this issue.

9.4.2 Elitist view

Elitists would see that both the protracted and efficient phases in the Pudong policy process resulted from the dominant role of those political elites, with the influences from other social elites. Although the Shanghai government raised the suggestion to develop Pudong in its overall development scheme which was submitted to the centre in 1984, and this idea was put forward again in 1986, Shanghai did not set forth a clear target or blueprint for Pudong. At that moment, Shanghai had already set up three ETDZs and obtained fruitful achievements, but what would be the direction of Pudong, an ETDZ or a SEZ? Shanghai did not explicitly ask the State Council. Similarly, in the two written replies to Shanghai's reports, the State Council also failed to offer a clear guidance and define an essential status for Pudong, but only generally agreed with Shanghai to develop Pudong. This non-decision situation did not change for six years until Deng's intervention in the early 1990. During this long period, the possibility of raising and deciding a more active plan for Pudong existed for both the leaderships in Shanghai and the State Council. The resources they controlled politically and economically could enable them to do so. But they failed to do so. The situation in the second half of the 1980s was that there were five SEZs and many ETDZs that had been set up, and a large numbers of Coastal Open Cities had been defined in China. Hence, there was no reason for them to consider the Pudong issue without thinking about the possibility of setting up SEZ or SEZ-like zone. Their inactive decision could be explained, conceivably, as either that Shanghai worried about the feasibility to do so for it needed huge capital, or that the State Council thought Shanghai was too important to China to conduct such an experiment, or that both of them simply did not really realise the far-reaching significance of developing Pudong for Shanghai and China's economic construction. The consequence of Shanghai's implicit requests and the State Council's inactive decisions was that the Pudong issue was protracted again and again.

Additionally, to a certain extent, the elitist view would also ascribe this prolonged and inactive policy process to the result of the possible hidden competition between those high level elites. At the brewing stage of the Pudong project, Zhao Zhiyang was in the core positions of both CPC centre and the State Council (premier 1980-87, General Secretary of CPC 1987-89). Zhao's base was Guangdong and the adjacent provinces. It is not clear whether Zhao had directly disagreed to grant Pudong an important status, but it had been an undeniable fact that the Pudong project was not given enough attention when Zhao was in the core position of power. Contrastively, the fortune of Pudong came soon after Jiang Zemin, the original secretary of Shanghai CPC Committee, became the General Secretary of CPC centre from the summer of 1989. Elitists see the formal official status as the important power resource of political elites, and so the changes of the power of Zhao and Jiang seem to have directly influenced the Pudong-related policy process.

Although Jiang's promotion might give impetus to the Pudong policy-making course, a fundamnetal change happened when Deng Xiaoping became involved in this event in the early 1990. Fully realising the value of Pudong project and Shanghai, Deng regretted not including Shanghai in the list of the first group of SEZ ten years ago. Hence, he strongly required the relevant leaders of both the centre and Shanghai to firmly grasp accelerating Pudong's construction. From his intervening in this event, the policy process for the Pudong project was speeded up marvellously. Within only two months a series of important study works were finished, which included an on-the-spot inspection conducted by a centre-dispatched group headed by a State Councillor, a feasibility study undertaken by a group headed by a vice premier. In this course Shanghai submitted its third report which specially requested developing Pudong. Then, the construction of Pudong New Zone as the State's project, to which a series of favourable policies would be granted, was formally embarked on in the middle April of 1990. Six years' prolonged and inactive policy-making process was ended immediately by Deng's instruction. Two years later, it was decided as the key project of China's economic development strategy in the 1990s. To elitists, this unmatchable decisive role exerted by Deng indicates the importance of the key elite in influencing the policy process of post-Mao China.

As confirming the significant impetus came from Deng in finally determining Pudong project, it is also not unreasonable to think it was a pity that Deng did not discover the special value of Pudong and Shanghai in promoting China's reform and opening-up course more earlier. Owing to Deng's status and authority, if he had supported Pudong five or ten years earlier, it would have been fortunate for both Shanghai and China. For this reason, Deng himself explicitly expressed his regret and admitted it was his mistake for failing to do so. These facts suggest that the key elites' role is important in advancing a policy issue; however, they could neither always obtain enough reliable data for their judgements nor always make correct decisions. If we re-think the performances of the State Council and the Shanghai authority in the early phase of the Pudong course, we can see a similar situation.

Elitists also view technological expertise and knowledge as the important resource of elites. To promote and develop the Pudong project, those experts contributed a lot in influencing policy-making. Before Deng's intervening in the event, the experts from home and abroad had done many works to demonstrate the necessity of developing Pudong, and to suggest methods to do so. Among which, Lin Tongyan's suggestion was very influential. Since the Pudong project was confirmed, those relevant experts were further involved with it. For example, in order to achieve the most brilliant design for the Lujiazhui, a tiny area that was defined as the financial centre of Pudong, those best designers from America, Japan, Italy, France and Britain were invited to join the work. This fact indicates the prominent extent to which those international experts could influence Pudong's development.

9.4.3 Institutional view

The institutional version would see the characteristic of the policy-making process for the Pudong project, which showed sharp contrast on the efficiency between the earlier and later stages, as the result shaped by China's existing political system and administrative mechanism. Institutionalists would agree that China's centralised power mechanism had greatly influenced the Pudong-related process. Since SEZ is a programme relating to many important policies and is one of the key parts of China's reform and opening-up strategy, the decision whether and where to set up a SEZ should be taken by the central power. If the centre agreed to a proposal, it could be advanced rapidly. This could be seen in the case of initiating the first group of SEZs, and the more particular case of the second stage of promoting the Pudong project in which very high efficiency had been shown. However, if the centre did not agree a proposal, or did not express a clear stance, it would be very difficult to change the situation and no substantial policy offer could be expected. In the first stage of the Pudong policy process, Shanghai did not obtain any substantial answer from the State Council, and so more than five years had been lost. Under this circumstance, Shanghai did not raise any different opinion for further argument, as Xu Shijie did for YP project in Hainan policy process. This may be explained as an indication of a more institutionalised power-operating mode in Shanghai — China's most important economic metropolis, in the post-Mao period.

The remarkable efficiency in the Pudong course since Deng's involvement suggests a strong impetus of a centralised power mechanism. As soon as the central leadership accepted Deng's suggestion, two central working groups went to Pudong and finished the investigation and feasibility study separately, and Shanghai submitted its explicit report for asking to develop Pudong. Then the Pudong project was formally adopted. All these works were completed within only two months, which noticeably showed the role of the institutionalised power characterised by centralised mechanism, as it started to operate. Further more, an institutional view would also confirm the significance of the special preferential policies and the direct financial assistance offered by the centre authority in promoting the development of the Pudong Project after it was launched. Pudong got some new preferential policies, besides enjoying those general items which had been implemented in other SEZs and ETDZs, such as the methods and conditions of tax reductions and exemptions, and the exemption from the industrial and commercial consolidated tax etc. These new policies include permitting foreign business people to build tertiary industries, to undertake financial, retail sales and other trades, for which foreign businessmen were banned or restricted from operating in other places at that time, and to set up foreign-funded banks in Shanghai and the zone. Moreover, within the bonded area of Pudong, foreign trade agencies are allowed to engage in entrepot trade. As for financial assistant to Pudong, the central government directly granted financial allocation and bank loan quotas for Pudong's infrastructure construction, which was also very special in China's SEZ policies. As we know without exception, all other China's SEZs and opening zones were only given policy privilege to facilitate local capital accumulation, but no direct grant from the central government. Thus, the special treatment to Pudong by the central government was a great impetus to Pudong's development. These policies were determined in a very short period after Pudong was decided upon as the state's project in 1990. To do so was unlike what happens in Western countries where usually to decide these policies needs a very long period to debate, negotiate and bargain among different policy-making organs. It was this highly centralised policy-making mechanism that promptly provided powerful policy support to Pudong and enabled Pudong to develop rapidly

An institutional approach would attach highly attention to the role of the paramount leader, which needs to be further discussed. As known to all Deng was China's paramount leader in the post-Mao period, as Mao was in the past. Deng's role in the Pudong course, in the major events of the SEZ policy process, and in China's political life as well, was related to the political system and the political philosophy. It is China's political system and China's ideology that provides and highlights the importance of a top leader or of a leadership core with a few top political elites. It has been beyond of controversy that Deng possessed great authority in influencing China's policy-making even after his retirement.

The institutional view would agree that the substance of admitting a paramount leader is actually accepting an absolute power and an absolute authority to a great extent. However, we know that the wisdom and ability of any talent or any elite, even the best one, are limited, compared with those possessed by numerous people and with a very complicated objective world in which the uncertainty could never to be ended. Hence, at any time and in any country, one top leader's idea could not replace those of other elites at different levels, and should not be dominant in all realms and all levels. To place too much power and hope in one or a few elites is unreasonable, and to concentrate too much power on one or a few elites is really taking a great risk. This has been demonstrated by PRC's history, especially in the first three decades. It was fortunate that in China's policy-making process in the post-Mao period, including the Pudong course and other SEZ programmes that most of Deng's decisions were mainly correct. However, if not, it would have been dangerous, for his power was decisive in most occasions.

9.4.4 Conclusions

The policy-making for setting up the Pudong New Zone indicates a changing process within which the extent to which different factors had influenced the event varied, which resulted in two sharp contrast periods in this peaceful-like course. The earlier phase was protracted and inactive whilst the later stage was accessing a high way. The pluralist approach explores that the Pudong project was promoted by a group of forces from different sides and different levels, and from home and abroad. The role of the participants involved in this event, influenced the policy process, passively or positively, to an extent that varied from one to another according to the resources each of them could control. Just as the State Council's inactive response protracted the course at the earlier stage, Deng's intervention turned aside and speeded up the process. The elitist view illustrates the substance of a wide involvement in the Pudong programme that it was those elites in different realms and different levels that dominated the policy-making process. From initiating the preliminary idea to determining the project, and from making the preferential policies to conducting the New Zone's design, those elites' roles were crucial. To institutionalists, the development of the Pudong policy process was actually shaped by China's existing political system and administrative mechanism. A centralised power structure and the rule of the game determined the earlier stage's prolongation and the later phase's acceleration. The role of the paramount leader, admitted by China's society, was decisive in Pudong course. It was an institutionalised tradition and social system that provided Deng with a good arena for his performance by which he brought about such a marvellous change, not only in Pudong, but also in other realms of China's reform and opening-up course.

9.5 Conclusions

The development of SEZ course indicates the significant influences of various elements upon policy-making processes in post-Mao China at different stages and in different events. During the period from 1979 to 1995, China's SEZ developed fast and obtained remarkable achievements, though deviations and setbacks occurred occasionally. In the new situation of the post-Mao period, the heavy internal and external pressures imposed on China had been turned around as powerful dynamics of promoting the changes of the thinking mode and the making of a series of new policies and new strategies. The efficiency and quality of Policy-making improved noticeably in view of diversified reasons, which include renewing the thinking mode and guiding thought of the policy makers, loosening the political environment, and adopting feasible and effective policy-making methods, etc. The occurrence of these elements had ensured that better policy outputs were produced and implemented, which brought about great achievement. To examine the applicability of those three selected theories and models concerning how policy is made in interpreting this SEZ-related policy process, what we can see varies from one to another.

To pluralists the rapid development of the SEZ course demonstrates that the powerful impetus stemmed from the involvement of multiple-interests at different levels. A pluralist view explores that both initiating the original SEZ programme and the project of developing Pudong were produced by a 'bottom up' pattern, in which interests interacted or were integrated and thereby influenced the policy processes. The development of Hainan involved much typical plural participation inside and outside the policy-making circle, in which the forces including those which were promoting and those were obstructing, positively exerted their roles respectively. The sharp conflicts, which occurred in this course, resulted in a tortuous and prolonged policy process. Although the Pudong project started later than all others, it obtained an important position in China's SEZ programmes. Besides the significant status of Shanghai in China, that the interest favoured this project possessed the most important resources politically and economically, is believed to be a noticeable reason. To be sure, pluralist explanation portrays a colourful picture of policy-making course in the post-Mao China, in which those involved interests performed actively to search for their desired targets, with the resources they could control. However, the applicability of this theoretical account to China's practice is still quite limited. Because, a plural tendency that occurred in the post-Mao period during the last two decades, is only at its preliminary stage. Moreover, its influences is also restricted by a centralised power system that seems to be less concentrated then than in the Mao era but is still rather strong. Additionally, it should be noticed that pluralist perspective itself also fails to probe exactly who dominates the SEZ policy process.

The elitist view shows us that the substance of conflicts and dynamics of the SEZ-related policy process was the competition among those political elites, especially those at and above the provincial level. The making of the reform and opening-up strategy, which was the precondition and guiding line of creating SEZ programme, came from the decisive victory of the reform-oriented elites group, headed by Deng. Without defeating the 'whatevers' group, headed by Hua, the then Chairman of the CPC centre, the leading group of CPC could not renew its thinking mode through turning down the old explanation about Marxism, and could not determine a range of new policies and programmes to speed up China's economic development. Without this turning, the SEZ programme could not be produced. In the three cases of the SEZ course, also, it was those elites who played the crucial role in influencing the policy processes, in which the impacts of the paramount leader was particularly prominent. Those elites' role, in this course, included those who promoted and those who obstructed, and both of which were noticeable in governing the policy process. In Hainan's YP case, the great pressures coming from different sides of society could not change the minds of those elites favouring the YP, and also, the will of the latter could not change the idea of those hidden opponents at central level. The eventual determination of this project three years later simply indicated the result of this competition. In the Pudong case, Deng's intervention immediately ended a protracted process for making Pudong's development, and embarked on this project with far-reaching significance. Although the elitist view is effective in interpreting the SEZ policy process to a considerable extent, it fails to explain why and how those elites could use their resources to govern the SEZ policy process, and what has shaped or structured the policy-making mechanism. To answer these questions, an institutional interpretation is applicable.

The institutional perspective sees the policy-making mode in the SEZ course as the product shaping by China's political system and administrative mechanism in the post-Mao period. It explores and demonstrates the following important issues. It was China's political system that granted those elites particular status and power, and enabled them to perform prominently in the SEZ course. It was China's political and administrative system that shaped a centralised power mechanism. The role of a centralised power mechanism is double-sided. It can restrict the enthusiasm and efficiency of the sub-state authority to a certain extent on the one hand, and also can secure a higher efficiency in making those important policy issues controlled by the centre, on the other hand. Though this power mode had been somewhat declined compared with the Mao era, it was still quite strong and its positive role in ensuring a relatively higher efficiency in SEZ-related policy-making is conspicuous. It was China's political system that permitted and admitted the prominent status of a paramount leader. For Deng, it did not matter whether he was or was not in the key positions of the Party and the State, he could influence the SEZ policy processes decisively in most occasions, except for dealing with the YP case in the earlier stage. It was China's political system that determined the crucial importance of the ideological controversy. The victory of fighting against 'Two whatevers' paved the road for China's development with reform and opening-up strategy as its central line, and stemmed from which SEZ programme came into being, in the post-Mao period. The ideological conflicts that occurred in the SEZ course often influenced the policy-making, for instance, the delay of adopting the YP project. To sum up, it could be said that the institutional interpretation is quite persuasive for showing us that the institutions are the resources and bases of China's power allocation and power operating mechanism, within which the SEZ-related policy-making took place. According to above analyses, the extent to which those three selected state theories could be used to interpret China's SEZ-related policy-making processes course, may be listed as below decreasingly: institutionalism, elitism and pluralism.

10 The applicability of the selected theories about how policy should be made

Examining China's SEZ course with selected state theories concerning how policy is made, in the preceding chapter, has helped us to understand the applicability of these theories and models and also China's policy processes from principle to practice, covering the aspects of motivation, participants, environment and resources in policy-making process. This chapter goes further to examine the applicability of four selected models about how policy should be made, to the SEZ-related policy process. These models comprise rational model, incremental model, optimal method and contingent theory.

As has been pointed out earlier, the creation of these policy-making models characterised by prescriptive analysis aimed at searching the way to improve policy process. Among these models, incrementalism is a critique of rationalism, and the others are attempts to find a middle ground. Then, are they applicable to interpret China's SEZ policy process, and to what extent and how can they be applied in this practice? These are the issues that we try to explore here.

10.1 Rationalist explanation

It has been demonstrated in a general analysis, in section 3.2.1, under the conditions of current China that the philosophical monism and absolutism are still affecting the political and ideological circles to a considerable extent, the individualistic arbitrariness and the personality cult have not been thoroughly cleared out, it is not only that to stress the importance of increasing the involvement of rationality is particular beneficial to China's practice, but the model is applicable in reality to a considerable extent. Applying this model is of great significance in reducing the influence of those passive elements mentioned above and promoting the development of a better policy-making pattern, even though both comprehensive rationality and bounded rationality models have their limits since they contain an idealistic content to different extents. This section further examines the applicability of the rational model to China's SEZ policy process.

10.1.1 Comprehensive rationality or bounded rationality?

To determine a policy, a comprehensive rationalist approach requires the selection of a suitable alternative that can maximise the decision-maker's value, based on considering all alternatives that are supported by necessary information, and analysing and evaluating all their consequences. (section 4.1.1) In the course of making SEZ-related policy decisions, was there any policy issue that had been decided in such a way? Was this approach ever effective in promoting SEZ cause? The available evidence suggests that usually the decision-makers tried lots of possibilities to pursue a solution or policy output that could meet their desired values, which appeared to be conducive to the SEZ course. In a general view, the basic decision-making processes of SEZ usually comprised the following steps:

- Raising a suggestion or a problem that wanted approval or solution, by local authority or a state's operating organ at department/ministry level.
- Identifying the substance of the suggestion or problem by the leaders of CPC or State at or above vice premier/secretariat levels, so as to see whether it needs to be put onto an agenda.
- If the issue has been considered necessary for further study, then an investigation group, headed by a senior leader, usually at least vice premier, was dispatched to conduct the on-the spot survey.
- Different forums or conferences were convened, by which to explore diverse opinions, and to discuss the possibilities and their consequences of various available alternatives.
- A solution or relevant policy was made after studying the feasibility of all those options.
- After holding a formal meeting by the State Council or CPC authority, an official document was issued either respectively or jointly by these two sides, and then a new programme or a new policy was put in force.

In the initiating stage of the first group of SEZ and the early-to-mid stages of brewing the Pudong New Zone, it could be seen quite clearly that the policy processes were conducted in this way. However, to analyse these two processes deeply, we can find some problems that are worth further discussion in detail. One of these problems occurred in initiating the first group of SEZs. In this course, 'a big mistake' (Deng's word) was made that Shanghai was not included in the short list of setting up SEZ. Ten years later, Deng Xiaoping publicly admitted with great regret that it was a fault which had lost one decade of good opportunity for both speeding up Shanghai and the whole country's economic development (see section 8.2.2). This fact suggests two possibilities: (1) in determining the programme of setting up the first group of SEZ, it seemed not all possible alternatives were considered; (2) the consideration for those alternatives, only focused on studying and evaluating their consequences on some aspects, for instance, the political geographic conditions, while Shanghai's best condition in both economic status and technological foundation in China was neglected.

The second problem occurred in the policy process of Pudong. The data indicates that as early as in 1984, the idea of developing Pudong had been put forward, through submitting a request report to the State Council, by the Shanghai authority. However, at that time the State Council only affirmed it as a local level's economic strategy. Two years later, in 1986, the State Council still did not consider Pudong as a state project, in its written reply to Shanghai's report 'The Overall Planning Scheme of Shanghai Municipality'. (ibid.) Pudong's significant status had not been recognised until the early 1990 when Deng did so. This course showed that within a six years' period the central policy authority failed to study and evaluate carefully the potential and possible future of Pudong with a broad view of China's overall situation, although it had at least two opportunities to consider Shanghai's reports. This issue was also related to the first problem: if Pudong were treated like Shenzhen in 1984 when Shanghai first raised the suggestion, then Deng Xiaoping's regret could be greatly reduced, for Pudong's six years earlier development could be conducted; and if it were decided in 1986, it would have been four years ahead of the late schedule. However, it failed to do so. This delaying of decision-making, and also the first problem of failing to selecting Pudong by the end of 1970s, persuasively demonstrated the limits of the rational model. It seems unreasonable to conclude, according to these facts, that the central decision-makers at that time did not work hard, or did not try their best to search for resources for their policy-making. Because, 'it is almost impossible to consider all alternatives during the process of decision; knowledge of the consequences of the various alternatives is necessarily incomplete; and evaluating these consequences involves considerable uncertainty' (Hill, M. 1997:100). This is the reason why an incremental approach seems more practical and applicable in many occasions, to which we will turn in the next section.

According to the above analysis, in further considering these two policy processes of the early stage of setting up the first group of SEZ and the early-to-mid stages of brewing the Pudong project, they are only able to be interpreted, to a certain extent, with a bounded rational model which emphasises not to maximise the decision makers' value, but to make it satisfactory or good enough, rather than a rational-comprehensive approach in which its requirements usually exceed the capability of human-beings. It means that, for the first case, it had been the good and successful decision-making that the idea of setting up industrial zone or exported-oriented zone was confirmed, deepened and legitimised, SEZ programme was soon launched and four advantaged and very promising places (maybe not all the best!) were selected. That the short list of SEZs finally did not include Shanghai then was a regret but not a big mistake which needs to be criticised acutely. With respect to the second case, likewise, it had been actually a good and satisfactory decision for Shanghai that its suggestion of setting Pudong New Zone was given attention and support by the central authority, from 1984 to the early 1990. Of course, to determine Pudong New Zone as a state project and even key project as happened later is much better; unfortunately, this recognition could not be reached in a short period. Obviously, these two cases suggest the limits of human rationality.

Nevertheless, the increasing involvement of rationality in China's policy processes was a noticeable progress. Compared with the past decades prior to the reform period, China has attached much importance to seeking better approaches for determining policies. Those usual steps of SEZ policy processes listed above and the data we had discussed in empirical chapters, indicate that the policy makers were ready to hear different opinions which embodied the opposing opinion, from various aspects which involved many experts and specialists inside and outside the party, home and abroad; they advocated and also actively conducted the investigation and feasibility study in an overall and deep way; and they determined a policy with much prudent attitude. All these changes marked the start of a new era that China has gradually departed from the old policy-making mode, which was characterised by empiricism, dogmatism, holism and idealism plus revolutionary fervour to different extents, which had prevailed to the different extent in the period before the end of 1970s.

If we consider the above two cases of SEZ policy processes using a bounded rationalist model to a certain extent, we also saw some other cases of SEZs policy-making actions, which involved rationalist approach to different extents. For instance, the overall development of Hainan's opening-up course was a relatively lower level rationality (actually it was an incremental process that will be discussed in the incrementalist interpreting part later). Then, did any policy event in SEZ course involve a relatively high level of rationality, and, was a higher level of rationalism applicable and effective in promoting SEZ course? To examine Pudong planning, we may find some answers for these.

10.1.2 Applicability of a higher level of rationality

In Chapter Eight, we saw that since the Pudong project was determined, in April 1992, as the state's key project of China's opening-up and economic development strategy of the 1990s, to make a good planning for its development became a crucial issue. That the requirement with a high starting point and a high standard for Pudong planning, which must reach the world's first-rank level, determined that to pursue the defined target Pudong planning must be conducted very carefully with the most advanced theories and technologies. For reaching the desired target, thus, Pudong's decision-makers had tried their best. In doing so, they adopted six major measures that were discussed in section 8.2.4. To be sure, these measures showed a higher level of rationalist approach, compared with the general mode of SEZ policy-making. It involved trying every possibility to realise a desired target, comparing all available alternatives and their consequences, and seeking to find the best option at one time. The overall development of the Pudong project, ever since its beginning, proved that both the guiding thought of the planning and the planning project itself could be affirmed, which had successfully led Pudong's construction to a healthy development course with high efficiency, and brought about a noticeable economic boom.

Concretely speaking, then, how and to what extent did the higher rationalist factors influence the policy process in Pudong planning? To explore this issue, the design of Lujiazhui district, the core area and the most important functional site of Pudong New Zone, provides us with a typical case. In order to search the best planning scheme for this tiny area which covers only 1.7 sq. Km., the planning authority had tried their best technologically and financially (section 8.2.4). It is no exaggeration to say that what the Pudong planning authority had done for Lujiazhui's design involved a highly rational approach, which included considering all the best alternatives and evaluating all their consequences. The producing of the final option came from the highest level's creation by combining the best schemes and ideas. These facts, accordingly, demonstrate that a relative higher rationalist model influenced the policy process of Pudong planning to a considerable extent. They also indicate that a higher level of rationalist approach could be applied, effectively, in those policy issues involving much more or pure technological factors.

In the above two sections, we have examined the involvement of the rationalist model in SEZ course at different levels and their influences on policy processes as well. As mentioned above, it was a noticeable progress of China's policy-making pattern. Then, why could this progress be achieved, or how could the involvement of rationality in policy processes increase remarkably in post-Mao China? This is what which next section tries to answer.

10.1.3 Why rationalism increased

To explore why the progress of China's policy-making pattern could be made, from the old pattern which was characterised by empiricism, dogmatism, holism and idealism plus revolutionary fervour, to the different extent, to the way which involved much more rational elements, we may analyse from four aspects.

Firstly, it was the logical consequence of China's thinking emancipation campaign that started from 1978. The debating about the criteria of testing truth greatly emancipated people's minds. The myth that leaders (particular the paramount leader) were omnipotent and always correct, fell through thoroughly. More and more policy makers began to understand the real meaning and importance of 'seeking truth from fact', and to understand the danger of only copying the words from the classical revolutionary works as guidance or only following the will of leaders regardless of the conditions in reality. These changes directly brought about the demand of pursuing rationalism, and resulted in the increase of rational thinking in the policy process. On the other hand, this emancipation campaign also provided the possibility to summarise China's historical lessons since 1949, on a comparatively objective basis, with the principle of 'seeking truth from fact'. It enabled people to face the past squarely and to realise that the main reason that caused so many failures in economic construction in the past decades, was the wrong policy-making (section 5.3). Thus, China's policy makers got to know more clearly that a state's policy-making, either economically or politically, or on any other aspect, is a work which required great prudence and carefulness, and any policy-making must be in accordance with objective reality (Deng, X. 1993, p. 22).

Moreover, realising the backward situation of China's economy compared with developed countries at the end of 1970s, China's leaders understood that they had no time to waste, which also increased their sense of urgency to speedily promote China's development. Hence, it became another impetus of pursuing rationality in policy-making.

Thirdly, a theoretical relation between rationality and the principle of 'seeking truth from facts', enabled the increasing involvement of rationality in policy-making. Fundamentally speaking, the essence of the bounded rationality model is somewhat like 'to seek truth from facts'. The bounded rationality suggests that policy makers need to search the major available alternatives and evaluate their consequences, so as to select one alternative that seems to be satisfactory or good enough. Similarly, the principle of 'seeking truth from facts', also emphasises to seek truth from available facts. From this angle of view, it can be said that the principle of 'seeking truth from fact' and the bounded rationality not only share the feature of emphasising the importance to find truth, but also the feature of emphasising the possibility of finding truth. The difference between them is that the former is more objective than the latter in seeking and recognising both truth and fact, because the former admits that its searching or probing can not surpass the limitation of objective conditions. Nevertheless, owing to these similarities or theoretical relations, when China began to re-advocate the principle of 'seeking truth from fact', it actually opened the door towards rationalism.

Furthermore, some other reasons also made it convenient to carry out rational approaches. These are China's centralised political system and the limitations on pluralism in current China. According to the practice in SEZ course, centralised power system seemed easier to implement a rational approach, for it can provide very effective means of making use of the available resources for policy-making. These powerful means include authority, data, finance and manpower, etc. For instance, in the policy process of setting up the first group of SEZ, the policy makers from central to local level could gather these resources to conduct various relevant works within a very short time, such as conducting repeated investigation by central authority, convening different conferences for feasibility study, etc. These efforts soon created the necessary conditions for final policy determination.

As discussed in chapter nine, since a pluralist tendency gradually occurred in China when the reform started, it faced some limitations from the existing political and ideological monism which constituted important parts of China's political institutions. On the contrary, these limitations actually increased the extent to which rationalism was involved, because, as for compensation, it forced policy makers to seek rationality more positively. Since making better policy so as to accelerate economic construction had been a defined target, the inadequacy of the widest participation in policy-making demanded much more rationality within a relatively small scope, so as to secure the reliability of a policy-making, especially for deciding those crucial policy issues which had overall and far-reaching influence to the country. We saw that in the processes of determining the first group of SEZ and the Pudong project, those relevant policy-making meetings were held again and again. These meetings were mainly at central level, but also sometimes at local level, which were small in scope. Usually, they were held by the leaders of the state Council or CPC centre. However, the NPC and CPPCC, the legitimate and consultative organs, were not involved, nor was public opinion. For this reason, it was natural that more importance was attached to the rationalist approach.

Nevertheless, as we see the roles of centralism and the political monism in promoting and strengthening the application of rational approach in a new situation of China's policy-making, we need to notice that this mechanism also easily enables the production of dogmatism and holism. This had been repeatedly demonstrated by the bitter lessons which occurred in the past.

To sum up, in this section, we have examined SEZ policy processes with rationalist model from different sides, and we have seen the involvement of rationality to a varied degree. The examination suggests a basic feature that the extent of applying rationalist approach varied from case to case, according to the requirement and environment of a policy-making issue. That is, the more massive a policy-making issue was and the more uncertainty involved, the lower the level rational approach which could be applied; and the more technological factors a policy-making issue involved and the more concrete a policy issue was, the higher level of rationalist approach could be adopted. The increase of the involvement of rationalist approach in policy processes in post-Mao China, was a logical development of China's reform since the end of 1970s. The rise of the thinking emancipation promoted the pursuing of rationalism; the pressures of economic construction strengthened this tendency; the feature of existing political institutions, such as centralised power system, and ideological monism, increased the necessity of adopting more rationalist elements for achieving better policy output.

However, as has been analysed, the most important condition which makes rationalist approach applicable is having the required resources as great as possible. Therefore, for those SEZ policy events, which involved many uncertainties, such as Hainan's development, the rationalist approach could not offer a reasonable interpretation. In those situations, it was impossible to apply a rational approach, even though the policy makers wanted to do so. To explain this situation is the task of the incremental model, to which we now turn.

10.2 Incremental explanation

The theoretical base of building up the incremental model, is affirming and stressing the uncertainties in a policy-making process, which are caused by the limits of the resources (section 4.1.2). These uncertainties determine that a policy-making action usually can not achieve the best output which can quickly lead to the desired goal, by a single application; instead, a series of incremental moves of continuously adjusting policies is necessary, by which to approach the target step by step.

The key concepts of the incrementalist model, according to Lindblom, the leading exponent of this theory which was discussed in section 3.1.2, include: the successive limited comparisons, disjointed incrementalism and the partisan mutual adjustment. The main difference of the first two is, the former requires continual adjustment aimed at achieving a definite goal; while the goal pursued by the latter through an indefinite sequence of policy moves involves continual changes, based on possibility and future desire. This section intends to analyse China's SEZ courses with these two approaches first and then an examination of the partisan mutual adjustment follows. In doing so, a general analysis and some selected case discussions are both engaged in, with which to see how and to what extent the incremental approach is applicable to China's practice.

10.2.1 A general examination of the SEZ course

The sixteen years from 1979 to 1995 witnessed a rapidly rise of China's SEZs. When examining this course which should be credited a lot in China's reform and opening-up strategy, a question will be inevitably raised as, what kinds of policy-making method played the key role in enabling this successful development, or, what effective approaches had been dominant in SEZ's policy processes? The available evidence suggests that it was the involvement of incrementalism that served as a leading method to ensure this noticeable progress. Is this conclusion reasonable, and how could incrementalism have dominated China's SEZ course? These are what the following sections try to answer in turn.

Observing the whole SEZ course, we notice a process that SEZ developed from zero to being in existence, from small size to large size, and the extent of opening-up from a relatively lower level to an increasingly high level. Obviously, this was an incremental policy process in which the features could be seen from three aspects: (1) that the idea of SEZ from brewing to completion was incremental; (2) the intensity of the policies granted to SEZ was incremental; (3) the target places which were selected as SEZ were incremental.

In the preceding part we pointed out that the initiating of SEZ is a lower level of rationalist process. Actually, fundamentally speaking, it was an incremental process. SEZ was a creation as a way of breaking-through in China's opening-up course. When the reform and opening-up strategy was formulated at the end of 1978, SEZ was not an existing concept of policy makers. Then, the raising of the idea to set up industrial zone or export-oriented zone, from different sides, made it possible to be considered gradually, and finally could be determined as an explicit policy output and programme of SEZ which serves as the window, bridge and experimental field of China's opening-up course. This was a disjointed incremental process. Because, at the very beginning, there was no concrete policy target, this was set up only by continuously search and adjustment in the policy-making process.

If we said that the process of creating the SEZ programme is a disjointed incremental course, then the overall development course of SEZ should be a successive limited comparison process. To analyse this process, we can examine it from the second and the third features of an incremental SEZ course, which have been listed above. They are: the intensity of the policies granted to SEZ was incremental, and the target places that were to be selected as SEZ were incremental.

With regard to the second feature, it mainly means that with the development of the SEZ course, the extent to which SEZs' opening-up to the outside world, in both depth and broadness, was remarkably increasing, and the level of supporting by the state was continuously increasing. Comparing the first group of SEZs and Hainan, for instance, some special policies were granted to the latter, which included that Hainan was allowed to conduct some political system reform of trying to set up the system of 'small government and big society' so as to promote economic construction, and to conduct the economic system reform which did not rely mainly on the development of the public-ownership economic sectors (section 7.4.2). More noticeably, Hainan was allowed to lease a large stretch of land to foreign investors for development for a long period.

Then, comparing Pudong New Zone and those early SEZs, the former was granted some very special and powerful policies. The main points of these policies included that foreign business investors were allowed to develop tertiary industries, to set up foreign-funded banks and to engage in entrepot trade, and central government gave direct and powerful financial support to Pudong and Shanghai for their development (see section 8.3.2). Therefore, Pudong was called 'the most special SEZ'.

These facts which are summarised above suggest a clear policy incremental process. In other words, as Deng said, a process of 'groping pebbles to cross the stream'. Why was it that those new policies which could be granted to the latter had not been in force in the former? It is simply because, during the period when those policies either had not been set forth or had not been proved feasible, they could not be implemented in practice. They needed to be probed step by step. For example, in Hainan, both to develop an economy which did not mainly rely on public-ownership economic sectors, and to lease a large stretch of land to foreign businessman for a long period were brand new issues in SEZ course, the former was raised according the experience of the first group of SEZ, and the latter from which Yangpu Incident occurred, took a long time to be solved and the relevant policy to be formulated. In the Pudong case, both being allowed to set up foreign banks and the tertiary industry, and directly offering financial support by central government, indicated a great increase of central government's determination in not only keeping on going but further expanding the opening-up course, and further strengthening the role of SEZ in China's economic construction.

With respect to the feature that the targets to be selected as SEZ were incremental, we saw that firstly those cities or regions adjoining to Hong Kong, Macao or Taiwan, were selected; then, Hainan, a large island with great natural resources, was involved; finally, Pudong, an important area of Shanghai, China's economic centre, was selected, although to do so involved considerable risk. In section 9.4, we have tried to explore the reason why Pudong could not be determined by the end of 1970s, nor in the mid-1980s, and nor in the end of 1980s, although the possibilities of considering it existed. To answer this question now, besides other reasons, it is because it needed time for China's decision-makers to realise the necessity and possibility of doing so. The practice had demonstrated that to reach this understanding was an incremental process.

To analyse these two incremental processes, some conclusions could be drawn as: the understanding of SEZ's importance was increased gradually as SEZs developed; the policies which could be in force in SEZs were strengthening continuously and reach more and more higher level of opening-up, as SEZ developed; the more policies which could be carried out effectively in SEZs, the more confidence and capability the policy makers had to make powerful policies to support SEZs' development; and so, finally, the better SEZs developed, the greater boldness and determination the decision makers would have. Then, why did we say that these are successive limited comparison incremental processes? Because the new policies were created only based on the situation of implementing the existing policies, and moved forward step by step with continuous exploration. In this way, the uncertainty that occurred in the SEZ course was solved gradually, continuously, and smoothly. When some acute contradictions occurred, such as the Yangpu Incident, they could also be handled eventually.

Observing the whole SEZ course with a macro-view, we see that it was a successive comparison process, for its general target was defined and all that was needed to promote the cause was a series of incremental adjusting actions. However, in some parts of the SEZ course, due to the existence of great uncertainty, the policy target was not clear, thus, the efforts which policy makers needed to make were continuously searching the goal according to the changing conditions, namely, a disjointed incremental approach was applied. To consider the integrated policy process of Pudong, this phenomenon is noticeable. Moreover, Hainan's development is a more typical case.

10.2.2 An integrated discussion of the Pudong case

As has been analysed in earlier sections, the development course of Pudong project policy-making can be divided in to two phases with the early 1990 as the boundary line. The first stage, from 1984 to 1990, a brewing period with a bottom-up method, was rather protracted; and the second stage, from 1990 to 1995, with Deng's intervention as its starting point and through a top-down method, developed fast. We understood that if we view these two phases separately, the first stage showed the rational element to a certain extent, and the second stage involved relatively higher level rationality, especially the Pudong planning.

Substantially, as has been pointed out, rationalism and incrementalism are the two ends of a continuum that shows the range scholars search the way to improve policy-making. Therefore, the lower level rationality involves the elements of incrementalism, and the preliminary incrementalism also contains the rational factors. To consider the Pudong case with an integrated way from end to end, it seems to be conceivable to view it as a disjointed incremental process to a certain extent in view of what follows. In 1984 and 1986, Shanghai raised its proposal to develop Pudong twice, but it did not directly or clearly ask for setting up a SEZ or other types' of development zone, in the context that four SEZs had been established in Guangdong and Fujian provinces. While, the replies from the State Council also did not give clear guidance for Pudong's development

Then, a clear target had not been determined until the early 1990 when Deng intervened in the event and confirmed Pudong's direction. In April 1990, Pudong was declared to develop as a New Zone with special SEZ policies, as the state's programme, when the Pudong project really began. Later, in 1992, Pudong's position was further emphasised and was determined as the state's key project of economic construction in the 1990s. This course indicates that the target for Pudong's development was not clear at early stage both to the Shanghai's government and the central authority. It needed to be searched step by step, instead of formulated at the very beginning or decided at one time. Incremental perspective would see this situation as the difficulty of solving the uncertainty that to determine Pudong's development mode often involved hesitated and protracted consideration due to Shanghai's crucial status economically and politically in China. Thus, a disjointed incremental policy process occurred, in which the uncertainties were handled gradually.

10.2.3 Hainan's road: a typical disjointed incremental process

Compared with the first group of SEZs, the development of Hainan's development experienced a tortuous road. It has been seen that SEZ was not set up in Hainan at the very beginning of Hainan's opening-up course. This target had not even been clearly determined until 1988 when eight years had passed since Hainan was decided to open to the outside world. In the early days of Hainan's opening-up course, it was ambiguous about what development mode or scheme was suitable to practise. As described from section 7.2 to 7.4, Hainan's opening-up course experienced three changeable stages: (1) a semi-SEZ referring to the policies experiences of the SEZs; (2) to be treated as a SEZ, but not a formal SEZ status; and (3) setting up a separate province in Hainan and setting up SEZ in the whole provinces. Since the issues of economic development direction and administrative status adjustment twisted together, it made the relevant policies more complicated and more difficult to be decided, especially when the latter issue had not been clearly identified, and its negative impacts on Hainan's development had not been clearly understood. Looking back on this process, we can see not only that the policies were continually changing, but that the goal or the direction of Hainan's development was also adjusting, or varying continually. In other words, this policy-making and implementing process was also a goal searching process.

Now Hainan's opening-up course had been put onto its right track for a long time. Like the early stage of the policy process of initiating SEZ programme which was discussed in the last section, Hainan's road suggests that, on many occasions when initiating a big and complicated programme, it is usually impossible for the decision makers to find the best policy, or solution, or even a clear target, at the very beginning or in a short period. Conversely, they need to keep exploring them in practice, and to keep on returning to and improving the existing problems, while adjusting the method and goal continuously towards a better direction; namely, a disjointed incremental approach is applicable. This method could also be considered as 'to search a correct target in actions', which seems an effective way to deal with uncertainty in many circumstances.

After examining the applicability of the first two elements of incremental approach, we now turn to the third one, partisan mutual adjustment, to see whether it works in the SEZ policy process.

10.2.4 Could 'partisan mutual adjustment' work?

Discussing the SEZ policy process with the partisan mutual adjustment approach, is to explore how those people involved in the policy action, approached each other and adjusted themselves to a possible policy, towards a policy target which could be accepted by most people. According to Lindblom, this method is introduced to achieve co-ordination between people in the absence of a central co-ordinator. However, in China's reality, the policy-making situation without a central co-ordinator only occurs on very rare occasions. The feature of China's centralised power system determines that all the policy-making authorities from Centre to the local level, have their co-ordinators, either individuals or organisations. For instance, the paramount leader can co-ordinate the politburo, a party secretary can co-ordinate the party committee which he heads, the higher level party authority can co-ordinate the lower level's party committee, etc. The situations without central co-ordinators can only refer to those in which the policy issue should be decided by voting, such as the election in the CPC and NPC Conference. Actually, even in this situation at different ranks, if an important policy issue needs to be determined by voting, the chief leader at or above that level and the higher authorities still have the power and channels to affect the tendency of the decisions. This is not like the situation in the Parliaments or the business companies' boards in Western countries. However, on the other hand, as we discussed in section 9.3.3, the feature of a fragmented authority in China's reality indicates the possibility of lower efficiency of co-ordination. Therefore, no matter in the situations with or without the co-ordinator, according to China's reality, for achieving co-ordination, the partisan mutual adjustment which involves negotiation and bargaining, is necessary.

Analysing the policy process of SEZ course with this approach, can we identify some sorts of relevant behaviours which have enabled partisan mutual adjustment at different levels? In central authority, this showed as the politburo meeting, State Council meeting, and the Centre's special working conference, in which the partisans shared an opportunity to communicate with each other, and exchange opinions. These ways could usually lead to the adjustment of policy decision more or less. For instance, a usual way to formulate SEZ-related policies which often concerned the affairs of various governmental sectors including economics, planning, finance, tax, foreign trade, bank and legislation etc., was to convene those people in charge from all the relevant ministries and commissions, by the leader of the State Council, to work together. With this way, in which much mutual-adjustment, including negotiation and bargaining, was involved, then a policy which could be accepted by multiple sides was mapped out.

Generally, the way of negotiation or bargaining was involved more in those policy processes in which the interest relations between centre and local, or between different local interests, needed to be solved. When the Yangpu Incident broke out, for searching for a solution, a special central working meeting was convened, to which those central leaders, provincial party leaders joined (section 7.4.4). Hainan's leaders, supported by some central and some other provincial leaders, had tried their best to achieve their desired goal through sharp debating, although the final result was unfavourable to them. This situation also often occurred at the province/ministry level. When some important policy issues needed to be solved, forums and conferences with focuses on given subjects provided chances to policy makers for their mutual adjustment while considering the opinions of those people inside and outside the policy-making circles. In the course of pushing ahead the SEZ development, many of them were held in different stages, in which experts and specialists were involved as consultants of the policy-making authorities, while the leaders in chief and relevant officials at different levels also participated. It has been proved that it was an important channel for the mutual adjustment between the policy-making authority and the specialists, and between the policy makers, for searching for a better policy output. One of the important reasons of attaching great importance to the Pudong project in the early 1990s was that the experts and specialists from home and abroad have positively promoted it. These promoters emphasised Pudong's significance and advised the authorities to seize the chance of developing Pudong again and again at different forums and conferences. To sum up, the three channels mentioned above are the basic methods to provide the policy makers with mutual adjustment, which have played their active part in SEZ policy processes.

According to the above analysis, we can see quite clearly that the incremental approach was not only highly applicable, but played an important role in China's SEZ policy-making processes. Why was incrementalism so popular, and what conditions enabled incrementalism to be significantly involved in the policy process of post-Mao China? This is what we now try to explore in the next section.

10.2.5 Why was incrementalism highly applicable?

The available facts suggest that the incremental approach was applied in SEZ policy processes in at least three aspects: the initiating of the concept and programme of SEZ; the general development of SEZ course; and the development of the SEZ-related policies. Therefore, it might be reasonable to say that the incrementalism was a basic policy-making approach in promoting the SEZ course. However, can we say that in all these policy processes, incrementalism was the best choice, and, was incrementalism the only choice? To answer these questions, we need to explore these policy processes from different sides.

We know that SEZ was one of the products and organic parts of China's reform and opening-up strategy, and so it was a new thing to a socialist China. There were neither ready-made experiences which could be used directly, nor any theoretical guidance from classical Marxist or Maoist works which could be followed. Therefore, all SEZ-related policies, including the concept and the programme of SEZ initiated as an experiment of the opening-up course, needed to be probed and created in practice step by step. In doing so, experiments were absolutely essential. This suggests the inevitability of applying an incremental approach in the policy process. For instance, the creating of the SEZ programme experienced three stages of consideration: industrial zone or exported-oriented zone ⇒ export-oriented special zone ⇒ special economic zone (section 6.2). This was a process in which policy makers gradually approached a clear and suitable target.

Besides the inevitability, a significant involvement of incremental approach in SEZ course was also necessary. In many occasions, a policy or a decision, which would be in force, might not be the best one, but seemed to be a necessary choice in that context. For example, now the determination of selecting the first group of SEZs could not be considered the best, for it did not include Pudong, which Deng regretted ten years later. Nevertheless, at that time, it was a good decision for it had considered all those places which were most adjacent to Hong Kong, Macao or Taiwan based on both economic and political consideration. The fact that Pudong could not be considered by the state until 1990 when ten years had passed since SEZ programme started, suggests that a good idea or a good policy is not easily produced, and time is needed to probe. But, a decision should be made when facing a policy issue, instead of waiting for 'the best'.

In the Hainan case, similarly, we can not say it was the best way at that time to use such an incremental method, because it took so much time to find a suitable way and suffered so many setbacks. However, under the circumstance that Hainan urgently needed development but a fully-studied and fully-reliable scheme was not available, the incremental approach was the only choice. Needless to say, it would be good if at the very beginning, a perfect general policy such as that decided later to set up SEZ in the whole island and change Hainan as a separate province, and all other relevant policies had been adopted. Unfortunately, this possibility was unrealistic.

Actually, to conclude, in a policy process which is always moving ahead, human rationality is limited, but 'the best' is boundless, so it can only make sense when 'the best' is considered in a given stage. This suggests the necessity of incrementalism which was shown in SEZ course. Deng's famous words, 'groping pebbles to cross the stream', not only summarises the essence of incremental approach which was applied in China's policy process, but also indicates its necessity. That means, you need to 'cross the stream', even by 'groping pebbles'; you can not wait until a bridge or boat is ready. To explain SEZ course with this view, indicates that when the opening-up cause and SEZ programme urgently need to be pushed ahead, those relevant policies should be made, even if facing many uncertainties and even if the policies might not be the best.

The necessity of adopting incrementalism in SEZ policy process also involved an historical reason. For preventing the mistakes of making rash and adventure policies, like the great leap forward, causing heavy loss in economic construction in the first three decades of PRC, required China's leaders to make policy decision with much prudence and careful attitude, in the post-Mao period.

Furthermore, we need to notice that China's adopting incrementalism in SEZ policy process did not mean or intend to slow down its work. While, advocating the method of 'Groping pebbles to cross the steam' to cope with the uncertainty in exploring the road for China's development, Deng also strongly encouraged China's leaders, cadres and masses to push ahead their works faster and more boldly many times, on many occasions. One of these most famous talks stated that,

> To engage the reform and opening-up cause must be more boldly, must have the courage to make trials. It should be not like the bound feet woman. To try boldly, to break the new path boldly, whenever an issue has been considered as right. The important experience of Shenzhen is daring to break a new path.

Without a fearless spirit of pathbreaker, without a spirit of venturing, without a momentum and vigour, it would be impossible to open a good path and break a new path, it would be impossible to build a new cause. To do anything could have fully possibility of success, no danger of anything going wrong, without any risk, who dares to say this words?... I never think in that way (Deng, X. 1993, p.372).

According to the words of the above paragraph, we can see the two sides of Deng's principles: adopting incremental approach in coping with the policy issue, and trying every possible way to go faster. This looks like a contradiction. However, it can be a balance. To stress the former is to avoid making big mistakes, and advocating the latter aims at rapidly pushing ahead China's reform and opening-up cause so as to narrow the gap between China and the developed countries and catch up with them as soon as possible. Therefore, the direction of China's policy-making behaviour should always be finding the solution to balance these two principles.

To sum up, according to the exploration in this part, the incremental approach was applicable in those SEZ policy processes that faced many uncertainties, to a great extent. Adopting this method had been conducive to avoiding or reducing the risk and loss, for it enabled more careful feasibility studies and experiments to be conducted, and widely expanded the participation from more aspects, so as to secure more reliable policy outputs to be obtained step by step. This significant involvement of the incremental approach resulted from four sides: the demands of conducting a series of new projects in pushing ahead the SEZ courses and relevant opening-up policies, in which many uncertainties existed, the seeking of a speedy and stable development of China's economy, the emancipation of thinking mode, and drawing lessons from the past.

However, when emphasising the importance and benefits of applying the incremental approach, it is necessary to point out that, in the final analysis, incrementalism is a balance between human rationality and the availability of resources for policy-making in coping with uncertainty, because both sides have their limitations. But under the circumstance that a policy relating to a significant great change is required, and while there is insufficient time to enable an incremental way to be engaged, then, adopting an incremental approach is not suitable for policy-making. This is the situation in which the optimal approach is applied. In SEZ course, some policy-making events can be interpreted with the optimal model, to which the following discussion turns.

10.3 Interpreting with optimal method

If we saw incrementalism as a balance between the limits of human rationality and the availability of resources in a policy process, then, other policy-making approaches, such as the optimal method, could be considered as the balance between rationality and incrementality, for it aims to search for a middle way between them. The key points of the optimal approach are extra-rational components, increase in the rational elements, and meta-policy-making. This section analyses China's policy-making practice of SEZ course with this approach, and examines how and to what extent and this approach is applicable to China's practice.

The available evidence suggests that the SEZ course saw a partial but significant involvement of the optimal approach in some events. With respect to the 'meta-policy-making' — to decide how to make policy, its importance and effectiveness can be seen quite clearly from the way of determining the theories and guiding principles for the SEZ course. We saw that SEZ was the product and organic part of China's reform and opening-up strategy, therefore, setting up all those theories and principles about reform and opening-up, and also the general policy of SEZ, was the starting point and basis to promote the SEZ course. Then, how could these theories and guiding thoughts be formulated successfully? Examining the reality at a macro-level, it can be interpreted with the reason of conducting a good meta-policy-making. That is, since the Third Plenary Session of the Eleventh Central Committee of CPC, China's policy makers had gradually set up a series of applicable principles and methods with which to guide policy-making. These principles, as we know, are, 'Seeking truth from fact', 'The practice is the sole criterion for testing truth', Deng's 'Cat theory', and later, the three criteria for judging the feasibility of adopting new programmes and new policies. These principles are not only the guiding thought of policy-making, but also the criteria for evaluating the consequences of policy options. Then, the policy-making methods, such as 'Groping pebbles to cross the stream', are more familiar with us. The policies made by the guidance of these principles and methods, had brought about the rise and development of China's SEZ, which had been beyond controversy.

Moreover, another partial involvement of optimal model is deciding the locations of the first groups of SEZs, in which extra-rational elements and rational elements were applied. A place, which can be selected as SEZ, generally speaking, should be the one that is located at the coastal area, so that an outward-looking economy could be developed conveniently. However, these kind of places, cities and towns, number more than one hundred. Why were those four cities chosen first to set up SEZs? Actually, the consideration did not only include the general geographic conditions, but a careful evaluation of the special geographic significance politically and economically. That was their greater possibility to set up connection with Hong Kong, Macao, Taiwan and overseas Chinese: to set up closer economic relations with them and also play political influence on them towards the target of promoting the reunification course (section 8.2.2). To determine these choices, policy makers' judgement, creative invention, brainstorming (considering those most important and sensitive aspects, according to policy makers' view then), and selective reviewing of options and some explication of goals (restricting consideration to some special cities, instead of all those cities in the coastal area), were involved.

The past eighteen years had proved that these selections were wise from the long-term view. For instance, Shenzhen, which is adjacent to Hong Kong, had been seen as the barometer of China's policy by Hong Kong citizens and investors for a long time. With Shenzhen's success and prosperity, in which a considerable rate of capitalist economy was involved, Hong Kong investors had greatly increased their confidence to expand their business in the mainland of China. At present, Hong Kong is the number one investor in capitals, among all other countries and regions investing in China. For example, it is only in Pudong New Zone, that both the numbers of projects and the capital of investment from Hong Kong comprise more than two fifths of the total of those coming from different countries and regions, respectively (*OCSE*, No. 126, 13 Jun. 1997). More importantly, Shenzhen's situation had greatly increased the confidence of Hong Kong's people in the policy of 'one country, two system', which had been very conducive to maintain Hong Kong's stability in the transition period and finally to the peaceful handover of Hong Kong's sovereignty. According to above analysis, we understand that to determine the locations of the SEZs is a decision-making in which extra-rational elements and rational elements were applied, for its decision-making based on the profound analysis of various elements economically, politically, and historically. With carefully assessing the influence of these elements and their inter-actions, then the selection of the locations of those SEZs, was finally determined.

What was discussed above enabled us to see that to interpret China's SEZ policy process with the optimal model, its applicability focuses on the situations that the policy issues with great significance and influence, must be explicitly decided in a given time, and the situation that to design procedures becomes necessary in order to achieve better policy outputs. Under these particular circumstances of SEZ course, an optimal approach had led to more reasonable and reliable policy decisions. As for other situations, the optimal method seemed not to be suitable. For example, when the resources for policy-making were good enough, like Pudong planning, it was not necessary to use this approach; and when the existing uncertainties were too much, it was impossible to apply this approach. This fact indicates that a policy-making model is effective only if it can meet the feature of a particular situation, which is emphasised by the contingent approach for which an analysis is conducted in the next section.

10.4 Interpreting with contingent approach

The essence of the contingent approach is: an appropriate model is effective only if it is used in a given policy process in which the contextual circumstance is appropriate for the application of the method. In the following pages, we first generally outline the situations of SEZ course in which different approaches were applied contingently, and then further discuss the applicability of different contingent theories in detail.

Reviewing SEZs' policy process, as we discussed in this and previous chapters, diversified approaches were applied in the light of the concrete situations, which had led to accomplishing the desired goals effectively to different extents. A brief classification can be listed as below.

- To determine the principles and methods, by which to formulate the SEZ-relevant policies, and to determine the locations of the first group of SEZs, the optimal model was applied;
- To formulate the macro-guiding-thought and the strategy of the reform and opening-up mainly involved the rational approaches;
- To map out the concrete schemes and the principal policies of the SEZ course, an incremental model — a successive comparison was applied;
- What Hainan's development experienced was a typical disjointed incremental process;
- In determining those concrete projects, especially those that involved concentrated higher technologies, a relative high level of rational approaches was applied, like Pudong planning.

These facts suggest that the contingent approach seems reasonable and applicable to interpret China's SEZ policy processes. Under different circumstances, decision-makers searched and discovered the distinct possibility and conditions so as to determine the essence and direction of the policy-making actions, and then adopted the suitable policy-making approaches, which had been conducive to producing better policy outcomes.

The contingent theories, as discussed in section 4.1.5, include three important models. (1) What Christensen put forward about four typical situations of decision-making and four corresponding methods to deal with them. (2) What John Forester raised that to view the policy-making background as a continuum from the rationalist's idealised situation to highly politically structured decision-making situation, and accordingly, to define the appropriate policy-making methods to match them. (3) What Patsy Healey suggested that policy process forms are the products of interest mediation around a specific set of issues, and so a continuum of process forms of decision-making are raised in the light of these variable relations, which are defined by three criteria. The following pages examine the applicability of these models in turn.

First, we discuss Christesen's model. The first situation Christensen defined is known technology; with an agreed goal. Under this circumstance, the decision-maker needs to match an effective technology to reach the goal according to the standard and the routine procedures. Reviewing the planning process of Pudong New Zone, we can find it is a typical case to be interpreted with this mode. During this course, the target of the planning is very clear that the first rank of world level of a modern metropolis had been defined, and the technologies were available which included the sources of finance and intelligence (see section 8.2.4). Therefore, the decision maker acted, as Christensen said, as programmer, standardizer, rule-setter, regulator, scheduler, optimiser and administrator, for their tasks are just formulating the programmes, setting the standards of the planning and regulation to reach the standards, selecting and optimising the alternative scheme, and administrating the planning.

Then, the second situation Christensen defined is unknown technology; with an agreed goal. Under this situation, the decision-maker needs to obtain the necessary knowledge and to search for the effective means with inventive and creative sensitivity, by moving incrementally. The shaping up of the CEDS (Coastal Economic Development Strategy, section 5.1.3), which was triggered by SEZ and then SEZ became one part of this strategy, indicates a process with this mode. As we have discussed, when the opening-up strategy was made the CEDS had not been raised. Opening-up to the outside world had been decided as a fixed target (agreed goal), but how to do this and by what ways were not clear. Consequently, the actual process to promote the opening-up course was to search for the way step by step continuously. It was just in this searching process, that the strategies of SEZ, ETDZ (Economic and Technological Development Zone), COC (Coastal Opening Cities), and CEDA (Coastal Economic Development Area) were made one after another, and finally the CEDS took shape. We now know that all these programmes, including the CEDS, had been formed as not only the important parts but also the important means of the opening-up strategy. However, they were not known in any policy makers' mind when the opening-up strategy was made. Thus, from the very beginning, in order to find the way to promote the opening-up course, the policy makers acted, in Christensen's words, as participation promoter, facilitator, mediator, constitution-writer and bargainer. From the case of the development process of CEDS, we see that the decision makers had done a lot of important jobs towards the general target (without a concrete means), in which they promoted the creating or discovering of ideas, identifying and formulating new schemes, summarising and introducing new experiences, shaping up and determining new policies and projects, and mediating and organising the economic and administrative force from different levels and different sides to carry out the new strategy. With all these efforts, those strategies mentioned above, starting from SEZ, were produced one by one, and finally the CEDS came into being, which became one of the important ways to push ahead the opening-up course.

The third situation defined by Christensen is known technology; with no agreed goal. Under this situation, the policy-making becomes a bargaining process. This bargaining needs to mediate conflicts of the interest and goal among the participators from all sides. The development of the Hainan SEZ suggests the applicability of this mode. As shown in chapter 7, Hainan's development experienced a very tortuous road. Why? Because, at the very beginning, the decision-maker simply did not have a clear goal or direction of how to develop Hainan. Thus, the searching for a suitable scheme had involved a series of bargaining among the decision-makers at and between different levels. These policy-searching processes concerned a lot of uncertainties (sections 7.2 to 7.4, and also 9.3) which covered the aspects of economic construction strategy and administrative system. These uncertainties caused many problems since the opening-up programme was sparked off, which needed to be identified and solved. For instance, the interest and power relations between centre, province and the Hainan region. During Hainan's development course, the policy makers acted, like Christensen said, as pragmatist, adjuster, researcher, experimenter and innovator. Hainan's tortuous experience suggested that the policy process involving exploration, research and bargaining, was mainly related to what direction Hainan should develop to and how the interest and power relations should be defined for speeding up Hainan's development. In this process, the decision-makers kept adjusting the goal and the power relations according to the demands of the practice, and finally a better and agreed goal was determined.

The fourth situation Christensen defined is unknown technology; with no agreed goal. Under this situation, the decision-making becomes the searching for order over both means and goal in a chaotic situation, and the decision maker acts as charismatic leader and problem-finder, and goes ahead pragmatically (incremental way), to deal with the uncertainty. The process of determining and pushing ahead of the SEZ programme could be interpreted in this way. As one of the important parts of China's opening-up strategy, the SEZs have been seen as the 'experiential fields', 'bridges' and 'windows' of China's opening-up cause for nearly two decades. However, before this programme was launched, as has been discussed, there was not a ready-made plan, and not even a clear concept about it. That means, that the situation is unknown technology with no agreed goal — the necessity of and how to set up these 'experiential field', 'bridges' and 'windows' was unknown. Then, under this circumstance, China's policy makers mobilised the participation of the masses to push ahead the opening-up course, discovered the original ideas created by the subordinates, formulated the policies and determined the programmes in time. During this course, the SEZs were developed from zero to coming into being, from few to more, from immature to mature, and have now become a key part of China's opening-up cause and play an important role in China's modernisation construction. Examining this process, it is not difficult to find that the policy maker exerted a crucial role in pushing ahead this great creative cause as participation promoter, initiative discoverer, relation mediator, and strategy maker.

To analyse the policy-making practice with Christensen's approach, the advantage can be summarised as: it clearly defines some sharp-cut contrasting situations, by which one can more easily to define the task and method of the decision maker. However, its problems are also prominent:

the situations of the policy-making can not be divided into those four sorts relating to the technology and goal with the clear-cut circumstances of known and unknown, agreed and not agreed; instead, the situations are diversified and complicated in which the degrees to which the decision makers have the technology or goal are varied at all possible levels. For instance, known technology may be about one third, half or more; and an agreed goal may have been approaching half way or nearly finished, or fixed at any point on the road towards the agreed goal. Therefore, it is not reasonable to use only yes or no to define the situation relating to the technology and goal, by which to analyse and select the policy-making approaches.

For defining the contextual situations of policy-making, the contingent approach which is set forth by Forester highlights a linear change in a continuum, which portrays the changes of the context from the rationalist's idealised situation to the highly political structured decision-making situation as a gradually reducing (former) and increasing (latter) process; and according to which the corresponding approaches for policy-making can be decided. Looking back on the SEZ development course, some major policy-making actions can be put into an order, according to the policy-making situations which varied along the above mentioned continuum. This list, which varies from highly rationalist's idealised situation to the highly political structured situation, would be: Pudong's planning ⇒ determining Pudong project ⇒ initiating SEZ programme ⇒ setting Shenzhen SEZ ⇒ determining Hainan's development direction. According to the facts we have discussed, this linear list indicates the policy-making situations, from the starting point to the end, the uncertainties increase gradually, and correspondingly the approach of dealing with the policy-making changes from more rationalism to more incrementalism, step by step.

Healey's model, which is comparable with the one of Forester, examines the policy-making styles according to a continuum in which interest mediation relations are changing, and stresses that the process forms are varied according to the changes of the relations of the latter. According to Healey's continuum and the corresponding process forms, those major policy events in SEZ's course can be listed, in terms of their interest mediation relations, as figure 10.1.

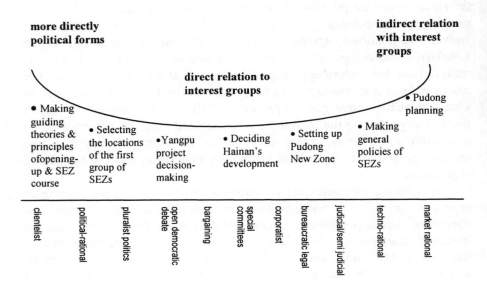

Figure 10.1 Examining policy processes of SEZ course with Healey's contingent model

The examination of SEZ policy processes with Healey's contingent model illustrates that the process forms were changing according to the context and substance of the policy issues. Those which had more direct link with interests, involved more open democratic debate and bargaining; those which contained more political elements, involved more political rationality; those which had more technological elements and were not directly linked with concrete interests, involved more tech-rationality and market rationality. This model throws light on the way from the another angle, which stresses the crucial influence of the relation of interest mediation on process forms, to observe and understand China's SEZ policy-making, which seems to be beneficial.

10.5 Conclusions

The results of examining SEZ course with four selected policy-making theories, in this chapter, suggest that they are applicable to China's practice to the different extent. As a root policy-making model, rationality had been increasingly involved in policy processes in post-Mao China, which was a logical development of China's reform cause since the end of 1970s. Compared with the situation when empiricism, dogmatism, holism and idealism plus revolutionary fervour prevailed for policy-making in the past, the increasing involvement of rationalist element is a significant progress, although its limits need to be recognised. However, the more important evolution of China's policy-making pattern should be the wide application of the incremental model. Summarising and advocating by Deng's word 'groping pebbles to across the stream', incrementalism became more and more popular theoretically and practically. Besides other reasons, the situation of facing massive uncertainty in reform and opening course in post-Mao China, greatly increased the necessity of adopting the incremental approach in order to reduce conflicts and loses, which had benefited China a lot in its development. Applying the optimal model was a choice by China's policy makers, under the circumstance when those significant policy issues need to be decided in a limited time, when it could be applied effectively. The contingent model offers a beneficial explanation to China's policy process from different ways. It illustrates that, in China's SEZ practice, those different policy-making methods had been effective only because they could match the given contextual situation in the aspects of either substance, or complexity, or the relations of interest mediation. Therefore, the result of this examination also suggests that the search for an applicable approach to solve a policy issue, must be adaptable to the reality which varies from case to case and from time to time.

11 Conclusion: a comprehensive analysis

Thus far, in this research, four tasks listed below have been performed. (1) A systematic discussion of the major theories and models in two groups on three sides, which covered the theories of how policy is made, including the relevant state theories and the models of how Chinese policy is made, and the major theories and models about how policy should be made. (2) A general exploration of the applicability of selected theories and models to China's practice, based on analysing China's power structure and its operating mechanism. (3) A review of the policy-making process of the SEZ course. (4) A particular analysis of the applicability of some selected theoretical models, to the SEZ-related policy-making processes, which is the focus of the research. These works have enabled us to understand a lot about the applicability of those theories and models, and also China's changing policy-making behaviour in post-Mao period, from different points of view at both the theoretical and practical levels.

As a concluding part, this chapter intends to conduct a further exploration with an integrated method, by which to analyse the applicability of those selected theories and models and to observe China's SEZ-related policy process in a comprehensive way. It is unlike the discussion in the preceding two chapters, in which basically each selected theory and model is used to analyse the policy process separately, and so each of them observes the practice from a special angle and emphasises the role of one element; instead, the exploration in this chapter uses a comprehensive method. It combines the approaches of description and prescription, and focuses its analysis on not only probing the role of each key element in policy-making, but also on the influences of interaction between those elements involved. This integrated exploration finally leads to a conclusion of the study, in which the main findings are summarised.

11.1 Further discussion: a comprehensive analysis with integrated theories

Drawing on the essential ideas from those theories and models that have been reviewed and examined in the previous chapters, a comprehensive analysis is conducted from three sides. (1) Examining the five key elements that play important roles in China's policy process. They are, the structure and mechanism of the policy-making authority, the participants in the policy process, the motivation (dynamics) for decision-making, the fundamental theories and methods used for making policy, and the political environment within which policy-making takes place. (2) Probing the extent to which each element affects the policy process, which varied in different periods. (3) Searching for the interactive relations among these elements, which also significantly affect the policy process.

Although some exploration of China's policy-making behaviour has been accessed when generally examining the applicability of those selected theories and models in the earlier chapters, the focus of the research has been the empirical studies of the SEZ course. Hence, before carrying out the comprehensive analysis, it is helpful to first engage in a brief review of the development and changes of China's policy-making behaviour in the period from 1949 to 1995, which is an essential contextual background to further the study. Then, an integrated analysis covering the role of each element, the relations and the changes among these elements, and the reasons of these two aspects as well, is conducted.

11.1.1 *A brief review of China's policy-making behaviour in different periods*

1949 — the mid-1957 It was a new period when the CPC became the ruling party and established a new regime. This is usually considered as the best period politically of new China before the start of the reform in the late 1970s. Within this stage the democratic atmosphere in the leadership was relatively good, and the macro political environment was comparatively loose. The leaders of the party and the State, either at the top, the provincial level, or the basic level, were readier to accept opinions and criticisms from inside or outside the policy-making circles. Three things characterised the policy-making process in this period.

• Personal worship had not obviously developed. Policy-making at top level had not become dominated by one paramount leader or by only a few people, and, a large numbers of politicians and senior officials, either inside and outside the CPC, were able to express their different viewpoints or even to criticise the top leader to some extent.

- The bureaucratic organisations, even though their development was at the early stage, did play some role in the policy process. The bureaucratic officials had the right to express their opinions to a certain extent.
- Public sentiment could be expressed through some normal channels.

The mid-1957— 1962   In this period there was a series of political movements, e.g. anti-bourgeois rightist and anti-right-deviations movements. Meanwhile, the so-called 'Great Leap Forward' was launched. The strengthening of political and ideological control resulted in some major features of the policy-making process as below.

- The role of individuals increased whilst the collective role gradually reduced both at the top level and the sub-national levels.
- The tendency that leaders became unwilling to listen to different opinions from inside or outside the party, was developing. This was especially prominent for the paramount leader.
- That the zeal and enthusiasm of the intellectuals, the part of a society which is most capable of offering constructive suggestions for the state's policy formulation, suffered setbacks. Hence, their possibility or courage to participate or influence the state's policy-making had been reduced to a considerable extent.

1963 — 1966   This was a readjusting period, when Mao quitted the forefront of the leadership, and Liu Shaoqi, the then president of the state, performed the major role as the chief leader of both the Party and State. The state's economic situation was improving through the adoption of some new policies which aimed at overcoming the mistakes caused by a series of leftist policies since 1957. The policy-making process in this stage seemed more open than in the previous period. However, on the other hand, the political situation was worrying. As the CPC centre clearly concluded later, in '*The Resolution about The Party's Several Historical Issues Since the Founding of PRC* (27th June 1981)', that since 'Mao Zhedong's erroneous theory about the class struggle in socialist society, became more and more serious. His personal arbitrary style gradually damaged the party's democratic centralism system, and the personality cult further developed. The party was unable to promptly correct these mistakes, whilst, careerists, such as Lin Biao, Jiang Qing and Kang Shen, promoted these mistakes with their hidden purpose. Thus, the final result was the launching of the "Cultural Revolution"' (*RF*, No. 13/1981, p. 12).

1966 — 1976 This was the period of the so called the 'Great Proletariat Cultural Revolution', when 'Comrade Mao Zhedong's personal leadership with leftist mistakes actually replaced the collective leadership of the Party Centre. The personality cult to comrade Mao Zhedong was advocated to a hysterical extent.'(ibid. p13) All important decisions, either political, economic, or diplomatic and all other key aspects of state affairs, were apparently made according to Mao's last instruction. Meanwhile, within the whole country from the top to the bottom only one kind of thinking and one kind of opinion (that being in accordance with Mao) was allowed to be expressed. No one was allowed to hold an idea that differed from that of the paramount leader. Under these circumstances, the policy-making approach was just the typical Mao-in-control model. Actually, owing to the limitation of personal energy, time, and the ability to clearly understand so many issues in different fields, Mao could not really respond to and cope with all those important policy-making issues by himself directly and efficiently. Thus, substantially, it provided those political careerists with the possibility to usurp the policy-making power for their own purposes.

1978 — 1990 Before this period, there was a short stage from the smash of the Gang of Four to the eve of the Third Plenary Session of the Eleventh Central Committee of CPC, which was held before the end of 1978. This was a short transition period. Afterwards, Deng definitely became the paramount leader of China's new generation leading group. In this stage, with the conducting of the reform policies, the political environment was gradually becoming looser and the democratic atmosphere was recovering step by step. Although the paramount leader still played a key role in policy-making, other members of the political elites were also important participators in the policy process. A plural tendency, especially in the economic realm, was gradually developing, which was conducive to the development of a better policy-making environment. Some better policy-making methods had been efficiently adopted. All these brought about a series of better policy outputs which resulted in many important achievements in speeding up the state's economic construction and strengthening the comprehensive national power.

1990 — 1995 The ongoing reform further developed and deepened, which touched or influenced almost all realms of China's society. Deng retired but retained an important influence on the top policy-making. More, better policy-making approaches and measures were adopted structurally and procedurally, by which to widely absorb those beneficial ideas and suggestions from different sides and from home and abroad, to speed up China's modernised course.

Through briefly tracing the changing and development of China's policy-making patterns in different periods, we gained a systematically understanding of the contextual and causal facts concerning our major analytical target. This provides us with a base for the further examination of the SEZ-related policy process, in a comprehensive way, and to which we now turn.

11.1.2 Analysing the influence of each key element in SEZ policy-making process

About the structure and mechanism of the policy-making power Confirming the importance of this element is based on the institutional theory. To discuss this element aims to probe the influence of allocation and the operating mode of China's policy-making power, which are determined by China's existing institutions. Examining this aspect of the SEZ course, the available evidence suggests that:

- The decisive power of determining the SEZ programmes and the related policies was concentrated in the central authority, instead of the ministry/province level. The merits of this centralised policy-making are inclusive of ensuring these programmes a high status as the state's development strategy, and enabling them to be decided and implemented with enough authority and impetus so as to reach a higher efficiency. Its weakness was disadvantageous to a certain extent for the local authorities to fully use their initiative and creative capacity.

- Party authority was in the core position of policy-making, while the state system's role was becoming more and more important. The major works for the policy-making were actually done by the governmental organs at different levels, but the Party leadership had the final say. This could be seen at all occasions of the SEZ policy-making, particularly for the key issues.

- Some strict procedures needed to be followed when examining and approving a policy issue, which sometimes could be used by the opposing force as a lawful means for realising their desired goals. For instance, in some occasions, policy issues could not be decided right away although those chief leaders had clearly confirmed their support, such as the delay in approving the Yangpu project for three years.

• Informal politics could influence the policy process to a certain extent. Some works, which Xu Shijie, Hainan's party secretary, did for saving the Yangpu project in the 'Yangpu Incident' were examples of this.

About the policy makers This is an elitism-basis element, which emphasises the role of political elites in China's SEZ policy-making process. The extent to which a decision-maker can affect the policy-making mainly depends on his or her political and professional ability, and his or her formal or informal status, on which an analysis in this section focuses.

Analysing the significance of the personal ability in policy-making, the case of Deng Xiaoping is a typical one. China's reform, opening-up and modernisation drive, in which the SEZ is an important component part, were all closely linked with him, for these programmes were not only mainly advocated by him, but were launched and promoted with his direct guidance. Now it has been widely acknowledged that Deng's outstanding ability, strong will, excellent wisdom and rich political experience had enabled him to be one of the best decision makers of the world and enjoyed a high prestige. With respect to the SEZ issues, the fact that he found and firmly supported the idea of setting up an industrial zone in Shenzhen and named it 'Special Zone' personally, unswervingly supported the Yangpu project, and clearly affirmed the crucial significance of Pudong project and promoted its development with all his efforts, prominently indicated his particular ability in discovering, analysing, judging and determining the key policy issues. Obviously, Deng's performances fully demonstrated the importance of the personal ability of a policy maker. Compared with Mao Zhedong, in the aspects of guiding the economic construction and the social development in a relative peaceful environment, Deng's ability in policy-making was much better than Mao's. Of course, the prominent difference between them in the methods and criteria for judging and determining the policy issues, was closely linked to their respective guiding thought (value, principles and the targets, etc.), which directly resulted in the distinct policy outputs. From the other point of view, setting up and insisting on a proper guiding thought for the state's development, which can meet the requirement of the era and society, is also an important personal ability of a decision-maker. In this aspect, Deng was also better than Mao.

At the provincial level, we saw that Xi Zhongxun and Yang Shangkun, the first and second party secretaries of Guangdong respectively in the late 1970s, had played key roles in finding and supporting the idea of setting up industrial zone in the early stage (section 6.2.1). Without their capable work then, it would have been impossible to put the idea on the state's agenda.

Comparing the development of Pudong and Hainan, we also can see the importance of the decision-makers' ability at the local level. Generally speaking, the development of Pudong New Zone was basically going well when it was formally decided as a state's project and started its overall construction. Besides other reasons, to a great extent, its smooth and proper development resulted from the role of its policy makers with relatively high quality. It was their effective work that enabled the policy processes of studying, planning, organising, and commanding the Pudong project, to be better conducted. As known to many people, since 1949, due to Shanghai's key important status in China politically and economically, as a municipality with provincial status, the leading cadres appointed to head Shanghai were usually those with stronger ability. For instance, at present, two standing members and one member of the politburo of CPC Centre, including Jiang Zemin, the party's General Secretary, Zhu Rongji, the premier, were originally Shanghai's chief leaders. In contrast, Hainan's situation was quite different. Although it is much bigger than Shanghai geographically, as a remote and isolated island, it was only an administrative region of Guangdong province before 1988, and so its leading group was relatively weak before the setting up of the new province and the SEZ. Then, after establishing the province and SEZ, it was still not easy to select and organise a capable and powerful leading cadre team to fill the positions from provincial to the primary levels in a short time. Consequently, this became one of the important reasons that the course Hainan's development experienced was zigzag, which involved many turns and twists and disturbances in all its three stages.

Another important issue, which needs to be discussed, is the impact of a decision-maker's status including his or her formal official status and informal status, upon the policy process. It has been a noticeable political phenomenon in post-Mao China that some crucial impacts of a decision-maker came from his or her informal status and they were even much greater than the impacts that could be produced from his or her formal status. Why did this situation occur? How did it influence a policy process? How should we evaluate the significance of a policy maker's status in a policy process? These issues are worthy of further analysis. Fundamentally speaking, it should be affirmed that a high-rank formal official status is important for a person involved in the state's policy-making actions. The rank of an official's formal status, usually, determines the extent to which he or she can influence a policy process at different levels. However, it is not all of the reality. China's political life of the last two decades witnessed that the influences upon the policy actions, which came from persons without corresponding formal official status, could never be disregarded or looked down on. Deng Xiaoping, as known to all, had never been a number one leader with formal status of either the Party or the state, since his rehabilitation in the late 1970s. His most important formal official status was only as a standing member of the politburo and the Chairman of the Central Military Commission. However, his real status and role, was undoubtedly the paramount leader of China in the last two decades, which had been always acknowledged by the world. After Deng retired from the politburo in 1987 and from the Chairmanship of the Central Military Commission in 1990, he still affected China's policy process on every key issue of the Party and the state affairs, through his powerful authority and great prestige in China. In the early 1990, it was Deng who raised the Pudong issue to the central leaders and instructed them to seize the task, after his inspection in Shanghai. Then, in the early 1992, it was Deng's famous South China inspection (mainly in the SEZs) and his series of speeches in this tour, in which he stated his thought of affirming the importance of setting up the market economy mechanism and accelerating China's reform and opening-up course, which gave great impetus to China's economic development. Deng's force which could powerfully affect the policy processes of China's reform and opening-up drive, did not only come from his authority, prestige, ability and his deeds of merit, but also from his close relations with those high-rank officials both in the party and the state's leading organs, and both in central and local authorities, which were set up during his more than seventy years' revolutionary and political career.

These facts demonstrate that not only the formal official status, but also a person's informal status building up by one's existing authority, prestige and social foundation, was the important resource of one's force to influence the policy-making. Actually, in the post-Mao China, not only Deng, but also many other veterans, regardless of whether they were in or not in the formal official status, could play important roles in China's policy-making process on different aspects. Why did this political phenomenon occur and exist for such a long period? It was caused by some historical reasons. Due to the upheaval of the Cultural Revolution, China had lost many important and capable leaders, and the work of cultivating new cadres was actually stopped for more than ten years. Then when the reform and modernisation drive sparked off in the late 1970s, the serious lack of cadres resulted in the veterans needing to either fill many important posts or to be advisors to offer advice for the new generation. No matter that those veterans had or did not have the formal official status, they were required to provide the party and state's organs at different levels with supervision and guidance. On the other hand, a person's position in power system usually depends on the time he or she serves and his or her contribution is a tradition of China's officialdom. Therefore, those people with senior qualifications at different levels could powerfully affect the policy-making action even though they were not in the relevant posts.

About the motivation (dynamics) of policy-making This element mainly involves the consideration of the influences of Marxist determinism and economic globalisation. If one raises a question: what was the main motivation of China to make state's policies in the post-Mao period? the answer undoubtedly must be to promote China's economic development as soon as possible. As has been analysed that this consideration resulted from the great economic and political pressures which came from both internal and external aspects, to the regime and the state. Since the 3rd Plenum of the 11th Central Committee of CPC, advocated by Deng Xiaoping, CPC Centre had formulated the Party's basic line of 'one central task, two basic points'. One central task is economic construction, and the two basic points are adhering to the four cardinal principles and adhering to the reform and opening-up (BR. vol. 40, No.10, 1997, pp. 8-9). This guiding thought is also indicated in the judging criteria of 'three whethers', which confirmed that the standards to judge the right and wrong of any issue in the reform and opening-up period, are to see whether it is conducive to promoting the development of the socialist productive force, whether it is conducive to strengthening the state's comprehensive force, and whether it is conducive to the improvement of people's living standard. It can be definitely said that never has China had such a clear and firm motivation or target to pursue the economic development prior to the reform period. Fortunately, this motivation has dominated China's policy-making actions for nearly twenty years. Thanks to this reason, China's economy has grown at more than nine percent for fifteen years, and an economically strong China is now arising.

While adhering to the opening-up and SEZ course, China's leadership also realised the possibility of the growing influences coming from the Western ideology and culture during the course of widely expanding the exchanges between China and the foreign countries and absorbing the advanced science, technology, managerial skill, capital and other useful elements from the latter. However, China's door opening to the outside world has never closed or become narrower since the end of the 1970s, for China's decision makers consider the opening-up and economic development as unchangeable targets which should take priority over all other issues. Because it was thought to relate directly to the state's destiny and future, preference was actually given to opening-up and economic development rather than to guarding against ideological invasion. Thus, in practice, in order to achieve a high-speed economic development, China's authority would rather take the risk of the possible ideological erosion coming from the foreign countries.

Analysing the motivation for promoting the SEZ course and the relevant opening-up programmes, another characteristic also needs to be noticed. That is, in making these programmes and policies, the motivation had combined both the economic and political pursuing. In other words, the economic and the political motives are fundamentally with one accord under this situation. It means that the opening-up and SEZ programme was needed both for promoting the state's economic development and improving people's living standard, and for maintaining social stability and promoting reunification course. The combining of these motivations in making policy, consequently, not only became the determination of the leadership, but also stirred up people's enthusiasm and support.

About the policy-making approaches Analysing this element aims at exploring how China improved its policy-making process. What approaches did China usually apply in the policy-making processes relating to the SEZ drive and the relevant opening-up programme? In examining the practice, we see that these approaches were mainly inclusive of democratic centralism, pragmatism, incrementalism, rationalism and optimism.

Democratic centralism is claimed as the fundamental principle of CPC, which requires that in all situations the minority must obey the majority, the subordinate must obey its higher authority, and the entire Party members and organs must obey the Party Centre. It is originally an organisational principle, but also serves as a principle of policy-making. However, actually, this method could not be easily implemented before the reform period, for the will of the chief leaders or the commanding official often played the decisive role in making decisions at different levels. This meant that the policy-making was more centralised, and less democratic; more power in the key authorities of the centre, less power in the local; more power in the leaders-in-chief, and less power in lower-ranks officials; and more power in the paramount leader, and less power in others. In the post-Mao era, this situation had changed remarkably. Theoretically, the participants of policy-making were encouraged to speak their minds freely and fully, and to boldly air their honest opinions. However, in practice, an important condition was always emphasised that the party members and cadres at all levels were required to keep unanimity with the Centre. This requirement was particularly strict in the political and ideological realms. Thus when we mention the progress in carrying out the democratic centralism, we mainly indicate the matters in the economic field.

China's democratic centralism system is often criticised as a model of paternalistic democracy. Whereas the Western individualistic tradition was considered to be liberal first and democratic later; in contrast, China sought to combine democracy with authority, dictatorship and centralism rather than with freedom (He, B. 1996, pp. 43-44). However, this system did show a higher efficiency in policy-making in many occasions, because it is beneficial in dealing with the policy-making promptly and efficiently in favour of the interest of the state. For highlighting this significance, Deng Xiaoping had clearly pointed out that:

> The greatest advantage of the socialist system is that when the central leadership makes a decision it is promptly implemented without interference from any other quarters. When we decided to reform the economic structure, the whole country responded; when we decided to establish the special economic zones, they were soon set up...From this point of view, our system is very efficient (Deng, X. 1983, p.75).

As we attach attention to the fact that centralised power is conducive to efficiency to a certain extent in China's practice, we also need to notice the importance of the development of the decentralised and democracy-oriented policy-making mode, the other side of the democratic centralism system. The ten-odd years' history of promoting the SEZ course and the relevant opening-up programmes witnessed the development of practising a better policy-making approach, in the economic and technological realms. In this course, as discussed in the empirical chapters, the participants from inside and outside the party, from local to the centre, from professional or non-professional fields, and from home and abroad, had been able to express their opinions comparatively freely, including opposing opinions. Up to now, no one had encountered trouble by expressing different opinions. To be sure, it is one of the important reasons that the SEZ course and the relevant opening-up programmes could be pushed ahead smoothly and promptly in a short period and obtained a remarkable achievement. This progress had enabled policy-making authorities to widely absorb the constructive opinions and suggestions from all possible aspects.

The term pragmatism has never been preferred in China's political and academic circles. However, the main policies China's leadership made in pushing ahead the reform and opening-up course has often been seen in Western countries as adopting pragmatism. Therefore, in the Western academic circles, it has been conventional to summarise Deng Xiaoping's political philosophy with this term (Pye, L. 1995, p. 32). Actually, in the Chinese view, the term pragmatism contains some vulgar connotation, for 'it is an euphemism for the ways of a corrupt politician who has no principles and is concerned only with his own self interest' on the one hand, and 'in a slight respectable vision, pragmatism suggests an operational code in which there are no higher values, nothing is sacred, and everything is up for "sale" if the price is right' (Pye, L. ibid.), on the other hand. To analyse the behaviours of pragmatism in an in-depth way, at least three of its manifestations can be found:
- Both the goal and the means are pragmatic;
- The goal is rational and conforms to one's basic value, but the means are pragmatic;
- The goal is pragmatic, but the means are rational.

According to China's reality, what we are discussing here is the second way: to use those methods or theories which can really solve the immediate problems, in order to pursue a rational target which conforms to the state's long-term and fundamental values. In determining and promoting the SEZ and the relevant opening-up programmes, this approach was always applied as the guiding thought and cardinal method. The essence of Deng's theory 'build socialism with Chinese characteristics', one of the two major contributions of Deng (BR. vol. 40, No. 10/1997, p. 8), actually provided the basis of doing so. The key point of this theory, substantially, is to determine China's policies in all realms, according to the reality of China (a country with a big population but with a comparatively backward economy and culture, etc.). These policies must be beneficial to the state's interest (conforming to the principle of 'three whethers'), instead of repeating the fault of dogmatism which occurred in the past that copied the principles and methods from the classic works or documents, or ready-made experiences and theories of other countries. So long as the policies meet the demands of China's reality (conditions and interests), they could be considered 'the socialist policies' with 'Chinese characteristics' and could be adopted. Thus, in a fundamental sense, the crucial significance of the theory 'build socialism with Chinese characteristics', is its providing a basis of flexibility for a wider policy choice for China's development. Deng's well known 'cat theory' just reflects the core of this thinking. Consequently, when China's decision makers were probing and analysing the feasibility of the SEZ and the relevant opening-up programmes, their judging criteria were the ideas of 'three whethers', which had made it much easier to find solutions without falling into time-consuming theoretical and ideological arguments. For instance, some common and intense debating issues were those that should the way or policy selected be socialism or capitalism, and was SEZ socialism or capitalism? These debates had occurred several times in the early 1980s, especially in Shenzhen SEZ when it was in progress of accelerating its development by adopting much more open policies. Fortunately, Deng Xiaoping always emphasised that we do not need to debate too much but refer to the principle of 'three whethers'. To follow this pragmatic guiding thought and method had made it convenient for China's decision-makers to keep boldly formulating the new policies with which to push ahead the opening-up and SEZ course.

The application of incrementalism, rationalism and optimism approaches has been discussed in detail in the previous chapters. Comparing these three, from the point of popularity and effectiveness in China's reality, as has been analysed, the incremental model is the first, and the rationalism and optimism follow in turn.

In considering the effects of applying diversified models in promoting the SEZ course and the relevant opening-up programs, one conclusion could be drawn that the application of the proper policy-making approaches has been very important in practice, for its leading to better policy outputs. The most noticeable success of this application is the using of the pragmatic and incremental approaches, which like the two wheels or two wings of the China's policy-making mechanism since the end of the 1970s, which had enabled China's policy-making behaviour to become much bolder, prudent and efficient.

About the political environment The element of the political environment for policy-making mainly examines to what extent a pluralist involvement can be realised. This environment is shaped by the political institutions, which concerns the possibility and extents of the interaction between the policy makers on one hand, and the interaction between the policy makers and public sentiment and popular feeling, on the other hand. For the first aspect, it examines how and to what extent the participants of the policy-making action can express their opinions freely and fully, and how and to what extent the correct opinions can be accepted. The second aspect examines how and to what extent public sentiment can influence the policy-making process, or how and to what extent the policy makers can accept opinions, demands and supervision from the public.

Generally speaking, this environment has been moving towards one with more forgiveness and toleration, especially in the economic policy-making realm. Reviewing briefly some main changes of China's political life, firstly, is beneficial to throw light upon the general context and background. Since the 3rd Plenum of the 11th Central Committee of CPC, the personality cult and personal arbitrariness had been reduced greatly, ideological toleration was increasing, and the progress of pluralist involvement in policy-making was noticeable. The obvious proofs include many aspects. It became no longer the practice to hang any leaders' pictures in public places, nor to call 'long life' for the paramount leaders; the ousted leading cadres with political views were no longer to be treated as class enemies suffering rude criticism and shame. The chief leaders of the centre are willing or good at listening to the opinions and suggestions from different aspects. The eight non-communist democratic parties have enjoyed a higher status they have never had before. The chief leaders of these non-CPC parties can access the state's crucial policy-making processes and are consulted on many major affairs relating to formulating those important documents of CPC, making the state's development strategies, and determining important personnel appointments, etc.

In the improvement of the political environment towards the direction with more plurality and tolerance, relating to the SEZ course, we saw that diversified opinions, including the opposing ones, had been allowed to be expressed in the policy-making processes. In Hainan's 'Yangpu Incident', many chief central leaders had publicly affirmed their support to the Yangpu project, Zhang Wei, a member of the CPPCC still delivered a speech strongly opposing the project. This would have been impossible in the past. Then, in the policy-making process of CPC centre about this issue involved arguments in which opinions opposing each other with equal harshness, which resulted in a deadlock. Although we still could not know the details about this process, but its output was clear that the Yangpu project failed to be approved even though many top leaders including Deng supported it. These phenomena signalled that China has been gradually departing from the old political environment and moving towards a comparatively open and tolerant political life, and this new environment has been much better to encourage people to participate in social and political life while actively expressing their opinions.

However, as mentioned above, at present, the improvement of the political environment for policy-making, is mainly in the economic field. As for making those ideological and political policies that are considered sensitive issues in China, it still does not encourage people to express their different ideas freely, especially those which obviously depart from the requirements and stipulations of the party centre.

11.1.3 Assessing the extent of each element's influence and their relations

After discussing the manifestations and roles of each element, this section further analyses and assesses the extents of their influences and their relations in China's policy-making process. The influence of each element, could be listed in turn, according to its importance to China's policy-making practice in the post-Mao period, as below:
- The structure and the mechanism;
- The policy makers;
- The motivation (dynamics);
- The approaches;
- The environment.

To understand why the five elements are listed in this order, some more analyses are essential. First, the structure and the mechanism of China's policy-making power, which embody the organisational structure and the operating mode, are closely connected with and shaped by the institutions. Simultaneously, on the other hand, the structure and the mechanism determine (1) the status, role, and power relations of the decision-makers, and (2) the basic procedures and methods of making a policy. They determine that the Party is in the core position of the state's leadership at different levels, and the centralised power system; they actually admits the powerful roles of a paramount leader; and they stipulate the procedures for examining and approving a policy or a programme. Thus, the structure and the mechanism occupy the most important place among the five elements.

Second, the important roles of the policy makers means that those political elites who are leaders at and above province/ministry level, especially the top leaders, were not only occupying central positions in policy-making process, but also playing the retroaction to China's power structure and power operating mechanism whenever the situation needed. In other words, they were not only passively affected or determined by the latter. In the reform period, for instance, the decisions of cancelling the position of the party chairman, abolishing the lifelong-hold-post system of leading cadre's appointment, and firmly promoting the power separation between party and the state administrative system, and between the party and enterprises, etc., were the measures reacted to the institutions through adjusting the power structure, power allocation method and the power balance relations. As reference to the SEZ course, setting the SEZ system, changing Hainan's regional status and setting up Hainan province, were also examples. Unquestionably, these measures were formulated mainly by high-rank policy makers, which are the prominent manifestations that the policy makers react to the power structure and the mechanism. These reactions had been beneficial in continuously improving the policy-making processes and accelerating China's development.

Third, then, setting up a good motivation (dynamics), namely, to promote China's economic construction and improve people's living stand as soon as possible so as to enable China's survival and development, which had became a great stress to China's leaders, was very significant in giving impetus to the SEZ-related policy-making. This dynamics was found and set up by China's key policy makers based on understanding the people's demands and the world's situation. Fourth, adopting those effective policy-making approaches, in which incrementalism and pragmatism were most popular, had been beneficial in producing better policy outputs, such as a series of SEZ-related policies which had brought about fruitful achievements. Fifth, the conspicuous improvement of the political environment, which was determined by the power structure and mechanism, and the decision makers as well, had significantly enlarged the plural involvement, in China's SEZ-related policy-making. This improvement also encouraged people to boldly express their opinions both inside and outside the policy-making circle, and to supervise the policy process. What happened around the YP Incident indicates the impact of this progress.

Finally, we may summarise the roles and relations of those five elements as follows.

- The structure and mechanism, which are shaped by China's institutions, are dominant among these five factors, for they determine the status and power relations of decision-makers, and the environment.
- Decision-makers play the key role in policy process, for they define the policy issues, set up the motivation, select approaches and affect the environment. Furthermore, they also can exert reactions to institutions.
- Motivation (dynamics) is important in setting up a proper policy-making target and pushing ahead an ongoing policy process.
- A proper approach is conducive to the better and more reliable policy output, in realising policy makers' target.
- Although the political environment is decided by the first two elements, its role in affecting policy process is noticeable, for it determines the possibility and extent of participation, expression and supervision in the policy-making process, which showed both inside and outside the policy-making circle.

Analysing China's SEZ course with a series of selected theories and models from different sides separately or integrally, and in a comprehensive way, has enabled us to know some basic features of China's policy-making behaviour in the post-Mao period, and the applicability of those theories and models as well. Now it is essential to go further to engage in a comparative discussion to examine the differences of the three cases (or three stages) of the SEZ course, by which to explore and evaluate the changes and development of China's policy-making behaviour in this period, and to further examine the applicability of those selected theories and models from another point of view.

11.2 A comparative analysis: the differences of the three cases

The time from the setting up of China's first SEZ Shenzhen to the rise of Pudong New Zone, spanned ten-odd years. During this long period, some prominent changes had been taking place in China's policy-making behaviour, which were influenced by many factors. Hence, comparing these three cases of the SEZ course, some different features of each one could be identified. The following pages analyse what policy-making models had been carried out in each case, and probe what progresses had been achieved in this course.

The feature of the policy-making mode, from a general viewpoint, in setting up the first group of SEZ involved multiple methods. The situation at that time was that China had just begun its first step of shifting the focus of the state's work to economic construction and searching for the way of opening-up course, when China had been basically isolated from the outside world for nearly three decades. The task to develop the economy and push ahead the opening-up course were urgent, but the means were unknown. Under this circumstance, what the policy makers did, as has been analysed, was to actively search for a way to break through. In doing so, they successfully discovered and seized the ideas of setting up export-oriented and industrial zones and then deepened and defined them as a new concept — special economic zone. Within a very short time, a series of intense works for developing this initiative, was completed (sections 6.2.2 and 6.2.3). This period saw the involvement of various policy-making modes. These included elitism, for the elites at different levels, especially the top level, played the key role, although the initiative of SEZ programme was produced by a bottom-up method, while other social forces were much less involved; rationalism, for the decision makers treated the policy issues very prudently and rationally (see section 6.2) as at the starting stage of the opening-up course, with drawing bitter lessons from the past; and a particular top-down approach, which means that all those important actions, after the original idea was initiated, to push ahead the following policy actions were firmly seized, commanded and supervised directly by the relevant central leaders. From the above analyses, some features of the policy process in this period can be identified: the motivation was clear-cut and urgent but the means to realise the target were not quite clear, the policy-making mode was contingent, central elites played a key role in promoting the policy action and therefore the determination and implementation of the policies were highly efficient.

Compared with the first group of SEZ, the policy-making process of setting up Hainan SEZ was sharply characterised by an incremental approach. We saw in chapter seven that the course of Hainan's development from starting opening-up course in the late 1980 to finally establishing the SEZ and setting up a new province in 1988, lasted a long time and experienced many twists and turns, including some great setbacks. Why did these happen? As we analysed in the contingent explanatory account (section 10.4), the policy process for Hainan's development faced too many uncertainties and problems for which it was not easy to find good solutions which were particular challenges to the central and provincial authorities; and simultaneously, the quality of Hainan's cadres team, especially the leading group, was still not good enough to be competent in responding to the difficult situation. Consequently, it resulted in a typical incremental way of 'groping pebbles to cross the stream' in policy-making, namely, to search for the suitable solutions step by step. More exactly, as analysed in section 10.2.2, therefore, the policy-making for Hainan's development, which experienced three stages, was a typical disjointed incremental process.

According to the theoretical relation between incrementalism and pluralism, the increasing involvement of the incremental approach, in Hainan case, indicates the inevitability of the increasing involvement of pluralist forces in the policy processes, for the existing uncertainties made it difficult for those elites to find solutions within a rational framework in a relatively short period. The development of the macro-political-environment then provided such a possibility for the plural involvement of interests and public sentiments. Hence, the major features of Hainan's policy process, besides adopting the incremental approaches, are the involvement of plural forces, and the prolonging of the decision-making.

The policy-making process for Pudong New Zone, the most special SEZ of China, was mainly characterised by rationalism. Compared with the first group of SEZ and Hainan SEZ, the policy-making context and background of Pudong were quite different. Namely, the conditions for Pudong's policy-making were much better than the first two, which could be seen in many ways. These included: some experiences for developing China's SEZ and promoting the opening-up course had accumulated; and Shanghai's advantageous conditions which could be beneficial to promoting Pudong's course, in the aspects of the quality of both leadership and cadres team, economic and technological foundations and status, financial base, and location. (sections 8.1) These beneficial conditions, therefore, enabled Pudong's policy-making process to be of higher efficiency and to produce better policy outputs when it was formally decided as a state project, which covered four aspects. (1) It reduced a lot of problems of trying out basic experiments in making the SEZ policies. (2) It ensured Pudong's development to be launched from a high starting point.

(3) It made it possible to set up a very high standard for Pudong's development. (4) It made it possible for policy makers to try to maximise the value they pursued. Owing to these reasons, it had been possible for Pudong's decision-makers including those at central and local authority, to mainly adopt the rational model in determining their policies. Furthermore, another feature of Pudong's policy-making was absorbing opinions and suggestions from a much wider range including academic and professional circles and involving people from home and abroad. To be sure, this stemmed from a much looser environment after ten-odd years' reform and economic development, and it had been conducive to further improve the policy-making quality prominently. However, as attaching attention to the conveniences and advantages of Pudong's development, we also notice another situation in its policy process. If we examine Pudong's policy process vertically, we can see the involvement of the incremental element, because the time for making the strategy of setting up Pudong New Zone had lasted from 1984 to 1990. In this course, covert competition among elites occurred, which resulted in a protracted process from the early consideration to the final determination.

According to above comparative discussions, it seems to be reasonable to draw a conclusion that during the ten-odd years' development course of promoting the SEZ programme, China's policy-making process has been on the way of keeping continuously improvement, which characterised by increasingly involvement of the elements of incrementalism, rationalism and pluralism.

Thus far, in studying the applicability of those major policy-making theories and models to China's practice, by which to explore the features of China's policy-making behaviour in the post-Mao period, we had accessed the analyses in four ways.

- A general examination of the applicability of selected theories and models to China's policy-making practice.
- A concrete analysis of the applicability of selected theories and models to China's SEZ-related policy-making process.
- A further exploration of the SEZ-related policy actions with a comprehensive method.
- A comparison of the features of the policy processes of the SEZs' three stages (or three cases), and their reasons.

Then, according to these multiform studies, to what extent have we understood China's policy-making behaviour in the post-Mao period with the help of those theories and models? The answer to this question is the conclusion of my study, which is summarised below.

11.3 The main findings

11.3.1 The existing institutions are decisive in shaping China's policy-making mode

How could the existing institutions shape China's policy mode? Currently China's main institutions include those at different levels, which determine the power structure and the power relations (section 11.1.2) within which the policy-making actions take place. Then, concretely, what policy-making-related elements are decided by existing institutions? They cover at least six aspects.

- CPC is the core force of the state's leadership and plays the key role in making the state's policies at all levels.
- The policy-making power is characterised by the centralised system, and subordinate organs and individuals are required to act in accordance with higher authorities, and with the centre.
- The authorities of party and state are separated in forms, but permeate each other with the party system in the key position.
- The crucial influence of the paramount leader is accepted and affirmed.
- Policy-making mechanism is administration-led (with the party as its core), instead of legislature-led.
- To parallel the importance of upholding the ideological principles and promoting economic development in making the state policy, with often giving more priority to the latter actually.

11.3.2 Political elites dominated China's policy-making process

Actually, in any modern country, the political elites play a key role in state's policy-making. Particular to current China was that, owing to the following reasons, these elites' dominant role was much more prominent. (1) The institutional background decided that people who either inside or outside the policy-making circle, still could not thoroughly speak out what they want to express, which particularly concerns those sensitive political and ideological issues. (2) The insufficiency of the power and mechanism, which can be used by the public to access the information about the state's policy issues and to monitor the policy process. (3) A weaker role of supervising the policy actions by the media. These deficiencies had enabled a much more superior status of those political elites, which included the prominent role of the chief leaders as individuals, the important influence of the higher-rank officials, the crucial role of the paramount leader, and the excessive intervention of the state organs to the society, etc.

The important status of the political elites in the state's policy-making actions also resulted from the influences of other factors. That the political system highlights the centralised system and the party's leading position at all levels of the regime, further strengthens the legal power of those elites. Moreover, China's current economic state as a developing country in general, determines that many people, even in the urban areas, still do not have a very strong sense of political participation. A relatively backward national education level also reduces, to a great extent, the possibility of public concerning, participating in and influencing the policy issues. Recent statistical data show that China's illiterate are 229 million, which accounts for 25.83 percent of the total of the world's illiterate; the entrance rate of the middle school is only 44 percent, which makes up the 66th of the world; and the entrance rate of university is 2 percent, which is listed as the number 102 of the world (Gao, G. 1997). Finally, historically speaking, since a complete and sophisticated feudal political and bureaucratic system had been developed for more than two thousand years in China, many passive elements remain, such as the sense of the absolute power of an emperor, the idea of considering an official as being more important than common people, the idea that a head-official's will is decisive, and calling the heads of a county, city and province the 'parents-like-officials', etc. All of these still produce impacts on the behaviour of current officials and common people as well, to different extents.

11.3.3 The rise of a pluralist tendency significantly influenced China's policy process

The substance of the rise of the pluralistic tendency in current China, is the increasing involvement of non-CPC and non-government political and social forces in China's policy-making. It also means the increasing involvement of the decentralised political forces in policy process. To affirm the significance of these progresses does not contradict what was discussed above that political elites still dominate China's policy-making, because a pluralist involvement has not reached a dominant position (it is usually impossible) although it has developed to a certain degree. This progress, comparing with the first three decades of PRC, included: those officials of non-CPC members had had more rights to participate in policy-making; the roles of the NPC (legislature organ) and CPPCC (political consultant organ), and those eight non-CPC democratic parties, were increasing significantly; people both inside and outside the policy-making circle were encouraged to express their opinion boldly, especially in the economic field. etc.

The appearance of this progress was a significant change in the post-Mao China, which signalled the start of China's moving towards a pluralistic society, which resulted from many reasons. Firstly, it was the consequence of the shifting of the state's work focus from the political and class struggle realms to economic construction, and so brought about speedy economic growth since 1980s. The fast economic growth had promoted the development of multiple social forces, which fundamentally changed the situation which existed in the past that only political leaders at all levels had power to control policy-making. The role of some leaders in the economic circle began to show their influences on policy-making. Moreover, with the rapid economic development, the incomes and interests of different social groups have been obviously distinguished and the gaps between them have even been greatly enlarged. This change became one of the reasons for the occurrence of the interests, which have started to express their different demands for their own desired goals.

Secondly, this pluralistic tendency was caused by the occurrence of the pluralistic economic sectors. With the development of the reform and the opening-up course, a great change in the structure of China's economic sectors had taken place. That means, the multiple economic components, including private sector, collective sector, joint-venture sectors and the sole foreign sectors, besides the pure public sector, had not only existed but also flourished in China. To distinguish them with the Marxism principle, they consist of socialist sector, mixed-socialist-and-capitalist sector and sole capitalist sector, etc. The appearance of this situation would have been absolutely impossible before the reform period. The existence of multiple-sectors in China's economy brought about the producing of multiple interest groups in the economic realm, which strongly strengthened China's tendency towards a pluralistic society.

Thirdly, it was influenced by the demands for political reform. Since the early 1980s, with the carrying out of the economic reform and opening-up policies, the movements asking for political reform and striving for more democratic rights have continued in China. Although these demands may have been too early or too radical to be accepted by current China's authority, they did influence the promotion of the political pluralistic and democratic progress.

Fourth, it also resulted from drawing lessons from history. During the period prior to the end of 1970s, there had been so many bitter lessons that many disastrous mistakes were caused by wrong decision-making modes (section 5.2.3). Therefore, to build up an environment with a more open and tolerant atmosphere, so as to promote a pluralistic way to widely absorb different opinions and also the public sentiment from inside and outside the policy-making participants, and from inside and outside the CPC, had been an inevitable choice for China's authority for accelerating China's modernisation drive.

11.3.4 The twin approaches of incrementalism and pragmatism were the foundation of China's policy-making mechanism, which powerfully promoted its successful operation

In the course of determining and promoting China's SEZ cause, and relevant reform and opening-up strategies, the most important approaches being applied were pragmatism and incrementalism, which were the foundation of China's policy-making mechanism. As has been discussed, what we mention here about pragmatism means to boldly apply the ways however effective for achieving a desired rational target, which is a thinking mode and also a policy-making model which has been popular in China as Deng's 'Cat Theory'. That the success of making and carrying out the SEZ-related policies which resulted from following the principle of 'three whethers' (Deng, X, 1993, p. 372), typically demonstrates the significance of applying this mode. Although the principle of 'three whethers' was formally put forward in 1992, its basic ideas and guiding thought had already been implemented since the launching of the reform, namely from the end of 1970s. Incrementalism, characterised by the idea of 'groping pebbles to cross the stream' which was advocated by Deng, was widely used in the policy-making process of post-Mao China, which enabled better policy outputs to be made. According to the SEZ course and others, to be sure, since the third Plenum of the Eleventh Central Committee of CPC, China has significantly reduced mistakes caused by the fault of decision-making, especially in the economic field.

Moreover, due to drawing lessons from the first three decades of the PRC, China has attached great attention to avoiding the mistakes of aiming too high, advancing too hastily, using the political principles to measure the economic policies or state's relations, and using political goal to replace the economic demands and targets, etc., which often occurred in the past. This has enabled the increasing involvement of the rational approaches whenever and wherever possible. Other useful approaches were also effectively employed whenever required by the circumstance.

11.3.5 Marxism was still the fundamental guiding thought of China's policy-making, but a great flexibility had been adopted

As a state upholding a socialist system, China was still taking Marxism as its guiding thought and basic principles. However, in the post-Mao period, the way China applied Marxism has been altered greatly, which has significantly influenced China's policy-making behaviour and mode. The available evidence suggests that the main change is adopting a greater flexibility and a realistic way in making policies. That is, the state's strategies and policies must be in accordance with China's reality: the demands of the people and the state, and the conditions and possibility economically, politically and socially; instead of copying the principles from books or from other countries' experiences. Since the end of 1970s, a series of new theories and policies had been made with this guiding thought, which included the theory of the primary stage of socialism, taking economic construction as the central task, building socialism with Chinese characteristics, reform and opening-up strategies which embodies the SEZ programmes, building up the socialist market economy mechanism, the theory of 'one country, two systems', and the whole set of the principles and policies in the fields of diplomacy, education, science and technology, military affairs, and so on. These new theories and policies had successfully promoted China's overall development towards the targets of modernisation and state's reunification, and greatly improved and strengthened China's status in the world. Unquestionably, none of these principles and policies is copied from Marxist classic works, or from China's former leaders' instructions or other countries' ready-made experiences. They are all new creations in the last two decades. To sum up, it was the renewing of the thinking mode that enabled China to adopt a flexible and realistic way to apply Marxism, through turning down those unreasonable explanations about Marxism, which had brought about the making of a range of new theories and policies.

Conversely, if a state could not determine its policy according to the reality, it would definitely cause trouble or even disaster. The awful situations that occurred in ex-Soviet Union and Albania, suggested this inevitability.

For affirming the significance of the flexibility and realistic method in applying Marxism, Liu Xila, a professor of Qinghua University and a member of CPPCC, pointed out that:

> Deng Xiaoping did not only bring to China the economic development and the social progress, more importantly, he taught Chinese a new thinking mode. That is, for the nation's destiny and future, we must conduct the creative thinking according to the principle of seeking the truth from the fact on one hand, and must accumulate our force through step by step's efforts with the spirit of down-to-earth, on the other hand (Gao, G. ibid.).

Objectively speaking, this comment is highly acceptable. The spirits of flexibility and seeking the truth from fact are just the basis of making a series of successful policies in the post-Mao period.

Bibliography

English sources

Alford, R. (1975), 'Paradigms of Relations between State and Society', in L. E. Lindberg, R. Alford, C. Crouch, and C. Offe (eds), *Stress and Contradictions in Modern Capitalism*, Lexington Books, Lexington Mass.

Anderson, J. E. (1975), *Public Policy-Making*, Preager Publishers Inc.

Anderson, J. E. (1984), *Public Policy-Making*, Hilt, 3rd edition, Rinehart & Winston, Inc. London.

Apter, D. E. (1991), 'Institutionalism Reconsidered', *International Social Science Journal*, (August) vol. 43, pp. 463-81.

Asia-Pacific Report: Trends, Issues, Challenges, (1986), Honolulu, East-West Centre.

Barnett, A D. (1968), *Cadres, Bureaucracy, and Political Power in Communist China*, New York.

Barnett, A. D. (1985), *The Making of Foreign Policy in China*, Westerview Press, Inc. Boulder.

Bell, D. (1960), *The End of Ideology*, Free Press, New York.

Berry, D. (1974), 'The Transfer of Planning Theory to Health Planning Practice', *Policy Science*, vol. 5, (September), pp. 343-61.

Binns, T. (1991), 'Shanghai's Pudong Development Project', *Geography*, October, vol. 76, pp. 362-65.

Blackstone, T. and Plowden, W. (1988), *Inside the Think Tank*, London, Heinemann.

Blowers, A. (1984), *Something in the Air: Corporate Power and the Environment*, Harper & Row Publishers, London.

Bogdanor, V. (ed.) (1987), *The Blackwell Encyclopaedia of Political Institution*, Basil Blackwell, Oxford.

Bogdanor, V. (ed.) (1992), *The Blackwell Encyclopaedia of Political Science*, Basil Blackwell, Oxford.

Bottomore, T. B. (1966), *Elites and Society*, Penguin, Harmondsworth.

BR (1987), 'Hainan Opens Wider to Outside World', *Beijing Review*, vol. 30, No.47, p. 30.

BR (1988), 'Hainan to Feature Market Economy', *Beijing Review*, vol.31, No.6, pp.5-6.

BR (1988), 'New Province, New Programmes', *Beijing Review*, vol. 31, No.37, pp.6-7.

BR (1988), 'Provisions of the State Council of the People's Republic of China for the Encouragement of Investment and Development in Hainan Island' (Promulgated on May 4, 1988), *Beijing Review*, vol. 31, No.35, pp. 26-28, 30.

BR (1988), 'Zhao Outlines Coastal Strategy', *Beijing Review*, vol. 31, No. 51, p. 5.

BR (1990), 'Hainan's Four Development Zones', *Beijing Review*, vol. 33, No.12, p. 30.

BR (1990), 'New Development Zones in Shanghai', *Beijing Review*, vol. 33, No. 36, pp. 29-30.

BR (1990), 'Preferential Policies on Pudong', *Beijing Review*, vol. 33, No. 29, p. 26.

BR (1990), 'Shanghai Mayor on Pudong Development', *Beijing Review*, vol. 33, No. 39, pp. 19-22.

BR (1991), 'Hainan Project to Begin Soon', *Beijing Review*, vol. 34, No. 18, p. 29.

BR (1991), 'Hainan SEZ Investment Rules', *Beijing Review*, vol. 34, No. 18, pp. 28-29.

BR (1991), 'Letter of Intent for Yangpu Zone', *Beijing Review*, vol. 34, No. 42, p. 29.

BR (1992) 'Yangpu EDZ Enjoys Preferential Police', *Beijing Review*, vol. 35, No.17, p. 31.

BR (1992), 'Making Decisions for Yangpu Development', *Beijing Review*, vol. 35, No. 41, p. 29.

BR (1992), 'Pudong Enters International Market', *Beijing Review*, vol. 35, No. 21, pp. 29-30.

BR (1992), 'Shanghai's Bold Move to Reform,' *Beijing Review*, vol. 35, No.12, pp. 5-7.

BR (1992), 'Yangpu Area to be Built Up with Foreign Funds', *Beijing Review*, vol. 35, No. 13, p. 30.

BR (1995), 'CPC Central Committee Proposal for Economic Development', *Beijing Review*, vol. 38, No. 46, pp. 12-6.

BR (1997), 'Message to the Whole Party, The Whole Army and The People of All Nationalities Throughout the Country', from the Central Committee of CPC, the Standing Committee of NPC, the State Council of PRC, the National Committee of CPPCC, and the Military Commissions of CPC Centre and the PRC, *Beijing Review*, vol. 40, No. 10, pp. 4-13.

Braybrooke, D. and Lindblom, C. E. (1963), *A Strategy of Decision*, The Free Press, New York.

'Bubbling along in Hainan', by a special correspondent of *The Economist*, *The Economist*, vol. 324, No. 775/1992, p. 73.

Burns, J. P. (1993), 'Book Review', *China Quarterly*, September 1993, vol. 135, pp. 573-4.

Carnoy, M. et al. (1993), *The New World Economy in the Information Age*, The Pennsylvania State University Press.

Castells, M. (1994) 'European Cities, the Informational Society, and the Global Economy', *New Left Review*, March/April, vol. 204, pp.18-32.

Cawson, A. (1986), *Corporatism and Political Theory*, Oxford, Blackwell Ltd.

Cawson, A. (1992), 'Corporatism', in Bogdanor, V. (eds), *The Blackwell Encyclopaedia of Political Science*, Basil Blackwell, Oxford.

Cawson, A. and Saunders, P. (1981), *Corporatism, Competitive Politics and Class Struggle*, paper prepared for a BSA/PSA Conference on Capital, Ideology and Politics.

Chan, T. et al. (1986), 'China's Special Economic Zone: Ideology, Policy and Practice', in Jao, Y. C. and Leung, C. K. (eds), *China's Special Economic Zones*, Oxford University Press.

Chan, T. M. H. (1991), 'The policy of opening and Special Economic Zones', in Kuan Hsin-Chi and Maurice Brossean (eds), *China Review*, The Chinese University Press, Hong Kong.

Chang, D.W. (1988), *China Under Deng Xiaoping*, Macmillan Press.

Chang, K. (ed.) (1990), *Mainland China after the Thirteenth Party Congress*, Westview Press, Oxford.

Chang, P. H. (1982), *Power and Policy in China*, second and large edition, the Pennsylvania State University Press.

Chao Yu-sun (1987), 'Why the Establishment of Hainan as a Province?', *Issues & Studies*, vol. 23, No. 10, pp. 7-10.

Cheng, Elizabeth (1988), 'No Plan For an Island — A new Chinese province develops in a chaotic fashion', *Far Eastern Economic Review*, vol. 140, No. 21, p. 96.

Cheng, Elizabeth (1989), 'No Treasure Island, — China's newest SEZ needs development funds', *Far Eastern Economic Review*, vol. 144, No. 20, pp. 58-9.

Cheng, Elizabeth (1992), 'Island Beach-Head — Kumagai wins approval for China trade zone', *Far Eastern Economic Review*, vol. 155, No. 17, pp. 64-5.

China's Foreign Economic Legislation, (1984), second edition, vol.1, Foreign Languages Press, Beijing.

Chossudovsky, M. (1986), *Towards Capitalist Restoration? - Chinese Socialism after Mao*, Macmillan, London.

Christensen, K. S. (1985), 'Coping With Uncertainty in Planning', *Journal of the American Planning Association*, No. 51 (1), pp. 63-73.

Cohen, M. D., March, J.G. and Olsen, J. P. (1972), 'A Garbage Can Model of Organisational Choice', *Administrative Science Quarterly*, No. 17, pp. 1-25.

Crane, G. (1990), *The political Economy of China's Special Economic Zone*, M. E. Sharpe, Inc., New York.

Cunningham, G. (1963), 'Policy and Practice', *Public Administration*, No. 41, pp. 229-38.

Dahl R. A. and Lindblom, C. E. (1953), *Politics, Economics and Welfare*, Harpers, New York.

Dahl, R. A. (1956), *A Preface to Democratic Theory*, Chicago University Press.

Dahl, R. A. (1961), *Who governs? Democracy and Power in an American City*, Yale University Press, New Haven, Conn.

Dahl, R. A. (1967), *Pluralist Democracy in the U.S.*, McNally, Chicago.

Dahl, R. A. (1982), *Dilemmas of Pluralist Democracy: Autonomy versus Control*, Yale University Press, New Haven, Conn.

Dai Gang, (1990), 'Shanghai's Pudong Project in Full Swing,' *Beijing Review*, vol. 33, No.43, pp. 16-20.

Dai Gang, (1991), 'A Bridge between Dream and Reality', *Beijing Review*, vol. 34, No. 29, pp. 23-6.

Dai Yannian, (1992), 'Hainan Improves Investment Environment', *Beijing Review*, vol. 35,No. 25, pp. 13-8.

David, B. (1991), *Bureaucracy, Economy and Leadership in China: the Institutional Origins of the Great Leap Forward*, Cambridge University Press.

Deng Xiaoping (1985b), *Building Socialism with Chinese Characteristic*, Foreign Language Press, Beijing.

Deng Xiaoping, (1984b), *Selected Works of Deng Xiaoping (1975-1982)*, *English edition*, Foreign Languages Press, Beijing.

Domes, J. (ed.) (1979), *Chinese Politics after Mao*, University College Cardiff Press, Cardiff.

Dreyer, J. (1993), *China's Political System: Modernisation and Tradition*, Macmillan Press Ltd.

Dror, Y. (1964), 'Muddling Through — 'Science' or Inertia? *'Public Administration Review*, No. 24, pp. 153-7.

Dror, Y. (1968), *Public Policy Making Re-examined*, Calif.: Chander, San Francisco.

Dunleavy, P. and O'Leary, B. (1987), *Theories of the State: the Politics of Libera Democracy*, Macmillan, London.

Dye, T. (1984), *Understanding Public Policy*, Prentice Hall.

Easton, D. (1953), *The Political System*, Knopf, New York.

Edmonds, R. L. (1989), 'Hainan Province and Its Impact on the Geography of China', *Geography*, vol.74, No. 32, pp. 165-9.

Engels, F. (1884), *The Origins of the Family, Private Property and the State*, Foreign Language press, Peking, 1978.

Etzioni, A. (1967), 'Mixed Scanning: A Third Approach to Decision-Making', *Public Administration Review*, No. 27, pp. 385-92.

Etzioni, A. (1968), *The Active Society: A Theory of Societal and Political Process*, Free Press.

Etzioni, A. (1986), 'Mixed Scanning Revisited,' *Public Administration Review*, vol. 47, pp. 8-14.

Evans, P. B. et al. (eds) (1985), *Bringing State Back in*, Cambridge University Press, London.

Fei Xiaotong, (1990), 'Turning Shanghai into a "Mainland Hong Kong"', *Beijing Review*, vol. 33, No. 43, PP. 21-3.

Forester, J (1984), 'Bounded Rationality and Politics of Muddling Through', *Public Administration Review*, Vol. 44, No, 1, Jan/Feb., pp. 23-31.

Forester, J. (1984), 'Bounded Rationality and the Politics of Muddling Through,'*Public Administration Review*, No. 44, pp. 23-31.

Franz Schurmann, (1966), *Ideology and Organisation in Communist China*, Berkeley.

Friend, J. K. et al. (1974), *Public Planning: The Inter-Corporate Dimension*, Tavistock, London.

Gao Shangquan (1996), *China's Economic Reform*, Macmillan Press Ltd, London.

Ge, W. (1990), 'Rules Add to Pudong's Appeal to Investors', *China*, vol. 33, No. 43, pp. 12-5.

Gerth, H.H. and C. Wright Mills (1958), 'Introduction: The Man and His Work', in Gerth and Mills (eds), *From Max Weber: Essays in Sociology*, pp. 3-74, New York, Oxford University Press.

Glassman, R. M. (1991), *China in Transition: Communism, Capitalism and Democracy*, Praeger Publisher, New York.

Goldstein, Avery (1990), 'Explaining Politics in the People's Republic of China: the Structural Alternative', *Comparative Politics*, April, pp. 301-322.

Goodman, D. S. G. (1989), *China's Regional Development*, Roultledge, London.

Goodman, D. S. G. (1994), *Deng Xiaoping and Chinese Revolution*, Poutledge, London.

Goodman, D. S. G. (1995), *Deng Xiaoping and the Chinese Revolution: a Political Biography*, Routledge, London.

Goodman, D. S. G. and Segal G. (eds) (1989), China at Forty: Mid-life Crisis? Clarendon Press, Oxford.

Goodman, D. S. G. and Segal, G. (eds) (1991), *China in the Nineties: Crisis Management and Beyond*, Clarendon Press, London.

Gorman, R. A. (ed.) (1985), *Biographical Dictionary of New-Marxism*, Greenwood Press, Wespoint Connecticut.

Grandner, M. J., Simon, H. A. and Guetzow, H. (1958), *Organisations*, Wiley.

Griffiths, F. (1971), 'A Tendency Analysis of Soviet Policy-Making', in Killing H. G. and Griffiths, F. (eds), *Interest Groups in Soviet Politics*, Pricenton University Press.

Gu, Z. (1991), *China Beyond Deng: Reform in the PRC*, Mcfarland & Company Inc. Publisher. Jefferson.

Hall, P. (1986), *Governing Economy: The Politics of State Intervention in Britain and France*, Oxford University Press, New York.

Hall, P. A. (1992), 'From Keynesianism to Monetarism: Institutional Analysis and British Economic policy in the 1970s', in Sven Steinmo, Kathleen Thelen and Frank Longstreth (eds), *Structuring Politics-Historical institutionalism in Comparative Analysis,* Cambridge University Press.

Ham, C. and M. J. Hill (1984), *The Policy Process in the Modern Capitalist State*, Harvester Wheatsheaf, London.

Ham, C. and M. J. Hill (1993),*The Policy Process in the Modern Capitalist State*, 2nd edition, Harvester Wheatsheaf, London.

Hanrin, C. L. (1990), *China and the Challenge of the Future*, Westview Press, London.

Harding, H. (1971), 'Maoist Theories of Policy-Making', in Robinson, T.W. (ed.), *The Cultural Revolution in China*, University of California Press, Berkeley.

Harding, H. (1981), *Organising China*, Stanford University Press.

Harding, H. (1984), 'Competing Models of the Chinese Communist Policy Process', *Issues and Studies*, February, pp. 13-36.

Harding, H. (1987), *China's Second Revolution: Reform after Mao*, The Brookings Institution, Washington, D. C.

He, Baogang (1996), *The Democratization Of China*, Routledge, London.

Healey, P. (1990), 'Policy Process in Planning', *Policy and Politics*, vol. 18, No.2, pp. 91-103.

Heath, A. (1981), *Social Mobility*, Fontana, London.

Heclo, H. (1972), 'Review Article: Policy Analysis', *British Journal of Political Science*, No. 2, pp. 83-108.

Hfferbert, R. I. (1974), *The Study of Public Policy*, Bobs-Merrill Company.

Hill, M. J. (1997), The Policy Process in the Modern State, third edition, Harvester Wheatsheaf, London.

Hill, M. J. (ed.) (1993), *New Agendas in the Study of Policy Process*, Harvester Wheatsheaf Press.

Hill, M. J. (ed.) (1993), *The Policy Process: A Reader*, Harvester Wheatsheaf Press.

Hirszowicz, M. (1980), *The Bureaucratic Leviathan: A Study in the Sociology of Communism*, Martin Robinson, Oxford.

Hogwood, B. W. and Gunn, L.A (1984), *Policy Analysis for the Real World*, Oxford University Press.

Hollingworth, C. (1984), 'Letter From the End of the World', *Far Eastern Economic Review*, vol. 123, No. 11, p. 27.

Hsu, I. C. Y. (1982), *China Without Mao*, Oxford Press.

Hsu, I. C.Y. (1995), *The Rise of Modern China*, 5th edition, Oxford University Press, New York.

Hu Qiaomu, (1978), 'Observe Economic Laws and Speed Up the Four Modernisation', *Beijing Review*, No. 47.

Hua Sheng, Zhang, X. and Luo, X. (1993), *China: From Revolution to Reform*, Macmillan Press Ltd., London.

Ian, D. (1991), *Politics in China: From Mao to Post-Deng Era*, W & R Chambers Ltd, Edinburgh.

Ikenberry, G. J. (1988), 'Conclusion: An Institutional Approach to American Foreign Economic Policy', in Ikenberry G. J, Lake, D. A. and Mastanduno, M. (eds). *The State and American Foreign Economic Policy*, Ithaca, Cornell University press, New York.

Janis, I. and Mann, L. (1977), *Decision Making*, Free Press.

Jao, Y. C. and Leung, C. K. (eds) (1986), *China's Special Economic Zones: Policies, Problems and Prospects,* Oxford University Press, New York.

Jenkins, W. I. (1978), *Policy Analysis*, Martin Robertson, London.

Jessop, B. (1979), Corporatism, Parliamentarism and Social Democracy, in Schmitter, P.C. and Lehmbruch, G. (eds), *Trends Toward Corporatism Intermediation*, Beverly Hills and London: Sage.

Jordan, A. G. and Richardson, J. J. (1987), 'The Contemporary Language of Policy Making', in Jordan, A. G. and Richardson, J. J (eds), *British Politics and Policy Process*, Unwin Hyman Ltd. London.

King, D. S. (1992), 'Work-welfare Programs', in Steinmo, S., Thelen, K. and Longstreth, F. (eds), *Structuring Politics-Historical institutionalism in Comparative Analysis*, Cambridge University Press.

Kleinbrg, R. (1990), *China's 'Opening' to the Outside World - the Experiment with Foreign Capitalism*, Westview Press, Boulder.

Kou Zhengling, (1990), 'Hainan to Lease Land-Use Right', *Beijing Review*, vol. 33, No. 17, p. 29.

Kuo, H. (1979), 'Patterns of Intra-elite Conflict', in Jurgen Domes (eds), *Chinese Politics after Mao*, University College Cardiff Press.

Lampton, D. M. (1987), 'Chinese Politics: The Bargaining Treadmill,' *Issue and Studies*, No. 3, pp. 11-41.

Lewis, J. W. (1963), *Leadership in Communist China*, Ithaca, New York.

Lieberthal, K. (1992), 'Introduction: The "Fragmented Authoritarianism" Model and It's Limitations', in Lieberthal, K. & Lampton, D. M. (eds), *Bureaucracy, Politics, and Decision Making in Post-Mao China*, 1992.

Lieberthal, K. and Oksenberg, M. (1986), 'Understanding China's Bureaucracy: The First Step to a Better Corporate Strategy', *China Business Review*, November-December, pp. 24-31.

Lieberthal, K. and Prahalad, C. K. (1989), 'Multinational Corporate Investment in China', *China Business Review*, March-April, pp. 47-51.

Lieberthal, K. G. and Lampton, D. M. (eds) (1992), *Bureaucracy, Politics, and Decision Making in Post-Mao China*, University of California Press.

Lieberthal, K. G. and Oksenberg, M. (1988), *Policy-making in China: Leaders, Structures, and Processes*, Princeton University Press.

Lieberthal, K. G. et al (eds) (1989), *Paths To Sino-US Automotive Co-operation*, Washington,U.S. Trade Development Program.

Lin Lianqi (1997), 'Yangpu: A New Hot Spot For Investment', *Beijing Review*, vol. 40, No. 49, pp. 9-12.

Lin, S. (1993), 'The New Pattern of Decentralisation in China: The Increase of Provincial Powers in Economic Legislation', *China Information*, vol. VII, No. 3 (winter 1992-3), Leiden.

Lindbeck, H. (ed.) (1972), *China: Management of a Revolutionary Society*, University of Washington Press.

Lindblom, C. E. (1959), 'The Science of "Muddling Through"', *Public Administration Review*, No. 19, pp. 78-88.

Lindblom, C. E. (1963), *A Strategy of Decision: Policy Evaluation as a Social Process*, Free Press.

Lindblom, C. E. (1964), 'Contexts for Change and Strategy: A Reply', *Public Administration Review*, No. 24.

Lindblom, C. E. (1965), *The Intelligence of Democracy*, The Free Press, New York.

Lindblom, C. E. (1977), *Politics and Markets*, Basic Books, New York.

Lindblom, C. E. (1979), 'Still Muddling, Not Yet Through', *Public Administration Review*, No. 39, pp. 517-25.

Liu, A. P. L. (1976), *Political Culture and Group Conflict in Communist China*, Clio Press, Inc. Oxford.

Louise do Rosario, (1989), 'North Wind Doth Blow — Peking sacks Hainan's governor and Guangdong trembles', *Far Eastern Economic Review*, vol. 145, No. 39, pp. 10-11.

Luard, E. (1990), *The Globalization of Politics: The changed focus of political action in the modern world*, Macmillan Press Ltd. London.

Macfarquhar, R. (1983), *The Origin of the Cultural Revolution*, Columbia University Press, New York.

Macfarquhar, R. (1983), *The Politics of China: 1949-1989*, Cambridge University Press, New York.

March, J. G. and Olsen, J. P. (1976), *Ambiguity and choice in organisations*, Bergen, Norway, Universitetsforlaget.

March, J. G. and Olsen, J. P. (1989), *Rediscovering Institutions, The Organisational Basis of Politics*, The Free Press, New York.

March, J. G. and P Olsen, J. P. (1986), 'Garbage Can Models of Decision Making in Organisation', in March, J. G. et al. (eds), *Ambiguity and*

Command: Organisational Perspectives on Military Decision Making, Cambridge, Mass. Ballinger.

March, J. G. and Simon, H. A. (1993), *Organisations*, second edition, Blackwell Business Press.

March, J. G. and. Olsen, J. P (1984), 'The New Institutionalism: Organisational Factors in Political life', *American Political Science Review*, No. 78, pp. 734-49.

Marsh, D. and Stoker, G. (1997), *Theory and Methods in Political Science*, Macmillam Press Ltd., New York.

Marx, K. (1859), *A Contribution to the Political Economy*, Preface, translated by McLellan, D.

Marx, K. (1977) *Selected Writings*, McLellan. D. (eds), Oxford University Press, Oxford.

Marx, K. and Engels, F. (1973), *Karl Marx and Frederick Engels Selected Works*, in one volume, Lawrence and Wishart, London.

Mckinlay, R. D. & Little, R. (1986), *Global Problems and World Order*, France Printer (Publishers), London.

Meyerson, M. and Christie, E. (1955), *Politics, Planning, and the Public Interest: the Case of Public Housing in Chicago*, Free Press.

Middlemas, K. (1979), *Politics in Industrial Society*, Andre Deutsch, London.

Miliband, R. (1969), *The State in Capitalist Society*, Weidenfeld & Niclson, London.

Miliband, R. (1977), *Marxism and Politics,* Oxford University Press, Oxford.

Miliband, R. (1983), 'State Power and Class Interests', in *New Left Review*, vol. 138 (March-April).

Montesquieu, C. (1746), 'Selections of "The spirit of the Law"', in M. Richter, (ed.), *The Political Theories of Montesquieu*, 1977, Cambridge Univ. Press.

Moody, P. R. (1977), *Opposition and Dissent in Contemporary China*, Hoover Institution Press, Stanford.

Moody, P. R. (1983), *Chinese Politics after Mao*, Praeger Publisher, New York.

Moody, P. R. (1984), 'Political Liberation in China: A Struggle between Two Lines', *Pacific Affairs*, January, pp. 26-44.

Mosca, G. (1896), *The Ruling Class*, trans. by Kahn, H. D. and Livingston (eds), A., New York, McGraw Hill (1939).

Nakamura, R. (1987), 'The Policy process and Implementation Research', *Policy Study Review*, No. 7, pp. 142-154.

Nathan, A. J. (1973), 'A Factionalism Model for CCP Politics', *China Quarterly*, vol. 53, pp. 34-66.

Nathan, A. J. (1976), 'Policy Oscillation in People's Republic of China: A Critique', *China Quarterly*, vol. 68, pp. 720-750.

Nolan, P. & Dong, F. (eds) (1990), *The Chinese Economy and its Future: Achievements and Problems of Post-Mao Reform*, Polity Press, Cambridge.

Nolan, P. (1993), *State and Market in Chinese Economy*, Macmillan Press Ltd.

O'Connor, J. (1973), *The Fiscal Crisis of the State*, St.Martin's Press, New York.

Oksenberg, M. (1968), 'Occupational Groups in Chinese Society and the Cultural Revolution', in Oksenberg, et al, *The Cultural Revolution: 1967 in Review*, Michigan Papers in Chinese Studies, No. 2 (Ann Arbor: Centre for Chinese Studies, University of Michigan)

Oksenberg, M. (1972), 'Policy Making Under Mao', in Lindbeck, M H (ed.), *Management of a Revolutionary Society*, University of Washington Press.

Oksenberg, M. (1982), 'Economic Policy-Making in China: Summer 1981', *China Quarterly*, vol. 90, pp. 165-94.

Oksenberg, M. and Goldstein, S. (1974), 'The Chinese Political Spectrum', *Problems of Communism*, March-April, No.2, pp. 1-13.

Panitch, L. (1980), 'Recent Theorisation of Corporatism: Reflections on a Growth Industry', *British Journal of Sociology*, vol. 31,No. 2, pp. 159-87.

Pareto, V. (1926), *Trattato di sociologia generale*, 2 vols. Trans. and (eds) by Livingston, A. and. Bongioro, A. as *The Mind and Society*, 4 vols, London, Cape, (1935).

Parsons, W. (1997), *Public Policy, An Introduction to the Theory and Practice of Policy Analysis*, Edward Elgar, Cheltenham.

Peter, B. Guy (1986), *American Public Policy*, Second edition. Chatham House Publishers Inc.

Poulantzas, N. (1973), *Political Power and Social Classes*, New Left Books, London.

Poulantzas, N. (1976), *Crisis of the Dictatorship*, New Left Books, London.

Poulantzas, N. (1978), *State, Power, Socialism*, New Left Books, London.

Pye, L. (1981), *The Dynamics of the Chinese Politics*, Cambridge University Press.

Pye, L. (1986), *The Dynamics of Factions and Consensus in Chinese Politics: A Model and Some Propositions*, The Rand Company.

Pye, L. (1991), *China: an Introduction*, fourth edition. Harper Collins Publisher.

Pye, L. (1995), 'An Introduction Profile: Deng Xiaoping and China's Political Culture', in David Shambaugh (ed.), *Deng Xiaoping — Portrait of a Chinese Statesman*, Clarendon Press, Oxford.

Rivett, P. (1979), *Model Building for Decision Making*, John Wiley & Sons, Chichester.

Robertson, D. (ed.). (1993), *A Dictionary of Modern Politics*, second edition, Europa Publication, London.

Robinson, T. W. (1971), *The Cultural Revolution in China*, University of California Press, Berkeley.

Rosario, L, (1989), 'Peking Sacks Hainan's Governor and Guangdong Trembles: North Wind Doth Blow', *Far Eastern Economic Review*, vol. 145, No. 39, pp. 10-11.

Sabatier, P. A. (1991), 'Toward Better Theories of the Policy Process', *Political Science & Politics*, No. 24, pp. 147-56.

Sabatier, P.A. (1988), 'An advocacy Coalition Framework of Policy Change and the Role of Policy-Oriented Learning Therein', *Policy Science*, vol. 21(fall), pp. 129-168.

Schmitter, P.C, (1974), 'Still the Century of Corporatism?' *Review of Politics*, vol. 36, pp. 85-131.

Schwarzmantel, J. (1994), *The State in Contemporary Society: An Introduction*, Harvester Wheatsheaf, London.

Shambaugh, D. (ed.). (1995), *Deng Xiaoping*, Clarendon Press, Oxford.

Shirk, S. L. (1993), *The Political Logic of Economic Reform in China*, University of California Press, Berkeley.

Shirk, S. L. (1993), *The Political Logic of Economic Reform in China*, University of California Press Berkeley.

Simon, H. A. (1947), *Administrative Behaviour*, Free Press.

Simon, H. A. (1975), *Administrative Behaviour*, third edition, Free Press.·

Simon, H. A. (1983), *Models of Bounded Rationality*, MIT Press, Massachusetts.

Simon, H. A. et.al. (1964), *Public Administration*, Knopt.

Skilling, H. G. (1968), 'Background to the Study of Opposition in Communist Eastern Europe', *Government and Opposition*, vol. 3 (spring), No.2, pp. 294-324.

Smith, G. and May, D. (1980), 'The Artificial Debate between Rationalist and Incrementalist Models of Decision Making', *Policy and Politics*, No. 8, pp. 147-61.

Solinger, D. (1982), 'The Fifth National People's Congress and the Process of Policymaking: Reform, Readjustment, and the Opposition', *Issues and Studies*, August, pp. 63-106.

Solinger, D. (1984), *Chinese Business under Socialism*, University of California Press.

Starkie, D. (1984), 'Policy Changes, Configurations, and Catastrophes', *Policy and Politics*, vol. 12, No.1, pp. 71-84.

Tai Ming Cheung, (1993), 'Life Is a Beach? — China's Hainan aspires to become an island paradise', *Far Eastern Economic Review*, vol. 156, No. 31, pp. 60-61.

Teiwes, F. C. (1972), 'Provincial Politics in China: Themes and Variations', in Lindbeck, H. (ed.), *China: Management of a Revolutionary Society*, University of Washington Press.

Teiwes, F. C. (1984), *Leadership, Legitimacy, and Conflict in China: From a Charismatic Mao to Politics of Succession*, Macmillan Press, London.

The Blackwell Encyclopaedia of Political Science (1992), Oxford.

Thelen, K. and Steinmo, S. (1992), 'Historical institutionalism in Comparative Politics', in Steinmo, S., Thelen K. and Longstreth, F. (eds), *Structuring Politics- Historical institutionalism in Comparative Analysis*, Cambridge University Press.

Thelen, K. and Steinmo, S. (1992), 'Historical institutionalism in Comparative Politics,' in Steinmo, S., Thelen, K. and Longstreth, F. (eds), *Structuring Politics- Historical Institutionalism in Comparative Analysis*, Cambridge University Press.

Vloeberghs, G. (1979), 'The Position of Hua Guofeng', in Jugen Domes (ed.), *Chinese politics after Mao*, University College Cardiff Press.

Whitson, W. W. (1972), 'Organisational Perspectives and Decision Making in the Chinese High Command', in Robert A Scalapino (ed.), *Elites In People's Republic of China*, University of Washington Press, pp. 381-415.

Wildavsky, A. (1980), *The Art and Craft of Policy Analysis*, Macmillan Press Ltd. London.

Winkler, J. T. (1976), Corporatism, in *European Journal of Sociology*, No. 17, pp. 100-136.

Wolfe, A. (1977), *The Limits of Legitimacy*, The Free Press, New York.

Yang Xiaobing, (1988), 'Hainan Province — China's Largest SEZ', *Beijing Review*, vol. 31, No. 18, pp. 14-18.

Yang Xiaobing, (1988), 'Hainan to Adopt More Special Policies', *Beijing Review*, vol. 31, No, 18: pp. 4-5

You Yuwen, (1995), 'Pudong and New Development in Shanghai', *China Today*, No. 10, pp. 10-12.

Chinese Sources

A Report Outline of Shenzhen SEZ, submitted to the Work Conference of SEZs which convened by the State Council in February 1990, by Shenzhen government.

Chang Huanli, (1992), 'The Establishment, Development and Features of Our Country's SEZs', *The Coastal Economy and Trade*, No. 6, pp. 15-8.

Cheng Yaoni (1996), 'Ecological City: A new Target of Shanghai within this Century', *Outlook*, No.49, pp. 27-31.

Cheng, E. (1992), 'Island Beach-Head', *Far Eastern Economic Review*, vol. 155, No. 17, pp. 64-5.

Chinese Statistical Yearbook (1988, 1989, 1990, 1990, 1991), Chinese Statistical Press, Beijing.

Chinese Yearbook (1988,1989, 1990, 1991,1992), China's Statistical Press, Beijing.

Deng Xiaoping (1984), *Selected Works of Deng Xiaoping (1975-1982)*, Chinese edition, People's Press, Beijing.

Deng Xiaoping (1985), 'The Magnificent Targets and the Basic Policies of Realising the Four Modernisation (October 6, 1984)', in *To Build the Socialism with Chinese Characteristics*, reversed and enlarged edition, 1985, Beijing, People's Press.

Deng Xiaoping (1987), 'To Develop Democracy in Politics and Carry out Reform in Economy (April 15, 1985)', in *To Build Socialism with Chinese Characteristics*, reversed and enlarged edition, People's Press, Beijing.

Deng Xiaoping (1993a), 'The Main Points of Deng Xiaoping's Talk in Wuchang, Shenzhen, Zhuhai and Shanghai (1992 Jan.18-Feb.21)', in *Selected Works of Deng Xiaoping*, vol. 3, People's Press, Beijing.

Deng Xiaoping (1993b), *Selected Works of Deng Xiaoping*, vol. 3, Chinese edition, People's Press, Beijing.

Dong, Furen (1982), 'Further Develop the Study of China's Economic Development Strategy', in *Jingjixue Wenzhai* (*Economics Digest*), No. 4.

ED (1988) 'Resolution of The First Session of The Seventh National People's Congress on Setting Up Hainan SEZ' (Adopted by the First Session of the Seventh NPC on 13 April), *Economic Daily*, 14 April, p. 2.

ED (1988), 'Resolution of The First Session of The Seventh National People's Congress on Setting Up Hainan Province' (adopted by the First Session of the Seventh NPC on 13 April), *Economic Daily*, 14 April, p. 2.

Gao Gang (1997), 'Post-Deng China: The Thinking of the Summit Consultants, A Report of Visiting the CPPCC Members', *Huasheng Monthly*, April, pp. 8-19.

Ge Wu (1990), 'Rules Add to Pudong's Appeal to Investors', *Beijing Review*, No. 43 pp. 12-5.

Guo Zhemin (1992), 'On the Development Types of China's SEZs', *The Economy of Asian and Pacific Region*, No.3, pp. 56-60.

Huang Ju (1990), 'To Celebrate Pudong's Development and Expand Opening Up to the Outside World', *Xinhua Monthly*, No. 9, pp. 54-56.

Ji Changwei (1989), 'The World's Economic Tendency and the Issue of Outward-Oriented Economy in China's Coastal Areas', *Development Studies*, No. 2, pp. 1-6.

Jiang Ji (1985), 'Several Relationships Concerning Opening Up Coastal Cities to the Outside World', *Economic Daily*, 13 May 1985, p3.

Jiang Shijie (1996), 'Yangpu, How Is Its Development Now?' *People's Daily*, overseas edition, 6 Jan. 1996, p. 2.

Jiang Zemin (1991), A Speech at the Reception of Celebrating the Tenth Anniversary of the Founding of Shenzhen SEZ, in *The Yearbook of China's Economic Management System Reform*, pp. 33-34.

Jiang Zemin (1996), 'Joining Forces to Create a Good Future of Friendship and Co-operation Between China and Kazakhstan', *People's Daily*, overseas edition, 6, Jul. 1996, p1.

Jiang, Wei (1981) The Origins of the Special Economic Zones, *World's Economic Introduction,* 2 February 1981, p. 2.

Jing, B. (1990), 'Pudong: An Open Policy Showcase', *Beijing Review*, vol. 33, No. 29, pp. 23-5.

Li Dahong at el. (1997), 'A Report of the Friendly Relation between the Third Generation Leadership Group of CPC and the Leaders of Democratic Parties', *Outlook*, No. 18, pp. 4-8.

Liang Xiang (1985), 'The Establishment and Development of Shenzhen Special Economic Zones', in *Shenzhen Yearbook*.

Liu Guoguang (1989), 'On the Several Issues of the Economy Development Strategy in China's Coastal Areas', in The Editorial Department of *The World Economy* (eds), *The Development Strategy of the Outward-Oriented Economy in China's Coastal Areas*, pp. 1-11.

Liu Peng (1985), 'We Must Revise Our Understanding of the Open Door Policy', *Outlook*, 18/April, pp. 9-11.

Liu Rongcang (1987), 'Increasing the Results in Funds Utilisation Is an Important Link in Increasing Production and Economising', *People's Daily*, 17 Apr. 1987, p. 2.

Liu Xiaolin (1996), 'China: to Turn Down Corruption', *People's Daily*, Overseas Edition, 13th, January 1996, p. 4.

Liu Yongbing (1992), 'The Development of the World's SEZs and the *Status Quo* of China's SEZs', in *Tactics and Countermeasures*, No. 11, pp. 31-3.

Lu Lin (ed.) (1995), *The Opening Forward Position Brimming with Charm*, The Law Press, Beijing.

Ma Chunhui & Feng Yuhui (1996), 'A Comparative Study of the Special Economic Zones Between the Developed and the Developing Countries', in *Special Zone Economy*, No. 2, pp. 49-50.

Ma Hong (1982), 'On Unified Financial Authority and Concentrated Financial Resources', in *Caijing Wenti Yanjiu (Research on finance and economic problems)*, No. 1.

Major, J. (1995), 'A Speech with Chinese Officers', *People's Daily*, Overseas edition, 27 December, p. 4.

Mao Zhedong (1943), 'Some Questions Concerning Methods of Leadership', in *Selected Readings from Works of Mao Zhedong*, Beijing, 1967.

Mao Zurong (1992), 'The Enlightenment form Visiting Shenzhen', *The Coastal Economy and Business*, No. 9, pp. 22-25.

Meng Jinghang and Yang Jianhe (1995), '"Three Unchanges" are the Fundamental Guiding Principles of Further Developing SEZs', *Special Zone Economy*, No. 10, pp.7-10.

Ni Tianzheng (1992), 'A Great Project Over Next Century', in the Department of Advanced Studies, CPC Central Party School (eds), *The Reports from SEZs*, The Press of CPC Central Party School, Beijing.

Ni Tu (1994a), 'Deng Xiaoping, Jiang Zemin and the Special Economic Zones', *Democracy and Law*, No. 9, pp. 4-8.

Ni Tu (1994b), 'The Origin of the Special Economic Zones: Deng Xiaoping, Jiang Zemin and SEZs', part 2, *The Democracy and Law*, No.10, pp. 6-9.

Ni Tu (1994c), 'The Origin of the Special Economic Zones: Deng Xiaoping, Jiang Zemin and SEZs', part 3, *The Democracy and Law*, No. 11, pp. 10-14.

OCSE (1997), 'Hong Kong is the Number One of the Foreign Investment in Pudong New Zone', *Overseas Chinese Scholars*, electronic edition, No. 126, 13, June.

OL (1996), 'Zhongnanhai and Pudong development', *Outlook*, Beijing, No. 17.

PD (1990), 'Jiang Zemin Inspects Hainan and Reaffirms that the Decision Making of Setting Up Hainan SEZ Is Correct and the Policies do not Change', *People's Daily*, 19 May, p. 1.

PD (1992), 'The State Council Further Relaxes the Policies for Hainan', *People's Daily*, 11 August, p. 1.

PDO (1995), Editorial: 'A New Example of Concentrating National Forces to Accomplish the Important Matter', *People's Daily*, overseas edition, 17 November, p. 1.

PDO (1996), 'Pudong Became the First Choice Area of Foreign Capital that Seeking Increasing in Value', *People's Daily*, overseas edition, 8 May, p. 2.

PDO (1997), 'Zhu Rongji Met Kirichy', *People's Daily*, overseas edition, 29, February, p. 1.

Peng Mingpang (1997), 'A Great Man of the Century', *Chinese Youth*, No. 3, pp. 4-13.

Qu Zhang (1989), 'China's Largest and Most Special SEZ — Hainan Province', *International Economic Cooperation*, No. 6, pp. 3-7.

Quan Qizhen (eds) (1992), *The Ten Years' General Situation of China's Coastal Economic Opening Zones*, Science Press, Beijing.

RF (1981), 'The Resolution about The Party's Several Historical Issues Since the Founding of PRC' (Adopted with one accord by the 6th Plenum of 11th Central Committee of CPC, June 27, 1981). *Red Flag*, No. 13, pp. 3-27.

Semi-month Talk, (Journal) Beijing. (1990-1995)

Sui Guangjun (1990), 'On the SEZs' Role in the Economic Cooperation between China and Foreign Countries', *Jinan Academic Journal*, No. 4, pp. 44-52, 62.

Sun Xiaogang (1991), 'On the Ten Relations in the Development of Shenzhen SEZ', *SEZ Economy*, No.1, pp. 12-14.

SZE, Editorial, *Special Zone Economy*, issue 4, 1992, Shenzhen, P.R. China

The Bulletin of the Third Plenum of the Eleventh Central Committee of CPC: 'The Regulations of Guangdong Special Economic Zones (Adopted on 26 August 1980 by the Standing Committee of the National People's Congress)', in Shenzhen Commission of Economic System Reform (eds), *The Selected Reform Documents of Shenzhen SEZ*, pp. 1-5.

The Research Office for Economic System Reform of CPC Hainan Committee (1989), 'The Reform and Opening-Up of Hainan Province', in The State's Commission for Economic System Reform (ed.), *Chinese Year Book of Economic System Reform*, Reform Press, Beijing, pp. 413-7.

The Selected Edition of the Important Documents since the Third Plenum of the Eleventh Central Committee of CPC, (1990), vol.1, People's Press, Beijing.

The SEZs Office of China's State Council (1988), 'China's Great Practice of Opening to the Outside World', in *The Ten Years of China's Economic System Reform*, Reform Press, Beijing.

'The Statistical Bulletin of the National Economic and Social Development of Shenzhen City in 1991' (1992) *The Economy of SEZs*, No. 3.

The Statistical Bureau of Shenzhen (1988), *A Combining Statistical Data of the Coastal Opening Cities, Special Economic Zones and the Cities with Special State Plans* (1980-1986), 1987, pp151-153, and 1988 edition, p. 100.

The Yearbook of Shenzhen Special Economic Zone, (1985), Shenzhen, China.

Wang Ruipu (ed.) (1995), *A General Review of China's Economic System Reform*, PLA Press, Beijing.

Wang Zhuo (1995), 'The Clarion Call of the Open Policy and the Sound of the SEZs: Congratulate the Ten Years Anniversary of the Open

Publication of "*The Special Zone Economy*"', *Special Zone Economy*, No. 9, pp. 6-9.

Xiamen's Statistical YearBook of Economy linked with Foreign Countries (1989), The Statistical Press of China.

Xiao Bing (1998), 'The Twenty Years of China's Political System Reform', *Xinhua Monthly*, No. 9, pp.37-38.

Xie Baisan (1991), *China's Economic Policies: Theories and Reforms Since 1949*, Fudan University Press, Shanghai.

Xie Jinghu (1995), 'Fifth Anniversary of Pudong's Development and Opening Up: the Harvest Besides the Figure', *Outlook*, No. 15, pp. 4-6.

Xie Jinghu, et al. (1996a), 'Zhongnanhai and Pudong Development', *Outlook*, No. 17, pp. 4-10.

Xie Jinghu, et al. (1996b), 'Pudong Become the First Choice Area of Foreign Capital's increment', *People's Daily*, overseas edition, May 8 1996, p. 2

Xinhua News Agency (1992), 'The State Council Approves Hainan Province to Introduce Investment from Foreign Businessmen for the Development and Construction of Yangpu Economic Development Zone', *People's Daily*, 14, 15 March.

Xu Long, (1991) 'The Ten Years of China's SEZs', *The Economy of Hong Kong and Macao*, No. 6: pp. 21-23.

Yan Bing (1995), 'A Tour through Beijing-Jiulong Railway (1)', *People's Daily*, overseas edition, 13th, November 1995, p. 1.

Zhan Qicheng (1989), 'On the Newly Development of the World's SEZs', *The Issue of International Trade*, No. 12, pp. 32-7.

Zhang Jianwei (1996), 'Xu Shijie and the Yangpu Disturbance', *The Successor of China,* overseas edition, No.1, pp. 34-41.

Zhang Shihong (1996), 'A Beautiful Blueprint and a New Contribution: An On-the-Spot Report of Pudong New Zone's Planning', *People's Daily*, Overseas Edition, 8 May 1996, p. 2.

Zhao Guobin, et al. (1992), 'A Study Report of Investigating Hainan, Shenzhen and Pudong', *Heihe Academic Journal*, No. 2, pp. 17-23.

Zhong Ekang (1986), On Some Issues of the Development Strategy of Shenzhen Special Economic Zone, *The Year Book of Shenzhen Special Economic Zone (1986)*, pp. 337-339.

Zhong Yechang (1989), *On the Economic Development of Hainan*, Hong Kong News Press.

Index